In this timely book Manuela Caiani and Ondřej Císař successfully develop a thoughtful and ambitious framework for analyzing the interaction between radical right-wing party politics and social movement mobilization, which is substantiated in empirically rich chapters. An important contribution that should be read widely.

*– **Jens Rydgren,** Professor of Sociology,*
Stockholm University, Sweden

Social movement studies have mainly addressed progressive movements. Focusing on the concept of movement parties, this interesting collection shows however that the toolkit of concepts and theories developed in the analysis of contentious politics can be usefully adapted to understand the contemporary challenges of regressive actors.

*– **Donatella della Porta,** Director of Centre of Social Movement*
Studies, Scuola Normale Superiore, Italy

By focusing on the movement qualities of radical right parties in West and East as well as party-movement interactions, this theoretically inspiring and empirically rich volume adds a significant piece of research to the comparative study of radical right politics in Europe.

*– **Michael Minkenberg,** European University*
Viadrina, Frankfurt (Oder), Germany

RADICAL RIGHT MOVEMENT PARTIES IN EUROPE

This book provides state of the art research by leading experts on the movement parties of the radical right. It examines the theoretical implications and empirical relevance of these organizations, comparing movement parties in time and space in Europe and beyond.

The editors provide a theoretical introduction to radical right movement parties, discussing analytical frameworks for interpreting their causes, forms, and effects. In the subsequent sections of the book, chapter authors examine a range of empirical case studies in Western, Central, and Eastern Europe, using a combination of qualitative and quantitative methodological approaches, and make a significant contribution to the literature on social movements and party politics.

This book is essential reading for scholars of European party politics and students in European politics, social movements, comparative politics, and political sociology.

Manuela Caiani is Associate Professor at the Department of Political Science and Sociology of the Scuola Normale Superiore (SNS) of Florence. Her research interests focus on: Radical Right, Populism, Europeanization and social movements, political mobilization and the Internet, qualitative methods of social research, political violence, and terrorism.

Ondřej Císař is Associate Professor at the Department of Sociology, Faculty of Social Sciences, Charles University, Prague, and is also affiliated to the Institute of Sociology of the Czech Academy of Sciences. He is editor-in-chief of the Czech edition of *Czech Sociological Review*. His research focus is on political mobilization, social movements, and political sociology.

Routledge Studies in Extremism and Democracy

Series Editors: Roger Eatwell, *University of Bath*, and **Matthew Goodwin**, *University of Kent*
Founding Series Editors: Roger Eatwell, *University of Bath*, and **Cas Mudde**, *University of Antwerp-UFSIA*

This new series encompasses academic studies within the broad fields of 'extremism' and 'democracy'. These topics have traditionally been considered largely in isolation by academics. A key focus of the series, therefore, is the interrelation between extremism and democracy. Works will seek to answer questions, such as to what extent 'extremist' groups pose a major threat to democratic parties, or how democracy can respond to extremism without undermining its own democratic credentials.

Radical Right-Wing Populist Parties in Western Europe
Into the Mainstream?
Edited by Tjitske Akkerman, Sarah L. de Lange, and Matthijs Rooduijn

The Populist Radical Reader
A Reader
Edited by Cas Mudde

The Far Right in America
Cas Mudde

Militant Democracy
The Limits of Democratic Tolerance
Bastiaan R. Rijpkema

Anti-Islamic Protest in the UK
Policy Responses to the Far Right
William Allchorn

Radical Right Movement Parties in Europe
Edited by Manuela Caiani and Ondřej Císař

For more information about this series, please visit: www.routledge.com/politics/series/ED

RADICAL RIGHT MOVEMENT PARTIES IN EUROPE

Edited by Manuela Caiani and Ondřej Císař

Routledge
Taylor & Francis Group

LONDON AND NEW YORK

First published 2019
by Routledge
2 Park Square, Milton Park, Abingdon, Oxon OX14 4RN

and by Routledge
52 Vanderbilt Avenue, New York, NY 10017

Routledge is an imprint of the Taylor & Francis Group, an informa business

British Library Cataloguing-in-Publication Data
A catalogue record for this book is available from the British Library

Library of Congress Cataloging-in-Publication Data
A catalog record has been requested for this book

ISBN: 978-1-138-56671-2 (hbk)
ISBN: 978-1-138-56676-7 (pbk)
ISBN: 978-1-315-12385-1 (ebk)

Typeset in Times New Roman
by Deanta Global Publishing Services, Chennai, India

CONTENTS

FIGURES

TABLES

CONTRIBUTORS

Editors:

Manuela Caiani is Associate Professor at the Institute of Scienze Umane e Sociali at the Scuola Normale Superiore (SNS) of Florence. Her research interests focus on: Europeanization and social movements, right wing extremism in Europe and the USA, political mobilization and the Internet, qualitative methods of social research, and political violence and terrorism. She has been involved in several international comparative research projects and coordinated research units for individual projects and grants. She has published in, among others, the following journals: *Mobilization, ActaPolitica, European Union Politics, South European Society and Politics*, and *RISP*; and for the following publishers: Oxford University Press, Ashgate, and Palgrave.

Ondřej Císař is Associate Professor at the Department of Sociology, Faculty of Social Sciences, Charles University and is also affiliated to the Institute of Sociology of the Czech Academy of Sciences. He is editor-in-chief of the Czech edition of *Czech Sociological Review*. His research focus is on political mobilization, social movements, and political sociology. He has been involved in several international comparative research projects and coordinated research units for individual projects and grants. He has published in, among others, the following journals: *Environmental Politics, Democratization, Poetics, European Union Politics*, and *Social Movements Studies*.

Chapter authors:

Lars Erik Berntzen is a PhD researcher in the Department of Political and Social Science, European University Institute and Researcher at the Center for Research on Extremism, University of Oslo. His research focuses on ideology, emotions, networks, and political violence, with an emphasis on the anti-Islamic far right in Western Europe and North America.

Joel Busher is a Research Fellow at the Centre for Trust, Peace and Social Relations (CTPSR), Coventry University, UK. His research addresses anti-minority movements, the dynamics of political violence, and the implementation and societal impacts of counter-terrorism policies. With Tufyal Choudhury and Paul Thomas he is the author of *What the Prevent Duty Means for Schools and Colleges in England: An Analysis of Educationalists' Experiences.* His book, *The Making of Anti-Muslim Protest: Grassroots Activism in the English Defence League*, published by Routledge, was awarded the British Sociological Association's Philip Abrams Memorial Prize, 2016.

Pietro Castelli Gattinara is Assistant Professor at the Centre for Research on Extremism (C-REX), University of Oslo, and a fellow of the Centre on Social Movement Studies, Scuola Normale Superiore, Florence. His research interests include comparative politics and the study of migration in Europe, with a particular focus on the far right, populism, and neo-Fascism. In previous years, he has been a teaching fellow of Comparative and European Politics at Sciences Po Paris and at Monash University. He holds a Master of Research and a PhD in Political and Social Sciences (2014) from the European University Institute, where he discussed a thesis on local politics and party competition on migration. He is a graduate of Political Science (University of Rome), and holds a Master of Science in Migration and Ethnic Relations from Utrecht University (2010). His work appeared in a number of international peer-reviewed journals and edited volumes. He is the author of the monograph *The Politics of Migration in Italy: Local, Party and Electoral Perspectives* (Routledge, 2016). He recently published 'Framing Exclusion in the Public Sphere: Far-Right Mobilization and the Debate on Charlie Hebdo' (*South European Society and Politics*, 2017) and 'The Refugee Crisis in Italy as a Crisis of Legitimacy' (*Contemporary Italian Politics*, 2017).

Maik Fielitz is a research associate at the Institute for Peace Studies and Security Policy at the University of Hamburg and a PhD candidate at Goethe University Frankfurt. His current research interests include far-right activism in Europe with a particular focus on Greece. Among his recent publications are: *Trouble on the Far Right* (Transcript, 2016) and *Knowledge, Normativity and Power in Academia* (Campus, 2018).

Gilles Frigoli is Senior Lecturer in Sociology at URMIS-University of Nice. His main research interests include social movements, state and local public policy, and the study of immigrant integration in French society. His previous research has appeared in numerous academic journals in France such as *Le temps des* *médias, Migrations Société, Revue Européenne des Migrations Internationales,* and *Déviance et Société*. He is currently working on various projects related to the politicization of immigration issues in French politics, society, and media.

Oľga Gyárfášová is an assistant professor and director in the Institute of European Studies and International Relations at the Comenius University in Bratislava. She studied sociology and holds a PhD in comparative politics. In her work, she focuses on public opinion, electoral studies, and political culture. Since 2004, she has been national coordinator of the European Election Studies (EES) and Comparative Studies of Electoral Systems (CSES). She has written extensively on transition development in Slovakia and other Central European states with a focus on voting behaviour, nationalism, and populism.

Jeanne Hanna is a PhD candidate in Public Anthropology and Graduate Fellow at American University in Washington, DC. Her research examines internal dynamics among supporters of the UK Independence Party in northern England after the June 2016 European Union Referendum. Her work focuses on issues related to race, immigration, and related policies within UKIP.

Gilles Ivaldi is CNRS Researcher in Political Science at URMIS-University of Nice. His main fields of research include French politics, the comparative study of radical right parties, and populism. He has published extensively on the Front National and his previous research has appeared in journals such as *Electoral Studies*, the *International Journal of Forecasting, French Politics* and *Political Research Quarterly*. He is currently the French project leader of the 'Sub-national context and radical right support in Europe' (SCoRE) international research program (2016–2018).

Jiří Navrátil is Assistant Professor at the Faculty of Economics and Administration, Masaryk University in Brno, Czech Republic. His research focus is on social movements and political protest, political networks, and civil societies in Eastern Europe. At the moment, he is working on an analysis of the transformation of inter-organizational networks of post-socialist trade unions and political parties. He has published in *Democratization, Studies in Social Justice* and *Social Movement Studies*. He is the author of *From Economic Globalization to the "War on Terror". Transformations of the Czech Left-Wing Activism at the Beginning of 21st Century* (2017) and co-author of *Dreams of Civil Society Two Decades Later: Civic Advocacy in the Czech Republic* (2014).

Abby Peterson is Professor Emerita of Sociology at the Department of Sociology and Work Science, University of Gothenburg, Sweden. She has published extensively within the fields of social movement research, cultural sociology, and criminology.

Andrea L.P. Pirro is a postdoctoral research fellow at the Department of Political and Social Sciences, Scuola Normale Superiore, Florence. He is editor of the journal *East European Politics* and convenor of the European Consortium for Political Research (ECPR) Standing Group on Extremism and Democracy. He has authored the monograph *The Populist Radical Right in Central and Eastern Europe: Ideology, Impact, and Electoral Performance* (Routledge, 2015) and edited three special issues.

Jakob Schwörer is a PhD student of political science at the Leuphana University of Lüneburg as part of the doctoral program "Democracy under stress". His research focuses on populist parties in Western Europe, particularly in Italy and Germany. In June 2016 his first book *Populismi. Il 'Movimento 5 Stelle' e la 'Alternativa per la Germania'* was published in cooperation with the *Fondazione Nenni.* It focuses on the specific character of populist sentiments and parties in Italy and Germany, analysing the causes of anti-political attitudes in the society, the electorates of the 5 Star Movement and the Alternative for Germany, as well as the ideological orientation of these parties. In his doctoral thesis, he focuses on the contagion effect of populism on mainstream parties in Italy, Spain, and Germany.

Ben Stanley is a Lecturer at SWPS University of Social Sciences and Humanities, Warsaw. His primary research interests are the theory and practice of populism and the party politics of Central and Eastern Europe (particularly Poland). He has published on these topics in the *Journal of Political Ideologies*, *Party Politics*, *Democratization*, *Communist and Post-Communist Studies*, and *Europe-Asia Studies*. He is currently working on populist attitudes and voting behaviour, and on the relationships between populist attitudes and conspiracy mentality.

Ivan Stefanovski holds a bachelor's degree in Law and an LLM degree in Constitutional Law, both from the Ss. Cyril and Methodius University in Skopje, Republic of Macedonia. At the beginning of his career, he started working as a member of the junior teaching staff at the Justinianus Primus Faculty of Law, giving classes and tutorials in Constitutional Law, Political Systems, and Political Parties and Interest Groups. He later worked for several domestic and international NGOs on issues such as elections and electoral models, media law, human rights, rule of law, freedom of information, free access to justice, and similar issues. He is also a member of several international foundations and groups. He started his PhD in Political Science and Sociology at the Scuola Normale Superiore, Florence in 2014, working on contemporary social movements in Southeast Europe.

Alma Vardari is the Postdoctoral Fellow at the Leonard Davis Institute for International Relations, at the Hebrew University, Jerusalem, conducting research on the topic of EU state building in the Western Balkans. She holds a PhD in Sociology from the Tel-Aviv University and an MA in Behavioral Sciences from the Ben-Gurion University, majoring in Political Sociology. During her academic life, she has won various international awards and research grants, such as: the Robert Schuman Doctoral research grant (2010), the Konrad Adenauer Doctoral Fellowship (2011), the Fulbright Postdoctoral Fellowship spent at Stanford University (2014–2015), and the Humboldt Fellowship (2016). Vardari is also an adjunct lecturer at the Deptartment of Politics and Government at the Ben-Gurion University. Since 2000, when she had the chance to work with Kosovar refugees, Balkan politics and societies have comprised her main research focus. Ever since, she has been building her professional expertise in Kosovo, Albania, Serbia, Macedonia, and USA as a researcher of contention politics, international state building, and European post-communist societies. She has also been teaching courses in Israel and abroad on Balkan politics, social movements, and international intervention, topics on which she has authored several articles and book chapters in English and Hebrew.

Manès Weisskircher is a researcher at the TU Dresden (MIDEM – Mercator Forum Migration and Democracy) and a PhD candidate at the European University Institute in Florence. His main research interests are comparative politics and political sociology, especially the study of social movements, political parties, and democracy. More specifically, he has written on the left, the radical right, animal rights, and the European Citizens' Initiative. His research has been published in *Government and Opposition* and in the *Journal of Intercultural Studies*. In addition, he has contributed to the Washington Post's Monkey Cage, openDemocracy, the LSE blog, the Jacobin, and science.orf.at, amongst others. Previously, he taught at the University of Vienna, the University of Bonn, the University of Düsseldorf, and the University of Bucharest.

ABBREVIATIONS

AFD	Alternative für Deutschland (Alternative for Germany)
AN	Alleanza Nazionale (National Alliance)
ANEL	Ανεξάρτητοι Έλληνες (Independent Greeks)
ANO	Akce nespokojených občanů (Action of Dissatisfied Citizens)
BB	Bündnis Bürgerwille (Alliance Citizenship)
BFB	Bund freier Bürger (Federation of Free Citizens)
BI	Bloc Identitaire (The Identitarians)
BK	Bürgerkonvent (Citizens' Convention)
BNP	British National Party
BPI	Blok proti Islámu (The Block against Islam)
CDU	Christlich Demokratische Union Deutschlands (Christian Democratic Union of Germany)
CEEC	Central Eastern European countries
CPI	CasaPound Italia (CasaPound Italy)
CR	Czech Republic
CSU	Christlich-Soziale Union in Bayern (Christian Social Union in Bavaria)
DLF	Debout la France (France Arise)
DOI	Declaration of Independence
DPS	Direktdemokratische Partei Schweiz (Direct Democratic Party of Switzerland)
DUP	Democratic Unionist Party
DVU	Deutsche Volksunion (German People's Union)
EP	European Parliament
EU	European Union
EULEX	European Union Rule of Law Mission in Kosovo

FANE	Fédération d'action nationale et européenne (Federation of National and European Action)
FDDV	Freiheitliche Direktdemokratische Volkspartei (Free Direct Democratic People's Party)
FDP	Freie Demokratische Partei (Free Democratic Party)
Fidesz	Magyar Polgári Szövetség (Hungarian Civic Alliance)
FN	Forza Nuova (New Force)
FN	Front national (National Front)
FPÖ	Freiheitliche Partei Österreichs (Freedom Party of Austria)
FW	Freie Wähler (Free Voters)
GNR	Groupes nationalistes-révolutionnaires (Revolutionary Nationalist Groups)
GO!	Grassroots Out
GRECE	Groupement de recherche et d'études pour la civilisation européenne (Research and Study Group for European Civilization)
GUD	Groupe Union Défense (Union Defense Group)
HSĽS	Hlinkova slovenská ľudová strana (Hlinka's Slovak People's Party)
HZDS	Hnutie za demokratické Slovensko (Movement for a Democratic Slovakia)
ICO	International Civilian Representative for Kosovo
IMF	International Monetary Fund
ISSB	Institut für strategische Studien Berlin (Institute for Strategic Studies in Berlin)
IVČRN	Islám v ČR nechceme (We Do Not Want Islam in the CR)
JOBBIK	Jobbik Magyarországért Mozgalom (Movement for a Better Hungary)
KAN	Kosovo Action Network
KDH	Kresťanskodemokratické hnutie (Christian Democratic Movement)
LAOS	Popular Orthodox Rally
LEGIDA	Leipziger Europäer gegen die Islamisierung des Abendlandes (Leipzig Europeans against the Islamization of the Occident)
LMP	Lehet Más a Politika (Politics Can Be Different)
LPR	Liga Polskich Rodzin (League of Polish Families)
ĽSNS	Ľudová strana Naše Slovensko (People's Party Our Slovakia)
M5S	Movimento 5 Stelle (Five Star Movement)
MDF	Magyar Demokrata Fórum (Hungarian Democratic Forum)
MEP	Member of European Parliament
MIÉP	Magyar Igazság és Élet Pártja (Hungarian Justice and Life Party)
MNR	Mouvement National Républicain (National Republican Movement)
MP	Member of Parliament

MPF	Mouvement pour la France (Movement for France)
MS-FT	Movimento Sociale – Fiamma Tricolore (Social Movement – Tricolour Flame)
MSI	Movimento Sociale Italiano (Italian Social Movement)
MSZP	Magyar Szocialista Párt (Hungarian Socialist Party)
NATO	North Atlantic Treaty Organization
ND	New Democracy
ND	Nouvelle Droite (New Right)
NHS	National Health Service
NMR	Nordisk Motståndsrörelsen (Nordic Resistance Movement)
NPD	Nationaldemokratische Partei Deutschlands (National Democratic Party of Germany)
OAS	Organisation armée secrète (Secret Army Organisation)
ODS	Občanská demokratická strana (Civic Democratic Party)
OF	Œuvre Française (French Work)
OFA	Ohrid Framework Agreement
OĽANO	Obyčajní Ľudia a nezávislé osobnosti (Ordinary People and Independent Personalities)
ON	Ordre Nouveau (New Order)
ONR	Obóz Narodowo-Radykalny (National-Radical Camp)
PACS	Pacte civil de solidarité (civil solidarity pact)
PASOK	Πανελλήνιο Σοσιαλιστικό Κίνημα (Panhellenic Socialist Movement)
PCA	Political Claims Analysis
PDF	Parti de la France (Party of France)
PEGIDA	Patriotische Europäer gegen die Islamisierung des Abendlandes (Patriotic Europeans against the Islamization of the Occident)
PIS	Prawo i Sprawiedliwość (Law and Justice)
PO	Platforma Obywatelska (Civic Platform)
POS	Political Opportunities Structure
PSL	Polskie Stronnictwo Ludowe (Polish Peasant Party)
PZPR	Polska Zjednoczona Partia Robotnicza (Polish United Workers' Party)
RBM	Rassemblement Bleu Marine (Marine Blue Gathering)
RN	Ruch Narodowy (National Movement)
SD	Sverigedemokraterna (Sweden Democrats)
SDSM	Social Democratic Union of Macedonia
SDU	Sverigedemokraternas Ungdomsförbund (Sweden Democrats Youth Organisation)
SFRJ	Socialist Federal Republic of Yugoslavia
SHO	Slovenské Hnutie Obrody (Slovak Movement of Revival)
SIEL	Souveraineté, Identité et Libertés (Sovereignty, Identity and Freedoms)

SLD	Sojusz Lewicy Demokratycznej (Democratic Left Alliance)
SĽS	Slovenská ľudová strana (Slovak People's Party)
SMER-SD	SMER – sociálna demokracia (Direction-Social Democracy)
SMK	Magyar Közösség Pártja (Party of the Hungarian Community)
SMO	social movement organization
SN	Stronnictwo Narodowe (National Party)
SND	Stronnictwo Narodowo-Demokratyczny (National-Democratic Party)
SNJ	Slovenská národná jednota (Slovak National Unity)
SNS	Slovenská národná strana (Slovak National Party)
SP	Slovenská pospolitosť (Slovak Togetherness)
SP-NS	Slovenská pospolitosť - Národná strana (Slovak Togetherness - the National Party)
SPD	Sozialdemokratische Partei Deutschlands (Social Democratic Party of Germany)
SPD	Svoboda a přímá demokracie (Freedom and Direct Democracy)
SPR-RSČ	Sdružení pro republiku - Republikánská strana Československa (Coalition for the Republic–Republican Party of Czechoslovakia)
SRP	Samoobrona Rzeczpospolitej Polskiej (Self-Defence)
SSO	Strana svobodných občanů (Free Citizens' Party)
SVP	Schweizerische Volkspartei (Swiss People's Party)
SVT	Sveriges Television Aktiebolag (Swedish Television)
SYRIZA	Συνασπισμός Ριζοσπαστικής Αριστεράς (Coalition of Radical Left)
TTIP	Transatlantic Trade and Investment Partnership
UK	United Kingdom
UKIP	United Kingdom Independence Party
UN	United Nations
UNDP	United Nations Development Program
UNMIK	United Nations Mission in Kosovo
ÚPD	Úsvit přímé demokracie (Dawn of Direct Democracy party)
UPR	Union Populaire Républicaine (Popular Republican Union)
USAID	United States of Agency for International Development
VMRO-DPMNE	Internal Macedonian Revolutionary Organization – Democratic Party for Macedonian National Unity
VV	Vetvendosje (Self-determination)
VV	Věci Veřejné (Public Affairs party)
WA2013	Verein zur Unterstützung der Wahlalternative 2013 (Association for the support of the Electoral Alternative 2013)
ZK	Zivile Koalition (Civilian Coalition)

PART I
Theory

1

RADICAL RIGHT MOVEMENT PARTIES IN EUROPE

An introduction[1]

Manuela Caiani and Ondřej Císař

This volume, exploring various radical right organizations in twelve European countries, presents the first comparative study of Radical Right Movement Parties in Europe. Based on a common analytical framework, chapters offer a highly differentiated view of how radical right politics develops across Europe through the interplay between radical right political parties and movements.

Movement parties, as a new type of political organization, have proved successful in mobilizing voters in many countries (Kitchelt 2006). Thus far, however, the academic focus has been mostly on left-wing movement parties and ideologically hybrid organizations, such as those that emerged in Southern Europe during the Eurozone crisis (for example Syriza, Podemos, and the Five Star Movement; della Porta et al. 2017). The radical right has as yet remained outside the focus of this research (although we list some exceptions below). Nevertheless, the radical right – in its populist and extreme variants – is one of the most researched objects in the social sciences (for example Mudde 2007; Caiani et al. 2012; Caiani 2017b), and seems to share features with other movement parties. In fact, some of these organizations have been seen to straddle the conceptual space between party and movement (Gunther and Diamond 2003) in that they contest elections in order to gain representation in office, yet seek to mobilize public support by framing contentious issues in particular ways (Minkenberg 2002). Whilst some attempts have been made to bridge the party political literature and social movement studies (for example Minkenberg 2003; McAdam and Tarrow 2010), the two branches of scholarship have only rarely crossed paths in analyses of the radical right (recently there have been new contributions such as papers in a forthcoming special issue of European Societies, see Gattinara and Pirro 2018; Minkenberg 2018).

In an attempt to bridge social movement and party politics studies within a wider concern with democratic theories, della Porta et al. (2017) present both new empirical evidence on left-wing political organizations such as Syriza and

Podemos that emerged after the 2008 crisis, and conceptual insights into these topical socio-political phenomena within a cross-national comparative perspective. Although their book is a ground-breaking work on movement parties, it does not focus on the radical right, nor does it include Eastern European cases. Similarly, in a recent work Hutter (2014) demonstrates the usefulness of studying both electoral and protest politics to better understand the impact of globalization on political mobilization, including the radical right. He particularly emphasizes how cleavage politics can be helpful to understanding the formation of new social movements and populist parties in Western Europe, but he relies only on quantitative evidence and does not include Eastern Europe either. Examining the collapse of the post-9/11 anti-war movement against the wars in Iraq and Afghanistan, Heaney and Rojas (2015) focus on activism and protest in the United States. They show that how people identify with social movements and political parties matters a great deal, and they consider the Tea Party and Occupy Wall Street cases for comparison. Theirs is an important book, but it includes only US movements.

As for right-wing groups, while the new right-wing populist parties' mobilization of the 'losers' in the processes of globalization is seen to be the driving force behind the restructuring of West European politics, some scholars have recently gone beyond party politics (for example see Kriesi et al. 2012) to show how the cleavage coalitions that are shaping up under the impact of globalization extend to state actors, interest groups, and social movement organizations, and how these various actors frame the new conflicts. However, these scholars do not pay specific attention to movement parties. Finally, Minkenberg (2015, 2017) focuses on the radical right's interaction in many Eastern European countries with other political actors, such as parties, governments, and interest groups, and underlines the effects of such interaction with regard to agenda-setting and policies in 'loaded' policy fields, namely minorities and immigration, law and order, religion, territorial issues, and democratization. However, he does not focus on movement parties and he does not include Western European cases.

In this book we aim at shedding light on this new object of investigation in the social sciences, by asking the following questions: what are the main features of movement parties on the radical right? What organizational and strategic features qualify these networks of organizations as movement parties rather than party movements? What is the lifecycle of movement parties, in terms of their emergence and breakthrough, the structuring of movement party relations, and the construction of shared collective identities?

Movement parties appear to be of particular scholarly (and social) relevance today in a 'Europe in crisis mode' (i.e. the euro debt/financial crisis, the migration crisis, the Greek crisis, the Ukraine crisis, the migrant crisis, Brexit, etc.) which has seen only moderate policy response from the political mainstream. Politics is indeed about the conflict between political interests and issues which are advocated by parties, social movements, and citizens' groups. The literature on political parties has conceptualized this terrain of contested political issues as a country's political interaction space. While the party literature has used this model to understand interactions among political parties and explain the mobilization of the radical right, we suggest extending this idea to include not only political parties, but also protest politics and social movements. Throughout the world, we can see street mobilizations turning into new political parties (such as Jobbik) and vice versa, i.e. established political figures spawning political mobilizations (Tea Party movement, Fidesz).

This volume focuses on one segment of these mobilizations that, alongside previous crises, has been gaining momentum against the backdrop of the current migrant crisis and that is *the interactions of radical right parties and movements*. As such, the volume seeks to bridge two types of literature – that on radical right parties and that on social movements. Social movement studies have tended to declare social movements the defining feature of established post-1968 democracies and have generally prioritized the protest arena of action. However, without taking political parties into account, it is hardly possible to make sense of radical right mobilization in most post-industrial countries. This type of interaction between movements and parties constitutes one of the most important challenges for the social sciences. At present, their interaction remains under-theorized. Therefore, this book investigates one of the most debated *theoretical and empirical problems* we face. It is hoped that it will also stimulate conversations across various research areas by bringing together scholars working on social movements and political parties.

Focusing on the interactions between electoral and protest politics seems especially important for studying the segments of the population that tend to express their grievances not through street protest, but through the protest vote, which is more common among people siding with the radical right than it is among movements on the political left (Hutter 2014). While the relationship between the electoral and protest arenas is one of reinforcement in the case of the left, on the political right, a substitutive effect seems to be at work. However, there are cases that exhibit a different pattern (see especially Chapters 8 and 9 on Germany and Sweden in this volume). There are examples where the electoral mobilization of the radical right was not accompanied by a decrease in political protest action. Although we lack a rigorous approach to explain this puzzle in the present volume, it seems that there are certain additional conditions that must be met in order for the substitutive effect to take place (see the concluding Chapter 15 in this volume).

Given that European societies are currently facing multiple challenges, such as the recent economic recession in some parts of the continent, the rise in political populism, and xenophobic mobilization against diverse 'others', this type of research that focuses not only on protest, but also on its electoral consequences is about to become even more important. This has been made all the more true by the European 'migrant crisis', which has clear potential to politically reconfigure not only the European political arena, but also national politics in many member states. In this respect, this volume focuses on a problem of a great relevance, seeking to engender a novel stream of research on the movement parties of the radical right addressing these issues. It examines the theoretical implications and empirical relevance of these organizations, comparing movement parties in time and space, drawing on empirical cases investigated with different methods, and trying to bridge the social movement and party politics literature.

The *first aim of this book* is therefore to fill the empirical gap that at present exists in the discussions of these dimensions of politics and political interactions, by providing a detailed map of emergent tendencies towards the formation of movement parties among European right-wing organizations. Focusing on Eastern as well as Western Europe, the volume offers a very wide perspective on the subject.

Moreover, although the volume's concern is with radical right organizations, its findings can be read in comparison to findings on other types of radicalism (e.g. religious radicalism) and the role of movement mobilization in them, offering in this way a valuable insight into one of the most recent and promising fields of investigation within extremism and radicalism research (i.e. the interactions of parties and movements).

Second, besides its descriptive side, this book offers a systematic study of different types of movement parties in different countries and is thereby able to reveal – and possibly explain – differences in the intensity, and especially in the forms of party movement interactions, while also offering reflections on developments, convergences, and divergences in these interactions. This is of crucial interest for the scientific discussion and literature on these political dimensions.

The volume makes a significant contribution to the research on radical right 'movement party organizations' in three ways: theoretically, by showing the importance of underexplored topics in the study of the radical right; methodologically, by expanding the scientific boundaries of this research field through an interdisciplinary approach and new methods of analysis; and empirically, by providing new evidence about radical right movement party organizations from Western, Eastern, and Central Europe. The book is divided into three sections. After discussing, in this introduction (Caiani and Císař), the new conceptual category of the movement party and its applicability to the radical right (underlining differences and similarities with left-wing organizations), this book reviews the scholarship on radical right parties and movements in Europe. It focuses on three strands of this extensive literature (for an overview, see Caiani 2017): first, the *political opportunity explanations* for the fortunes of these parties and movements; second, *internal supply-side approaches*, referring to internal organizational resources, leadership, communication, and propaganda, etc.; and third, the *cultural dimension* of the emergence and the rise of radical right parties and movements (framing and cultural resources). The goal of this book is to shed light on all these aspects (*contextual opportunities*, *resources*, and *culture*) in each chapter, with empirical evidence drawn from different case studies in Europe: Western Europe (including Northern Europe), and Central and Eastern Europe (including the Balkans). More specifically, in Chapter 2 Caiani and Císař illustrate the theoretical framework of the book, within which all chapters could be located; conceptualizing radical right movement parties, and discussing an analytical framework and some hypotheses for interpreting (and explaining) their mobilization. From Chapter 3, the book focuses on Western Europe. In particular, Chapter 3 (Schwörer) investigates the successful new German party 'Alternative für Deutschland' (AfD), tracing its development starting on the street and ending up in Parliament. As the chapter's author notes, since the post-war era, the German Federal Republic has mostly been 'spared' successful parties and movements on the radical right, but the emergence of the AfD, often considered a right-wing populist phenomenon, has put an end to that. The analysis, based on party documents and speeches, reveals how the party's ideological character has changed and moved from being a moderate right to a radical right populist party. In Chapter 4, Hanna and Busher argue that the concepts of movement parties and party movements provide a useful lens through which to enrich understanding of the evolution of the radical right in the UK. Specifically, such concepts enable a better description and analysis of the complex and shifting relationships between the main political actor in this space, UKIP, and both the loose network of smaller radical right groups, and mainstream political parties and their activists. This argument is developed by tracing the trajectory of UKIP and its interactions with cognate actors from the early 1990s through to the 'Brexit' referendum and its immediate aftermath. Chapter 5 (Frigoli and Ivaldi) is devoted to the French case, and questions whether the Front National (FN) can still be considered (with respect to its origin and developments) an example of a radical right movement party. The authors suggest that the FN's contentious frames have achieved greater resonance in mainstream politics, media, and society as a result of the mainstreaming of the party itself, and of the radicalization of the mainstream. They conclude that, while increasingly bridging radical right and mainstream politics, the FN has retained its profile as a movement party, exploiting the resources and initiatives provided by the broader 'reactionary' movement within which it functions.

Chapters 6 and 7 move to Southern Europe. In Chapter 6, Castelli Gattinara focuses on the radical right in contemporary Italy, describing its main ingredients as: subcultural identification, street mobilization, and electoral participation. In Chapter 7, Fielitz focuses on a neglected political party: the radical right Independent Greeks (ANEL), which can be considered one of the most visible symptoms of the representative crisis of Greek democracy. The chapter argues that while much attention is being paid to the electoral fate of Syriza and the rise and persistence of the neo-Nazi Golden Dawn, little is known about the political performance of ANEL, which in fact represents a unique case of rapid ascendance from an indignant right-wing movement into a governmental force in conditions of political and economic crisis.

Weisskircher and Berntzen (Chapter 8) direct their attention to the anti-Islamic PEGIDA mobilization and its relationship to party politics (especially the AfD mobilization). They identify three different dimensions of movement party relations: First, a number of activists tried to enter the arena of party politics in subnational politics, but overwhelmingly failed to do so. Second, extra-parliamentary radical right mobilization did not grow particularly weaker, at least in the case of PEGIDA, when radical right parties were getting stronger. There is no substitutive effect (under the conditions of crisis) like that described in the literature. Third, in the rest of Germany, as well as in other Northern and Central European countries, PEGIDA was often associated with 'subcultural milieus' that included individuals from minor and sometimes major political parties, whose support was sometimes essential for organizing small-scale street activism. Ultimately, the chapter assesses the relevance of party politics for understanding the biggest anti-Islamic social movement in contemporary Europe.

Finally, Chapter 9 (Peterson) analyses the relationship between a movement party and its radical fringe in Sweden. The author examines in depth the Swedish Democrats and the militant factions within the Swedish radical right movement, and shows that the radical right movement in Sweden, both its more moderate party arm and its militant fringe factions, share similar goals – the difference lies in their choice of tactics and rhetoric. The party 'make-over' process resulted in new additions to the fringe – two splinter parties, which were only ostensibly in competition with their 'mother party', and rather mobilized the more 'untameable' supporters of the goals of the wider movement. In terms of more general dynamics, the Swedish chapter demonstrates that the successful electoral mobilization of the radical right has not had a substitutive effect on the radical fringe; in Sweden these two arms instead strengthen each other.

In the second part of the book (from Chapter 10 onwards), the book addresses the rise of new radical right party movements in East-Central Europe and their politics and policies. More specifically, in Chapter 10 Pirro focuses on the organizational and ideological transformation of the radical right in Hungary. Using primary and secondary data, the chapter demonstrates that Jobbik is today one of the most successful radical right organizations effectively contesting elections in Europe. It has upheld its movement party profile and contributed to the rejuvenation of the radical right by politicizing and mainstreaming issues such as 'Roma crime' and 'political crime'. The author concludes that the radical right in Hungary can still be regarded as being in the movement party phase, which in no way contradicts its institutionalizing trajectory. In Chapter 11 on Poland, Stanley shows that the – still ongoing – consolidation of the Polish party system has created both constraints and opportunities for radical right movement parties. Indeed, it is argued that the philosophy of the right-wing Law and Justice Party, taken as a case study, has been to 'leave nothing between us and the wall', as it attempts to cater to radical right concerns and adopt elements of the movement repertoire of action, even during its time in power.

Císař and Navrátil (Chapter 12) focus on the emergence of radical right parties in the Czech Republic, with a focus on the period of migrant crisis (2015 and after). It is argued that the period of migrant crisis offers a unique opportunity to investigate possible transformations of radical right organizations, since the crisis forms the most likely case of the transformation of extra-parliamentary organizations into parties. However, unlike Hungary, the Czech case presents a different path to the mobilization of radical right parties, as its radical right parties are not based on any movement in the country. A number of important radical right parties seem to have originated in the sector of private business rather than from the mobilization of social movements. In this respect, the Czech case enriches our understanding of the multiple paths radical right party mobilization has taken in Eastern Europe. Chapter 13 (Gyarfášová) on Slovakia stresses the role of 'nativist' movements and parties in the political process of the country. They illustrate that although nativist movements and right-wing national political parties have been an integral part of Slovakia's politics since the earliest years of the democratic transition, this phenomenon has been through several metamorphoses in terms of actors, organizations, appeal, and electoral success. The latest stage of this development is the radical right People's Party Our Slovakia Party that entered the national parliament after the 2016 general election. Although the party has no coalition potential, since it is isolated in the parliament and its role is limited to opposition, it has nevertheless a relevant impact on the political process and political discourse in the country.

Finally, Chapter 14 of the book concerns South-Eastern Europe (i.e. the Balkans). Here, Stefanovski and Vardari, compare two 'hybrid' movement parties, as the authors call them, in two countries very much neglected by Western scholars and research, namely: Kosovo and Macedonia. By conducting discourse analyses of in-depth interviews, newspaper articles, and materials produced by the organizations themselves in these two countries, the chapter investigates and compares the similar socio-political configurations that enabled the emergence of two social movements and their development into political parties located at different points on the left-wing axis: the (movement) party 'Vetëvendosje' in Kosovo and 'Levica' in Macedonia. The political opportunity structure (POS) approach is used to interpret the empirical findings. The chapter also points out that it is the formation of a domestic–foreign alliance that creates a closed political structure which is inaccessible to local actors, and they in turn evolve into movement parties in order to overcome marginalization and gain access to the new decision-making process.

In the concluding chapter of this book (Chapter 15), a typology for interpreting the possible 'types of relations between (radical right) parties and movements' is proposed, together with empirical evidence derived from the case studies presented in the book and beyond (Caiani and Císař). More specifically, on the basis of a typology that presents nine types of possible relations between parties and movements, case studies of recent waves of radical right mobilization in European countries are interpreted. These different possible patterns of interaction between political parties and movements are further debated and problematized. Future research is still needed, along with more theorizing on the consequences of radical right mobilization for democracy.

Note

1 This book was supported by the Charles University Research Programme Progress Q18: *Social Sciences*.

References

Albanese, M., Bulli, G., Gattinara, P.C., and Froio, C. (2015) *Fascisti di un Altro Millennio? Crisi e Partecipazione in CasaPound Italia*, Roma: Bonanno.

Caiani, M. (2017) 'Radical Right Wing Movements: Who, When, How and Why?' In Sociopedia, *Sociopedia.isa*

Caiani, M. and Parenti, L. (2013) Web Nero: *Organizzazioni di estrema destra ed Internet*, Bologna, Il Mulino.

Caiani, M., della Porta, D., and Wagemann, C. (2012) *Mobilizing on the Extreme Right: Germany, Italy, and the United States*, Oxford, Oxford University Press.

della Porta, D., Fernández, J., Kouki, H., and Mosca, L. (2017) *Movement Parties Against Austerity*, Cambridge: Polity.

Gattinara, P. C. and Pirro, A. (2018) 'The Far Right as Social Movement.' *European Societies*, https://doi.org/10.1080/14616696.2018.1494301

Gunther, R. and Diamond, L. (2003) 'Species of Political Parties: A New Typology', *Party Politics*, 9(2): 167–199.

Heaney, M.T. and Rojas, F. (2015) *Party in the Street: The Antiwar Movement and the Democratic Party after 9/11*, Cambridge: Cambridge University Press.

Hutter, S. (2014) *Protesting Culture and Economics in Western Europe. New Cleavages in Left and Right Politics*, Minneapolis, MN: University of Minnesota Press.

Kitschelt, H. (2006) 'Movement Parties', in Katz, R.S. and Crotty, W. (eds) *Handbook of Party Politics*, Thousand Oaks, CA: Sage, 278–290.

Kriesi, H., Grande, E., Dolezal, M., Helbling, M., Höglinger, D., Hutter, S., and Wüest, B. (2012) *Political Conflict in Western Europe*, Cambridge: Cambridge University Press.

McAdam, D. and Tarrow, S. (2010) 'Ballots and Barricades: On the Reciprocal Relationship between Elections and Social Movements', *Perspectives on Politics*, 8(2): 529–542.

Minkenberg, M. (2002) 'The Radical Right in Post-Socialist Central and Eastern Europe: Comparative Observations and Interpretations', *East European Politics and Societies*, 16(2): 335–362.

Minkenberg, M. (2003) 'The West European Radical Right as a Collective Actor: Modeling the Impact of Cultural and Structural Variables on Party Formation and Movement Mobilization', *Comparative European Politics*, 1(2): 149–170.

Minkenberg, M. (ed) (2015) *Transforming the Transformation? The East European Radical Right in the Political Process*, London: Routledge.

Minkenberg, M. (2018) 'Between Party and Movement: Conceptual and Empirical Considerations of the Radical Right's Organizational Boundaries and Mobilization Processes.' *European Societies*, https://doi.org/10.1080/14616696.2018.1494296.

Mudde, C. (2007) *Populist Radical Right Parties in Europe*, Cambridge: Cambridge University Press.

2

MOVEMENTS, PARTIES, AND MOVEMENT PARTIES OF THE RADICAL RIGHT

Towards a unified approach?[1]

Manuela Caiani and Ondřej Císař

Introduction: background story

Social dissatisfaction, together with the corresponding political backlash, in a time when European democracies are in economic and political crisis, is one of the central concerns of contemporary political and scholarly debate. A particular focus of scholarly attention has been the support expressed for (populist) radical right[2] parties and movements, which has been increasing rapidly in recent decades. Citizens increasingly give their support to parties and movements that promote xenophobia, ethno-nationalism, and anti-system populism (Caiani 2017a). The election of Donald Trump as President of the United States has been taken as further evidence of the 'mainstreaming of radical right politics' which has affected Western democracies beyond Europe (Mudde 2016).

Recently, growing concerns over the austerity programmes adopted by European governments in response to the financial crisis, immigration, and multiculturalism, combined with disillusionment with mainstream politics and representative democracy, have given rise to strong criticism from civil society groups (see, for example, Kriesi and Pappas 2016). The reactions to EU integration, economic crisis, and globalization have, however, taken various forms:

> the radical left opposition to the opening up of the borders is mainly an opposition to economic liberalization and to the threat it poses to the left's achievement at the national level. The populist right's opposition to the opening up of the borders is first of all an opposition to the social and cultural forms of competition and the threat they pose to national identity.
>
> *(ibid.: 18; see also Wodak 2015)*

The success of the radical right and its 'mobilization of the losers', at least in some party systems, is considered to be responsible for a shift in the right's emphasis away from the economic questions of the 1970s to today's questions of culture (Kriesi et al. 2008: 265; see also Caiani 2017b). All this is leading to a revitalization of radical right-wing actors in both Europe and the United States. At the same time, a new 'category' beyond 'strict' radical right-wing political parties on the one hand, and extreme right-wing movements and subcultures on the other (Bjorgo 2005; Caiani 2017b) seems to have emerged on the political scene: namely radical right movement parties. In terms of academic debates, we can see them as one possible expression of the currently widely studied repertoire of party movement interactions.

Radical right movement parties

Movement parties, as a new breed of political actor, have proved successful in mobilising voters in times of crisis. While it has often been noted that parties are important for movements and *vice versa*, previous research has used the concept of movement party to refer to actors that are in transition from extra-institutional movements to partisan electoral competition 'as their primary vehicle to bring societal interests to bear on policy-making' (Kitschelt 2006: 278).

Scholars have labelled these new parties movement parties, stressing their hybrid nature and their origins in the transformation of social movements into political parties (Kitschelt 2006). It has already been argued that they are likely to emerge in times of political and economic crisis, when traditional cleavage structures are transformed and new societal grievances are not addressed by the existing parties (della Porta 2017; Kitschelt 1989). 'New' movement parties usually exhibit a strongly anti-establishment attitude, deploying a populist discourse of 'us' (the people) against 'them' (the political elite), and drawing on society's mistrust of the dominant political class in times of crisis (Lanzone and Woods 2015). As della Porta (2017: 15) points out,

> the use of an 'anti-political' language by leaders in contrast with parties and professional politicians (...) becomes an instrument for reinforcing personalized leadership by politicians that underline, paradoxically, their estrangement from politics.
>
> Other typical features of newly founded movement parties include weak organizational cultures and a lack of ideological core, because of which they often change political stances or leadership.
>
> *(Gunther and Diamond 2003)*

So far, however, the academic focus has mostly been limited to left-wing and ideologically hybrid organizations, such as those that emerged in Southern Europe amid the Eurozone crisis (for example, Syriza, Podemos, and the Five Star Movement; della Porta et al. 2017), thus neglecting developments on the (radical) right. However, the radical right – in its populist, radical, and extreme variants – is one of the most successful objects of inquiry in the social sciences (see, for example, Mudde 2000, 2007), and seemingly shares organizational features with other movement parties. In fact, there is no doubt that recent developments in Europe, including the economic crisis and the subsequent refugee emergency, have created favourable conditions for the emergence and consolidation of populist parties, either on the right or on the left.

In many ways, the AfD resembles the new left-wing parties that were created through social movements during the economic crisis, such as Syriza in Greece, Podemos in Spain, and the Five Star Movement in Italy (della Porta 2017); the main striking difference is that it promotes an 'exclusive', rather than 'inclusive' populism (Mudde and Kaltwasser 2013). However, we can identify various other movement parties that have mobilized on the (radical) right in Europe. We can probably even find (self-proclaimed) movement parties that have successfully connected mainstream and extreme variants of right-wing ideology, as is the case in some Eastern European countries (Herman 2016; Císař and Štětka 2016; Císař 2017). Almost without exception, these organizations have been trying to straddle the conceptual space between party and movement (Gunther and Diamond 2003), in that they contest elections in order to gain representation in office, yet seek to mobilize public support by providing particular frames to contentious issues (Minkenberg 2002). While some attempts have been made to bridge the party politics literature and social movement studies in the analysis of collective actors of this type (see Minkenberg 2003; McAdam and Tarrow 2010; Kriesi at al. 2012; Hutter 2014), the two branches of scholarship have only rarely crossed paths.

Research in social movement studies has tended to declare social movements the defining feature of established post-1968 democracies (Meyer and Tarrow 1998) and generally prioritized the protest arena of action (for exceptions, see Meyer and Lupo 2007: 120–122). However, important recent contributions to social movement studies have pointed out the need to focus on the electoral arena, political parties, and their interactions with social movements and protest politics (see Goldstone 2003; McAdam and Tarrow 2010, 2013; Kriesi at al. 2012; Hutter 2014; Heaney and Rojas 2015; della Porta et al. 2017). This type of inter-arena interaction constitutes one of the most important challenges of current social movement research (Císař 2015).

Focusing on the interactions between electoral and protest politics seems especially important for studying those segments of the population that tend to express their grievances through the protest vote rather than through street protest – segments that are more common on the (radical) right than on the left (Koopmans et al. 2005). Given that European societies currently face multiple challenges, such as the recent economic recession in some parts of the continent, the rise in political populism, and xenophobic mobilization against diverse representatives of the supposed European 'other', research that focuses not only on protest, but also on its electoral consequences is about to become even more important.

Party–movement interactions

Politics is about conflicting political interests and issues that are advocated by parties, social movements, citizens' groups etc. The available literature on political parties has conceptualized this terrain of contested political issues as a country's political space (see, for example, Marks et al. 2006; Kriesi et al. 2008; Vachudova and Hooghe 2009; Rovny and Edwards 2012). While the party literature has used a spatial model to understand interactions among political parties, it has been suggested that this idea of the political space should be extended to include not only political parties, but also protest politics (Hutter 2014; Císař and Vráblíková 2019). Simply put, political space is a structure of issues that are relevant in various societies, on which political actors take positions and compete for public support (Rovny and Edwards 2012: 57). Similarly, the currently burgeoning literature on social fields (drawing on Bourdieu – see, for example, Bourdieu 1991; but not just him – for social-movement theory-based approaches, see also Fligstein and McAdam 2012 and Goldstone 2004) has developed a related concept of the political field as the site in which collective agents articulate their visions of the world and thereby transform 'the world itself' (Thompson 1991: 26). By producing slogans, programmes, and the like, political actors seek both to construe and impose a particular vision of the world and to mobilize the support of those who should serve as the base of their political power to accumulate political capital.

This perspective has been used to explain the countervailing or disalignment effect between parties and movements. Authors focusing on xenophobic and extreme right claim-making (Koopmans et al. 2005: 185–187; Giugni et al. 2005: 146; Koopmans and Statham 1999) explain that, if there is an established party that articulates a similarly radical agenda and that is even able to participate in the government and implement its programme, the space for radicals decreases, since most potential supporters will channel their concerns through this established party. The available space for radical protest contracts, or even closes completely (see Kriesi et al. 2012 and Hutter 2014 for a more general application of this logic in the context of Western Europe; on Central-Eastern Europe, see Císař and Navrátil 2015a; Císař and Vráblíková 2019).

However, it is not clear whether the same mechanism characterizes the relationship between party and protest politics in general. According to Hutter's (2014) findings on Western Europe, summarized in the form of the differing logics hypothesis, while the countervailing mechanism defines the political right, in case of the left, there is congruence between parties in power and political protest. Unlike the political right, whose success in formal politics tends to decrease protest, left-wing governments tend to reinforce the protests of allied movement forces. Moreover, in summarizing developments in US politics in the 20th century, McAdam and Tarrow (2013) found congruence for both the political right and left. While dominance of the party left triggers liberal and left movements, the hegemony of conservative forces helps right-wing movements; in general, the institutionally prevailing political forces open up opportunities for their potential movement allies in the political system. Conversely, focusing on the whole political spectrum in post-1989 Central-Eastern Europe, Císař and his collaborators (Císař and Navrátil 2015a; Císař and Vráblíková 2019) demonstrate the existence of a countervailing relationship between the arenas of party and protest politics.

The present volume should also open up an opportunity for different conceptualizations of these interactions, with a focus on movement parties of the radical right. Obviously, one such conceptualization is in the form of niche parties. Such a role can be played by radical right forces, which tend to be newer political actors marginalized in relation to the main (socioeconomic for Western Europe) political conflict (Meguid 2005, 2008). In general, the countervailing dynamics between parties and protest changes into congruence, and the emergence of niche parties, when the balance of competition among the mainstream parties on the main socioeconomic issue dimension is destabilized. When this occurs, opportunities open up for protest actors to put their demands onto the agenda in the party field. In terms of the classical apparatus of the political-opportunity structure (the political process model), this is an instance of shifting alignments. Shifting alignments cause party leaders to look for new sources of support outside of the established camps; as a result, opportunities for new (niche party and protest) actors open up (Tarrow 2011: 165).

Similarly, the saliency of political issues might be reconfigured because of external developments, such as the appearance of a new social cleavage (such as today's demarcation-integration due to globalization; see Kriesi et al. 2008, 2012; Hutter 2014) and/or the occurrence of some significant threat leading to a major crisis, such as the current economic and migrant crises (Bermeo and Bertels 2004; Giugni and Grasso 2015). In such moments, the equilibrium supported by the mainstream parties is lost, and a new space for other actors opens up; the party and protest fields become aligned, and new types of actors, such as movement parties, can emerge. If we look at the ability of general protest actors to add their issues to the political agenda, Jack Goldstone (2004: 355) shows that it is 'triggered by major society-wide crises, such as military or economic challenges that weaken support for a government'. Contemporary Europe is going through at least two types of crises right now. The Great Recession has been accompanied by a massive inflow of refugees, for which the continent was unprepared. Will the current crises lead to new types of political mobilization and electoral action? Will they lead to an ever more closely connected mobilization in the form of movement parties?

While largely still under-specified theoretically, hybrid organizations such as movement parties of the radical right are also under-researched in terms of their main characteristics, i.e. membership, internal structures, resource mobilization, and repertoires of action (cf. Kitschelt 2006; Albanese et al. 2015). What are the main traits of movement parties on the (radical) right across various countries? What organizational and strategic features (or combination thereof) qualify these networks of organizations as movement parties rather than 'party movements'? What is the lifecycle of movement parties, in terms of emergence and breakthrough, the structuring of movement party relations, and the construction of shared collective identities? In addition, if applicable, a historical conceptualization of the existing movement parties in each country needs to be provided, in order to understand their 'novelty', or the lack of it.

Our framework

In order to provide our volume with theoretical consistency, we opt for concepts derived from social movement theory. This will give the volume basic consistency, but at the same time, it will give individual authors enough flexibility to use the theory according to their desired research goals, which may differ across the chapters. Thus, while the readers will encounter political opportunities, resources, and cultural factors in all chapters, they may be used for various research goals. In essence, we differentiate between analytical description, theory/concept development, and explanation, i.e. theory testing (see, for example, King et al. 1994; van Evera 1997; George and Bennett 2005). If an author opts for the first one, she will use the theoretical concepts for a structured descriptive analysis of the theoretically relevant dimensions of radical right movement parties. If she opts for the second one, she will still organize the chapter according to these dimensions, but based on her data, she will try to either modify the concepts, or extend the original three dimensions relevant for the analysis of radical right movement parties. Provided a proper design is in place, the third strategy is to use theories of social movements to explain the emergence of movement parties in a given context. If we combine the three basic concepts of social movement theory with three possible research goals, we get the following table of what possible chapters may look like (see Table 2.1). In the remainder of this chapter we will outline basic theoretical concepts/dimensions, which will structure the presentation of the forthcoming chapters.

I. Political and discursive opportunities and (radical right) movement parties

Although there has been a lot of debate regarding both the concrete conceptualization of environmental variables and their subsequent operationalization (see Kitschelt 1986; Gamson and Meyer 1996; Kriesi et al. 1995; Tilly 1995; Tilly and Tarrow 2007; Tarrow 2011), these discussions notwithstanding, the core of the concept is made up of both formal and informal political institutions (Kriesi et al. 1995; Kriesi 2004). The basic idea of the approach based on political opportunity structure is that open political institutions facilitate mobilization, and closed institutions impede it. The level of their openness or closedness is a function of the number of access points available to social movement organizations and other non-state actors in a political system at a given point in time. Thus, open opportunities can be operationalized as the existence of formal and informal mechanisms and procedures of inclusion of non-state actors in the policy process of a given polity. Closed opportunities display the opposite value. While open access facilitates political mobilization and invites non-state actors to become integrated into the political process, closed opportunities exclude them from the process and increase the costs of collective action (see Tarrow 2011).

TABLE 2.1 Movement parties: possible analytical strategies

	Analytical Strategy 1: Analytical Description	Analytical Strategy 2: Theory/Concept Development	Analytical Strategy 3: Explanation/ Theory Testing
Context (Political and Discursive Opportunities)	Descriptive analysis of the context (of movement-parties' emergence/ success)	Modification or extension of the concept of political and cultural opportunities (to be applied to movement-parties' emergence/ success)	Test of expectations (hypotheses) derived from the political process theory
Resource Mobilization	Descriptive analysis of the way resources are mobilized and employed (by movement parties)	Modification or extension of the resource mobilization concept	Test of expectations (hypotheses) derived from resource mobilization theory
Cultural and Symbolic Tools (Framing)	Descriptive analysis of the way cultural resources and symbols are employed (by movement parties)	Modification or extension of framing (and related) analysis	Test of expectations (hypotheses) derived from framing literature

Political mobilization is not determined only by the level of institutional access: the structures in which non-state actors interact possess a symbolic dimension, i.e. 'the cultural side of opportunity' (Gamson and Mayer 1996: 279). Accordingly, Koopmans and Statham (1999) propose we should include cultural properties of the political context in the analysis based on the notion of political opportunity structure. They coin the term 'discursive opportunity structure' to highlight the idea that the context of political mobilization is not only shaped by formal political institutions, but is also formed by prevailing interpretative schemata that make some ideas and claims generally acceptable, 'sensible', 'realistic', and '"legitimate" within a certain polity at a specific time' (ibid.: 228). Prevailing political discourse provides 'a language in which policy can be described within the political arena and the terms in which policies are judged there' (Hall 1989: 383). At the same time, discursive conditions limit political actors and provide them with cultural resources to draw upon when making their claims: in other words, they provide them with a particular repertoire of legitimate claims and action forms (Steinberg 1998, 1999; Tilly 1995). How does this relate to the radical right?

The political opportunity structure (see, for example, Arzheimer and Carter 2006; Mudde 2007) available in a specific time and country, refers to both the stable and the dynamic characteristics of the political context, such as the institutional framework of a country, the functional and territorial distribution of powers, the party system, or the form of government; the shift in the configuration of allies and opposition, new laws, and so on (see Mudde 2007), can strongly influence the emergence and impact of the radical right (beyond its mobilization). This concept, traditionally used to understand the mobilization of the left, has more recently also been applied to radical right-wing movements and parties (see Koopmans et al. 2005; Caiani et al. 2012; for radical right-wing parties in particular, see the review by Muis and Immezel 2016).

In particular, for what concerns the contextual opportunities for the radical right, the economic and social dimensions of the context can integrate the traditional notion of political opportunity structure (for a more general argument, see Císař and Navrátil 2017). More specifically, economic and social crises in particular have been discussed in connection with the success of radical right parties and movements (Prowe 2004). However, political instability, allies in power (Koopmans 2005), the legacy of an authoritarian past, youth subcultures and hooliganism, and the spread of xenophobic views within society have also all been discussed in this regard (Mudde 2007; Rydgren 2005). Koopmans (2005), for instance, argues that right-wing radicalism in Europe tends to be motivated more by a lack of opportunities (e.g. through established political channels of expression) than by the presence of grievances in society (e.g. the presence of immigrants or economic difficulties). As far as Central and Eastern Europe is concerned, the role of the former communist regime has been cited as favouring greater acceptance of right-wing discourses and ideologies (Minkenberg 2015).

Moreover, the idea of the political opportunity structure has been integrated with the notion of 'discursive opportunities', which determine what kind of ideas become visible for the public, resonate with public opinion, and are held to be '"legitimate" by the audience' (Koopmans et al. 2005; Kriesi 2004: 72; for a literature review on the concept, see McCammon 2013). In this regard, stress has been placed both on the importance of 'frames' and discourses (see also below) as mediating factors for mobilization between the individuals and their context (Furlow and Goodall 2011; Morrow 2015; Wodak 2015), and on the importance of public discourse and media debates for radical right-wing movements (e.g. Ellinas 2010). Likewise, theories on diffusion and social contagion stress the importance of cognitive elements for the spread of right-wing radical mobilization (Jäckle and König 2016; Koopmans and Olzak 2004; Muis 2015). On the basis of a longitudinal, cross-country study of five European democracies, Koopmans et al. (2005) found that both the mobilization and the success of radical right-wing actors were affected more by the cultural and historical policies of the country (i.e. its conception of 'citizenship'), and by the prevailing discourses on migration and ethnic diversity in the country than they are by other variables within the context.

II. Resources and (radical right) movement parties

As the adherents of the resource mobilization paradigm pointed out long ago, contemporary organized political activism is based on the availability of resources, such as money, time, leadership skills, expert knowledge, and cultural and human capital (McCarthy and Zald 1977; Jenkins 1983; Zald 1992; Edwards and McCarthy 2004). While the availability of resources fosters mobilization, their shortage disables it. There are a variety of resources that are available for political activists at a particular point in time. At the same time, not all resources are accessible to all activists. Rather, activists are always limited in what resources they can get hold of. The resources instrumental to successful mobilization are always unequally distributed within societies and among them.

Edwards and McCarthy (2004) define four bundles of resource-access mechanisms, which determine (or shape) political activism in particular ways: aggregation, self-production, appropriation/co-optation, and patronage. Aggregation defines the mechanisms by which resources are generated *from individuals*, such as individual contributions. Self-production refers to the mechanisms by which resources are created *by movements themselves*: social movement organizations 'create cultural products like collective-action frames, tactical repertoires, music, literature, and organizational templates for enacting specific types of collective events or issue campaigns' (ibid.: 134). They also self-produce other resources, such as human capital, via training and economic resources by merchandising their own products. Appropriation/co-optation includes the mechanisms of *strategic appropriation of already existing institutions and organizations* for the movements' purposes. Patronage describes 'the bestowal of resources upon an SMO by an individual or an organization that often specializes in patronage … Government contracts, foundation grants, and large private donations are the most common forms of financial patronage … ' (ibid.: 135).

For radical right-wing organizations, this approach (or line of explanation for collective actors' emergence and success) focuses mostly on internal factors, such as organizations' dynamics, leaders, resource-access mechanisms, ideologies, and propaganda, to explain the emergence, survival, and endurance of the radical right. Among organizational resources, the role of ideology in current right-wing movements is important. Because right-wing extremists generally dehumanize their enemies, attacks on target groups, such as black people or enclaves of foreign workers in Europe, are justified according to their ideology (Caiani et al. 2012). Griffin (2003) underlines the role of 'dream time' in radical right-wing political violence. Moreover, charismatic leadership is also a prominent supply-side explanation for radical right mobilization in the academic literature (e.g. Eatwell 2005). It has been argued that charismatic leaders who are able to maintain peace in an organization can instigate an upward spiral of organizational strength (Klandermans and Mayer 2006). Also, the networks that radical right organizations are able to build, either at the national or at the international level, are considered important for right-wing mobilization (e.g. on networks built online, see Burris et al. 2000; Gerstenfeld et al. 2003; Qin et al. 2007; Zhou et al. 2005). All in all, they point to a combination of underlying (individual and contextual) motives for contention with organizations and their networks as the basis for movement recruitment and the eventual path to popular mobilization (Caiani et al. 2012; Diani 2015; on the post-communist situation, see Císař and Navrátil 2015b).

At the same time, radical organizations in particular may not be based on mass mobilization of resources and individuals. Radical activism is based mainly, although not exclusively, on loose organizational platforms and individual activists, who may not be members of any particular group. Their ability to network and cooperate is similarly limited, since radical movements 'explicitly articulate their critiques of the extant, and the dimensions of the desired future society' (Williams 2004: 103). As a result, radicals' demands often approximate the boundaries of the established discourse, 'falling outside what many people are able to "hear" as acceptable visions of society', which limits the resonance of their message among individual supporters (ibid.; see also the next section). Therefore, this type of activism is often based on few participants and militant strategies (Císař 2013).

III. Frames, discourses and (radical right) movement parties

Frames are defined as cognitive instruments that allow us to make sense of external reality (Snow and Benford 1992). They are very often produced by organizational leadership, and they provide the necessary background within which individual activists can locate their actions (Snow et al. 1986; Gamson 1988). As is the case of any collective actor, extreme-right organizations have to motivate individuals to action – even if they are organizations with only limited resonance – and provide followers and potential followers with the rationale for joining and supporting their organizations. Depending on the cultural conditions that prevail in each context, some frames will resonate while others will not

(Benford and Snow 2000). Frame resonance 'concerns the relationship between a movement organization's interpretative work and its ability to influence broader public understandings' (Keck and Sikkink 1998: 17). As every public discourse is bounded, there is only a limited set of claims that can be deemed legitimate at a particular point in time. If activists wish to be successful, either their claims must fall within this set, or they must be able to reinterpret the set in a way that fits their goals. The boundaries of what is regarded as 'legitimate' change over time: for example, Ellingson (1995) has shown that discursive conditions change in response to particular events, marking the temporal development of political mobilization. In this respect, current economic and cultural crises can bring about visible changes in discursive conditions, which determine the frame resonance of the radical right (see also the section on discursive opportunities).

At the same time, the concept of 'frame' allows us to stress both the fragmentation of the extreme-right discourse (whose eclecticism has often been stressed) and the cognitive function of the discourse, which can fruitfully be analysed to understand the new generation of (right-wing) movement parties, as it provides the voters and sympathizers of right-wing organizations with an immediate instrument to make sense of the reality they perceive.

The discourse of the extreme right has been addressed by several subfields of the social sciences. Studies in political communication have looked at political campaigns, stressing that, by making use of an anti-establishment and antiparty rhetoric, radical right populist parties and movements are able to gain visibility and mobilize citizens' feelings of disaffection toward the national and European political class (for example, Caiani and della Porta 2011). Electoral studies have explored extreme-right party manifestos (for example, the influence of the left/right dimension on party position toward European integration; for a summary, see Statham 2008). Social constructivist studies have addressed the discourse of the extreme right as 'a site of the construction' of extreme-right identity; 'exploring how meaning works in discourse' (Ferber 1998: 48). Further, the success/failure of extreme-right parties has been linked to their discourse and frames (for example, Rydgren 2008). Indeed, the ideology and propaganda of xenophobic parties or movements 'may influence people's frame of thought' (Rydgren 2003: 52–53), offering 'a theory guidance in black-box situations' and a 'powerful tool to reframe unsolved political problems'.

Recently, two different theoretical developments have brought about some shifts in attention. On the one hand, there has been a growing focus on the cultural and symbolic dimension of social movements (Jasper, Goodwin, and Polletta 2001; Flam and King 2005). On the other hand, a more relational vision of protest has been promoted, with attention paid to social mechanisms that intervene between macro-causes and macro-effects (McAdam, Tarrow, and Tilly 2001). In a critique of the 'structuralist bias' of previous approaches, attention has moved toward the relational, cognitive, and affective mechanisms through which contextual input is filtered and acquires meaning. In this process, cultural frames play an ever-important role.

Notes

1 This chapter was written as part of work on the research project 'Activism in Hard Times' funded by the Czech Science Foundation (No. 16-10163S).
2 Even though the terms 'extreme right', 'far right', and 'populist radical right' are often used in the literature to refer to the same empirical object, in this work we use 'radical right' to refer to those groups that exhibit in their common ideological core the characteristics of nationalism, xenophobia (ethno-nationalist xenophobia), anti-establishment critiques, and socio-cultural authoritarianism (law and order, family values) (Mudde 2007). The term extreme right is avoided by many scholars and we will avoid it here too, because it can also include groups well beyond the legal boundaries of democratic politics (e.g. violent direct actions or even terrorist attacks), while the parties studied in this book are limited to those using conventional, mostly electoral, channels. Therefore, we prefer to use the label 'radical right' to describe those parties that are located toward one pole on the standard ideological left–right scale.

References

Albanese, M., Bulli, G., Castelli Gattinara, P., and Froio, C. (2015) *Fascisti di un Altro Millennio? Crisi e Partecipazione in CasaPound Italia*, Roma: Bonanno.
Arzheimer, K. and Carter, E. (2006) 'Political opportunity structures and right-wing extremist party success', *European Journal of Political Research*, 45(3): 419–443.
Benford, R. and Snow, D. (2000) 'Framing Processes and Social Movements: An Overview and Assessment', *Annual Review of Sociology*, 26: 611–639.
Bermeo, N. and Bartels, L.M. (eds) (2014) *Mass Politics in Tough Times*, Oxford: Oxford University Press.
Bourdieu, P. (1991) 'Political Representation: Elements of a Theory of the Political Field', in Thompson, J. (ed.) *Language and Symbolic Power*, Cambridge, MA: Harvard University Press, 171–202.
Burris, V., Smith, E., and Strahm, A. (2000) 'White Supremacist Networks on the Internet', *Sociological Focus*, 33(2): 215–235.
Caiani, M. (2017a) 'Nationalism, Populism and the Ri-Birth of Nationhood in Europe', in Grimmel, A. (ed.) *The Crisis of the European Union: Challenges, Analyses, Solutions*, Oxon: Routledge, 91–103.
Caiani, M. (2017b) 'Radical Right Wing Movements: Who, When, How and Why?', *Sociopedia.isa*.
Caiani, M. and della Porta, D. (2011) 'The Elitist Populism of the Extreme Right: A Frame Analysis of Extreme Right Wing Discourses in Italy and Germany', *Acta Politica*, 46(2): 180–202.
Císař, O. (2013) 'A Typology of Extra-parliamentary Political Activism in Post-communist Settings: The Case of the Czech Republic', in Jacobsson, K. and Saxonberg, S. (eds) *Beyond NGO-ization: The Development of Social Movements in Central and Eastern Europe*, Aldershot: Ashgate Publishing, 139–167.
Císař, O. (2015) 'Social Movements in Political Science', in della Porta, D. and Diani, M. (eds) *Oxford Handbook of Social Movements*, Oxford: Oxford University Press, 50–67.
Císař, O. (2017) *Czech Republic: From Postcommunist Idealism to Economic Populism (International Policy Analysis)*, Berlin: FES.
Císař, O. and Navrátil, J. (2015a) 'At the Ballot Boxes or in the Streets and Factories: Economic Contention in the Visegrad Group', in Giugni, M. and Grasso, M. (eds) *Austerity and Protest: Popular Contention in Times of Economic Crisis*, Aldershot: Ashgate Publishing, 35–53.

Císař, O. and Navrátil, J. (2015b) 'Promoting Competition or Cooperation? The Impact of EU Funding on Czech Advocacy Organizations', *Democratization*, 22(3): 536–559.

Císař, O. and Štětka, V. (2016) 'Czech Republic: The Rise of Populism from the Fringes to the Mainstream', in Aalberg, T., Esser, F., Reinemann, C., Stromback, J., and De Vreese, C. (eds) *Populist Political Communication in Europe*, London: Routledge, 285–298.

Císař, O. and Navrátil, J. (2017) 'Polanyi, Political Economic Opportunity Structure and Protest: Capitalism and Contention in the Post-communist Czech Republic', *Social Movement Studies* 16(1): 82–100.

Císař, O. and Vráblíková, K. (2019) ''National Protest Agenda and the Dimensionality of Party Politics: Evidence from East-Central European Democracies', *European Journal of Political Research*, forthcoming.

della Porta, D. (2017) 'Movement Parties in Times of (Anti)Austerity: An Introduction', in della Porta, D., Fernández, J., Kouki, H., and Mosca, L. (eds) *Movement Parties against Austerity*, London: Wiley.

della Porta, D., Fernandez, J., Kouki, H., and Mosca, L. (2017) *Movement Parties*, Cambridge: Polity Press.

Diani, M. (2015) *The Cement of Civil Society*, Cambridge: Cambridge University Press.

Edwards, B. and McCarthy, J. (2004) 'Resources and Social Movement Mobilization', in Snow, D., Soule, S., and Kriesi, H. (eds) *The Blackwell Companion to Social Movements*, Malden, MA: Blackwell Publishing, 116–152.

Ellinas, A. (2010) *The Media and the Far Right in Western Europe: Playing the Nationalist Card*, New York: Cambridge University Press.

Ellingson, S. (1995) 'Understanding the Dialectic of Discourse and Collective Action: Public Debate and Rioting in Antebellum Cincinnati', *American Journal of Sociology*, 101: 100–144.

Ferber, A.L. (1998) 'Constructing whiteness: The intersections of race and gender in US white supremacist discourse', *Ethnic and Racial Studies*, 21(1): 48–63.

Flam, H. and King, D. (eds) (2005) *Emotions and Social Movements*, London: Routledge.

Fligstein, N. and McAdam, D. (2012) *A Theory of Fields*, Oxford: Oxford University Press.

Furlow, R.B. and Goodall, H.L. (2011) 'The War of Ideas and the Battle of Narratives: A Comparison of Extremist Storytelling Structures', *Cultural Studies Critical Methodologies*, 11(3): 215–223.

Gamson, W. and Mayer, D. (1996) 'Framing Political Opportunity', in McAdam, D., McCarthy, J., and Zald, M. (eds) *Comparative Perspectives on Social Movements. Political Opportunities, Mobilizing Structures, and Cultural Framings*, Cambridge: Cambridge University Press, 275–290.

George, A.L. and Bennett, A. (2005) *Case Studies and Theory Development in the Social Sciences*, Cambridge MA: MIT Press.

Gerstenfeld, P.B., Grant, D.R., and Chiang, C. (2003) 'Hate Online: A Content Analysis of Extremist Internet Sites', *Analysis of Social Issues and Public Policy*, 3(1): 29–44.

Giugni, M., Koopmans, R., Passy, F., and Statham, P. (2005) 'Institutional and Discursive Opportunities for Extreme-Right Mobilization in Five Countries', *Mobilization: An International Quarterly*, 10(1): 145–162.

Giugni, M. and Grasso, M. (eds) (2015) *Austerity and Protest: Popular Contention in Times of Economic Crisis*, Aldershot: Ashgate Publishing.

Goldstone, J. (ed.) (2003) *States, Parties, and Social Movements*, Cambridge: Cambridge University Press.

Goldstone, J. (2004) 'More Social Movements or Fewer? Beyond Political Opportunity Structures to Relational Fields', *Theory and Society*, 33(3/4): 333–365.

Griffin, R. (2003) 'Shattering crystals: The role of 'dream time' in radical right-wing political violence', *Terrorism and Political Violence*, 15(1): 57–95.

Hall, P. (1989) 'Conclusion: The Politics of Keynesian Ideas', in McAdam, D., Tarrow, S., and Tilly, C. (eds) *The Political Power of Economic Ideas: Keynesianism across Nations*, Cambridge: Cambridge University Press.

Heaney, M.T. and Rojas, F. (2015) *Party in the Street: The Antiwar Movement and the Democratic Party after 9/11*, Cambridge: Cambridge University Press.

Herman, L.E. (2016) 'Re-evaluating the Post-communist Success Story: Party Elite Loyalty, Citizen Mobilization and the Erosion of Hungarian Democracy', *European Political Science Review*, 8(2): 251–284.

Hutter, S. (2014) *Protesting Culture and Economics in Western Europe. New Cleavages in Left and Right Politics*, Minneapolis, London: University of Minnesota Press.

Jäckle, S. and König, P.D. (2016) 'The Dark Side of the German 'Welcome Culture': Investigating the Causes Behind Attacks on Refugees in 2015', *West European Politics*, 40(2): 223–251.

Jasper, J., Goodwin, J., and Polletta, F. (2001) *Passionate Politics. Emotions and Social Movements*. Chicago, IL: The University of Chicago Press.

Jenkins, C.J. (1983) 'Resource Mobilization Theory and the Study of Social Movements', *Annual Review of Sociology*, 9: 527–553.

Keck, M. and Sikkink, K. (1998) *Activists Beyond Borders: Advocacy Networks in International Politics*, Ithaca, NY: Cornell University Press.

King, G., Keohane, R., and Verba, S. (1994) *Designing Social Inquiry. Scientific Inference in Qualitative Research*, Princeton, NJ: Princeton University Press.

Kitschelt, H. (1986) 'Political Opportunity Structures and Political Protest: Anti-Nuclear Movements in Four Democracies', *British Journal of Political Science*, 16: 57–85.

Kitschelt, H. (1989) *The Logics of Party Formation: Ecological Parties in Belgium and West Germany*, Ithaca, NY: Cornell University Press.

Kitschelt, H. (2006) 'Movement Parties', in Katz, R.S. and Crotty, W. (eds) *Handbook of Party Politics*, Thousand Oaks, CA: Sage, 278–290.

Klandermans, B. and Mayer, N. (2006) 'Through the Magnifying Glass. The World of Extreme Right Activists', in Klandermans, B. and Mayer, N. (eds) *Extreme Right Activists in Europe. Through the Magnifying Glass*, London and New York: Routledge, 269–276.

Koopmans, R. and Statham, P. (1999) 'Ethnic and Civic Conceptions of Nationhood and the Differential Success of the Extreme Right in Germany and Italy', in Giugni, M., McAdam, D., and Tilly, C. (eds) *How Social Movements Matter*, Minneapolis, MN: University of Minnesota Press, 225–252.

Koopmans, R. and Rucht, D. (2002) 'Protest Event Analysis', *Methods of Social Movement Research*, 16: 231–259.

Koopmans, R. and Olzak, S. (2004) 'Discursive Opportunities and the Evolution of Right-Wing Violence in Germany', *American Journal of Sociology*, 110(1): 198–230.

Koopmans, R., Statham, P., Giugni, M., and Passy, F. (2005) *Contested Citizenship: Immigration and Cultural Diversity in Europe*, Minneapolis, MN: University of Minnesota Press.

Kriesi, H., Koopmans, R., Duyvendak, J.W., and Giugni, M. (1995) *New Social Movements in Western Europe: A Comparative Analysis*, London: UCL Press.

Kriesi, H., Grande, E., Lachat, R., Dolezal, M., Bornschier, S., and Frey, T. (2008) *West European Politics in the Age of Globalization*, Cambridge: Cambridge University Press.

Kriesi, H. (2004) 'Political Context and Opportunity' in Snow, D., Soule, S., and Kriesi, H. (eds) *The Blackwell Companion to Social Movements*, Malden, MA: Blackwell Publishing, 67–90.

Kriesi, H., Grande, E., Dolezal, M., Helbling, M., Höglinger, D., Hutter, S., and Wüest, B. (2012) *Political Conflict in Western Europe*, Cambridge: Cambridge University Press.

Kriesi, H. and Pappas, T.S. (eds) (2015) *European Populism in the Shadow of the Great Recession*, Colchester: ECPR Press.

Lanzone, L. and Woods, D. (2015) 'Riding the Populist Web: Contextualizing the Five Star Movement (M5S) in Italy', *Politics and Governance*, 3(2): 56.

Marks, G., Hooghe, L., Edwards, E., and Nelson, M. (2006) 'Party Competition and European Integration in the East and West: Different Structure, Same Causality', *Comparative Political Studies*, 39(2): 155–175.

McAdam, D. and Tarrow, S. (2010) 'Ballots and Barricades: On the Reciprocal Relationship between Elections and Social Movements', *Perspectives on Politics*, 8(2): 529–542.

McAdam, D. and Tarrow, S. (2013) 'Social Movements and Elections: Toward a Broader Understanding of the Political Context of Contention', in Van Stekelenburg, J., Rogeband, C., and Klandermans, B. (eds) *The Future of Social Movement Research: Dynamics, Mechanisms, and Processes*, Minneapolis, MN: University of Minnesota Press, 325–346.

McCammon, H. (2013) 'Discursive Opportunity Structure', in Snow, D.A., della Porta D., Klandermans, B., and McAdam, D. (eds) *The Wiley-Blackwell Encyclopedia of Social and Political Movements*, Malden, MA: Wiley.

McCarthy, J. and Zald, M. (1977) 'Resource Mobilization and Social Movements: A Partial Theory', *American Journal of Sociology*, 82(6): 1212–1241.

Meguid, B. (2005) 'Competition Between Unequals: The Role of Mainstream Party Strategy in Niche Party Success', *American Political Science Review*, 99(3): 347–359.

Meguid, B. (2008) *Party Competition between Unequals: Strategies and Electoral Fortunes in Western Europe*, Cambridge: Cambridge University Press.

Meyer, D. and Tarrow, S. (eds) (1998) *The Social Movement Society*, Lanham, MD: Rowman and Littlefield.

Meyer, D. and Lupo, L. (2007) 'Assessing the Politics of Protest. Political Science and the Study of Social Movements', in Klandermans, B. and Roggeband, C. (eds) *Handbook of Social Movements across Disciplines*, Berlin: Springer, 111–156.

Minkenberg, M. (2002) 'The Radical Right in Post-Socialist Central and Eastern Europe: Comparative Observations and Interpretations', *East European Politics and Societies*, 16(2): 335–362.

Minkenberg, M. (2003) 'The West European Radical Right as a Collective Actor: Modeling the Impact of Cultural and Structural Variables on Party Formation and Movement Mobilization', *Comparative European Politics*, 1(2): 149–170.

Morrow, E. (2015) 'Framing, Counter-Framing and Mobilisation: An Ethnographic Study of the English Defence League', unpublished thesis, King's College London: London.

Mudde, C. (2000) *The Ideology of the Extreme Right*, Manchester: Manchester University Press.

Mudde, C. (2007) *Populist Radical Right Parties in Europe*, Cambridge: Cambridge University Press.

Mudde, C. (2016) *On Extremism and Democracy in Europe*, London: Routledge.

Mudde, C. and Kaltwasser, C.R. (2013) 'Exclusionary vs. Inclusionary Populism: Comparing Contemporary Europe and Latin America', *Government and Opposition*, 48(2): 147–174.

Muis, J. and Tim, I. (2016) 'Radical Right Populism', *Sociopedia.isa*, DOI:10.1177/2056846016121.

Prowe, D. (2004) 'The Fascist Phantom and Anti-Immigrant Violence', in Weitz, E. and Fenner A. (eds) *Fascism and Neofascism*, New York: Palgrave Macmillan, 125–140.

Qin, J., Zhou, Y., Reid, E., Lai, G., and Hsinchun, C. (2007) 'Analyzing Terror Campaigns on the Internet: Technical Sophistication, Content Richness, and Web Interactivity', *International Journal of Human–Computer Studies*, 65(1): 71–84.

Rovny, J. and Edwards, E. (2012) 'Struggle over Dimensionality: Party Competition in Western and Eastern Europe', *East European Politics and Societies*, 26(1): 56–74.

Rydgren, J. (2007) 'The Sociology of the Radical Right', *Annual Review of Sociology*, 33: 241–262.

Snow, D.A., Rochford, E.B., Jr., Worden, S.K., and Benford, R.D. (1986) 'Frame Alignment Processes, Micromobilization, and Movement Participation', *American Sociological Review*, 51(4): 464–481.

Statham, P. (2008) 'Political Party Contestation over Europe in Public Discourses: Emergent Euroscepticism?', *Arena Working Papers Series*.

Steinberg, M. (1998) 'Tilting the Frame: Considerations on Collective Action Framing from a Discursive Turn', *Theory and Society*, 27(6): 845–872.

Steinberg, M. (1999) 'The Talk and Back Talk of Collective Action: A Dialogic Analysis of Repertoires of Discourse among Nineteenth-Century English Cotton Spinners', *American Journal of Sociology*, 105(3): 736–780.

Tarrow, S. (2011) *Power in Movement. Social Movements and Contentious Politics*, Cambridge: Cambridge University Press.

Thompson, J. (1991) 'Editor's Introduction', in Thompson, J. (ed.) *Language and Symbolic Power*, Cambridge, MA: Harvard University Press, 1–32.

Tilly, C. (1995) *Popular Contention in Great Britain 1758–1834*, Cambridge, MA: Harvard University Press.

Tilly, C. and Tarrow, S. (2007) *Contentious Politics*, Boulder, London: Paradigm Publishers.

Vachudova, M. and Hooghe, L. (2009) 'Postcommunist Politics in a Magnetic Field: How Transition and EU Accession Structure Party Competition on European Integration', *Comparative European Politics*, 7: 179–212.

Van Evera, S. (1997) *Guide to Methods for Students of Political Science*, Ithaca, NY: Cornell University Press.

Williams, R. (2004) 'The Cultural Contexts of Collective Action: Constraints, Opportunities, and Symbolic Life of Social Movements', in Snow, D., Soule, S., and Kriesi, H. (eds) *The Blackwell Companion to Social Movements*, Malden, MA: Blackwell Publishing, 91–115.

Wodak, R. (2015) *The Politics of Fear: What Right-Wing Populist Discourses Mean*, London: Sage.

Zald, M. (1992) 'Looking Backward to Look Forward: Reflections on the Past and Future of the Resource Mobilization Program', in Morris, A. and Mueller, C.M. (eds) *Frontiers in Social Movement Theory*, New Heaven, CT: Yale University Press, 326–348.

Zhou, Y., Reid, E., Qin, J., Chen, H., and Lai, G. (2005) 'U.S. Domestic Extremist Groups on the Web: Link and Content Analysis', *IEEE Intelligent Systems*, 20(5): 44–51.

PART II
Western Europe

3

ALTERNATIVE FÜR DEUTSCHLAND

From the streets to the Parliament?

Jakob Schwörer

Introduction

Right-wing populism is on the increase. This is a fact illustrated by the victory of Donald Trump in the most recent US presidential election, the UK's Brexit (which was supported by right-wing populist parties and politicians), and by the rising electoral success of right-wing populist parties throughout the rest of Europe (Boros, Freitas, Kadlót, and Stetter 2017). The increasing success of right-wing populist parties is also reflected in the growing interest of the media and social scientific research. As a result of constant new publications, it is getting more and more difficult to maintain an up-to-date overview of literature regarding right-wing populism already in German-speaking countries, not to mention the large number of publications in English.[1]

In Germany, the increased interest in right-wing populism can also explain the success of the Alternative for Germany (AfD), which is already represented in 14 parliaments of the states (end of 2017), and entered the German Bundestag in September 2017, winning 12.6% of the electoral votes. Since the end of the Second World War, the Federal Republic of Germany had been one of the few European countries free of successful right-wing (populist) parties, until the recent success of the AfD. It is, therefore, not surprising that the supposed establishment of a right-wing populist party in the Federal Republic has aroused and/ or strengthened the interest of many political scientists regarding the phenomenon of right-wing populism.

The AfD claims to be different to traditional parties, not to belong to the establishment 'old parties', and to act in the interest of the German people. This chapter seeks to explain the causes for the success of the AfD. Therefore, three theoretical dimensions outlined in Chapter 2 of this book will be addressed: political opportunities, resource mobilization, and frames and discourses. Linked to these dimensions, three batteries of questions will be discussed: First, whether the AfD can rather be understood as a political actor that emerged through social movements, or as a traditional party. In this regard, this contribution is going to examine the hypothesis that the party has made it 'from the streets to the parliament', and that it can therefore be seen as a movement party. Furthermore, it will be illustrated what kind of opportunity window the AfD took advantage of, in order to be so successful. To answer these questions, the history and the emergence of the party will be illustrated, as well as the two central opportunity structures the AfD benefited from. In order to understand the party's strategy and discourses, which mobilized a large number of voters, the party's program as well as its electorate will be delineated in a second step. Finally, since party programs are not sufficient to understand in which ways parties appeal to the public, the discourse and the strategy which enabled the party to attract the attention of the media and a considerable voter base, will be presented. I therefore refer to the results of my recent study which analyzed, among other things, the public discourse of the Italian Five Star Movement and the AfD according to both parties' websites or press releases (Schwörer 2016).

In what follows, a short history of populism in the Federal Republic of Germany is briefly discussed, in order to understand the difficult cultural and political opportunities for parties from the far right in Germany to emerge and be successful. In the subsequent section, I will point out the origins of the AfD and the context of political and discursive opportunities that emerged between 2013 and 2016. Following that, the resources of the AfD or its program and electorate are presented in order to understand its discourse and political strategy – demonstrated in the subsequent section – which can be seen as the AfD's recipe for successfully attracting a large amount of voters.

Populism in Germany – difficult cultural opportunities

Since the end of the Second World War, populist parties in the Federal Republic have had a hard time gaining ground. It was only in the 1980s that some right-wing populist parties succeeded in attracting attention. However, their success was usually only of short duration, and limited to a few states. The most successful among these right-wing populist parties in the Federal Republic were The Republicans, founded by two former politicians of the Christian Democratic Union (CDU), Franz Handlos and Ekkehard Voigt, in 1983 (Decker and Hartleb 2006, 193). The core demands of The Republicans were: a more direct democracy; facilitated deportation of unemployed and criminal foreigners; financial support for German families; and the withdrawal of Germany from the European Union (Schoofs 2014). During the elections in the state of Baden-Württemberg in 1992, the party achieved a remarkable 10.9% of the overall vote, and four years later again achieved 9.1%. In the elections to the European Parliament of 1989, The Republicans won 7.1% of the votes, an above-average result for a populist party in the Federal Republic, a result which was only again achieved by the AfD during the 2014 European elections. Disputes within the party and the inability (or lack of will) to distance themselves from right-wing extremist parties eventually led to the decline of The Republicans in the following years.

The second most successful populist party in the Federal Republic – until the founding of the AfD – was that commonly called the 'Schill Party', named after its founder Ronald Schill. Only one year after its establishment, the party won 19% of the votes during the elections in Hamburg in 2001. The party propagated a zero tolerance policy towards crime and designated Hamburg as 'the capital of crime' (Decker and Hartleb 2006, 197). Schill himself, who rose as the undisputed leader of the party, had made a name for himself in the years before his political career as a 'merciless judge' at the Hamburg district court. After the election, the Schill Party, together with the CDU and the Liberals, even set up a government in Hamburg; however, it collapsed after a mere two years. Similar to the case of The Republicans, internal disputes in the subsequent years led to the eventual decline of the Schill Party. The party failed to repeat its spectacular success in the following years and received a disappointing 0.8% of the votes in the Bundestag elections of 2002.

Thus, right-wing populist parties never had any great success in Germany. In general, it can be said that the German cultural environment did not offer large opportunity structures for radical right-wing parties. To put it in the words of Koopmans (1999, 96), the options offered by far-right parties in Germany were excluded by the cultural environment because they were 'unacceptable'. More specifically – according to Münkler (2012, 7) – the Germans are protected against right-wing populist temptations because the terror of their national socialist past is still always 'at their necks'. Decker (2012, 22) also argues that the haunted national socialist past means that not only right-wing extremists, but also right-wing populists are subject to a general stigma in the Federal Republic. In particular, the media in Germany has reservations about any close contact with right-wing populist parties and movements. Additionally, right-wing populists have to be afraid of being trampled by extreme-right groups, who would like to use these parties as a stepping-stone. The public image of such a party would, therefore, be ruined sooner or later as a result of inner-party battles.

Nevertheless, Decker and Münkler also agree that corresponding moods and resentments in the population, which may benefit the populist parties, also exist in the Federal Republic (Münkler 2012, 6). According to Decker, populism can be understood as a protest phenomenon, which has to do with the consequences of individualization and reflects crises in the process of identity construction (Decker 2012, 22). The Federal Republic is suffering no less from the consequences of modernization processes than other European states. Moreover, the underlying conflict structures do not differ significantly from those in other European countries. Nevertheless, the Germans were, and are, more satisfied with their national democracy, at least when compared to other member states of the European Community/Union, as polls of the Eurobarometer from the 1970s and 1980s indicate (Schwörer 2016, 48). However, this satisfaction has diminished over time (especially after German unification), although it is still more widespread than in the EU average (see also the next pages).

Given these poor conditions for the success of right-wing parties in Germany, the question to answer is: why is the AfD so successful, while former populist parties in Germany have failed? In the following, the emergence of the party and the new opportunity structures which formed the preconditions for the success of the AfD are described.

Origins of the AfD and context of political and discursive opportunities

Regarding their origin, parties can arise from spin-offs, through mergers or unifications of different parties (Lucardie 2013, 67f). Alternatively, parties can emerge completely new from social movements, as the German Greens, and, in a certain way also the Southern European 'Movement-Parties' Podemos and the Five Star Movement did (Della Porta, Fernández, Kouki, and Mosca 2017). However, the AfD cannot be understood as a party whose origin is to be found in social movements, as will become clear from the following exemplification.

At its beginning, the AfD was able to fall back on an already existing network of economic, as well as conservative and fundamental Christian, associations. Therefore, it did not start from ground zero at its foundation in February 2013 (Bebnowsky 2015, 19ff). Among other economic initiatives and organizations, the Alliance Citizenship[2] (BB) and the Association for the support of the Electoral Alternative 2013[3] (WA2013) are worth mentioning as the most important movements in the run-up to the AfD, who brought together many of the later party founders and members (ibid., 19). The BB was founded in early 2012 as a result of an online petition against the European Stability Mechanism and brought together many eurocritic economists. The WA2013 was founded by Bernd Lucke and other former CDU members or politicians, such as Konrad Adam and Alexander Gauland, during the run-up to the Lower Saxony parliamentary elections in 2013. During this election, the WA2013 joined with the party of the Free Voters (FW).[4] But, due to the poor election results, the cooperation with the FW was terminated, and consequently, the party Alternative für Deutschland was founded on February 6, 2013. In addition to their spokesman Lucke, the later AfD top politicians Hans-Olaf Henkel and Joachim Starbatty, as well as a large part of their later economic supporters, participated in the BB and in the WA2013. At the first AfD party conference in Berlin on April 14, 2013, Bernd Lucke, Frauke Petry and Konrad Adam were elected as the party leaders.

The conservative, market-liberal economists, however, formed only one part (albeit for the emergence of the AfD, a central one) of the party. The AfD occasionally awakens the impression of being a party 'from below', originating from conservative citizens' initiatives, mostly because of the many ultraconservative initiatives, whose positions are reflected in today's AfD. Thus, the party may share features with movement parties (Bebnowsky 2015, 27). However, the impression that many conservative initiatives have emerged independently or 'from below' is a deceptive one. In fact, all of these initiatives, such as the 'Institute for Strategic Studies in Berlin' (ISSB),[5] the online paper 'Freie Welt', or the 'Family Protection Initiative',[6] are part of the 'Civilian Coalition' (ZK)[7] which is a network of various conservative and market-radical initiatives founded in 2004 with the decisive participation of Beatrix von Storch and her husband Sven von Storch. Beatrix von Storch has been a member of the AfD since 2013. The ZK 'is the strategic center of the AfD politician, and was deliberately split up by von Storch – the individual initiatives thus gave the impression of being normal citizens' initiatives, although they were in fact professionally managed campaigns'[8] (Bebnowsky 2015, 26).

The Citizens' Convention (BK)[9] must also be mentioned as a further central unit for the formation of the AfD. The BK, in turn, is close to the civilian coalition. The members of its Executive Board are largely active in the ZK as well. The substantive positions of the BK are aimed at a more passive role for the state, and contain fewer state-oriented precautionary measures (Speth 2003, 6). Hans-Olaf Henkel, who was deputy spokesman for the AfD from March 2014 until his departure in July 2015, also took part in this initiative. Frequently, the 'Federation of Free Citizens' (BfB),[10] founded by former liberal politician Manfred Brunner in 1994, is also regarded as a kind of predecessor party of the AfD (Bebnowsky and Förster 2014, 9f.). After the founding of the AfD, three former members of the BfB became members or supporters of the AfD: Joachim Starbatty, Karl Albrecht Schachtschneider, and Bruno Bandulet.

At the Essen party conference in early July 2015, Petry defeated Lucke in an inner-party struggle for the chairman position. There had been bitter disputes between Lucke and Petry about the future direction of the party, but also about Lucke's claim to leadership. With the initiation of a 'wake-up call', the Lucke-wing attempted to gather its economic supporters in the party, and to implement political guidelines against the party leaders through a collection of signatures. However, most of the members of the AfD saw this action as a dictatorial one, with party-splitting intentions (Häusler 2016, 241). After the Essen party conference, large parts of the economic wing and Lucke himself left the AfD and founded the party ALFA (later the Liberal Conservative Reformers). While ALFA was not able to gain electoral successes, the AfD, which has now moved sharply to the right, succeeded to an unprecedented degree in the following months. At the party conference held in Cologne on April 22, 2017, the new leadership of the party was elected after months of internal struggles, and the manifesto for the Bundestag elections 2017 was passed. Similar to the conference two years before, the determining questions were who to choose as the party's leader, and how to deal with the rightist currents within the party. Petry wanted to lead the party on her own and – in the long run – to form coalitions with the CDU/CSU. She also wanted to banish the far-right currents from within the party. However, Petry appeared to be increasingly isolated, and she had Alexander Gauland and co-chair Jörg Meuthen, among others, as powerful opponents. Shortly before the congress, Petry stepped down from being a candidate for the party's leadership and her motion to follow a more moderate and less polarizing strategy was not even put to the vote at the congress. Alexander Gauland and Alice Weigel, a less-known board member of the party with liberal economic visions, were elected as the new leadership of the party. In the aftermath of the congress in Cologne and after the elections for the German Bundestag in September 2017, when Petry announced her withdrawal from the AfD, the party seems to shift even more to the right.

As Bebnowski describes appropriately, the founding of the AfD was 'a process planned with military precision, not a spontaneous convergence of swarm-intelligent conservative grass roots' (Bebnowsky 2015, 34). Therefore, the AfD can be understood rather as a federation of well-organized conservative activists and economists, as well as former members and politicians from other parties. However, the AfD seems to move more and more in the direction of a right-wing movement party, which can be seen especially in the AfD regional associations of the States Thuringia and Saxony-Anhalt (Häusler 2015, 15). In the context of the PEGIDA marches, the AfD also started campaigning and demonstrating against the asylum policy of Chancellor Merkel. A large number of demonstrations and rallies started in September 2015, not only, but especially, in Thuringia. In this regard, Björn Höcke, the local AfD faction chairman, demanded: 'Get out on the streets, get out on the squares! The AfD must now be omnipresent, out in the streets and on the squares!' (quoted in: ibid., 15). Furthermore, there was an increasing number of rallies, info-stations, lectures, placards, and a larger demonstration of the AfD against the asylum policy of the Federal Government under the slogan 'Autumn offensive' at the end of 2015 in Berlin. In particular the 'Patriotic Platform' and 'The Wing', currents that are far-right within the party, often requested direct collaborations with PEGIDA. Markus Pretzell, (ex-)regional chairman of the AfD in North Rhine-Westphalia, even claimed that the AfD is also a 'Pegida-party'[11] (Steiner 2015).

Höcke and the leader of the 'Patriotic Platform' Hans-Thomas Tillschneider, both members of the far-right party wing, are close to the PEGIDA movement. The latter was once even closely connected with the more radical Leipzig offshoot Legida. Although the party leadership still do not publicly acknowledge their support for PEGIDA, it is clear that many AfD politicians, members, and sympathizers are already involved in these protest marches. In the 'Erfurter Resolution', passed by the right wing of the party, it is even written that thousands of AfD members are already participating in these marches (Der Flügel 2015, 1). Hence, it can be said that the AfD is in fact not a party that made it 'from the streets to the parliament', but rather, more and more so, from the parliaments to the streets.

As mentioned above, the question to answer can be expressed as follows: Why is the AfD so successful, while former right-wing parties sooner or later became irrelevant? Therefore, it is necessary to focus on the windows of opportunity, which paved the way for the party's success. Parties such as the AfD often need a certain social crisis, which Lawrence Goodwyn (1976) called the 'populist moment'. The European financial crisis opened an opportunity window for an

EU-critical party. When the topic of the euro lost momentum, the issue of refugees became topical, which the AfD used as a political opportunity to put itself once again into the gap to the right of the CDU/CSU, formulating drastic demands (Decker 2016, 14). Added to this is the important fact that the theses of the famous SPD politician Thilo Sarrazin on the alleged failure of the immigration and integration policy of the German government have already made a significant contribution to opening the discursive space for right-wing actors in the year 2010. The AfD was founded in a period in which some of the former taboos concerning immigration and immigrants have already been broken (ibid., 15).

That explains why the media lost their fear of making contact with representatives of the AfD and its demands: in 2016, 54% of the political talk shows in German television approached typical AfD-themes like 'refugees' (40 of 141 shows), 'Islam and terror' (15), or 'populism' (21), and politicians of the AfD were often invited (Restle, El Moussaoui, and Maus 2017). During the televised debate between Angela Merkel and Martin Schulz on September 3, 2017, the topics of migration, refugees, and terrorism took over half of the broadcasting time (Hildebrand 2017). Furthermore, in social scientific literature, the success of right-wing populist parties is often explained by fears of social decline (Spier 2010) and dissatisfaction with the political establishment (Mayer 1999). Looking at the former, however, it is noticeable that these fears do not seem to be particularly widespread in Germany (Figure 3.1; in fact, both fear of social decline and

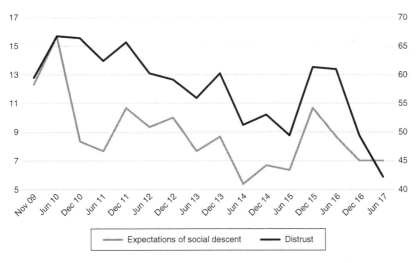

FIGURE 3.1 Expectations of social descent and distrust against political institutions in Germany.

Own graph based on data from the Eurobarometer.[12] Gray line and left axis: average values from the number of Germans surveyed who have negative expectations regarding their professional, financial, and general situation in one year. Black line and right axis: percentage of Germans surveyed who 'tend not to trust' their own national parties, parliament and the government (average-value).

distrust against the political establishment are less marked than the EU average). But the value in December 2015 was as high as it had not been in almost six years. The same is true for the generally widespread mistrust against the parties, the government, and the parliament: the value in December 2015 was exceeded the last time in 2011. Actually, the AfD was able to achieve double-digit survey results during the exact same period in which the mistrust of politics and expectations of social descent were particularly strong, especially during the time when 'Syrian refugee' immigration to Germany peaked.

From opportunities to resources: program and voters of the AfD

As mentioned in the first chapter of this book, the mobilization of resources is an important task for parties which emerged from social movements. Since the AfD started rather as a professional political party than a social movement, this question seems less important with regard to the AfD. Many resources such as money, time, leadership skills, expert knowledge, and experience in daily party work were available right from the beginning. Absent were a strategy and a discourse to gain support from the German electorate. But first of all, the question of how the AfD can exactly be described in ideological terms and which social groups vote for the AfD must be addressed. Following up on this, the strategies and discourse with which the AfD appeals to the people are outlined in the next section of this chapter.

Political parties can be characterized by the political left-right axis, which describes two basic social conflicts: the socio-cultural conflict of values with conservative authoritarian values on the right and libertarian values on the left, and the socio-economic conflict of distribution with the right pole of free market and the left pole of social justice (Decker 2016, 11). The unique thing about populist parties is that they construct a new axis, whose central poles are the political elite on the one hand, and the 'ordinary' people on the other. The connecting element of all populist parties is not their position on social or ecological issues, but rather their anti-establishment orientation, and their claim to be the only legitimate voice for honest people. In the basic program of the AfD, some typical populist claims, such as more direct democracy (AfD 2016, 9), and the limitation of the power of political parties (ibid., 11), are clearly articulated. On p.8 of the program, it is written that the 'secret Sovereign is a small, powerful political leadership group within the parties. It has been responsible for the mistakes of the past decades. A political class of professional policymakers has developed, whose urgent interest is their power, status, and material well-being' (ibid., 8).

Furthermore, according to its program, the AfD can be characterized as a right-wing party, both in socio-economic and sociocultural terms. Despite the withdrawal of large parts of the economic liberal wing as a result of the Essen party conference in July 2015, the basic program of April 2016 can at least in parts be described as neo-liberal: 'Across a broad front' (AfD 2016, 68), the economy is to be deregulated and state interventions should be limited (ibid., 67). Property and inheritance taxes are to be abolished, and commercial taxes have to be reviewed as well (ibid., 75). However, there are also signs of an SME-oriented, national protectionist policy (Botsch 2016, 11), which, for example, rejects free trade agreements such as TTIP (AfD 2016, 68). Recently, some groups emerged within the party that represent the interests of employees. But they still have little impact on the party's agenda (Hensel, Finkbeiner, and Dudek: 2017, 16). With regard to socio-cultural positions, the controversial passage 'Islam does not belong to Germany' (AfD 2016, 49) has in fact made it into the basic program, and also into the manifesto for the Bundestag elections 2017. The right of asylum should be abolished and asylum applications should no longer be processed in Germany, but in 'asylum centers' in the respective home or neighboring country of the potential refugee exclusively (ibid., 59f). 'Gender mainstreaming' is rejected, and the AfD adheres to the traditional family values of man, woman, and child (ibid., 41). Concerning the party's original issues, the EU is to be restored to an 'economic and interest community of sovereign, loosely connected individual states' (ibid., 16), and a national referendum on the maintenance of the euro is to be carried out (ibid., 18).

To a certain point, the composition of the AfD's electorate seems to fit the party's program: the voters are dissatisfied with the country's current democracy and political decision-makers. Moreover, they worry about their financial future as well as about the influx of immigrants to Germany. For the absolute majority of AfD voters in all five state elections in 2016, the 'refugee' issue was crucial and the number one deciding factor, and in the election of the German Bundestag in September 2017, the topics 'terror', 'crime', and 'refugees' were crucial, too. The decision to vote for the AfD is caused primarily by a disappointment with the other political actors, which will be explained in the next part of this section. When the AfD started its political career, its electorate did not show any great peculiarity in terms of its socio-demographic characteristics (Schwörer 2016, 76ff). But, at least since 2016, a typical right-wing populist profile of the electorate has emerged, as is suggested by electoral surveys in the context of the states' elections (ibid., 139ff). In particular, young men with a rather low educational level, blue-collar workers, and the unemployed, especially in former East Germany, are now the core of the AfD's electorate. In the election of the German Bundestag in September 2017, however, the AfD also attracted older voters, especially those between 35 and 59 years[13] (Table 3.1).

However, it seems difficult to combine the liberal economic, employer-friendly program of the party with the socio-demographic characteristics of the AfD's voters. Logically, they should be more interested in a well-functioning welfare state, since many of them come from low income and educationally alienated classes. In the following section, it will be explained how the AfD could solve this contradiction, choosing a strategy that allows to attract large parts of the low income classes.

TABLE 3.1 'Typical' AfD-voter

	'Typical' AfD-voter
Age	35–59
Sex	Male
Profession	Classical worker, unemployed
Education	Low/average
Political origin	Non-voters, CDU, minor parties, SPD, The Left
Satisfaction with democracy and parties	Low
Fear about immigration	Widespread
Expectations of social descent	Widespread
Crucial topic	Terror, crime, refugees

Own table based on Data from Infratest Dimap (see also Schwörer 2016, 141).[14]

The recipe for success: strategy and discourses of the AfD

In the previous sections, the opportunity structures the AfD benefited from have been discussed, as well as its voters and political concerns. However, this alone does not explain the success of the AfD, but rather the chances or preconditions for it. The question to be answered in this section is which discourses and strategies the AfD uses to appeal successfully to the public. It is argued that, although in its history, ideology, and program, economic liberalism as well as the interest of employers have had a high significance, the party does not promote these political views publicly. Rather, the AfD focuses on social-cultural claims and on anti-establishment discourses. This strategy seems to be very successful, since large parts of the AfD-voters would hardly agree with the party's pro-employers' attitude.

According to Ernesto Laclau, a collective political identity – the people – is created by identifying opponents or 'enemies' who do not belong to them (Laclau 2005). Laclau states that people are more likely to develop a sense of belonging by defining themselves in contrast to certain outgroups. Populism can be understood as a strategy or 'thin-centred' ideology, which – as indicated above – excludes certain groups from its conception of the people (Mudde 2004, 544). While so-called left populist parties, such as Podemos or Syriza, apart from the political establishment, may exclude specific economic groups or members of upper classes, they do not exclude religious, cultural, or ethnic groups. The exclusion of the latter groups, however, is the main characteristic of the right-wing populists (Table 3.2).

The AfD is constructing its conception of the people by excluding some cultural, religious, and ethnic groups from 'its people', and tries to create a community of 'honest Germans' who stand together against the threat of immigration and against the malicious politicians and parties. As indicated above, since the split of the party, the socio-cultural demands are particularly apparent in the public sphere, and the 'most important campaign theme is the agitation against refugees and immigrants' (Botsch 2016, 9). What was regarded as the right wing of the party in Lucke's time has now become a majority in the AfD. The current right

TABLE 3.2 Three types of populism

	'Inclusive' Populism	*Right-wing Populism*	*Left-wing Populism*
Enemy: Political Establishment	+	+	+
Enemy: Immigrants/ethnic, religious or cultural groups	–	+	–
Enemy: Economic players/the upper class	–	+/–	+
Appeal to the people	+	+	+

+ compulsory position; – impossible position; +/– not compulsory but possible position. Own table (Schwörer, 2016).

wing, around the Thuringian faction leader Björn Höcke and the AfD faction leader André Poggenburg in Saxony-Anhalt, has a completely different quality – and their position seems to have been strengthened after the party congress of Cologne – as the following examples show: the comparison of differing reproduction habits of Africans and Europeans and the explanation of these differences by evolutionary biology (Hurtz 2016), or Höcke raging against the Holocaust monument in Berlin calling it a 'monument of shame' (Pastebin 2017). Some weeks after a speech given by Höcke, which criticized the dealings with Nazi history, Petry and the majority of the directorate decided to begin the process of excluding Höcke from the AfD. However, after the elections to the Bundestag and the withdrawal of Petry, Gauland and Weidel will probably stop the process of excluding Höcke (Pittelkow and Riedel 2017). Furthermore, statements by the AfD-European deputy Beatrix von Storch and the AfD-chairwoman Frauke Petry herself, that border patrols should make use of guns, in order to keep 'illegal' immigrants from entering the country, would not have been conceivable during Lucke's time. Alexander Gauland even demanded that the Germans should have the right to be proud of the achievements of German soldiers in the two world wars (Zeit Online 2017). There have been countless examples of such provocative statements from the ranks of the AfD. However, it would be deceptive to assert that elements of right-wing thinking did not exist before the rightward shift of the party. The economic structure of argumentation has already been a self-evident component and an anchor point for right-wing populist positions in the AfD. The 'competition populism' (Wettbewerbspopulismus) of Lucke was already based on the fact that there were subordinate and superior people (hard-working Germans and lazy Southerners), which was not justified by a racial superiority of individual peoples, but rather by the economic superiority of individual economies (Bebnowsky 2015, 23).

In the following, some more examples of the political discourse of the AfD will be displayed, based on the articles from the party's website that I have analyzed in my book *Populismi. Il Movimento 5 Stelle e la Alternativa per la Germania* (Schwörer 2016). The analyzed articles on the party website were ultimately press releases of the top politicians of the AfD on – according to the AfD – politically relevant topics. Recently, the website has changed somewhat and articles on the period before 2016 can no longer be accessed. I made use of a non-computer-based content analysis. Following the concept of populism, presented in Table 3.2, I tried to observe how often and in which contexts and quality certain groups (political establishment; religious, cultural, ethnic groups; economic actors) are presented as enemies or as a threat to the true people.[15] Furthermore, I tried to identify how often and in which context the AfD (and the M5S) refer to the people.

My analysis also illustrates the change of the party's discourse in favor of a more right-wing, anti-establishment rhetoric after the split of the party in the beginning of July 2015 (Table 3.3). While in July 2015, only 7% of the articles published on the party's website were about the negative impact of immigration, in September of the same year, the topic was addressed in more than every second contribution. Though to a smaller extent, an increase is also observable in articles that criticize the political establishment by moral accusations. Nevertheless, two accusations which are expressed by many other European populist parties towards the political establishment could not be identified in the contributions of the AfD: corruptibility and a lack of work-motivation. The AfD accuses the 'old parties' of acting against the people's interest, of being dishonest, of having a defective democratic awareness, and of being unable to solve the people's problems (Schwörer 2016, 124): 'That she [Angela Merkel] acts against the will of most Germans seems to be totally indifferent for her, especially as she knows that the citizens de facto do not have a chance to resist her politics' per Frauke Petry (quoted in: Schwörer 2016, 113). Furthermore, as claimed in another article, the German government 'is insidiously cheating its own people' (quoted in: ibid.). Interestingly, economic actors are not portrayed as threats or enemies in the website contributions, which seems to confirm the party's orientation towards the employers. This orientation did not change in the months following the split of the party.

In some articles, the German people are said to be 'captured by the politicians' (quoted in: Schwörer 2016, 114). Moreover, Merkel is accused of a planned population exchange, a common conspiracy theory, which states that since the

TABLE 3.3 'Enemies' of the AfD according to its articles from the website

	July 2015	August 2015	September 2015	Share in all website's articles
Enemy: Political Establishment	12 (42,86%)	16 (50%)	25 (55,56%)	53 (50,48%)
Appeal to the people	11 (39,29%)	9 (28,13%)	11 (24,45%)	31 (29,52%)
Enemy: Economic players/ the upper class	0	0	0	0
Enemy: Immigrants/ ethnic, religious or cultural groups	2 (7,14%)	14 (43,75%)	25 (55,56%)	41 (39.05%)
Total articles	28	32	45	105

Schwörer 2016: 112.

Germans have now seen through Merkel's harmful policies, she was trying to build up a new, loyal electorate among the immigrated refugees (ibid., 122). According to the AfD, the Germans are, in principle, victims who are trampled insidiously by the Merkel government. The AfD argues that the German people should be given the opportunity to vote for or against the agenda of the government. Whether or not the question of more citizen participation is credible, is, however, doubtful. On basis of the website's contributions, the aim of the AfD does not seem to be to establish a radically new form of politics, as the Five Star Movement in Italy tries to accomplish, but merely to introduce referenda on issues where the majority of the population could agree with the position the AfD takes. In the statements from the website I analyzed, the demand for more referenda or more participation of citizens is never separated from topics like 'The Salvation of Greece' or 'Immigration'.

Furthermore, the threat of the 'refugees' is probably the most important part in the discourse of the AfD. According to the AfD, refugees are receiving more favorable treatment than the Germans, and they supposedly get everything they want: food, accommodation, and support from activists, whereas for Germans, this is not the case: therefore, as stated in one article, 'Hansjörg Müller came up with the idea of personally welcoming our border policemen and brought them food and drinks, what usually only happens to refugees' (quoted in: Schwörer 2016, 119). Other articles from the website construct a threat scenario, as, for instance, one contribution by Frauke Petry: 'In Africa alone, several hundred million people live below the poverty line, where are they supposed to be resettled and to be provided with work in Germany?' (quoted in: ibid., 121).

Thus, on the one hand, the AfD is successfully adopting a typical right-wing populist discourse, which in the last years and decades brought success to many European anti-establishment parties but, on the other hand, the AfD is hiding its unpopular, enterprise-friendly demands. The combination of an anti-immigration discourse with a populist rhetoric against the 'old' parties and politicians seems to be the recipe for success in mobilizing voters, especially because – as mentioned above – right-wing populist rhetoric is no longer a taboo in Germany. However, it must be noticed that most of the voters of the AfD do not vote for the party because they feel very close to it, but, most of all, because they want to score off the traditional parties. In the elections for the parliaments of the states Baden-Württemberg, Rhineland-Palatinate, and Saxony-Anhalt in 2016, and in the election for the German Bundestag in September 2017, between 60% and 70% of the interviewed AfD-voters stated they had voted for the AfD because they were disappointed with the other parties. Only between 21% and 30% voted for the party because they were convinced of its agenda.[16] Thus, a vote for the AfD is a protest vote more often than not. However, without its anti-immigration and populist discourse, the AfD probably would not attract these protest voters because, as mentioned above, these issues seem to be very important for the AfD's electorate.

Since the AfD is also involved in marches, demonstrations, and extra-parliamentary actions, it not only needs voters, but also supporters and activists

who identify themselves with the party. As discussed previously, the far right eastern branches of the party seem especially to be strongly involved in activities
together with PEGIDA, as, for instance, in Dresden in May 2017, even though the
demonstrations officially did not take place at the same stage and the same time
and place. Though the AfD does not put forward one central charismatic leader,
those from the far right of the party, like the Young Alternative, identify with
agitators like Björn Höcke, who became their unofficial spokesperson, and an
important person for attracting people from the far right. So, beside the populist
ideology and anti-immigration discourses, certain charismatic persons are important, in order to achieve identification of people with the party.

Conclusions

The AfD succeeded in using the opportunity of the European economic and
financial crisis and established a Euro-critical party to the right of the Christian
Democratic Parties. When the topic lost its relevance or salience, the AfD succeeded in finding a new core identity, at least since the victory of the right over the
more liberal party wing. Through the right-wing populist exploitation of the now
predominant topic of refugees, the AfD was able to achieve clear two-digit survey
results, also because – since Sarrazin published his theses – taboos regarding far-
right demands had already been partially broken.

The AfD is not a party created by social movements from below. It was founded
on a well-organized network of market-liberal economists and professional right-
wing conservative initiatives. However, the AfD behaves in an anti-elitist way
and is increasingly distancing itself from the traditional parties, accusing them of
not acting in the interest of the German people. Even though right-wing populist
parties do not originate from movements, they are sometimes referred to as movement parties, since they seek to 'create or displace social movement practices'
(Kitschelt 2006, 286), often by means of 'marches and demonstrations' (ibid.,
288). Moreover, movement parties and populist parties 'are hostile to party and
the Establishment.' They distance themselves from the political establishment by
proclaiming to be different and to represent the true will of the people, while
the establishment is only interested in its own well-being (Gunther and Diamond
2003, 189). It is from these points of view that the AfD can also be regarded as a
right-wing populist movement party. In the meantime, the AfD no longer appeals
only to the people, but acts more and more outside of the parliaments. In addition, well-known AfD politicians, particularly in the eastern part of the Republic,
advocate a commitment to PEGIDA. Some members and currents within the party
are even in touch with further movements on the right, such as the 'Identitarian
Movement'. According to Alexander Häusler (2016, 242), the AfD already
provides a partisan political anchor for nationalist and right-wing protests, for
instance, PEGIDA, and other initiatives directed against immigrants and refugees.

The change in the AfD's electorate also shows that the party has evolved from a
party of elitist professors to a 'common man' type party. Although, paradoxically,

the economic demands certainly hardly reflect the will of the workers and the unemployed who vote for the AfD. However, the party seems to be hiding its unpopular points of view successfully. Moreover, other alleged problems have more relevance for the voters, in particular, immigration and the 'Islamization' of Germany. The AfD's anti-establishment discourse, combined with chauvinistic and anti-immigration rhetoric, is its recipe for success.

What the AfD will evolve into is open. The current facts show that, since July 2015, the party has moved farther and farther to the right and is focusing on polarization. This last point was clearly demonstrated by the conference held in Koblenz with other European right-wing populists, such as Marine Le Pen from the French Front National, Matteo Salvini from the Italian Lega Nord, and Gerd Wilders from the Party for Freedom in the Netherlands. The AfD's party congress in April 2017 seems to confirm the shift to the farer right.

The fact that the AfD entered the Bundestag after the election in 2017 was not surprising. But the future of the AfD will depend on whether the topics of Islam and refugees will remain relevant for the German people, how the AfD will act in the German Bundestag, and on the relationship between the more moderate and the far right wings of the party. Short after the elections of the Bundestag, Petry declared that she will leave the party, and will not be part of the parliamentary group of the AfD in the German parliament, even though she obtained a seat for the party. It is open, whether, and how many, deputies will follow her. The day after the election, it is no longer clear how many of the elected deputies will in the future be part of the AfD Group (September 27, 2017). Thus, the tensions between the far right and the more moderate party wing have not yet been resolved, and still have considerable potential for conflict. In this respect, little can be predicted about the further development of the party, but a split-off of parts of the more moderate party wing is conceivable. However, this would probably not threaten the existence of the party: the electorate of the AfD seems to favor the shift to the far right. It is true that about half of the AfD voters believe that the party does not distance itself enough from right-wing extremism, but this has not kept them from voting for the AfD. And even if more moderate voters turn away from the party, it is unlikely that the party will fall below the 5% hurdle in the short or medium term.

Notes

1 In the large German meta-catalog "KVK", the keyword search for the term "Populism" illustrates a significant increase in publications in the major German libraries and library networks: While the search for the year of publication delivers 322 hits in 2010, this number increases each year and comes in 2016 with 534 new publications to the previous peak. URL: http://kvk.bibliothek.kit.edu/.
2 Bündnis Bürgerwille.
3 Verein zur Unterstützung der Wahlalternative 2013.
4 Freie Wähler.
5 Institut für strategische Studien Berlin.
6 Initiative Familienschutz.

7 Zivile Koalition.
8 All originally German citations used in this work have been translated into English by the author of this chapter.
9 Bürgerkonvent.
10 Bund freier Bürger.
11 However, short after the withdrawal of Petry, also Pretzell (who is her husband) announced his withdrawal from the AfD's parliamentary group in the Landtag of North Rhine-Westphalia and from the party.
12 Data is accessible at URL: http://ec.europa.eu/commfrontoffice/publicopinion/index. cfm/Survey/index#p=1&instruments=STANDARD.
13 The data is accessible at URL: http://wahl.tagesschau.de/wahlen/2017-09-24-BT-DE/ umfrage-alter.shtml.
14 Data is accessible at URL: http://wahl.tagesschau.de/landtag.shtml and http://wahl. tagesschau.de/wahlen/2017-09-24-BT-DE/index.shtml.
15 The analysis was carried out for the period July-September 2015. The Website of the AfD now is accessible under: https://www.afd.de/.
16 The data is accessible at URL: http://wahl.tagesschau.de/wahlen/2016-09-04-LT-DE-MV/index.shtml and wahl.tagesschau.de/wahlen/2017-09-24-BT-DE/umfrage-afd.shtml.

References

AfD (2016) *Programm für Deutschland*. Available at: https://www.alternativefuer.de/wp-content/uploads/sites/7/2016/05/2016-06-27_afd-grundsatzprogramm_web-version.pdf.
Bebnowsky, D. (2015) *Die Alternative für Deutschland. Aufstieg und gesellschaftliche Repräsentanz einer rechten populistischen Partei*, Wiesbaden: Springer.
Bebnowsky, D. and Förster, L.J. (2014) *Wettbewerbspopulismus. Die Alternative für Deutschland und die Rolle der Ökonomen*, Frankfurt on the Main: Otto-Brenner-Stiftung.
Bíró-Nagy, A., Győri, G., and Kadlót, T. (2015) *Populism, the new zeitgeist? The situation of European populist parties in 2015*, Budapest: Friedrich-Ebert-Stiftung.
Boros, T., Freitas, M., Kadlót, T., and Stetter, E. (2017) *The State of Populism in the European Union 2016*, Brussels: Foundation for European Progressive Studies.
Botsch, G. (2016) 'Populismus plus Programm: Das Dilemma der AfD', *Blätter für deutsche und internationale Politik*, 6(17), 9–12.
Decker, F. (2012) 'Warum der parteiförmige Rechtspopulismus in Deutschland so erfolglos ist', *Vorgänge*, 1(197): 21–28.
Decker, F. (2016) 'Die »Alternative für Deutschland« aus der Sicht der vergleichenden Parteienforschung', in Häusler, A. *Die Alternative für Deutschland. Programmatik, Entwicklung und politische Verortung*, 7–24.
Decker, F. and Hartleb, F. (2006) 'Populismus auf schwierigem Terrain. Die rechten und linken Herausfordererparteien in der Bundesrepublik', in Decker, F. *Populismus. Gefahr für die Demokratie oder nützliches Korrektiv?*, Wiesbaden: VS Verlag, 191–215.
Della Porta, D., Fernández, J., Kouki, H., and Mosca, L. (2017) *Movement Parties Against Austerity.* Hoboken, NJ: John Wiley & Sons.
Der Flügel (2015) *Erfurter Resolution.* Available at: http://derfluegel.de/erfurterresolution. pdf.
Goodwyn, L. (1976) *Democratic Promise. The Populist Moment in America*, New York: Oxford University Press.
Gunther, R. and Diamond, L. (2003) 'Species of Political Parties', *Party Politics*, 2(9): 167–199.

Häusler, A. (2015) *Die AfD: Eine rechtspopulistische Partei im Wandel. Ein Zwischenbericht*, Berlin: Deutscher Gewerkschaftsbund.

Häusler, A. (2016) 'Ausblick', in Häusler, A. *Die Alternative für Deutschland. Programmatik, Entwicklung und politische Verortung*, Wiesbaden: Springer 239–246.

Hensel, A., Finkbeiner, F., and Dudek, P. (2017) *Die AfD vor der Bundestagswahl 2017. Vom Protest zur parlamentarischen Opposition*, Frankfurt on the Main: Otto-Brenner-Stiftung.

Hurtz, S. (2016) '„Blanker Rassismus": Höcke und die Fortpflanzung der Afrikaner', *Süddeutsche Zeitung*, December 12. Available at: http://www.sueddeutsche.de/politik/afd-thueringen-blanker-rassismus-hoecke-und-die-fortpflanzung-der-afrikaner-1.2780159.

Kitschelt, H. (2006) 'Movement Parties', in R. Katz and W. Crotty *Handbook of Party Politics*, London, Thousand Oaks, CA, New Delhi: Sage, 278–290.

Koopmans, R. (1999) 'Political. Opportunity. Structure. Some Splitting to Balance the Lumping', *Sociological Forum*, 14(1): 93–105.

Laclau, E. (2005) *On Populist Reason*, London: Verso.

Lucardie, P. (2013) 'Zur Typologie der politischen Parteien', in Decker F. and Neu, V. *Handbuch der politischen Parteien*, Bonn: Bundeszentrale für politische Bildung, 61–76.

Mayer, N. (1999) *Ces francais qui votent FN*, Paris: Flammarion.

Meny, Y. and Surel, Y. (2009) *Populismo e democrazia*, Bologna: Il Mulino.

Mudde, C. (2004) 'The populis Zeitgeist', *Government and Opposition*, 39(4): 541–563.

Münkler, H. (2012) *Populismus in Deutschland. Eine Geschichte seiner Mentalitäten, Mythen und Symbole*, London: Counterpoint.

Pastebin (2017) *Transkript Höcke, Dresden-Rede*, January. Available at: http://pastebin.com/jQujwe89.7.

Pittelkow, S. and Riedel, K. (2017) 'AfD-Spitze will Höcke halten. Aus für den Ausschluss', *Tagesschau.de*, September 30. Available at: http://www.tagesschau.de/inland/afd-hoecke-113.html.

Restle, G., El Moussaoui, N., and Maus, A. (2017) 'Talkshows: Bühne frei für Populisten. Monitor'. Available at: http://www1.wdr.de/daserste/monitor/sendungen/talkshows-102.html.

Schoofs, J. (2014) 'Bundeszentrale für politische Bildung'. Available at: http://www.bpb.de/politik/wahlen/wer-steht-zur-wahl/europawahl-2014/180947/rep.

Schwörer, J. (2016) *Il "Movimento 5 Stelle" e la "Alternativa per la Germania"*, Rome: Bibiotheka.

Speth, R. (2003) *Der BürgerKonvent – Kampagnenprotest von oben ohne Transparenz und Bürgerbeteiligung*, Düsseldorf: Hans-Böckler-Stiftung.

Spier, T. (2010) *Modernisierungsverlierer? Die Wählerschaft rechtspopulistischer Parteien in Westeuropa*. Wiesbaden: VS Verlag.

Steiner, T. (2015). Die AfD stellt sich neu auf: "Wir sind die Pegida-Partei". *Badische Zeitung*, July 6. Available at: http://www.badische-zeitung.de/deutschland-1/die-afd-stellt-sich-neu-auf-wir-sind-die-pegida-partei--107238994.html.

Zeit Online (2017) 'Gauland provoziert mit Äußerung zur Nazizeit', *Zeit Online*, September 14. Available at: http://www.zeit.de/politik/deutschland/2017-09/afd-alexander-gauland-nazi-zeit-neubewertung.

4

UKIP AND THE UK'S RADICAL RIGHT

A tale of movement party success?

Jeanne Hanna and Joel Busher

Introduction

Among the political upsets laid at the feet of right-wing groups in recent years, the United Kingdom's vote to exit the European Union (EU) in June 2016 was perhaps the most unexpected, and among those with the most far-reaching implications. While the 'Brexit' vote was driven by a variety of actors (Clarke, Goodwin, and Whiteley 2017), few, if any, were as important as the UK Independence Party (UKIP) who, over the twenty years preceding the referendum, had become one of the most forthright and prominent proponents of Euroscepticism in the UK and beyond (Ford and Goodwin 2014; Goodwin and Milazzo 2015). UKIP's role as an impetus of the EU referendum and as active, grassroots campaigners for the Leave vote represent the group's pinnacle triumph, and the (at least partial) fulfilment of its founding purpose. Analysis of this victory, however, also throws light on the struggles of UKIP's members to mobilize around other issues, and reveals the disorder in UKIP's ranks both before and since the referendum.

In this chapter, we show how the concept of movement parties (Kitschelt 2006) provides a useful lens through which to surface and interpret the hybrid nature of political actors such as UKIP, and argue that UKIP's role in British politics – as both a political party and, at times, as a constituent part of a wider movement – provides a salient case through which to understand the opportunities and perils that organizing as a hybrid movement party might pose for actors on the right of the political spectrum. In developing this argument, we also invite reflection on three issues that require careful consideration if the concept of a movement party is to help us to better comprehend right-wing politics at its more radical fringes. The first concerns the question of which movement UKIP functions as a vehicle. As we describe below, while UKIP was founded as a result of particular political and constitutional concerns, over time, it has been a vehicle for a range of different and, at times, competing movements with distinct and occasionally conflicting interests and ideas. This raises an intriguing possibility: is it possible that a movement party can serve simultaneously as a vehicle for the interests of more than one movement, or for a series of movements over time?

The second issue concerns the non-linearity of UKIP's organizational journey. Unlike the broadly left-wing groups that Kitschelt initially analyzed as movement parties, which emerged initially as social movements, and later adopted a more party-like form in order to operate in new arenas (2006: 281–2), UKIP has in practice wavered between functioning and organizing as a party, a movement party, and a movement throughout the past 25 years, sometimes functioning and organising simultaneously as all three – at times a source of considerable intra-group tension. This raises important questions about whether such non-linearity might be typical of movement parties on the right, and, if so, what implications it might have for how the concept is deployed.

The third issue concerns the slipperiness of notions of organizational 'success', whether in the analyses of external actors (academics, journalists, other political parties, etc.) or internal actors (activists, leaders, members). Given that the success of political parties is usually assessed primarily in terms of numbers of votes and representatives, it is unsurprising that such measures have been prominent in discussions about UKIP's fortunes, particularly among external actors. Yet attention to internal actors' perspectives reveals more hybrid and fluid notions of success. As discussed below, UKIP's leaders have frequently focused more on moving the political debate and pressuring rival parties, rather than replacing them. At the same time, however, UKIP has always participated in, at a minimum, national elections, and when its polling numbers have been favourable, touted its success on those terms. Arguably, such diverse and flexible definitions of success have comprised an asset for UKIP, enabling leaders and activists alike to sustain movement morale and media attention by claiming victories or dismissing losses even when the facts on the ground appeared to suggest otherwise. Yet they have also provided a point of potential rupture, as different definitions of success have revealed different and sometimes conflicting aims: something brought home most starkly in the fallout from the EU referendum. As one long-time UKIP member opined at a branch meeting in Rotherham, South Yorkshire, less than a year after the EU referendum, 'In many ways we would have been better off if we *just* lost the referendum, rather than *just* won it' (Hanna 2017).

We explore these issues by tracing UKIP's history across four periods: (1) from its founding in 1993 to 2010, when UKIP operated largely as a fringe party; (2) from 2010 to 2015, when UKIP began to gain significant electoral support and eventually achieved the promise of an EU referendum; (3) the year-long referendum campaign and its impact on UKIP's understanding of its own purpose; and (4) UKIP's trajectory after the EU referendum and what it means for a movement party to potentially have its greatest accomplishment behind it.

This chapter draws on a combination of the academic literature regarding UKIP, media reporting, and primary ethnographic research carried out among

UKIP activists and supporters before, during, and after the UK's referendum on EU membership in June 2016. Overt ethnographic observation was conducted by the lead author at over sixty UKIP meetings, campaigns, conferences, electoral events, and social gatherings, both formal and informal, across South Yorkshire between May 2015 and May 2017. Forty-five semi-structured interviews were carried out with UKIP activists, local party leaders, councillors, and activists working with anti-racist and anti-fascist organizations, as well as countless informal interviews and conversations with people connected directly or peripherally with UKIP. The fieldwork was undertaken with ethical approval from the American University in Washington, DC, the lead author's host institution.

1993–2010: survival on the political fringe

UKIP was founded as a political party in 1993 by Alan Sked, a London School of Economics historian, in response to the failure of the Anti-Federalist League, an earlier cross-party organization also led by Sked, to gain significant support in their efforts to prevent the ratification of the Maastricht Treaty. As has been well-documented (most notably by Ford and Goodwin 2014: 20–106), in its early years UKIP experienced more lows than highs, particularly in electoral terms. In its earliest election contests, UKIP was outstripped at times even by the satirical Monster Raving Loony Party, and while UKIP enjoyed notable success in the European Parliament (EP) elections of 2004 and 2009, coming third and second with 15.6% and 16% of the national vote respectively, such successes took a long time to arrive and did not translate into other electoral arenas. UKIP did not enjoy a significant breakthrough in local elections until 2013, and had to wait until 2014 to win their first seat in the UK Parliament. Furthermore, these victories were always swiftly followed by an eruption of internal divisions that threatened to pull the organization apart (Ford and Goodwin 2014: 20–106).

Indeed, the 2004 EP elections aside, it was only towards the end of 2008 that UKIP emerged clearly as the leading party committed to Euroscepticism in the UK.[1] During the mid-1990s, Sir James Goldsmith's Referendum Party, founded in 1994 to advocate for a nationwide referendum on the UK's membership of the EU, was better funded than UKIP, able to field more candidates, and more adept at garnering recognition with the press and public (Carter, Evans, Alderman, and Gorham 1998). The Referendum Party collapsed after the death of Goldsmith in 1997, leading many supporters to switch their allegiances to UKIP. This, along with a shift to proportional representation in EP elections as of 1999, and the fact that as a 'second order election' (Reif and Schmitt 1980), the EP elections favoured UKIP due to lower voter turnout and voters' propensity to use such elections to evince dissatisfaction with the larger parties, all contributed to UKIP's first relative electoral success, coming fourth, and achieving three seats. From this point on, EP elections would prove both an electoral and financial boon for UKIP, due to the financial resources granted to UKIP by the EP as a function of their EP representatives – although as discussed below, these resources would eventually also become a source of internal conflict. However, in local and national elections, UKIP still found itself trailing the extreme right British National Party (BNP), which promoted a long-standing nativist and anti-immigrant platform, and was also thoroughly hostile to the UK's membership in the transnational EU. UKIP was beaten by the BNP in 80% of the constituencies in which both parties stood candidates in 2005, and the BNP won two to three times as many votes as UKIP in a series of local elections between 2006 and 2008 (Ford and Goodwin 2014).

So how did UKIP operate during this period? In some respects at least, in this period UKIP resembles most closely what Kitschelt describes as a movement-party. As described above, UKIP emerged out of the conviction of Sked and colleagues that a fully-fledged political party was required to advance Eurosceptic positions that they believed were not represented by the main parties. Yet despite registering as a political party, analysis of UKIP's policy platform, mode of organising and strategic aims make clear that it functioned throughout much of its early years essentially as a single-issue pressure group.

As early as the 1997 General Election, UKIP's policy platform begins to expand beyond withdrawal from the EU to include positions on healthcare, education, defence, and other policy areas. However, both the 1997 and 2001 manifestos were ultimately framed around the perceived financial and regulatory burdens of UK membership of the EU. Indeed, during elections through the early 2000s, UKIP's leaders resisted internal pressure to further expand the party's platform or emphasize issues beyond withdrawal from the EU. They instead encouraged supporters to use elections and election hustings to discuss the perils of the EU, and focused their energies on pressuring mainstream parties to support EU withdrawal (Ford and Goodwin 2014). What broadening of their policy platform did take place appears largely to have been instrumental: driven by party leaders' recognition of the difficulty of folding together tenuous support from a wide swath of British politics on the sole basis of shared antipathy to the EU (Lynch and Whitaker 2013). As discussed further below, there was an emerging view among party leadership, particularly Nigel Farage, one of their first MEPs and a media savvy campaigner who would become one of their longest serving and, arguably, most successful leaders, that that they would only be able to compete with parties such as the BNP by expanding their policy base (Ford and Goodwin 2014: 89–92).

During this period, UKIP's mode of organising also resembled what Kitschelt describes as that of a movement party. While UKIP quickly developed a cohort of activists operating primarily at the national level, there was little investment in developing the type of party infrastructure, particularly at the local level, required to build lasting electoral support at all levels of representation. In fact, the contrast between their failure to do so and the BNP's Liberal Democrat-inspired strategy of building local pockets of support through community politics (Copsey 2007; John and Margetts 2009; Goodwin 2011) is likely to be one of the reasons why the BNP, despite significant stigma, was able to outperform UKIP at local and national elections for as long as it did.

Crucially, the narrow policy focus on opposition to the EU also shaped UKIP's strategic aims during this period. While UKIP entered the electoral arena from the outset, electoral contests were seen primarily as an opportunity to fan pervasive anxieties over the EU and, later, the new euro currency, driving this issue into greater public prominence. Even within electoral contexts their aim, at least initially, was not to replace the Conservative Party, itself internally divided on the issue of the EU, but to pressure more Conservative MPs into adopting Eurosceptic positions by undermining their ability to compete against other main party candidates (Ford and Goodwin 2014: 32–38) – arguably a more realistic aim within the UK's first-past-the-post electoral system. During UKIP's first nationwide electoral campaigns they specifically targeted seats in the south of England held by pro-EU Conservative MPs, a strategy that remained largely unchanged over the next decade.

By 2007, a new strategic direction appeared to be emerging. Party staffers, including Liverpool-born future party leader Paul Nuttall, urged leaders to expand UKIP's focus to Labour-leaning constituencies in the north of England (Ford and Goodwin 2014: 108–109). Following Nuttall's advice, in the run-up to the 2009 EP elections then-leader, Nigel Farage, committed to contesting every seat in the upcoming race, including those in working class constituencies in the Midlands and North of England where the BNP had previously been more successful at challenging Labour's dominance in local elections (John and Margetts 2009). This strategic shift was not uncontroversial, particularly among UKIP's more single-minded Eurosceptics. However, it was deemed successful when UKIP not only gained one further MEP, bringing the party's total to thirteen, but also narrowly defeated the Labour Party to place second for the first time, securing more than twice as many votes as the BNP (Ford and Goodwin 2014: 76–78).

Yet even after such spectacular electoral success, the single-issue focus of some within UKIP would soon shape party strategy again. Farage, to the surprise of many, resigned as leader after the 2009 EP elections. No sooner was the new incumbent, Lord Pearson, in the post than he attempted to form an electoral alliance with the Conservatives for the upcoming 2010 general election (Ford and Goodwin 2014: 80–81). In a seemingly bizarre move as the leader of a political party, Pearson offered to disband UKIP entirely if David Cameron would pledge to hold a referendum on British membership of the EU as part of the Conservative Party's election platform (Hough and Prince 2009). Although the proposal was rejected, the news undermined UKIP's fledgling position as a genuine and independent political contender and reinforced public perception that UKIP was essentially a single-issue party.

The events that followed help to illustrate how, even at this relatively early stage, UKIP had become a vehicle for different movements with sometimes competing interests and aspirations. Pearson's offer of a deal with the Conservative Party made sense within a conceptualization of UKIP as a single-issue protest group broadly aligned with the Eurosceptic wing of the Conservative Party and one that defined success primarily in terms of UK withdrawal from the EU.

Many of UKIP's supporters and activists, however, had latched onto a wider set of political ideas and aspirations that were only realistically attainable if they could achieve a more direct role in policy and governance. As such, while Pearson was trying, and failing, to strike an electoral deal with the Conservative Party, another increasingly influential faction now favoured a more radical anti-immigrant and anti-Islamic agenda which, they believed, would appeal to disaffected working class voters in the Labour heartlands of deindustrializing northern towns (Ford and Goodwin 2014: 83–85). The result was one of the most wide-ranging manifestos published by UKIP to date. For the first time, UKIP's campaign literature openly opposed 'multiculturalism', and referred to tackling 'extremist Islam,' implying that Islam was antithetical to 'Britishness', and advocated policies targeting Muslims, including bans on face veils, 'radical preachers', and 'sharia courts' (UKIP 2010). This manifesto also contained statements challenging climate science and related policies, as well as proposals to decentralize the NHS and implement an opt-out voucher system for patients. Such radical proposals and language unnerved some of UKIP's more moderate supporters.

UKIP went into the May 2010 election in a state of disarray. While Pearson continued to make open attempts to strike deals with Eurosceptic Conservative candidates, some UKIP candidates in Conservative constituencies who opposed such moves refused party orders to stand down against their Eurosceptic rivals (Ford and Goodwin 2014: 84–86). Yet even with such confusion, the electoral fruits of broadening their policy platform and expanding their ambitions were evident. While the total votes cast for UKIP dropped from almost 2.5 million in the EP election in 2009 to under one million in the 2010 General Election, something important had happened in terms of the distribution of their support: they had begun to make inroads in Labour heartlands in the North and Midlands (Ford and Goodwin 2010: 80–85).

2010–2015: UKIP as a serious electoral challenger

Two developments dominate this period: a drive to build local and national structures in order to professionalize UKIP as a political party; and the growing prominence of opposition to 'mass immigration' as a focus of policy attention.

Recognising that UKIP could not compete meaningfully as a political party without developing its infrastructure, Farage, who reassumed leadership after the 2010 election, ensured that UKIP hired regional organizers and began to make substantial investments in local campaigning. In some respects, the move was a resounding success. Party membership more than doubled between 2010 and 2013 – providing a significant increase both in human and financial resources – and UKIP made significant electoral gains at a series of local elections, becoming the official opposition, or even gaining control of several local authorities (Ford and Goodwin 2014: 92–93). Then, in 2014, an ascendant UKIP won an historic victory over both the Labour and Conservative Parties in the EP elections with 26.6% of the vote.

This formalization of party infrastructure could be read as a sign of UKIP's transition from being a movement party to a fully-fledged political party. Yet in other ways, UKIP continued to resemble a movement party. While UKIP developed local and national structures across the country, party leaders, including Farage, still did relatively little to meaningfully incorporate the new members within the party, or to reconcile the different political interests and ideas driving UKIP support in different parts of the country and across different sections of the electorate.

UKIP's traditional support-base in the South of England was more middle class than their new supporters. They were concerned with lowering taxes and mitigating perceived economic ill-effects of immigration. Many of UKIP's new supporters in the North and Midlands, however, had more in common with the BNP's traditional base (Ford et al. 2012; Cutts et al. 2011). They were more likely to have grown up in working class, Labour-supporting families (Ford et al. 2012), and their concerns about immigration, while not divorced from economic circumstances, were more frequently articulated in terms of cultural difference and integration (Ford and Goodwin 2014: 117–126). In South Yorkshire, for example, where the fieldwork underpinning this study took place, UKIP supporters' explanations of what had motivated them to join the party were often framed in terms of the supposed effects of immigrants on British culture. Furthermore, northern UKIP activists were typically more concerned about dwindling public safety nets, the closure of local care homes for elderly or disabled family members, the de-funding of home-based care services, and the perceived vulnerabilities of the National Health Service (NHS) than they were about levels of taxation.

The balancing of such different interests was never going to be easy, but was made more difficult by the fact that, whatever Farage's intentions, the growth of UKIP's party infrastructure neither kept pace with nor evolved to represent the growing diversity of interests and local realities in which activists were operating. Some grassroots members, particularly in the North, complained that the national leadership was 'parachuting in' organizers and candidates from other areas of the country, often one of the party's growing list of MEPs, rather than recruiting and training local activists – a practice that many believed reflected a growing dominance of the party by its MEPs as a result of the EP funding they brought in.

UKIP supporters in South Yorkshire also evinced frustration with the management style of the still largely southern-based party leadership, frequently citing the lack of adequate support for local council elections. Even while local leaders in Rotherham celebrated winning 14 council seats in 2014, they simultaneously bemoaned the scant financial or logistical assistance they received from party headquarters. Local supporters complained that when a senior party figure did come to Yorkshire to speak on behalf of UKIP's national interests, the newcomer would inevitably commit a regionally specific political faux pas, whether it was praising Margaret Thatcher, still much reviled in this former mining and industrial region, or proposing further cuts to social services, including the NHS, which many northern UKIP activists were committed to protecting and even expanding.

Meanwhile, the party also became increasingly riven by debates about the adoption of a more radical populist and anti-immigrant agenda. While antipathy towards the EU provided a unifying policy theme, those who wanted the withdrawal from the EU to remain the party's primary focus clashed with those pushing for the party to give greater policy focus to issues related to Islam, immigration, and multiculturalism. These clashes would intensify in 2014 when Raheem Kassam, editor-in-chief of the right-wing news outlet Breitbart London, was hired as a senior advisor to Nigel Farage, further unsettling those who wanted to retain withdrawal from the EU as UKIP's primary focus. Some prominent party figures, including deputy leader Suzanne Evans, openly expressed concern that Kassam was pushing Farage, and therefore the party, towards a radical right agenda, as well as encouraging increasingly personal attacks against Farage's rivals, both inside and outside the party (Mason 2015).

By this stage, however, such tension had arguably become inherent to the party, inscribed in the political logics shaping UKIP's strategy. Electoral success, and therefore a greater role in shaping debates around the EU, required an expanded policy platform to attract and capitalize on greater support. At the same time, emphasizing UKIP's expanded policy positions risked highlighting fault lines within the support base that could be exploited by their opponents.

In order to retain a modicum of control over the party, UKIP's leaders continued to foreground the issue of the EU, while deflecting critical examinations of their own ideological and political disunity with attacks on their main political competitors. This balancing act brought the party notable success, at least in the short-term – generating a sense of considerable momentum among party activists and supporters, and alarm among their political opponents. In 2014, there was UKIP's historic win in the EP elections, which was followed by two defections from Conservative Party MPs, Douglas Carswell and Mike Reckless, who won successive by-elections, and helped to further expand UKIP's professional political organization. After standing candidates in four separate national elections for seats in Westminster, and failing each time, UKIP had two seats and expected to take more. With a national profile, expanded issue base, and voters willing to support them in both the North and South, UKIP was at the height of its influence in the lead-up to the 2015 general election. Rumours and polling data hinted at a hung parliament, with the prospect of a coalition government between a further handful of UKIP MPs and the Conservative Party seemingly a realistic prospect (Neather 2015).

As such, with tensions between UKIP's various factions and local branches simmering just beneath the surface, UKIP, arguably aided by heightened media and public interest in the so-called 'refugee crisis' that reached a peak in 2015 (Poushter 2016), nonetheless played a major role in shaping the political debate in the run-up to the 2015 general election. The Labour Party, wary of the threat to its seats in northern England, placed uncharacteristic emphasis on promises to control immigration (Helm 2015). Yet it was the Conservative Party's response to the perceived UKIP threat that would have the most dramatic effects.

UKIP, acting more like a pressure-group while under the control of Lord Pearson, had failed just a few years earlier to extract the promise of an EU referendum from David Cameron. However, in 2015, with the burgeoning electoral organization of a serious political party, UKIP was a key player in pressuring Cameron to pledge a nationwide referendum on the UK's membership of the EU.

Despite winning more than 12 percent (3.9 million) of votes cast that year, the UK's first-past-the-post voting system left UKIP with just one MP, Douglas Carswell – a bitter pill when the Liberal Democrats achieved eight seats with less than eight percent of the vote and the Scottish National Party fifty-six seats with less than five percent of the vote (Electoral Commission 2015). Despite UKIP achieving close second place losses behind Conservative and Labour Party rivals in more than 90 constituencies, UKIP was, by many traditional definitions, still a minor political party, with just one MP and control of just one local council. Yet 2015 was also a success for UKIP, certainly as a movement. They had shaped the debate, securing a campaign promise on their central political cause. They had followed an unconventional path to an unconventional success, but had nevertheless helped to generate enough anti-EU pressure to persuade the now-ruling Conservative Party to take one of the biggest gambles in recent British history.

UKIP during the EU referendum: the shift into movement politics

As we have argued, in its early years UKIP closely resembled what Kitschelt describes as a movement-party, gradually becoming more like a fully-fledged political party as they sought to build and sustain public support and exercise policy influence. UKIP's strategies during the referendum, however, shifted again, and became more similar to those of a political or social movement (see Diani 1992). UKIP's key organizers, and eventually the party's very identity, were subsumed into a more pluralistic network of groups with a shared ambition for UK withdrawal from the EU. While UKIP formally remained a distinct political party, and UKIP supporters were key activists in the Leave campaign, the group's tactics changed significantly during the referendum. The ideological and organisational conflicts that UKIP's leaders had struggled to control during the lead up to the 2015 election persisted, and threatened to collapse the fragile sense of party unity engendered by their limited successes. However, the singular and imminent goal of the larger Leave movement provided its own political infrastructure and allowed UKIP's leaders and supporters greater latitude for containing their differences than did the more multifaceted demands of operating as a political party.

The potential for internal division was present from the outset as UKIP's key figures aligned themselves with three different campaigns for leaving the EU. While Nigel Farage, along with Conservative, Labour, and Northern Irish DUP Eurosceptic MPs, founded Grassroots Out (GO!) (Harris 2016), Arron Banks, a major UKIP donor, founded Leave.EU in the summer of 2015[2] (BBC 2015), and finally, Vote Leave was launched in October 2015 by Conservative Party activists with the support of UKIP's only MP, Douglas Carswell, and UKIP's deputy chair, Suzanne Evans (Carswell 2015). The rivalries between these Leave-supporting groups echoed many of the differences that had divided UKIP in the past. Grassroots Out and Leave.EU advocated for a campaign more overtly focused on immigration and cultural values, while Vote Leave claimed to focus more on economic arguments against EU membership (Sparrow 2016). Though Vote Leave did, in April 2016, win the Electoral Commission mandate to officially represent the Leave campaign, the other groups did not disappear, nor did the ideas that they represented. However, these differences did not in practice stop activists from the various campaigns collaborating with one another. Where similar conflicts had stymied UKIP's growth as a party, as part of the Leave movement, with its clearly defined common purpose, they were absorbed more successfully.

This dynamic was apparent among local UKIP activists. In early June 2016, two middle-aged women, Nicole[3] and Wendy, distributed Vote Leave leaflets as part of a large group of UKIP supporters in the Sheffield city centre. Both were well-versed in the Vote Leave literature's talking points, but they had also donned lime green, high vis jackets that loudly declared 'Grassroots OUT!'. When asked about this discrepancy, Nicole said she and Wendy had supported 'Nigel's group', and while they used and largely agreed with the Vote Leave materials, they still thought GO! had a more persuasive message. Like Grassroots Out, Nicole and Wendy frequently framed their arguments against the EU around immigration, despite the fact this was not a focus of the Vote Leave literature they distributed. Late in the afternoon, Wendy struck up a conversation with a younger woman who looked around furtively before saying in a confessional tone, 'I don't want to sound racist … '. Wendy interrupted her emphatically, 'You're not racist!' The woman continued, 'But if Turkey get in, we're all dead. Because we'll be a Muslim country.' Wendy nodded enthusiastically as the woman spoke and told her that 'control' over borders and immigration would be returned to the UK outside the European Union. While such issues were not a focus of the Vote Leave literature they handed out, Nicole and Wendy felt free to frame their appeals to voters around issues about which they were obviously more personally passionate.

Some of UKIP's supporters went even further off-script in attempts to persuade people to vote Leave, even if it meant endorsing views antithetical to their general political positions as UKIP members. For example, at another UKIP-organized campaign event in South Yorkshire, one man, Dean, brought a pamphlet that a local branch of the Communist Party had delivered throughout his neighbourhood, setting out the left-wing arguments to vote Leave. Despite agreeing with little of what the pamphlet said, apart from the headline message of voting Leave, Dean had committed its key points to memory, and attempted to use them when speaking to people he thought may have a more leftist political worldview.

The most striking example of how participation in the wider Leave movement shaped UKIP's own strategy was the party's own branding policy during the referendum campaign. UKIP-organized Leave events mainly made use of official Vote Leave literature, with GO! and Leave.EU materials used less frequently.

Furthermore, in March 2016, UKIP leaders advised all local branches to avoid wearing, using, or even speaking about UKIP's name or logo when campaigning on the EU referendum, for fear of tainting Vote Leave and the other groups with any stigma associated with UKIP (Bennett 2016). These orders were not uncontroversial. Many UKIP activists were reluctant at first to relegate their political affiliation in favour of the movement campaign against the EU. Over time, however, some UKIP supporters began to think differently. Andrew, a late-middle-aged man on the board of a local UKIP branch in Doncaster, said he had initially disagreed with the branding decision. He was proud to be a member of UKIP, and saw no need to hide that fact. However, as the referendum campaign progressed, he accepted the 'wisdom' of this tactic. Fewer people were shouting at him or shutting doors in his face, leading him to marvel at how much more positively people responded to the Vote Leave name as compared with that of UKIP.

Where UKIP, alone, had only ever been able to persuade four million or so voters to back their cause, as part of the Leave movement, UKIP was a central player in a campaign that gained the support of more than four times that number. UKIP's abdication of its political autonomy, identity, name, and logo in favour of the wider Leave-supporting movement had contributed to one of the biggest political upsets in a generation. Few people were more surprised by the Vote Leave's success than UKIP's own activists. It was a shock for which they and their party were thoroughly unprepared.

The price of success: UKIP fractures after the 'Brexit' vote

It took a while for the shock and disbelief among UKIP's supporters in South Yorkshire to fade. It was replaced, at first, by optimistic determination. UKIP, they thought, was in a prime position. The party's supporters had played a crucial role in providing the opportunity for more than 17 million people to vote to leave the EU. Local activists and branch leaders were determined to turn every one of them into a UKIP voter. Not only did this prove to be unrealistic, but UKIP was soon struggling to simply hold onto the base of support it had developed in the years leading up to the referendum. Neither did UKIP's success erase the discord within its ranks. Indeed, it is in the fallout from this apparent victory that competing interests, aspirations and interpretations of success are laid particularly bare. No longer subsumed under the Leave movement, UKIP was once again a small political party divided amongst itself, but now without its unifying purpose.

When Farage announced his intention to resign as UKIP's leader less than two weeks after the referendum, the reaction among the party faithful was mixed. Despite the barely disguised tensions within the national leadership, Farage was still considered by many to have acted as a unifying force for the party, and he was generally popular among grassroots members of every stripe. However, a change in party leadership was seen, at first, as an opportunity to successfully refresh the party's message and prepare their organisational infrastructure for the new political landscape wrought by the referendum. The desire for a new message and updated party structures were common refrains as the campaign for UKIP's next leader began. Activists were aware that outsiders in the media and other parties expected UKIP to vanish now that its founding goal had been achieved. They were desperate to prove them wrong and demonstrate they were, as one long-time activist put it, 'a real political party … not a one trick pony'.

Defining UKIP's post-referendum purpose would, however, turn out to be more challenging than most activists had imagined. As we now discuss, Leaders and supporters alike were divided. Discussions of UKIP's new political focus, beyond the EU, were highly contentious, as were deliberations over the level of significance the ongoing Brexit negotiations should play in future UKIP policy and campaigning. As UKIP's leaders and members struggled to resolve these disputes, it became clear that UKIP had become a vehicle for two different movements: a straightforward Eurosceptic movement, and a radical right, anti-Islam movement. Following the referendum and the loss of the unifying forces of both the EU and Farage's leadership, the precarious alliance between these factions quickly unravelled. Their competing visions of UKIP's future would dominate the party for at least the next 15 months, shaping not one but three leadership elections, as the party lurched through a series of public relations disasters and electoral failures.

During the first of these leadership elections, the eventual winner, Diane James, sought to address the issue of UKIP's future political focus by proposing a consultation with the party's members. James' proposal deflected potential conflict and helped catapult her, however briefly, to the top role in UKIP. These conflicts could not be held at bay for long, however, as UKIP's supporters began clamouring for a cohesive new party platform, the basis of which remained unclear. James resigned just 18 days after being elected leader, citing concerns that she did not have 'sufficient authority' or 'the full support of all my MEP colleagues and party officers' (Wilkinson 2016). Her departure was swiftly followed by a physical altercation between two UKIP MEPs that left one popular candidate for James' successor briefly hospitalized. UKIP's more EU-focused leaders, including Douglas Carswell and Suzanne Evans, both former Conservative Party politicians, advocated restoring focus and order within the party by prioritising the government's negotiations with the EU, positioning themselves, and by extension UKIP, as the stewards of Brexit. This position, reminiscent of UKIP's earlier behaviour as a single-issue pressure group, was swiftly challenged by other leaders and party members who believed UKIP should capitalize on its role in the referendum victory by expanding, not narrowing, its political aims.

When a new leadership race was called following James' resignation, Raheem Kassam, former advisor to Nigel Farage, became a contentious candidate both inside and outside the party when he announced his intention to run for leader under the Donald Trump-inspired slogan 'Make UKIP Great Again' (Mason 2016). His rivals in the leadership race raised concerns that moves such as Kassam's verbal attacks on Muslim schools, and call for a national referendum on Muslim women's clothing would lead the party toward the far right (Merrick 2016); part of wider concerns about the increasing closeness between Kassam, UKIP, and Breitbart (Kirchgaessner and Hopkins 2017). While anxieties about the supposed threats from Islam had begun to appear in UKIP's longlist of political concerns in 2010, it was never a central point of organization or agreement across the party. Yet this shift clearly resonated with some elements of UKIP's grassroots. Certainly, Breitbart was often referenced by UKIP supporters in South Yorkshire, with some citing discussions on the website's comment section as a major influence in their decision to join UKIP. Although Kassam withdrew from the leadership race, debates over the adoption of anti-Islam positions, and the potential for UKIP to lurch toward the right continued as long-time UKIP organizer Paul Nuttall, positioning himself as the party unity candidate, was elected leader in November 2016.

Nuttall's spell as leader began poorly and never really improved. He suffered an embarrassing by-election defeat in a pro-Brexit Stoke-on-Trent constituency in February 2017. That same month, nearly half of UKIP's MEPs were reported to be under investigation by EU financial regulators for misuse of EU funding to support national level political campaigning, giving credence to rumours that had previously been a source of resentment among the party's grassroots members (Rankin 2017). Less than two months later, in April 2017, UKIP lost 145 local council seats. Fending off calls for his resignation, Nuttall debuted a controversial 'Integration Agenda' in April 2017 that proposed, among other things, burqa bans, annual and compulsory genital mutilation exams, and a moratorium on Muslim faith schools (UKIP 2017). While UKIP supporters who favoured a more radical policy platform welcomed the announcement, others, including Tariq Mahmood, one of the party's few, high-profile Muslims members, denounced the agenda as too extreme, setting off a wave of resignations among senior party figures (Maguire 2017; Hope 2017).

The divide between UKIP's more EU-focused members and the anti-Islam faction was soon further compounded. After UKIP was resoundingly defeated in the June 2017 snap general election, returning its worst national election performance since 2001, Jonathan Arnott, a UKIP MEP was among those who criticized UKIP's recent 'anti-Islam messages' (Heffer 2017). Paul Nuttall resigned as UKIP leader, yet there remained support within the party for his 'Integration Agenda', support that Anne Marie Waters sought to expand and deepen, as she looked to replace Nuttall as leader. Breaking with UKIP's history of seeking to clearly distinguish itself from the far right, Waters, the co-founder of anti-Islam social movement PEGIDA UK and chair of Sharia Watch, controversially welcomed support from both the BNP and activists affiliated with the anti-Muslim English Defence League. She was the first UKIP leadership candidate to openly propose rebuilding their political platform primarily around anti-Islam positions rather than opposition to UK membership of the EU, prompting former UKIP leaders, including Farage and Nuttall, to caution that such a myopic focus on Islam would render UKIP unelectable (Bloodworth 2017).

Waters was narrowly defeated by Henry Bolton, a former Army captain, police officer, and Liberal Democrat, who had warned during the campaign that UKIP could become the 'UK Nazi Party' should they choose the wrong candidate to replace Nuttall (Walker 2017). Bolton, who had campaigned on a platform that appealed to the party's more moderate Eurosceptic members, used his acceptance speech to declare, 'Brexit is our core task' (Mance 2017). Waters promptly left UKIP, apparently with the intention of forming a new party. Meanwhile, rumours continue to circulate that Aaron Banks might launch a new political movement. UKIP's future is uncertain.

Conclusion

UKIP's journey is often told like a political Cinderella story. The UKIP of this fairy-tale was once a small, single-minded, largely unsuccessful party, whose obsession with the EU was easily mocked and dismissed, until it suddenly burst upon the scene as a force in British politics, with a base of voters pulled from both the traditional right and left of the political spectrum, and helped to create one of the biggest political upsets in British history. As we have shown here, UKIP's journey was not nearly so simple. Persistently torn between the strategic logics of a single-issue movement and a fully-fledged political party, even at the moment of what arguably comprized its greatest triumph, UKIP was riven with discordant understandings of the party's fundamental purpose.

UKIP was founded as a political party, yet operated for much of its history without strong organizational infrastructure or a broad policy platform. While these apparent deficiencies as a political party often inhibited UKIP's growth and its ability to achieve electoral success, its ideological ambiguity also created opportunities for the party to draw support from diverse sections of British society, in turn enabling it to generate far greater policy pressure on both the Conservative and Labour parties. In doing so, however, the party itself became increasingly fractured, a process exacerbated by the failure of the party leadership to ever fully incorporate new members and supporters within the party's ideological and organisational structures.

By 2015, UKIP had become a vehicle for at least two distinct movements, each with their own understandings of success, pulling the party in different, often contradictory directions. For UKIP's more straightforward Eurosceptics, often drawn from primarily Conservative-dominated regions of southern England, success entailed removing the UK from the EU by any means necessary, even if it meant sacrificing UKIP's political autonomy and survival. For this faction, elections were a means of raising the profile of their criticisms of EU membership, and pressuring political competitors to adopt positions more hostile to the EU. They were wary of association with groups perceived as more politically extreme, and of policies that might distract from the European issue. For supporters of UKIP's more radical and anti-Islam faction, the EU was also important, but was far from their sole political focus. Members of this faction aspired to make UKIP a competitive political party in order to advocate more wide-sweeping reforms to UK immigration law and a refocusing of policy priorities onto the supposed threats posed to the UK by Islam and Muslims. United by little more than their common antipathy to the EU, these factions within UKIP were tenuously united while the EU remained a central focus of the party's platform. Tensions between them were largely set aside as attention centred on the imminent cause of achieving victory in the 2016 referendum. In the wake of the Leave movement's victory, however, these divisions soon re-surfaced, and the delicate balance between diverse interests and strategic logic unravelled.

Examining UKIP as a movement party can help us articulate a more complicated and less linear understanding of UKIP's history: one that can help reveal the possibilities and liabilities facing movement parties on the right. As we have sought to demonstrate, of particular salience in this regard are issues about how the hybrid nature of movement parties can fuel and, at least temporarily, accommodate diverse interpretations of success and, related to this, the way movement parties can become vehicles for the interests of more than one movement, sometimes at the same time.

Notes

1 While the Conservative Party has become increasingly dominated by Eurosceptic positions, particularly since William Hague's leadership (1997–2001), it has never as a party been dedicated to Euroscepticism.
2 Leave.EU was originally called The Know, but changed when the referendum wording 'Leave/Remain' was chosen over 'Yes/No' (BBC 2015).
3 All names used in this chapter in the descriptions of primary data are pseudonyms.

References

BBC News (2015) 'The Battle to Be the Official EU Referendum Leave Campaign'. Available at: http://www.bbc.com/news/uk-politics-34484687. Accessed 30 October 2017.

Bennett, O. (2016) 'Ukip Activists Told Not to Use Party Logo When Campaigning for Brexit', *Huffington Post UK.* Available at: http://www.huffingtonpost.co.uk/2016/03/01/ukip-brexit-campaigning-evans-farage_n_9357148.html. Accessed 30 October 2017.

Bloodworth, J. (2017) 'Meet Anne Marie Waters – the Ukip Politician Too Extreme for Nigel Farage', *New Statesman.* Available at: https://www.newstatesman.com/culture/2017/08/meet-anne-marie-waters-ukip-politician-too-extreme-nigel-farage. Accessed 30 October 2017.

Carswell, D. (2015) 'Douglas Carswell: Why I'm backing Vote Leave in the EU referendum', *The Telegraph.* Available at: http://www.telegraph.co.uk/news/newstopics/eureferendum/11922172/Douglas-Carswell-Why-Im-backing-Vote-Leave-in-the-EU-referendum.html. Accessed 30 October 2017.

Carter, N., Evans, M., Alderman, K., and Gorham, S. (1998) 'Europe, Goldsmith and the Referendum Party', *Parliamentary Affairs,* 51(3): 470–85.

Clarke, H., Goodwin, M., and Whiteley, P. (2017) *Brexit: Why Britain Voted to Leave the European Union,* Cambridge: Cambridge University Press.

Copsey, N. (2007) 'Changing Course or Changing Clothes? Reflections on the Ideological Evolution of the British National Party 1999–2006', *Patterns of Prejudice*, 41(1): 61–82.

Diani, M. (1992) 'The Concept of Social Movement', *The Sociological Review*, 40(1):1–25.

Electoral Commission (2015) '2015 UK General Election Results'. Available at: https://www.electoralcommission.org.uk/find-information-by-subject/elections-and-referendums/past-elections-and-referendums/uk-general-elections/2015-uk-general-election-results. Accessed 30 October 2017.

Ford, R. and Goodwin, M. (2014) *Revolt on the Right*, London: Routledge.

Goodwin, M. and Milazzo, C. (2015) *UKIP: Inside the Campaign to Redraw the Map of British Politics*, Oxford: Oxford University Press.

Hanna, J. (2017) 'UKIP After the Referendum', *Anthropology News.*

Harris, S. (2016) 'Brexit Campaign 'Grassroots Out' Unites 'Political Foes' to Push for UK to Leave European Union', *Huffington Post UK*. Available at: http://www.huffingtonpost.co.uk/2016/01/23/brexit-campaign-grassroots-out-uk-leave-european-union_n_9058344.html. Accessed 30 October 2017.

Heffer, G. (2017) 'Jonathan Arnott quits UKIP role over party's 'anti-Islam' stance', *SkyNews*. Available at: http://news.sky.com/story/jonathan-arnott-quits-ukip-role-over-partys-anti-islam-stance-10910078. Accessed 30 October 2017.

Helm, T. (2015) 'Ed Miliband to set his promises in stone', *The Guardian*. Available at: https://www.theguardian.com/politics/2015/may/03/ed-miliband-sets-promises-in-stone. Accessed 30 October 2017.

Hope, C. (2017) 'Ukip frontbencher quits over 'burka ban' as Paul Nuttall says policy came from Ukip members', *The Telegraph*. Available at: http://www.telegraph.co.uk/news/2017/04/25/ukip-frontbencher-quits-burka-ban-paul-nuttall-says-policy-came/. Accessed 30 October 2017.

Hough, A. and Prince, R. (2009) 'New Ukip Leader 'Offered to Disband Party if David Cameron Agreed to EU Referendum', *The Telegraph*. Available at: http://www.telegraph.co.uk/news/newstopics/eureferendum/6674458/New-Ukip-leader-offered-to-disband-party-if-David-Cameron-agreed-to-EU-referendum.html. Accessed 30 October 2017.

John, P. and Margetts, H. (2009) 'The latent support for the Extreme Right in British politics', *West European Politics*, 32(3): 496–513.

Kirchgaessner, S. and Hopkins, N. (2017) 'Revealed: Ukip Whistleblowers Raised Fears about Breitbart Influence on Brexit', *The Guardian*. Available at: https://www.theguardian.com/politics/2017/oct/30/revealed-ukip-whistleblowers-raised-fears-about-breitbart-influence-on-brexit?CMP=share_btn_link. Accessed 31 October 2017.

Kitschelt, H. (2006) 'Movement Parties', in R.S. Katz and W. Crotty (eds) *Handbook of Party Politics*, Thousand Oaks, CA: Sage, 278–290.

Lynch, P. and Whitaker, R. (2013) 'Rivalry on the right: The Conservatives, the UK Independence Party (UKIP) and the EU issue', *British Politics*, 8(3): 285–312.

Maguire, P (2017) 'Ukip's 'Integration Agenda' Is Another Lurch Away from the Mainstream', *New Statesman*. Available at: https://www.newstatesman.com/politics/uk/2017/04/ukips-integration-agenda-another-lurch-away-mainstream. Accessed 30 October 2017.

Mance, H. (2017) 'Henry Bolton becomes Ukip leader with Nigel Farage's backing', *Financial Times*. Available at: https://www.ft.com/content/1919431c-a530-11e7-9e4f-7f5e6a7c98a2. Accessed 30 October 2017.

Mason, R. (2015) 'Ukip Insider Raheem Kassam: 'We Had to Lock HQ Doors Because Some People Were Too Embarrassing to Be Seen', *The Guardian*. Available at:

https://www.theguardian.com/politics/2015/jun/10/ukip-insider-raheem-kassam-we-had-to-lock-hq-doors-because-some-people-were-too-embarrassing-to-be-seen. Accessed 30 October 2017.

Mason, R. (2016) 'Ukip Leadership Contest: Five Likely Contenders to Succeed Diane James', *The Guardian*. Available at: https://www.theguardian.com/politics/2016/oct/05/ukip-leadership-contest-steven-woolfe-raheem-kassam-paul-nuttall-suzanne-evans-lisa-duffy. Accessed 30 October 2017.

Merrick, R. (2016) 'Ukip at War Again as Two More Leadership Candidates Put Themselves Forward', *The Independent*. Available at: http://www.independent.co.uk/news/uk/politics/ukip-at-war-again-as-two-more-leadership-candidates-put-themselves-forward-a7376851.html. Accessed 30 October 2017.

Neather, A. (2015) 'Who Will Form a Coalition Government After the General Election?', *The Evening Standard*. Available at: https://www.standard.co.uk/lifestyle/london-life/who-will-form-a-coalition-after-the-general-election-10201442.html. Accessed 15 December 2017.

Poushter, J. (2016) 'European Opinions of the Refugee Crisis in 5 Charts', Pew Research Center. Available at: http://www.pewresearch.org/fact-tank/2016/09/16/european-opinions-of-the-refugee-crisis-in-5-charts/. Accessed 15 December 2017.

Rankins, J. (2017) 'Nigel Farage among UKIP MEPs accused of misusing EU funds', *The Guardian*. Available at: https://www.theguardian.com/politics/2017/feb/01/nigel-farage-among-ukip-meps-accused-of-misusing-eu-funds. Accessed 15 December 2017.

Reif, K. and Schmitt, H. (1980) 'Nine Second-Order National Elections – A Conceptual Framework for the Analysis of European Election Results', *European Journal of Political Research*, 8(1): 3–34.

Sparrow, A. (2016) 'EU Referendum: Vote Leave Chosen to Lead Official Brexit Campaign – as it Happened', *The Guardian*. Available at: https://www.theguardian.com/politics/blog/live/2016/apr/13/labour-says-whittingdale-should-lose-control-of-press-regulation-after-sex-worker-revelation-politics-live. Accessed 30 October 2017.

UKIP (2010) *Empowering the People: UKIP Manifesto 2010.*

UKIP (2017) 'Our Bold New Integration Agenda Aims to Bring Communities Together'. Available at: http://www.ukip.org/our_integration_agenda_aims_to_bring_communities_together#. Accessed 30 October 2017.

Walker, P. (2017) 'Ukip Risks Becoming 'UK Nazi Party' if it Selects Wrong Leader', *The Guardian*. Available at: https://www.theguardian.com/politics/2017/sep/11/leadership-hopeful-warns-wrong-leader-could-turn-ukip-into-uks-nazi-party-henry-bolton. Accessed 30 October 2017.

Wilkinson, M. (2016) 'Diane James Quits as Ukip Leader after Just 18 Days as Nigel Farage Rules Out a Comeback', *The Telegraph*. Available at: http://www.telegraph.co.uk/news/2016/10/04/diane-james-quits-as-ukip-leader-after-just-18-days-as-successor/. Accessed 30 October 2017.

5

STILL A RADICAL RIGHT MOVEMENT PARTY?

Political opportunities, party strategy and the cultural context of the Front National in France

Gilles Frigoli and Gilles Ivaldi

Introduction

The French Front National (FN) is a prominent example of the West European radical right (Mudde 2007). The FN was founded in 1972 as a coalition of small nationalist and neo-fascist movements which sought to compete in national elections. Whilst this resulted in the dominance of a party-oriented structure, the FN retained its previous organizational and strategic profile as radical right movement party i.e. a hybrid type of actor in transition from an extra-institutional movement stemming from the extreme right subculture into partisan electoral competition (Gunther and Diamond 2003).

During the 1980s and the 1990s, anti-establishment populism and the politicization of new contentious 'cultural' issues of immigration and law and order helped the FN create an electoral niche and establish itself as a major player in the French party system, galvanizing voters from both sides of the political spectrum (Rydgren 2005). Electoral support for the FN peaked in the 2002 presidential elections where Jean-Marie Le Pen progressed into the second-round run-off against the incumbent right-wing president Jacques Chirac, marking a dramatic turn in the history of the far-right movement in post-war France. Reflecting the FN's lack of credibility, however, the 2002 performance was followed by a series of electoral setbacks, most notably the 2007 elections, which produced strong incentives for party change, resulting in Marine Le Pen's accession to leadership in January 2011.

Since her accession, Marine Le Pen has set a new trajectory for her party, seeking to shed its extremist profile in order to reclaim legitimacy, and to maximize electoral support for the FN. Changes in the party's strategic and programmatic profile have been embedded in the so-called strategy of '*dédiabolisation*' (de-demonization). Whilst certainly not the only factor of FN success, the political rejuvenation of Jean-Marie Le Pen's 'old' extreme right has recently helped the FN reach new electoral heights. In the 2017 presidential elections, Marine Le Pen captured 21.3 per cent of the first-round vote, and progressed into the run-off against Emmanuel Macron, winning 33.9 per cent of the vote, over 10.6 million votes, by far the highest level of support ever achieved by the FN.

At the same time, important changes have occurred in the political environment of the FN, providing new cultural resources and 'discursive opportunity structures' for radical right mobilization in France. Since the early 2000s, public discourse and media debates in France have seen the development of a larger 'reactionary' movement outside the realm of the FN (Lindenberg 2002). This movement is embodied by cultural elites whose national profile and notoriety have helped heighten the prominence of FN issues in the mainstream political space and media. Reflecting further the diversification in the political arenas of radical right mobilization in France, FN themes are also diffused by an informal network of small extreme-right groups and sub-cultural milieus operating primarily on the internet, which are referred to as the French '*fachosphère*' (fascist-sphere) (Albertini and Doucet 2016), and which interact with the more mainstream manifestations of the radical right.

Looking at changes that have occurred in both the party and the social movement, this chapter examines the current context for radical-right mobilization in France, and the extent to which these changes may have altered the FN's profile as a movement party operating across both intra and extra-parliamentary spheres. We examine the conditions and forms under which radical right mobilization manifests itself across both party and movement in contemporary France, looking in particular at inter-arena interactions between party formation and/or change, on the one hand, and movement mobilization, on the other. The French FN is currently at the center of this informal, heterogeneous, and porous interaction network which produces a specific set of discursive opportunities and shared collective identities, thereby providing the FN with intellectual assets, mobilization initiatives, and grassroots activists.

As regards the general framework proposed in this volume, this chapter employs the first analytical strategy which seeks to provide a description of the current context for radical right mobilization by the FN in France. We look primarily at the ideational and organizational resources that are mobilized by political actors in order to frame their political strategies and communication. Following Minkenberg (2003), the main focus of this chapter is on how cultural resources and symbols are produced through interactions between the FN as institutionalized party, the broader and more fluid 'reactionary' movement in which the FN operates, and the informal network of groups, intellectuals and activists in the far-right subcultural milieu of French politics, which represent a 'micro-mobilization potential' for the radical right.

This chapter is organized into two main sections. We begin by looking at the internal supply-side variables and external incentives for the strategic recalibration of the FN, and the new mobilization frames and strategies employed by the party in the electoral arena. We then move onto examining the collective identity frames, strategies, and topography of the current context for radical right mobilization by the FN. We examine the specific sets of discursive opportunity structures that are produced within the right-wing cultural movement and the more informal network of far-right groups and activists.

1. From 'old' to 'new': the parameters of FN recalibration

This first section looks at the main features of the political space for radical right politics in France since the early 1980s. We then describe the aims and parameters of the strategic recalibration of the FN by Marine Le Pen.

1.1. The political space for radical right politics in France

The French FN epitomizes the West European radical right (Mudde 2007). During the 1970s and the early 1980s, the FN exemplified the radical right movement party, that is, a hybrid type of actor progressively transforming itself from an extra-institutional far-right movement into a more established political party. The FN emerged in the early 1970s as a coalition of small nationalist and neo-fascist movements, accommodating former pro-French Algeria activists and OAS members such as Roger Holeindre, national-revolutionary groups such as *Ordre Nouveau* and François Duprat's *Groupes nationalistes-révolutionnaires* (GNR), as well as nostalgics of the collaborationist Vichy regime, such as Pierre Bousquet. In the late 1970s, FN membership also included small neo-Nazi groups, such as Mark Frederiksen's FANE (Ivaldi 1998).

In the first decade following its inception, the FN remained a fringe party, essentially operating in the far-right sub-cultural milieu. It was largely irrelevant to electoral politics, winning less than one per cent of the vote in national elections. During the 1980s, however, the FN began to mobilize support on political discontent with the established political parties, while simultaneously politicizing new contentious 'cultural' issues of immigration and law and order (Rydgren 2005). This helped create an electoral niche, and galvanize voters from both sides of the political spectrum, most notably amongst working-class and lower education voters (Perrineau 2017). The party consolidated further electorally during the 1990s, adopting a Eurosceptic and anti-globalization platform (Zaslove 2008).

Ideologically, the FN took its inspiration from the political and philosophical framework of the French New Right (*Nouvelle Droite*, ND), embodied notably by the GRECE movement. The GRECE was founded by Alain de Benoist in reaction to the 1968 social movement in France, strongly opposing egalitarianism and socialism. It was primarily conceived as a 'metapolitical' project, rejecting direct participation in the electoral arena. FN discourse and policies on immigration and 'national preference' were significantly influenced by the ND's ethnopluralist agenda and claims to fundamental rights to 'cultural identity' (Taguieff 1994). During the 1980s, the FN accommodated a number of former GRECE members such as Pierre Vial, Yvan Blot and Jean-Claude Valla, while also establishing links with leaders of the neo-conservative faction of the ND, namely the *Club de l'Horloge*, such as Jean-Yves Le Gallou and Bruno Mégret who later joined the FN, providing the party with a more comprehensive and sophisticated set of themes and policies (Ivaldi 1998).

Finally, the FN exhibited the main organizational features of the movement party, showing a relatively weak party structure, and a strong 'leadership principle'. Ivaldi and Lanzone (2016) define the FN under Jean-Marie Le Pen as a 'charismatic party' characterized by centralization of power, a highly personalized leadership and a confrontational anti-establishment rhetoric. As Gunther and Diamond (2003: 189) suggest, extreme right movement parties typically embrace a strong leader and 'they are hostile to 'party' and 'establishment', more generally'. The FN showed also a high degree of elite turnover and internal factionalism (Ivaldi 1998). During the 1990s, a significant organizational split occurred, as the FN Delegate General Bruno Mégret, left the party, together with about half of its grassroots and cadres, later founding the *Mouvement National Républicain* (MNR), which, however, failed to achieve electoral relevance.

Notwithstanding a short-lived period of co-operation with the moderate right in the late 1980s, the FN has been primarily characterized by its status as a political pariah. The FN outsider status has been reinforced by France's majoritarian electoral system which is traditionally detrimental to minor party alternatives. The FN's extreme right heritage and profile have significantly restricted its ability to co-operate with other political parties in France. The FN has been politically ostracized by parties of the mainstream, and it has been secluded behind a 'cordon sanitaire', playing mostly a nuisance role vis-à-vis other actors in the party system (Ivaldi 2016).

1.2. Reframing radical right politics

Since her accession, Marine Le Pen has set a new trajectory for her party. Marine Le Pen was elected as party leader with 67 per cent of the membership vote against Bruno Gollnisch at the FN party congress in Tours in January 2011, advocating a strategy of modernization and professionalization, and claiming to depollute the FN from its extremist heritage.

These party goals are embedded in Marine Le Pen's concept of 'de-demonization'. Current de-demonization replicates previous strategic adjustments conducted by modernist factions in the FN during the 1990s, most notably under the influence of former party delegate General Bruno Mégret. As Ivaldi (2016) suggests, de-demonization is primarily a vote-maximizing strategy which mainly aims to change the party's reputation to improve its credibility, while simultaneously preserving its radical right-wing populist potential for voter mobilization.

First, the FN is seeking to shed its extremist profile in order to reclaim legitimacy and to maximize electoral support. An important aspect is the attempt by the FN to dissociate itself from extreme right heritage, and it concerns the filtering by the party of its political communication. Since her accession, Marine Le Pen has notably repudiated anti-Semitism, Holocaust denial, and overt racism, which were customary of the FN under Jean-Marie Le Pen, and which have been the principal causes for FN stigmatization in the past. On several occasions since 2012, she has publicly condemned Nazism and anti-Semitism. In August 2015, Jean-Marie Le Pen was expelled from the FN after he reiterated his controversial comments that Nazi gas chambers were 'a detail of the history of the second world war'.[1] Moreover, the FN has been increasingly incorporating moderate pro-Israel themes and policies since 2011, as revealed in the positions taken by FN elites such as Gilbert Collard and Louis Aliot. The FN is seeking to reach out to the Jewish community in France by exploiting growing fears of Islamic fundamentalism. However, during the presidential campaign of 2017, Marine Le Pen was heavily criticized for denying that the French state was responsible for the round-up of Jews at Vel' d'Hiv during the War,[2] while FN vice-president Jean-François Jalkh had to step down after allegedly casting doubt on Nazi gas chambers.[3]

De-demonization has produced new interpretative frames for contentious issues of immigration and Islam, which are primarily a tactical reformulation of the traditional radical right policies and themes (Frigoli and Ivaldi 2016). While continuing with its previous ethnopluralist agenda, the FN under Marine Le Pen has co-opted the French Republican model of integration and secularism. FN republican narratives target primarily Muslims, emphasizing the alleged stand-off between Islam and secularism. Islam is instrumentalized as a threat to liberal democratic values, and the FN now claims to defend France's laicity against the dangers of 'communitarism' which, the party argues, would be the breeding ground for Islamic terrorism.

Additionally, the FN is seeking to appropriate feminism and the defense of women's rights, showing deviation from the organic and paternalistic ideology of the far right, which emphasizes family and traditional moral values. In 2017, Le Pen's manifesto claimed to promote gender equality, and defend women's fundamental rights and freedom which, as is the case with laicity, are mostly seen as being under threat from Islam. The current FN has also moved away from its previous socially conservative themes, moderating its views on issues such as abortion, homosexuality, and civil union contracts (PACS), which marks a significant departure from the past (Crépon 2015). During 2013, the FN was deeply divided over the new law on same-sex marriage by the socialist government, showing an opposition between conservative factions embodied by Marion Maréchal-Le Pen and more 'liberal' elites within the party such as Florian Philippot, Sophie Montel, and Marine Le Pen.

Finally, the FN has adopted left-wing domestic economics, and it has accentuated anti-capitalist themes and policies, rejecting international financial and economic powers (Ivaldi 2015). The FN under Marine Le Pen has espoused economic populism, claiming to represent all the left-behind (*les oubliés*) at the bottom of society against the economic oligarchy. The FN attacks large multinational corporations and the power of financial markets. It opposes neoliberalism and free trade, while denouncing the 'savageness' of unbridled globalization, of which the European Union would be the 'Trojan Horse'.

1.3. Organizational strategies

Organizationally, the FN under Marine Le Pen is seeking to sever its ties with the nationalist subcultural milieu and extreme right groups. In the lead up to the 2011 FN leadership election, Marine Le Pen had publicly distanced herself from the extremist milieu, announcing that she would put an end to dual membership, which had traditionally allowed for FN activists to remain members of other far-right groups and parties.

Support from extremist groups was found primarily in Gollnisch's camp during the 2011 internal election. A longstanding FN member, Gollnisch was a member of the *Solidariste* faction, a nationalist group led by Jean-Pierre Stirbois and Roland Gaucher, which had joined the party in the late 1970s. In 2011, Gollnisch's party leadership campaign had the backing of a number of nationalist groups, newspapers – e.g. *Présent*, *Minute*, and *Rivarol* – and activists such as Pierre Sidos and Yvan Benedetti's *Oeuvre Française*, Bernard Antony's Catholic fundamentalists, as well as former cadres of the FN, such as Carl Lang and Jacques Bompard, who had left the party in the mid-2000s in opposition to the growing influence of Marine Le Pen.

The dissociation by the FN from traditional extreme right subjects and groups reflects the change in the factional balance within the party, and the rise of Marine Le Pen's faction organized through the *Générations Le Pen* think-tank that she had created in 1998. A significant generational turnover has occurred in the national leadership since 2011, showing the rise of a younger and more 'pragmatic' cohort of elites such as Louis Aliot, David Rachline, Stéphane Ravier, Nicolas Bay, Sébastien Chenu, and Julien Rochedy, as well as the marginalization of the 'old' nationalist guard e.g. Bruno Gollnisch, Marie-Christine Arnautu, and Jean-Marie Le Pen himself.

Since 2011, FN national executive bodies have been progressive populated by pro-Marine elites and supporters of her de-demonization strategy, which has helped Marine Le Pen establish a strong and personalized leadership (Ivaldi and Lanzone 2016). In the 2012 elections, the FN sought to open itself up to more 'respectable' parties and groups to the right of French politics, through the founding of the *Rassemblement Bleu Marine* (RBM) electoral umbrella, which accommodated minor Eurosceptic parties such as Karim Ouchikh's *Souveraineté, Identité et Libertés* (SIEL), as well as right-wing personalities such as Gilbert Collard, FN deputy in the Gard, and Robert Ménard, mayor of Béziers. In the 2017 presidential election, Marine Le Pen managed to seal a significant electoral pact with Nicolas Dupont-Aignan's *Debout la France* (DLF), a mainstream right-wing Eurosceptic party. The current FN retains the typical features of the movement party, however. The party continues to operate on a confrontational anti-establishment rhetoric, which is characteristic of extreme right movement parties (Gunther and Diamond 2003: 189). The FN portrays itself as a third competitive bloc in French politics, violently opposing both the left and the right – the so-called 'UMPS caste' (Ivaldi 2016).

Let us note also here that the FN has not severed its ties with all extremist groups and far-right milieus, however. Nationalist groups such as the *Groupe Union Défense* (GUD) still play an active role in Marine Le Pen's entourage, as exemplified by Axel Loustau and Frédéric Chatillon. At grassroots level, racist and homophobic social media postings by FN candidates suggest extreme right continuity in the party's cadres and local elites.[4] In the Southern region, FN elites such as Marion Maréchal-Le Pen and Stéphane Ravier notoriously embody the hard-line approach that was shaped by Jean-Marie Le Pen during his time as party leader. They co-operate locally with far-right extreme groups such as the *Identitaires* (formerly the *Bloc Identitaire*, BI) and Jacques Bompard's *Ligue du Sud*. In 2015, former leaders of the BI such as Philippe Vardon and Benoît Loeuillet were selected by the FN to stand in the regional elections in Provence-Alpes-Côte d'Azur, and Vardon is now a member of the national leadership.

Finally, one last dimension of de-demonization is credibility. The current FN seeks to improve its credibility as agency through party modernization and professionalization. The claim to embody a credible governmental alternative to mainstream parties has been central to the party's rhetoric since the mid-1990s. Under the influence of Mégret, in particular, the FN sought to expand its ideological appeal beyond its focus on core issues of immigration, to encompass a broader range of socio-economic themes. Similarly, Marine Le Pen has been seeking to reduce the FN's socio-cultural 'nicheness' by broadening its electoral agenda and appeal, which has notably resulted in a significant increase in socio-economic relevance since 2012 (Ivaldi 2016). Economic and credibility issues have been prioritized in the 2012 and 2017 presidential campaigns, and the FN has founded a number of think-tanks such as Louis Aliot's *Idées Nation*, which provide for policy expertise and networks of politically likeminded members of the national administration. Additionally, the FN is increasingly seeking to reach out to civil society through the founding of flanking organizations (*Collectifs*) which target specific socio-economic groups and interests, most notably amongst entrepreneurs and small business organizations.

Under Marine Le Pen, the electoral consolidation of the FN has been accompanied by the reinforcement of its party apparatus and the development of the party's local base of power, from 22,400 registered members in the 2011 internal election up to 51,500 at the time of adopting the new party statutes in July 2015. During the last electoral cycle, the FN has won a large number of seats across local and regional elections, progressively rebuilding its pool of mid-level elites (Ivaldi and Lanzone 2016).

Access to political institutions at the sub-national level has made the FN eligible for more public funding, thus increasing its financial assets. While the FN relied originally on Jean-Marie Le Pen's personal fortune inherited from the Lambert family in the late 1970s, political revenue is currently collected from a variety of sources such as membership fees, loans, and private donations. Other sources include subsidies from the state, and from the European Union. In 2015, the FN received a total 5.5 million euros from the state, and it collected about 2 million euros from its members.[5] Additionally, since 2014, the European Parliament has become a valuable source of revenue for the party, providing about 570,000 euros each year for personnel. Party financing has become an important, and somewhat controversial, aspect of the current FN. Marine Le Pen has tried to undermine the influence of her father's COTELEC by setting her own micro-party, Jeanne, to collect funds. In 2014, the FN received a loan of 9.4 million euros from a Russian bank. In 2015, Marine Le Pen was charged with misuse of assets and complicity in fraud in a continuing campaign finance inquiry, which concerned her 2012 campaign and the role of Frédéric Chatillon's Riwal company. In June 2017, Le Pen was charged over misappropriation of European Parliament funds.[6]

2. A new political space for radical right politics

The current FN is able to exploit new opportunities, interpretative frames, and symbolic resources provided by the broader cultural and political context. As Koopmans and Statham (1999: 228) suggest, we must consider the 'discursive opportunity structure' in which political parties operate and compete, and which shape the context of political mobilization. This second section looks at the reconfiguration that has occurred in the heterogeneous cultural and political movement to the right of French politics.

2.1. The development of a 'reactionary' movement

Since the early 2000s, significant changes have occurred in public discourse and media debates in France. A broad conservative movement has developed, which consists of a variety of intellectuals on the right, including journalists such as Yvan Rioufol and Elisabeth Lévy, essayists such as Eric Zemmour, and philosophers such as Alain Finkielkraut. These right-wing intellectuals have been defined, somewhat controversially, as 'new reactionaries' (Lindenberg 2002). They produce a profusion of literature, public discourses, and media debates, offering new interpretative frames for socio-economic and cultural issues, which tend to transgress the boundaries of legitimate political discourse.

While partly espousing the views of the FN, this movement has grown outside the realm of the FN and relatively independently from it. It can primarily be characterized as a reconfiguration of the 'intellectual field', which has produced new right-wing public discourses and media debates. Moreover, the movement's disconnection from electoral politics has helped sustain its actors' pledge for a complete change of paradigm, seemingly ignoring the history and current development of the far right in France.

The current 'reactionary' movement can be analyzed from a history of cultural counter-hegemonies in France, looking at how political and intellectual actors periodically engage in contesting what they refer to as the 'dominant ideology'. As such, the rehabilitation during the 2000s by the conservative movement of concepts such as heritage and rootedness can be seen as a backlash against what has been defined by scholars as the legacy of the '1968 ideology' (Ferry and Renaut 1988) embodied in the cultural and intellectual movement (e.g. Foucault, Deleuze, and Derrida), which has been associated with the radical social and cultural revolution of 1968 in France. The latter is criticized by conservative thinking for its alleged impact on the traditional social order, and for having precipitated the advent of a socially disenfranchised individual condemned to hedonism, relativism, and the 'tiredness of being oneself' (Ehrenberg 1998).

2.1.1. Mobilization frames

Since the early 2000s, the right-wing intellectual movement has engaged in a cultural critique of what is deemed the 'idealistic' political and ideological left, producing new interpretative frames and repertoires of legitimate claims for radical right mobilization. Whilst heterogeneous as regards the diversity of its actors, trajectories, milieus, and modes of expression, the current right-wing cultural movement is characterized by its open hostility to left-wing thinking, criticizing left-wing intellectuals and elites for their alleged sense of 'self-righteousness' and claim to be on the side of good (see, for instance, Finkielkraut 2013; Lévy 2017).

As Durand and Sindaco (2015) argue, the movement's critique is fixated on the 'intellectual project' of the left, that is, the systematic deconstruction of values, traditions, and social hierarchies inherited from the past. According to right-wing thinkers, the demolition of social norms and values is legitimated by new theories – e.g. French Theory, Cultural Studies, and Gender Studies – which have progressively transformed into philosophical *doxa*, instilling a new religion of the 'otherness'. This moral prescription by the left would emphasize alterity and claims to enhance minority status and rights, while simultaneously demonizing any majority expectation or identity claim (e.g. Zemmour 2014).

A second target of criticism concerns the so-called 'political correctness' which is vilipended by right-wing intellectuals as a form of social control that would be enforced by imposing censorship on their values and ideas. These include, for instance, the attempt to address the needs of the majority rather than 'flattering' minorities, to re-establish verticality in society, and to construct a concept of the people truly connected with their identity and roots against the so-called culturally globalized elites (Finkielkraut 2013; Rioufol 2014). Right-wing intellectuals claim that they are socially stigmatized for defending the 'real people' against the myth of individualism and moral relativism that underpins the concept of successful 'living together' which, they argue, is in fact disembodied and artificial.

Finally, a third aspect refers to those who are accused by right-wing intellectuals of propagating 'cultural leftism', namely journalists, academics, intellectuals, human rights activists, and politicians, such as the so-called Champagne Socialists who, out of moral idealism or self-interest, would be the zealous advocates of this new moral order, leading to nothing but social alienation disguised in individual emancipation. Because they are disconnected from electoral and parliamentary politics, right-wing actors may further claim their status as political pariahs ostracized by the mainstream. Moreover, by symbolically constructing a hegemonic political adversary, right-wing intellectuals, and media pundits produce a coherent and systematic worldview whereby they portray themselves as the visionary 'vanguard' i.e. those able to unmask the false pretense of the dominant progressive ideology. They notably denounce the 'single mindset' (*pensée unique*) in French politics, and they depict themselves as those who are willing to assume their ideas in public.

2.1.2. Re-interpreting critical events

Conservative assaults on the ideology of 1968 go beyond the critique of the social revolution that shook up patriarchal post-war France, however, to include a series of 'critical events' which are interpreted through the prism of the anti-'68 cultural values and ideas, and which are seen as providing additional justifications for the need for political and cultural action. While contesting in particular the idea of an 'end of history', the current conservative movement is able to politicize specific events and incorporate a set of different temporalities – including for instance pre-1968 events and changes – to systematically celebrate the 'world from before', and condemn the world as it is today.

The conservative critique is embedded, for instance, in a post-1989 thinking which sees the end of the Cold War as the trigger for the rise of a cultural 'new left' disconnected from the old left's more traditional focus on socio-economic issues, and which has endorsed economic liberalism and globalization. As right-wing conservatives argue, individualism and the global market have produced social atomization which needs be reversed by returning to organic social bonds and hierarchies. Similarly, the terrorist attacks of 9/11 in the United States are seen as the beginning of a new area of civilizational war, whereby new hostile forces would put Western values under threat, therefore attesting to the very existence of a Western civilization that would need to be defended. In the French context, the specter of a war of cultures has been raised further by the suburban riots of 2005, which, according to conservative intellectuals, revealed the failure of the French model of immigrant assimilation and the dominance of what is described as its perversion by the ideological 'tyranny of minorities'.

These frames have strong roots in France's history of decolonization, and the national trauma caused by the Algerian war of independence. Right-wing conservative intellectuals object to what they see as the excesses of the trend towards 'repentance', and critical examination of France's colonial past, which, as argued by right-wing thinkers, would ultimately result in 'self-hatred'. More generally, the current conservative movement draws ideologically from the older literary and intellectual heritage of the French reactionary tradition, at times reactivating old counter-revolutionary themes dating back to the 1789 revolution in France, and which had been durably delegitimized by fascism in the 1930s, and by the episode of Vichy's collaborationist regime during World War II.

The breadth and scope of the current conservative worldview goes beyond cultural issues to embrace socio-economic themes. Current right-wing thinking evokes, for instance, the liberal U-turn by François Mitterrand's Socialist government in 1983 as a symbol of how the French left has abandoned the working class to adopt social liberalism. Similarly, the 2005 referendum on the European Constitutional Treaty is regarded as one example of the collusion of political elites against the people's will and interests. Left-wing elites, in particular, are criticized for their embrace of neoliberal globalization and the increase in social inequality which has been associated with the development of the global market economy during the 2000s, thus providing opportunities and frames for a critique of left-wing progressivism.

2.2. Movement heterogeneity

Whilst they unite in their critique of left-wing progressivism, individuals and groups in the current conservative movement are characterized by the diversity of their political backgrounds and policy preferences. These actors show weak organizational links beyond mutual ideological affinities and sporadically lending support to one another in the press and media. Their diverging values and strategies form a complex set of intertwined ideological cleavages, cross-cutting traditional left–right ideological affiliations.

Actors and groups within the current right-wing conservative movement hold substantively different economic policy positions. The movement includes, for instance, French Thatcherites and national-conservatives such as Henri de Lesquen, which support market liberal economics embedded in social conservatism and traditional values.[7] These actors differ from more radical left-wing revolutionary anti-capitalist activists, such as Alain Soral, who proclaim the demolition of the old bourgeois social order (Soral 2011). This second group of actors echoes the rhetorical arsenal of the anti-capitalist left in attacking capitalism and neoliberal globalization, which they see as the result of the historical convergence between political and economic liberalism. They advocate a return to traditional organic social structures against the commercialization of the world.

Another significant line of conflict concerns religion and moral values. The movement includes a variety of religious elements, such as Catholic fundamentalists in Civitas and the *Renouveau Français*, for instance, who are doctrinally opposed to the Second Vatican Council of the 1960s.[8] They diverge from those such as Pierre Vial advocating Neopaganism,[9] as well as from other groups and actors such as *Résistance Républicaine*,[10] which see themselves as heirs of the Enlightenment, and those such as *Riposte Laïque* which emphasize France's Republican principle of secularism (*laïcité*),[11] and, for some of them, advocate atheism as a founding political principle. As regards moral values, the traditionalist wing of the movement champions traditional family values, which they say have been under attack in 1968, while others show a greater interest in promoting women's rights, and the recognition of sexual minority rights as civilizational achievements. Polemists such as Renaud Camus, for instance, believe these rights should be defended against the dominant cultural relativism of the Left. Because of fighting racism, the Left is accused of being too lenient against the patriarchy and intolerance towards women and sexual minorities which allegedly is found amongst French Muslims.

There are other significant differences as well, which concern how actors in the movement appropriate traditional extreme right repertoires, such as racism and anti-Semitism, and how these are articulated with their growing animosity towards Muslims (Frigoli and Ivaldi 2016). An assimilationist definition of Frenchness, which is devoid of any ethno-racial connotation, is found, for instance, amongst those such as Paul-Marie Coûteaux and the SIEL who situate themselves within France's tradition of Republican Jacobinism. They differ substantially from more radical groups such as *Terre et Peuple*, which continue to articulate the defense of a 'White Europe' that stretches back for millennia, thus perpetuating classic far-right racism. Cultural and civilizationist themes are also predominant in theories of 'the great replacement', such as that propagated by Renaud Camus, whereby non-Western immigration is seen as a demographic threat to France's identity (Camus 2011). These ideas were endorsed by Aymeric Chauprade (2015), a former foreign policy adviser to Marine Le Pen, as well as by Marion Maréchal-Le Pen, and the 'identitarian' faction within the FN. An ethno-racial approach to immigration is found also in the *Bloc Identitaire* (BI),[12] a far-right extreme group which puts a strong emphasis on regional identity and which is notorious for lashing out at Islam by organizing 'wine-and-pork' events and by actively campaigning against the building of mosques. These themes increasingly find their way into the literary field, as revealed for instance by Michel Houellebecq's controversial novel *Soumission* (2015) as well as by the previous writings of Maurice G. Dantec (2002) and Richard Millet (2012).

Anti-Semitism is another important driver of debates, which splits the movement. The movement accommodates an array of groups and personalities which repudiate anti-Semitism, and increasingly show pro-Israel positions; however, this is primarily as a means to expand the anti-Muslim coalition. Such a posture is found, for instance, in former GRECE member, Guillaume Faye (2015) and it is strongly opposed by those such as Hervé Ryssen, Robert Faurisson, and the *Rivarol* newspaper, which continue to profess traditional far-right anti-Zionism and anti-Semitism (e.g. Ryssen 2010). Given the social stigma attached to the themes and ideas they manipulate, these actors continue to be banished from mainstream media, and they operate mostly at the radical margins of the movement, notably enjoying the numerous opportunities offered by the internet and social media.

2.3. New arenas and opportunities

Contentious politics may take place across a variety of arenas where right-wing intellectuals interact with other actors, showing diverging sets of opportunities, strategic options, and goals. Unlike the *Nouvelle Droite* in the 1970s and the 1980s, which had relatively little public visibility, the current conservative movement operates within the mainstream, with regular access to major media outlets. A number of right-wing intellectuals have achieved a national profile and notoriety, therefore increasing the degree of visibility and resonance of FN themes and discourses in the political space.

This reflects deep changes that have occurred during the 2000s in what the French sociologist Pierre Bourdieu has referred to as the 'intellectual field'. The latter, Bourdieu argues, is not only semiotic, but also institutional and material. The production and the reception of new ideas and themes are socially embedded, reflecting competition over social power, capital, and benefits (Bourdieu 1999: 7). The transformation of the intellectual field and its growing connection with the mass media are important aspects of the current deployment of conservative thinking in France, showing a relationship of mutual dependence. While mocking mainstream medias for their alleged 'conformism', reactionary intellectuals and media pundits enjoy growing access to major television and radio networks.

Right-wing writers and journalists such as Eric Zemmour, Élisabeth Lévy, and Ivan Rioufol, for instance, show a good deal of adaptation to the new media environment and 'infotainment' culture, which feature predominantly being politically offensive, while also performing ad hominem attacks on reality shows to generate 'buzz'. These actors exemplify a new type of media figure, juxtaposing political commentary, ideological combat, and infotainment, fully seizing the new opportunities produced by the cultural transformation of mass media during the 2000s. The success of this new type of intellectual, which meets the expectations of the dominant media culture of spectacle, has contributed to the weakening of traditional experts and elites, thus opposing the figure of the 'prophetic intellectual' (Sapiro 2011) to that of the 'specific intellectual' advocated for instance by Foucault (2001).

Reflecting further the diversification of political arenas, the internet has become an important force in the practice of right-wing politics in France, as it has elsewhere in Europe and America (Caiani and Parenti 2013). The internet is host to a vast array of right-wing conservative and extremist actors, providing a favorable social and political space for the diffusion of their critique of the progressive left. These actors exploit web resources to propagate counter-cultural discourses whereby they define themselves as the alternative to the 'system' and to the 'single mindset'. The internet provides a forum where these actors denounce the censorship allegedly imposed by the leftist bias in the 'dominant media', and against which they are empowered.

The diffusion of right-wing ideas on the internet is achieved strategically through a variety of social networks, YouTube channels, blogs, web-magazines, TVs, and so-called 're-information' websites, such as Alain de Benoist's *TV Libertés*. This online political community, which is often referred to as the French *'fachosphère'* (fascist-sphere) (Albertini et Doucet 2016), is a loose association of bloggers, YouTube monologists, and smaller political groups which do not exhibit formal organizational structures. This cyber-community brings together various sectors of the extreme right, such as conspiracy theorists, neofascists, identitarians, and nostalgics of the monarchy such as *Action Française*. It targets primarily disenfranchised social groups, in particular, young voters, who are increasingly moving away from traditional media and political affiliations. As exemplified by the recent launch of Meta TV, performers of the YouTube extreme right community have adopted the communication tools of modern mass media, producing talk-shows, music, and entertainment, often adopting the soft humorous tone and political jokes which have become predominant in mainstream broadcasting.

Most of these actors remain independent operators, such as Daniel Conversano, for instance, and they are not officially associated with the leading public figures of the conservative movement. Links remain mostly indirect, and they are established through mutual referencing and social media dissemination of books, essays, and major media broadcasts and performances, essentially promoting a community of debate. These actors are, however, connected to the other sectors of right-wing mobilization by shared ideas, priorities, and sensibilities, showing a dual relationship. On the one hand, the radical sphere provides mainstream intellectuals and media pundits with a seal of political 'subversiveness', which is key to maintaining their profile as outsiders, while simultaneously allowing them to appear somewhat more 'moderate'. On the other hand, leading right-wing intellectuals help diffuse extremist ideas and theses into the mainstream, thus expanding the space of opportunity for radical right mobilization.

Notably, some actors are able to circulate across different arenas, adapting to the specific forms of communication and message framing that dominate each specific arena, thus achieving a delicate balance between mainstream and extreme right politics. Recently, new arenas have emerged, which facilitate links between the various sectors of the movement. This is the case, for instance, of the *Cercle Iéna*, a think tank founded by former members of the ultra-nationalist movement *Ordre Nouveau* such as José Bruneau de la Salle and Alain Robert, which promotes right-wing reactionary writers such as Eric Zemmour and Jean Raspail, and which has links with FN's cadres such as Philippe Péninque, a personal advisor to Marine Le Pen.[13] Other examples include Charles Millon's *Avant-Garde* conservative think tank, Henry de Lesquen's *Radio Courtoisie*, the *L'incorrect* magazine recently created by members of Marion Maréchal-Le Pen's entourage such as Jacques de Guillebon and Arnaud Stephan, Alain de Benoist's *TV Libertés*, as well as the more mainstream *Causeur* magazine.

Finally, a variety of groups and actors are found in the electoral arena where other more marginal far-right parties compete against the FN. These include, for instance, a number of organizations founded by former FN cadres and leaders, such as Jean-Marie Le Pen's *Jeanne Committees*, Carl Lang's *Parti de la France* (PDF), Karim Ouchikh's SIEL, and Jacques Bompard's *Ligue du Sud*. In the 2017 legislative elections, these parties and groups formed an ad hoc electoral coalition under the umbrella of the *Union des Patriotes* (UP), and ran in 160 constituencies. Further to the mainstream, various 'sovereignist' Eurosceptic parties such as

Dupont-Aignan's DLF, Philippe de Villiers' *Mouvement pour la France* (MPF), and the *Union Populaire Républicaine* (UPR) led by François Asselineau function as bridges between the mainstream right and the FN.

Conclusion

As the analysis in this chapter suggests, the contentious interpretative frames propagated by the FN have acquired greater resonance in mainstream politics, media and society in France. This proliferation must be seen as the product of the interaction and convergence between party and movement, that is, between the FN as institutionalized party and the broader and more informal cultural movement within which it functions, and which, we argue, has developed relatively independently outside the realm of the FN since the early 2000s.

While becoming more institutionalized, the FN has retained its profile as a movement party, and it currently finds itself occupying the center of an informal interaction network which consists of a plurality of movements, groups and individuals. The current FN connects mainstream and extreme variants of the French right, and this can be seen as a result of a dual process. On the one hand, the FN under Marine Le Pen has been gradually moving towards the mainstream, although not entirely severing its ties with the far-right milieu. On the other hand, mainstream politics and media have been progressively radicalizing, showing a complexification of the political space within which the FN operates. The FN is bridging the gap between far-right and mainstream politics, exploiting the discursive opportunities that are produced by the broader subcultural milieu within which it functions. This social movement provides with the FN with activists, intellectual assets, and initiatives, which help politicize contentious issues with the aim of influencing public discourses and mainstream party strategies, thus increasingly achieving cultural hegemony.

However, both party and movement are increasingly confronting challenges arising from the widening of the 'space of ambiguity' that exists between conflicting political strategies and goals, i.e. differentiation versus normalization, and homogeneity versus diversity. As regards first the FN, de-demonization concerns predominantly the packaging of FN narratives and strategy, and it has not yet changed the core of the party's radical right ideology. Ideologically, the appropriation by the FN of Republican narratives, feminism, and leftist economic policies, together with the moderation of its social conservative agenda, have increased policy heterogeneity, significantly hampering the FN's efforts to portray itself as a credible alternative to mainstream parties in French politics. Internal fights have revealed factionalism within the party, ultimately leading to the exit of Florian Philippot's modernist faction in September 2017, which may signal a return to previous radical right strategies and themes.

Similarly, today's conservative movement in France is taking the form of a cultural nebula which aggregates groups and individuals from very different backgrounds. Beyond their shared concept of a 'civilizational crisis', and opposition to the cultural dominance of the 'self-righteous' left in French politics and society, today's proponents of right-wing conservative thinking exhibit different sets of ideological preferences and strategies. They diverge deeply in the discursive constructions of their collective identities, both culturally and ideologically (e.g. Republican, Royalist, Socialist, Liberal, etc.). Moreover, these identities are conflated into multiple and often contradictory combinations which produce greater ideological heterogeneity and ambiguity. Such diversity of actors and positions within the movement impedes significantly its ability to translate its ideological maelstrom into a more coherent set of policies. So far, the reactionary movement in France has failed to create a unitary political force, which would, however, be crucial to FN mobilization and electoral success in the future.

Notes

1 French National Front expels founder Jean-Marie Le Pen, *BBC*, 20 August 2015 (http://www.bbc.com/news/world-europe-34009901).
2 https://www.theguardian.com/world/2017/apr/09/marine-le-pen-denies-french-role-wartime-roundup-paris-jews.
3 https://www.theguardian.com/world/2017/apr/27/le-pens-replacement-as-fn-leader-questioned-existence-of-gas-chambers.
4 http://www.huffingtonpost.fr/2015/03/23/resultats-departementales-2015-derapages-candidats-fn-pas-penalises_n_6921814.html.
5 http://www.cnccfp.fr/docs/commission/cnccfp_rapport_activite_2016.pdf.
6 http://www.lemonde.fr/les-decodeurs/article/2017/02/02/les-trois-affaires-qui-menacent-marine-le-pen-et-le-front-national_5073473_4355770.html.
7 https://henrydelesquen.fr/.
8 http://www.civitas-institut.com/; http://renouveau-francais.com/.
9 http://www.terreetpeuple.com/chroniques-par-pierre-vial.html.
10 http://resistancerepublicaine.eu/.
11 https://ripostelaique.com/.
12 http://www.les-identitaires.com.
13 http://droites-extremes.blog.lemonde.fr/2016/02/12/le-cercle-iena-au-rendez-vous-des-anciens-dordre-nouveau-et-du-gud/.

References

Albertini, D. and Doucet, D. (2016) *La fachosphère. Comment l'extrême-droite remporte la bataille du net*, Paris: Flammarion.
Bourdieu, P. (1999) 'Le fonctionnement du champ intellectual', *Regards sociologiques*: 17–18, 5–27.
Caiani, M. and Parenti, L. (2013) *European and American Extreme Right Groups and the Internet*, London: Routledge.
Camus, R. (2011) *Le grand remplacement, introduction au remplacisme global*, Paris: Eds. David Reinharc.
Chauprade, A. (2015) *Chronique du choc des civilisations : Du 11 septembre 2001 à la guerre contre l'État islamique, analyses géopolitiques et cartes pour comprendre le monde d'aujourd'hui*, Paris: Éditions Chronique.
Crépon, S. (2015) 'La politique des mœurs au Front National', in *Les faux-semblants du Front national*, Paris: Presses de Sciences Po, 185–206.

Dantec, M.G. (2002) *Le théatre des opérations, journal métaphysique et polémique 1999*, Paris: Gallimard.

della Porta, D., Fernandez, J., Kouki, H., and Mosca, L. (2017) *Movement Parties*, Cambridge: Polity Press.

Durand, P. and Sindaco, S. (2015) *Le discours néo-réactionnaire*, Paris: CNRS éditions.

Ehrenberg, A. (1998) *La fatigue d'être soi. Dépression et société*, Paris: Odile Jacob.

Faye, G. (2015) *Comprendre l'Islam*, Paris: Tatamis.

Ferry, L. and Renaut, A. (1988) *La pensée 68. Essai sur l'anti-humanisme contemporain*, Paris: Gallimard.

Finkielkraut, A. (2013) *L'identité malheureuse*, Paris: Stock.

Foucault, M. (2001) *Dits et écrits II, 1976-1988*, Paris: Gallimard.

Frigoli, G. and Ivaldi, G. (2016) 'L'extrême droite et l'islam: fractures idéologiques et stratégies électorales', *Hommes & Migrations*, 1316: 27–34.

Gunther, R. and Diamond, L. (2003) 'Species of Political Parties: A New Typology', *Party Politics*, 9(2): 167–199.

Houellebecq, M. (2015) *Soumission*, Paris: Flammarion.

Ivaldi, G. (1998) 'The National Front: The Making of an Authoritarian Party', in Ignazi, P. and Ysmal, C. (eds) *The Organization of Political Parties in Southern Europe*, Westport: Greenwood-Praeger, 43–69.

Ivaldi, G. (2015) 'Towards the Median Economic Crisis Voter? The New Leftist Economic Agenda of the Front National in France', *French Politics*, 13(4): 346–369.

Ivaldi, G. (2016) 'A new course for the French radical-right? The Front National and 'de-demonization'', in Akkerman, T., de Lange, S., and Rooduijn, M. (eds) *Radical Right-Wing Populist Parties in Western Europe. Into the Mainstream?*, London: Routledge, 231–253.

Ivaldi, G. and Lanzone, M.E. (2016) 'From Jean-Marie to Marine Le Pen: organizational change and adaptation in the French Front National', in Heinisch, R. and Mazzoleni, O. (eds) *Understanding Populist Party Organization: a Comparative Analysis*, London: Palgrave, 131–158.

Koopmans, R. and Statham, P. (1999) 'Ethnic and Civic Conceptions of Nationhood and the Differential Success of the Extreme Right in Germany and Italy', in Giugni, M., McAdam, D., and Tilly, C. (eds) *How Social Movements Matter*, Minneapolis, MN: University of Minnesota Press, 225–252.

Lévy, E. (2017) *Les rien-pensants*, Paris: Cerf.

Lindenberg, D. (2002) *Le rappel à l'ordre. Enquête sur les nouveaux réactionnaires*, Paris: La république des idées.

Millet, R. (2012) *Langue fantôme; suivi de Éloge littéraire d'Anders Breivik*, Paris: Pierre-Guillaume de Roux.

Minkenberg, M. (2003) 'The West European Radical Right as a Collective Actor: Modeling the Impact of Cultural and Structural Variables on Party Formation and Movement Mobilization', *Comparative European Politics*, 1(2): 149–170.

Mudde, C. (2007) *Populist Radical Right Parties in Europe*, Cambridge: Cambridge University Press.

Perrineau, P. (2017) *Cette France de gauche qui vote FN*, Paris: Seuil.

Rioufol, I. (2014) *Touche pas à ma France*, Paris: Éditions de Passy.

Rydgren, J. (2005) 'Is Extreme Right-Wing Populism Contagious? Explaining the Emergence of a New Party Family', *European Journal of Political Research*, 44(3): 413–437.

Ryssen, H. (2010) *Histoire de l'antisémitisme: vue par un goy et remise à l'endroit*, Paris: Baskerville.

Sapiro, G. (2011) *La responsabilité de l'écrivain. Littérature, droit et morale en France (XIXe-XXIe siècles)*, Paris: Editions du Seuil.

Soral, A. (2011) *Comprendre l'Empire: demain la gouvernance globale ou la révolte des nations*, Paris: Blanche.

Taguieff, P. (1994) *Sur la Nouvelle Droite. Jalons d'une analyse critique*, Paris: Descartes and Cia.

Zaslove, A. (2008) 'Exclusion, Community, and a Populist Political Economy: The Radical Right as an Anti-Globalization Movement', *Comparative European Politics*, 6(2): 169–189.

Zemmour, E. (2014) *Le suicide français*, Paris: Albin Michel.

6

NEO-FASCIST MOVEMENT PARTIES IN ITALY

The extreme right between electoral and protest politics

Pietro Castelli Gattinara

Introduction

Extant literature on political cleavages in Europe suggests that the relationship between the electoral and protest arenas is generally substitutive, rather than reinforcing, for the political Right (Hutter and Kriesi 2013; Hutter 2014b). This implies that the presence of radical right parties in the institutional arena reduces the space available for right-wing street actors. Put differently, right-wing protest would decrease in a context characterized by a strong established political party (Koopmans et al. 2005, 185–187; Giugni et al. 2005; Kriesi 2012). In this chapter, I set out to illustrate how this 'trade-off hypothesis' (Pedahzur and Weinberg 2001) neglects the role of intersectional actors transitioning from the extra-institutional to the electoral arena. In line with the remit of this edited collection, the analytical strategy focuses on ideological factors and political opportunities as explanations for the interpenetration of activism across arenas of conflict (Castelli Gattinara and Pirro 2018; see also Froio 2018). I focus on Italy as a case study, addressing two specific political and cultural factors expected to facilitate the development of far-right movement parties.

First, Italy has been at the core of the three major crises that have revitalized far-right street politics in recent years: the Eurozone crisis, the so-called migration crisis, and the crisis of representation in established democracies (Kriesi and Pappas 2015; Castelli Gattinara 2018). As shown by previous research, these events have shaped far-right politics, both quantitatively and qualitatively (Mudde 2016, 612), and thus might have offered right-wing actors opportunities to mobilize across political arenas. Indeed, during political crises, far-right parties may recognize that street organizations can help them in rooting in society, facilitating co-existence, and even co-operation across arenas (Pedahzur and Weinberg 2001). The crises might thus disrupt pre-existing opportunity structures, triggering new 'brands' of actors, ideally bridging the forms, organization, and practices of political parties and social movements (Castelli Gattinara and Pirro 2018).

Second, Italy's neo-fascist milieu enables the embedding of contemporary manifestations of far-right politics in their historical and cultural context (Mammone 2009), most notably in terms of Fascism's outspoken mistrust of party politics (Payne 1995; Gentile 2008). A crucial stream of Italian fascism is, in fact, the one described by Renzo De Felice (1969) as 'fascism as a movement', which is characterized by revolutionary anti-capitalist and secular tendencies, as opposed to the conservative, institutional 'fascism as a regime'. If conservative streams of neo-fascism emphasized order and tradition, fascism as a movement pursued revolutionary ideals based on dynamism, youth activism, and the rejection of modernity and democracy (Ignazi 2003). While this tension has characterized neo-fascism since its inception, here I look at its manifestation in terms of repertoires of action in contemporary activism. Thus, by addressing the legacy of fascism as part of the opportunity structure for far-right mobilization in Italy, I intend to tackle the ideological and cultural evolution of extreme right actors transitioning from movement to party politics.

Empirically, this chapter focuses on the three most visible neo-fascist actors in contemporary Italy, with the goal of assessing if, and to what extent, their mobilization can be likened to that of social movements, rather than political parties. The groups – *Movimento Sociale – Fiamma Tricolore* (MS-FT),[1] *Forza Nuova* (FN),[2] and *CasaPound Italia* (CPI)[3] – share many ideological traits: a fascist legacy, nativism, and opposition to liberal democracy. They stand out as hybrid political organizations in that they originally emerged in the extra-institutional arena, but eventually opted to contest electoral campaigns. Still, they differ considerably in terms of their organization and mobilization. MS-FT represents a prototypical example of a political party: it self-defines as such, it regularly contests elections, and it has long been involved in routinized politics. In contrast, CPI is a network of political and cultural movements, which is deeply involved in Italy's neo-fascist youth subculture, and thus privileges the rhetoric and imagery of social movements (Rao 2014). Between these extremes, the FN presents itself as a 'political movement'. Unlike the MS-FT, it can count on established ties with subcultural milieus and street-based groups, yet it is also considerably more institutionalized than CPI, and it regularly contests elections (see Caldiron 2013).

In the next sections, I shall compare the claims-making and repertoires of action of the three groups over time, looking at the way in which they relate to the domain of protest and party politics. As political parties, they are expected to be office seeking, to act as representatives of citizens' interests, and to compete with other parties for votes by means of electoral contests (Mudge and Chen 2014). As social movements, they are primarily agenda-setters, and they engage in contentious non-institutional political action based on shared beliefs and identities (Diani 1992). Yet neo-fascist actors can also qualify as hybrid political organizations that are ideally located at the intersection between these two configurational types. In this respect, while these actors have progressively transitioned from the extra-institutional to the electoral arena, I expect that their transition remained incomplete due to the ideological legacy of fascism as a movement. To address these expectations, in the next sections, I present the data and methods of the study, and offer an overview of Italy's neo-fascist parties and movements. I then move on to the empirical analysis, which will shed some light on how neo-fascist actors have been able to bridge the office-seeking logic of political parties with the agenda-setting one of social movement action.

Data and methods

The empirical study uses new quantitative data on the repertoires of action of the extreme right,[4] collected through an extensive Political Claims Analysis (PCA) of right-wing collective action in Italy, 1992–2015. Claims-making implies 'the purposive and public articulation of political demands, calls to action, proposals, criticisms, or physical attacks, which, actually or potentially, affect the interests or integrity of the claimants and/or other collective actors' (Koopmans et al. 2005, 254). The news stories originate from the *Factiva* digital archive of the daily broadsheet *Il Corriere della Sera,* and capture all articles containing references to the three extreme right organizations. Considering all claims initiated by one of these actors, as well as events attributed to their sympathisers, the political field of extreme right politics in Italy amounts to 2,209 instances of claims-making. While some have raised doubts about using newspaper data to measure public events, previous research has proved the robustness of PCA to systematize and assess collective action (e.g. Kriesi 1995; Koopmans et al. 2005; Hutter 2014a). Unlike other quantitative methods of data collection and analysis, in fact, PCA accounts for all types of intervention in the public sphere, while also emphasizing their thematic focus (Koopmans and Statham 1999).

Since a political claim might refer to a speech act, but also to various forms of collective mobilization, PCA is most suited to studying actors at the intersection between protest and institutional politics. To account for mobilization taking place at the intersection between protest and conventional action, each non-verbal claim was coded according to its degree of radicalism (Tarrow 1989; Caiani and Borri 2013). Repertoires of action are categorized as follows: conventional forms of contention (electoral campaigning, petitions); demonstrative actions (demonstrations, rallies); expressive actions (commemorations, cultural events, and other internal meetings); confrontational actions (blockades and occupations); and violent actions (including symbolic and physical violence). In addition, the coding accounts for the two main issues at the core of each public intervention, resulting in six broad issue fields of right-wing claims-making: socio-economic affairs, cultural liberalism, Europe, immigration, law and order, and ideological statements (see Kriesi 2012).

Political and cultural opportunities for far-right mobilization: Italy's post-war fascism

Building upon the symbolic dimension of political opportunity structures, this section focuses on cultural aspects of Italian neo-fascism. Specifically, I focus on the cultural and symbolic legacy of the fascist ideology, which had a profound influence on the identity of extreme right parties and movements in the post-war years (Cento Bull 2007).

While the neo-fascist camp had initially envisaged itself as a militia-style organization, it abandoned this idea soon after the war in favour of a party organization, and became the *Movimento Sociale Italiano* in 1946 (MSI). The MSI was configured as a legal political party organized along the mass-party model, and contested elections with a programme combining vague calls to national pacification, and nostalgia for the symbols and culture of the regime (Ignazi 1998). From its origins, the party was torn between two main factions, which can be likened to De Felice's (1969) famous differentiation between the fascist 'movement' and 'regime'. The 'movement' faction claimed continuity with the revolutionary, non-conformist, and anti-bourgeois style of the republican fascism of the mid-1940s, opposing the principles of the democratic system. The moderate faction, instead preferred the clerical, corporatist, and conservative tendencies of the fascist regime: it was more inclined to access the party system, supporting NATO and the ruling parties against Communism.

If the moderate politics of the MSI proved electorally rewarding in the 1950s and early 1960s, the progressive isolation of the party enfeebled the moderate leadership and revitalized the radical faction in subsequent years. On the one hand, this fostered the development of new groups calling for hard-line clashes on the streets with opponents. On the other, it paved the way for ideological renovation within the movement faction of the party, mainly inspired by the French *Nouvelle Droite*'s critique of the liberal-capitalist system, individualism, and consumerism (Bar-On 2012). Of considerable impact on younger generations was the organization of a series of communitarian summer camps, which aimed at taking the MSI out of the gloomy neo-fascist ghetto, to take an active role in the Italian society.

The attempts by the radical faction would, however, fall short in solving the MSI's isolation, due to the party's enduring nostalgia for the regime, and its complicity with street violence and terrorism. If the 1980 Bologna railway station massacre led to the dismantlement of most extra-parliamentary right-wing organizations, the changing global context progressively made confrontation with communism and street violence lose momentum. By the early 1990s, the MSI had gradually turned into a collector of protest by legal means, unambiguously denouncing violence, and clearly distancing itself from the extreme right fringes. As MSI candidates achieved resounding success in local elections, the party greatly improved its coalition potential (Ignazi 1998). Taking advantage of these opportunities, the 1995 congress marked the transition of the MSI into a modern European conservative party, allegedly detached from its fascist legacy. *Alleanza Nazionale* (National Alliance – AN) could now present itself as a legitimate ally for the emerging mainstream right coalitions that would rule Italy in the following decades (Campani 2016).

However, several MSI activists and officials did not support the transition and the rejection of the revolutionary features of fascism. A group of prominent members of MSI's movement faction thus founded *Movimento Sociale-Fiamma Tricolore* (Social Movement – Tricolour Flame – MS-FT). While AN progressively took a clear stand against biological racism and anti-Semitism, MS-FT did not renounce its fascist legacy, especially its 'social' revolutionary principles (Castelli Gattinara, Froio, and Albanese 2013). Its radical positions against globalization, immigration, and liberal economy contributed to its popularity among marginal groups in metropolitan areas, qualifying the party as a clear example of extreme right politics (Ignazi 2003). The splinter group managed to elect one MP at the 1996 national elections, and one Euro-MP at the 1999 European Parliament elections. Over the years, however, the party lost momentum, as other actors in the same area increasingly challenged its distinctive profile.

In the same years, in fact, former members of neo-fascist militant organizations founded the party *Forza Nuova* (New Force – FN). Originally, the group was the grassroots faction of the MS-FT. After splintering, thus, FN primarily focused on street activism, with a series of campaigns against abortion, euthanasia and same-sex marriage. Despite this propensity for social movement activism, FN's politics combined fascist ideals with ultra-Catholic values, which set it apart from the secularist tradition of Italy's neo-fascist movement faction. During the 1990s and early 2000s, FN infiltrated organized soccer clubs to recruit militants among hooligans, and the subcultural music milieu to attract young skinheads (Caldiron 2013). While the link between neo-fascism, hooliganism, and skinhead culture soon became the trademark of FN, the group also tried to gain legitimacy in the electoral arena, by collaborating with small splinter groups originating from AN. From 2008 onwards, however, FN has run its own independent candidates in national and local elections, generally with little success. Thus, similar to the factions that characterized Italian neo-fascism in the post-war years, FN displays a conflicted nature, seeking respectability as a political party, while claiming to be 'revolutionary', and open to violence, in the protest arena (Campani 2016).

In the early 2000s, MS-FT progressively transitioned to the electoral arena, where it repeatedly established alliances with the mainstream right coalition of Silvio Berlusconi. The electoral turn led to internal tensions, especially with the youth branch of the party, which demanded more flexibility in the decision-making process, while also contesting the rigidity of the party apparatus. This eventually led to a split, as a small group of militants left the party in 2008, under the leadership of a recognized public figure in the neo-fascist music subculture. In the following months, the group started the 'metapolitical' project of *CasaPound Italia* (CPI), as a youth cultural centre promoting alternative music events alongside demonstrative political actions. In a few years, CPI has been able to develop an innovative political language and imagery, largely inspired by the experiences of 1970s youth neo-fascism, thus attracting both the nostalgic neo-fascists and youth cultures. By the late 2000s, CPI was actively engaged not only on the web and in the neo-fascist subculture, but also with demonstrative political actions, occupations, as well as street clashes (Albanese et al. 2014). Only in 2013 did CPI decide to run in elections with its own candidates.

The Italian extreme right: electoral and protest politics

As observed, the three actors can be reconciled with the ideological tradition of Italian neo-fascism that considered street activism and electoral politics complementary, rather than incompatible. Initially, the three actors represented the 'social movement' wing of broader and more institutionalized political parties. Over time, moreover, they all progressively transitioned from the extra-institutional to the electoral arena, which is in line with the operational definition of movement parties used in this volume. In order to offer an in-depth account of the extent to which MS-FT, FN, and CPI have accomplished this transition, this section shall observe their choice of repertoires of action and the focus of their mobilization empirically.

The general picture: patterns of extreme right mobilization in Italy

First, I look at the overall claims making of the three actors over time, as reported in newspaper articles (Figure 6.1). MS-FT first appears in 1995, whereas FN and CPI only appear in 1998 and 2004 respectively. The figure offers three crucial insights for our understanding of the extreme right along the party–movement continuum. First, it shows that extreme right claims-making in Italy is punctuated. None of the actors displays a clearly identifiable upward or downward historical trend in visibility in the mass media, nor do they show an extended period of stasis. Rather, claims-making by all three actors varies considerably on a yearly basis.

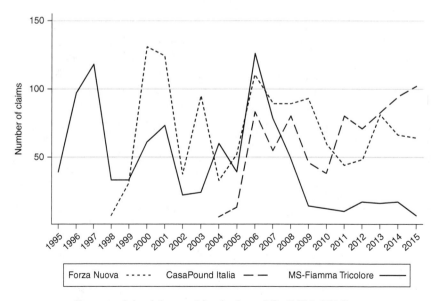

FIGURE 6.1 Extreme right claims making in the public (1995–2015).

Second, peaks in claims-making are associated with the years of Italy's national elections: 1996, 2001, 2006, 2008, and 2013. This suggests that extreme right mobilization takes advantage of available electoral opportunities. While only MS-FT presented its lists in 1996, FN contested the elections in 2001, and CPI filed its candidates from 2013. The nature of their electoral participation, however, changed over time. At times, they signed alliances with mainstream parties. For instance, MS-FT reached strategic agreements with the representatives of Italy's mainstream right, to avoid competition with them at the 1996 and 2001 elections. At other times, instead, they joined forces with other extreme right organizations or presented independent candidates. In 2003–2006, FN successfully joined forces with other minor organizations of its area, forming the cartel *Alternativa Sociale* (Social Alternative). The group managed to elect one EMP, and ultimately allied with the mainstream right coalition in 2006, albeit failing to elect any MPs. As for CPI, its first experiences in national and European elections were rather unsuccessful, but the group was later able to elect local representatives, and managed to attract much media attention with its communicative and expressive style of political campaigning.

Third, the mobilization capacity of the three organizations is considerably different. While obviously in the early years MS-FT, and then FN, took the lion's share of extreme right claims-making in the public sphere, the visibility of MS-FT has progressively declined after 2006. Conversely, CPI emerged rapidly in the early 2000s, and acquired increasing importance from 2010 onwards. More specifically, the figure suggests that the outbreak of the economic and political crisis in Italy might have provided new opportunities for social movement actors of the extreme right, such as FN and CPI, which became more active in the last few years.

Moving on to the comparative analysis, Table 6.1 displays the different repertoires of action of extreme right mobilization for MS-FT, FN and CPI. At one extreme are conventional actions, corresponding to the most traditional and routinized forms of mobilization typical of political parties. At the other end of the spectrum there are social movement actions, including demonstrative, as well as confrontational, actions against the police and opponents, and all types of violent actions.

TABLE 6.1 Form of action of extreme right mobilization (aggregate)

Form of action	Forza Nuova	Fiamma Tricolore	CasaPound Italia
Expressive	13.7	11.5	18.8
Conventional	22.7	53.5	13.1
Demonstrative	22.1	14.7	18.3
Confrontational	21.9	9.3	24.0
Violent	19.6	10.9	25.9
Tot	100%	100%	100%
N	943	686	580

MS-FT displays a clear tendency towards conventional forms of activism, accounting for more than half of the public interventions. These include electoral campaign activities, and participation in the policy process through elected officials, especially at the local level. Demonstrative actions account for only 15 per cent of the mobilization, whereas confrontational and violent actions account for an additional 10 per cent. The latter mainly took place in the early years of MS-FT's activity, when the group was more frequently engaged in street confrontations.

Only 13 per cent of CPI's mobilization, instead, takes place by means of conventional action, although the group is rather active in the promotion of cultural and music events for members and sympathizers. Social movement repertoires, such as demonstrations, and confrontational and violent actions, account for almost 70 per cent of CPI activism. Over one quarter of CPI's actions involved at least some degree of either symbolic or physical violence, and an additional 25 per cent entailed confrontational actions. Indeed, especially in its early years, CPI gained visibility after a series of episodes of street violence, and with the occupation of abandoned buildings in Rome, which at times also led to physical clashes with law enforcement agencies.

Finally, FN holds an intermediate position. On the one hand, it is relatively more engaged in conventional forms of actions than CPI (22 per cent), including the routinized participation in local and national elections. On the other, it is more prone to social movement actions than MS-FT: 45 per cent of FN's actions correspond to demonstrative and confrontational protests, and 19 per cent to violent actions. These mainly had to do with cycles of counter-mobilization. On some occasions, because of clashes with anti-fascist movements. In others, because FN militants stormed demonstrations by their opponents, especially during gay prides and civil rights protests.

The transition: from the social movement arena to electoral competition

Following Kitschelt's definition (2006), movement parties are transitional configurations of political actors which have developed in the social movement arena, but are progressively shifting to electoral competition as a primary means of political engagement (see also: Pirro and Castelli Gattinara 2018). To see whether this proposition stands up to empirical scrutiny, Figure 6.2 below displays extreme right claims-making, singling out protest actions (demonstrative, confrontational, and violent actions) from other conventional repertoires of action. For each year, the figure thus reports the share of protest actions for all the activities promoted by each of the three organizations.

Once more, the figure shows a different pattern for MS-FT, on the one hand, and FN and CPI, on the other. In the first case, protest actions account for less than half of the repertoires of action of MS-FT. Furthermore, three years stand out for increased shares of protest actions in MS-FT's mobilization: 1998, 2006, and 2015. The observations for 1998 and 2015 (i.e. the absolute number of

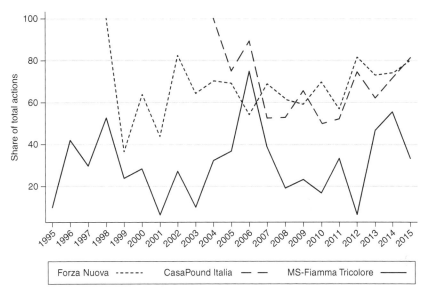

FIGURE 6.2   Share of protest actions in extreme right mobilization, by actor (1995–2015).

claims promoted by MS-FT) are too few to draw any substantial conclusion from this finding. However, the figure for 2006 suggests that electoral opportunities (national elections) triggered mobilization also in the streets. Indeed, in 2006, MS-FT filed its candidates in the lists supporting Berlusconi's mainstream right coalition; while the electoral returns of this choice were scarce, it appears that MS-FT took advantage of available opportunities in the electoral arena to mobilize in the protest one as well.

FN and CPI, instead, display a considerably higher propensity for street protest. As is illustrated by the preferred forms of mobilization in the early years, the two groups first emerged as protest actors. Over time, they progressively 'normalized' their strategies of contention, arguably finding an equilibrium between street politics and routinized forms of electoral competition. In recent years, however, both FN and CPI seem to have returned to protest activism as a primary form of engagement, especially with the outbreak of the economic crisis in Italy (2011), and even more so during the so-called European migration crisis (2015).

To elaborate on this, Figure 6.3 reports extreme right claims-making, this time singling out violent actions from all other conventional and protest repertoires. The figure shows unequivocally that the use of violence is a viable option for extreme right organizations in Italy. In particular, FN and CPI display a high propensity for violence, and they are considerably more likely to engage in violent actions than the more institutionalized MS-FT. Furthermore, violent episodes by FN and CPI appear to be on the rise, especially after 2011 and in 2015. Once again, street activism appears to be responsive to the socio-political circumstances, irrespective of previous electoral choices.

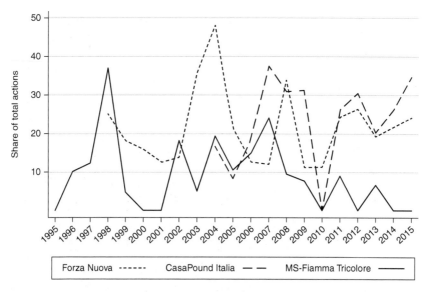

FIGURE 6.3 Share of violent actions in extreme right mobilization, by actor (1995–2015).

Regarding Kitschelt's assessment, the findings outlined so far suggest that the three extreme right groups under observation qualify as movement-parties, defined as hybrid actors located in between the protest and electoral arena (Kitschelt 2006; Pirro and Castelli Gattinara 2018). Yet, it also appears that FN and CPI, unlike MS-FT, are still far from completing the transition from social movement to political party. Furthermore, the analysis suggests that the trajectory of the 'transition' from one arena to the other is neither unidirectional nor irreversible. On the contrary, it is highly sensitive to external circumstances and, as discussed below, strategic choices, which might actually reverse the expected direction and drive actors that opted for electoral competition back to the social movement arena.

Movement party transition as strategic choice: issue focus and repertoires of actions

As discussed in the theory chapter of this volume (Chapter 2), the choice of repertoires of action does not respond exclusively to external circumstances (such as political opportunities), and internal incentives (such as ideology and values), but also to strategic factors linked to the issue focus of claims-making. If this is indeed the case, it is reasonable to expect some issues to dominate when the extreme right engages in conventional politics, and others when it opts for street mobilization. Accordingly, Table 6.2 reports data on the issue focus of the claims-making by FN, MS-FT, and CPI.

TABLE 6.2 Issue focus of extreme right mobilization, by actor

Issue	Forza Nuova	Fiamma Tricolore	CasaPound Italia
Socio-economic affairs	9.2	15.9	20.3
Cultural liberalism	19.6	13.7	18.4
Europe and the EU	3.1	4.2	5.7
Migration and integration	35.4	12.6	14.7
Law and order	4.2	11.3	4.3
Ideological statements	26.7	36.1	33.8
Other issues	1.8	6.2	2.9
Tot	100%	100%	100%
N	872	452	512

At a most general level, the analysis of thematic fields offers interesting insights on the similarities and differences in claims-making by the neo-fascist right. A considerable share of the public interventions by all three groups focus on strictly ideological statements, by which they simply claim a connection with the historical experience of Italian fascism, without referring to any substantial policy issue. CPI and MS-FT are relatively more prone than FN to engage on socio-economic issues, especially through political campaigns that call for strong state intervention in the economy, and criticize financial capitalism for depriving the nation of its sovereignty. Conversely, FN engages the most on migration affairs, as over a third of its claims-making deals with either immigration or integration politics. In this respect, FN is the only actor that could resemble, at least to a certain extent, the idea of a 'single-issue' party developed in the literature on the far right (Mudde 1999).

To complement this information, Table 6.3 compares the forms of actions of each of the three actors across issue fields. MS-FT adopts conventional repertoires of action on all issue areas, confirming that the group has completed its transition to standardized and routinized politics. The opposite holds for CPI: on all issue areas, CPI makes the least use of conventional repertoires, and is most likely to engage in street violence. While for CPI, social movement repertoires are especially predominant when it comes to socioeconomic issues, migration, and law and order issues, for FN they prevail in actions focusing on cultural liberalism and Europe.

Overall, the analysis outlined in this section could not identify a clear-cut differentiation between preferred forms of activism, and the content of claims-making. Still, the findings provide further evidence that neo-fascist actors are hybrid political actors. Specifically, the three organizations are located at distinct stages in the transition from social movement to the electoral arena. MS-FT displays the typical traits of a political party, engaging in routinized forms of activism irrespective of the policy issue at stake. FN displays the traits of an institutionalising movement: it focuses almost exclusively on one issue, which it approaches through multiple means, including election campaigns and policy proposals, as well as demonstrative actions and street violence. Finally, CPI mainly qualifies as a street-based movement: it prioritises the activism and narrative of social movements, while also occasionally participating in elections, and interacting with the party arena. In this

TABLE 6.3 Form of action and issue focus, by actor

Issue	Conventional actions	Social movement actions	Violent actions	Tot	N
Forza Nuova					
Socio-economic affairs	30.0	53.3	16.7		60
Cultural liberalism	21.3	58.2	20.5		122
Europe and the EU	34.8	56.5	8.7		23
Migration and integration	25.5	56.7	17.9	100%	224
Law and order	28.6	60.7	10.7		28
Ideological statements	42.4	41.8	15.8		165
Other issues	53.8	38.5	7.7		13
Fiamma Tricolore					
Socio-economic affairs	76.3	20.3	3.4		59
Cultural liberalism	50.0	39.1	10.9		46
Europe and the EU	76.9	23.1	0.0		13
Migration and integration	39.0	46.3	14.6	100%	41
Law and order	53.4	33.3	13.3		30
Ideological statements	42.7	39.1	18.2		110
Other issues	80.0	20.0	0.0		20
CasaPound Italia					
Socio-economic affairs	22.5	67.5	10.0		80
Cultural liberalism	30.7	44.0	25.3		75
Europe and the EU	25.0	55.0	20.0		20
Migration and integration	7.4	68.5	24.1	100%	54
Law and order	27.3	72.7	0.0		22
Ideological statements	55.1	27.2	17.6		136
Other issues	42.9	42.9	14.3		14

respect, it would appear that FN differs from CPI, in that it engages in street politics to obtain electoral gains – thus applying the office-seeking logic of political parties. Conversely, CPI differs from FN in that it participates in the electoral arena with the goal of driving attention to its extra-parliamentary activities and issues – thus applying the agenda-setting logic that characterizes social movement politics.

Conclusion

This chapter has appraised neo-fascist actors in Italy as hybrid political organizations located at the intersection between the party and social movement forms. Building upon the political process theory, and focusing on both external and internal factors, I analyzed the Italian far right as a movement party (Castelli Gattinara and Pirro 2018). Focusing on political and discursive opportunities, I have stressed the importance of the contextual circumstances in which the choice of repertoires of actions across different arenas of engagement takes place. Furthermore, by looking at the ideology of the groups, I have discussed how the legacy of fascism defines extreme right political activism in terms of social movement and political party practices. Specifically, in line with Kitschelt's definition of movement parties

(2006), I anticipated that neo-fascist actors emerging in the extra-institutional arena would progressively transition to electoral politics, depending on the available political opportunities for institutionalization (Pirro and Castelli Gattinara 2018). At the same time, I also expected that their transition would remain incomplete, mainly due to the ideological legacy of fascism as a movement.

I have then tested the expectations empirically, looking at claims-making by three neo-fascist actors in Italy that I considered susceptible to qualify as movement parties: *Movimento Sociale-Fiamma Tricolore*, *Forza Nuova*, and *CasaPound*. Emerging from the radical wing of post-war neo-fascism, in fact, these groups splintered from pre-existing political parties due to their stated preference for social movement activism. Their emergence is thus closely tied with ideological motivations, most notably a professed proximity to the spirit of the 'fascism as a movement' as opposed to the party-oriented tendency of the conservative faction of the Italian far right (De Felice 1969; Ignazi 2003).

Based on an extensive quantitative data analysis, I have then illustrated empirically the main features of the repertoires of action of MS-FT, FN, and CPI. The empirical evidence confirmed that none of the three actors under examination has ever been exclusively involved in either the electoral or the social movement arena. Rather, all three actors participate selectively and strategically in both electoral and protest politics. As hybrid actors, they engage in politics by means of different repertoires throughout their history of mobilization, promoting actions that are typical of social movements, as well as routinized and standardized actions that normally pertain to established political parties.

While confirming the main definitional criteria of movement parties as hybrid actors transitioning from the extra-institutional to the electoral arena, the analysis has also shown some crucial differences in how extreme right actors relate to social movement and party politics. Most notably, the analysis has suggested that the transition from one arena to the other is neither unidirectional nor irreversible, and that changing political opportunities might influence the extent to which actors engage in electoral, rather than street, activism. As a result, if MS-FT has fully transitioned to the arena of party politics, CPI seems to consider the electoral arena a corollary to social movement activism, whereas FN displays a more balanced propensity for social movement politics as well as electoral campaigning.

The finding that there might be an interpenetration between different arenas of conflict has paved the way to conceptualizing alternative configurations within the movement party paradigm, which are likely to apply beyond the specific case of Italy's neo-fascist right. Even if only illustratively, I have suggested appraising movement parties not only based on the extent of their transition from one arena to the other, but also in terms of their underlying motivations for activism. Rather than as a univocal and unidirectional process, the transition from the social movement to the electoral arena ought in fact to be understood as a reversible pattern shaped by external circumstances and strategic choices. On the one hand, movement parties might thus apply the office-seeking logic of political parties, and therefore engage in street politics with the goal of attracting voters, and gain an electoral advantage over their competitors. On the other, they might apply the agenda-setting logic of social movements, and thus participate in electoral politics with the primary goal of attracting attention to their extra-parliamentary activities. Future empirical research at the intersection between party politics and social movement studies is thus needed to assess whether and how collective actors can successfully bridge the logics of protest and those of electoral competition.

Notes

1 http://www.fiammatricolore.com (accessed 17.11.2017).
2 http://www.forzanuova.eu (accessed 17.11.2017).
3 http://www.casapounditalia.org (accessed 17.11.2017).
4 *Neo-fascist* organizations belong to the category of the extreme right, which opposes democratic principles and ultimately aims at subverting the democratic order. This is distinct from the radical right, which generally subscribes to the rules of parliamentary democracy. Both categories, however, can be appraised as 'far-right' (e.g. Mudde 1996).

References

Albanese, M., Bulli, G., Castelli Gattinara, P. and Froio, C. (2014) *Fascisti Di Un Altro Millennio? Crisi e Partecipazione in CasaPound Italia*, Rome: Bonanno Editore.

Bar-On, T. (2012) 'The French New Right's Quest for Alternative Modernity', *Fascism*, 1(1): 18–52. doi:10.1163/221162512X631198.

Bulli, G. and Castelli Gattinara, P. (2013) 'Tra Vecchie e Nuove Identità. L'estrema Destra in Movimento Nell'esempio Di Casapound Italia', in Alteri, L. and Raffini, L. (ed) *La Nuova Politica. Mobilitazioni, Movimenti e Conflitti in Italia*, Naples: Edises.

Busher, J. (2015) *The Making of Anti-Muslim Protest: Grassroots Activism in the English Defence League*, London: Routledge.

Caiani, M. and Borri R. (2013) "The Extreme Right, Violence and Other Action Repertoires: An Empirical Study on Two European Countries', *Perspectives on European Politics and Society*, 14(4): 562–581. doi:10.1080/15705854.2013.793532.

Caldiron, G. (2013) *Estrema destra*, Rome: Newton Compton Editori.

Campani, G. (2016) 'Neo-Fascism from the Twentieth Century to the Third Millennium: The Case of Italy', in Lazaridis, G. Campani, G. and Benventiste, A. (eds) *The Rise of the Far Right in Europe. Populist Shifts and 'Othering'*, London: Palgrave Macmillan UK, 25–54.

Castelli Gattinara, P. (2018) 'Europeans, Shut the Borders! Anti-Refugee Mobilization in Italy and France', in della Porta, D. (Forthcoming) *Contentious Moves: Solidarity Mobilizations in the 'Refugee Crisis'*, London: Palgrave Macmillan.Castelli Gattinara, P. and Pirro, A.L.P. (2018) 'The Far Right as Social Movement', *European Societies*, Online First, doi:10.1080/14616696.2018.1494301.

Castelli Gattinara, P., Froio, C. and Albanese, M. (2013) 'The Appeal of Neo-Fascism in Times of Crisis. The Experience of CasaPound Italia', *Fascism*, 2(2): 234–258. doi:10.1163/22116257-00202007.

Cento Bull, A. (2007) *The Strategy of Tension and the Politics of Nonreconciliation*, Oxford and New York: Berghahn Books.

De Felice, R. (1969) *Le interpretazioni del fascismo*. 1995th ed. Bari: Laterza.

Di Nunzio, D. and Toscano E. (2011) *Dentro e Fuori CasaPound: Capire Il Fascismo Del Terzo Millennio*, Rome: Armando Editore.

Diani, M. (1992) 'The Concept of Social Movement', *The Sociological Review*, 40(1): 1–25. doi:10.1111/j.1467-954X.1992.tb02943.x.

Froio, C. (2018) 'Race, Religion, or Culture? Framing Islam between Racism and Neo-Racism in the Online Network of the French Far Right', *Perspectives on Politics,* 16(3): 696–709.

Gentile, E. (2008) *Modernità totalitaria: il fascismo italiano*. Rome: Laterza.

Giugni, M., Koopmans, R., Passy, F., and Statham, P. (2005) 'Institutional and Discursive Opportunities for Extreme-Right Mobilization in Five Countries', *Mobilization: An International Quarterly*, 10(1): 145–162. doi:10.17813/maiq.10.1.n40611874k23l1v7.

Hutter, S. (2014a) 'Protest Event Analysis and Its Offspring', in della Porta, D. *Methodological Practices in Social Movement Research*, Oxford: Oxford University Press, 335–367.

Hutter, S. (2014b) *Protesting Culture and Economics in Western Europe: New Cleavages in Left and Right Politics*, Minneapolis, MN: University of Minnesota Press.

Hutter, S. and Kriesi, H. (2013) 'Movements of the Left, Movements of the Right Reconsidered', in van Stekelenburg, J., Roggeband, C., and Klandermans, B. *The Future of Social Movement Research: Dynamics, Mechanisms, and Processes*, Minneapolis, MN and London: University of Minnesota Press.

Ignazi, P. (1998) *Il Polo escluso: profilo storico del Movimiento Sociale Italiano*, Bologna: Il Mulino.

Ignazi, P. (2003) *Extreme Right Parties in Western Europe*, Oxford: Oxford University Press.

Kitschelt, H. (2006) 'Movement Parties', in Katz, R.S. and Crotty, W. *Handbook of Party Politics*, Thousand Oaks, CA: SAGE, 278–290.

Koopmans, R. and Statham, P. (1999) 'Political Claims Analysis: Integrating Protest Event and Political Discourse Approaches', *Mobilization: An International Quarterly*, 4(2): 203–221. doi:10.17813/maiq.4.2.d759337060716756.

Koopmans, R., Statham, P., Giugni, M., and Passy, F. (2005) *Contested Citizenship: Immigration and Cultural Diversity in Europe*, Minneapolis, MN: University of Minnesota Press.

Kriesi, H. (1995) *New Social Movements in Western Europe:* A Comparative Analysis, UCL Press.

Kriesi, H. (ed.) (2012) *Political Conflict in Western Europe*, Cambridge; New York: Cambridge University Press.

Kriesi, H. and Pappas, T.S. (2015) *European Populism in the Shadow of the Great Recession*, ECPR Press.

Mammone, A. (2009) 'The Eternal Return? Faux Populism and Contemporarization of Neo-Fascism across Britain, France and Italy', *Journal of Contemporary European Studies*, 17(2): 171–192. doi:10.1080/14782800903108635.

Mudde, C. (1996) 'The War of Words Defining the Extreme Right Party Family', *West European Politics*, 19(2): 225–248. doi:10.1080/01402389608425132.

Mudde, C. (1999) 'The Single-issue Party Thesis: Extreme Right Parties and the Immigration Issue', *West European Politics*, 22(3): 182–197. doi:10.1080/01402389908425321.

Mudde, C. (2016) *The Populist Radical Right: A Reader*, London: Routledge.

Mudge, S.L. and Chen, A.S. (2014) 'Political Parties and the Sociological Imagination: Past, Present, and Future Directions', *Annual Review of Sociology*, 40(1): 305–330. doi:10.1146/annurev-soc-071312-145632.

Payne, S.G. (1995) *A History of Fascism, 1914–1945*, Madison, WI: University of Wisconsin Press.

Pedahzur, A. and Weinberg, L. (2001) 'Modern European Democracy and Its Enemies: The Threat of the Extreme Right', *Totalitarian Movements and Political Religions*, 2(1): 52–72. doi:10.1080/714005438.

Pirro, A.L.P. and Castelli Gattinara, P. (2018) 'Movement parties of the far right: The organisation and strategies of nativist collective actors', *Mobilization*, 23(3): 367–383.

Rao, N. (2014) *Trilogia della celtica*, Milan: Sperling & Kupfer.

Tarrow, S.G. (1989) *Democracy and Disorder: Protest and Politics in Italy, 1965–1975*, New York: Oxford University Press.

Virchow, F. (2015) 'The 'Identitarian Movement': What Kind of Identity? Is It Really a Movement', inSimpson, P.A. andDruxes, H., *Digital Media Strategies of the Far Right in Europe and the United States*, Lanham, MD: Lexington Books, 179–189.

7

FROM INDIGNATION TO POWER

The genesis of the Independent Greeks

Maik Fielitz

> Good morning. Our movement has been born. May Virgin Mary be our aide and guardian. WE ARE MANY, WE ARE INDEPENDENT, WE ARE GREEKS![1]

On 20 February 2012, one of the most idiosyncratic crisis phenomena in Greece was born through a short post on Twitter and on Facebook, namely: the Independent Greeks (ANEL). Tracing its roots to online platforms, and the reactionary part of the Greek Indignant People's Movement (*aganaktismenoi*), members of the movement (party) made headlines with provocative public interventions, as well as by fomenting anti-German sentiment. With its nationalist pathos and populist rhetoric, ANEL vehemently opposes the crisis governance promoted by international institutions, and it has vowed to regain control of 'national sovereignty'.[2]

As a response to the crisis in Greece, ANEL's chairperson, Panos Kammenos – a former MP of the conservative New Democracy (ND) – proclaimed a new style of movement. With the 'citizen's movement' of ANEL, he stated, 'we are witnessing a revolution of post-dictatorial Greece.'[3] He added that, for the first time since the fall of the Regime of the Colonels in 1974, his movement would overcome ideological divides, be open for everyone who stands against foreign interventions in the country's economy, and be a proponent of traditional values such as family, church, and nation. As such, national independence was the battle cry of the newly founded movement that would quickly transform itself into a political party, and claim 7.5 per cent of the vote for the Greek parliament just four months later. Less than three years after its inception, ANEL even managed to join the ranks of government in 2015 (Aslanidis and Kaltwasser 2016).

While much attention has been paid to the electoral fate of SYRIZA, as well as the rise and persistence of the neo-Nazi organisation Golden Dawn, little is known about the context, resources, and mobilising frames of ANEL (Verney 2014: 31).

This dearth of research on the party, along with the fact that it represents a unique case of rapid ascendance from an indignant right-wing movement to a governmental force, merits further careful investigation, which is one of the aims of this chapter. Compared to other far-right movement parties in Europe, ANEL is on course to directly influence the political setting of the Greek party system in the medium-term, and political culture in the long-term. Despite its peculiarity, multiple parallels exist in relation to other (far-right) movement parties that emerged during the same period: catch-all policies, an alleged embodiment of the people's will, and the personalisation of leadership, just to name a few (see Della Porta et al. 2017).

As it was first established in 2012, ANEL emerged amidst the Greek debt crisis, a time during which the bipartisan political system was collapsing, and a political void was imminent (see Douzinas 2013). Hence, opportunities emerged for marginal and new political actors, as austerity was prevailing, and the economic situation was deteriorating for the vast majority of the population (Karyotis and Gerodimos 2015). Similarly, public discourse shifted strongly to the topos of national independence, one filled with right-wing and even with leftist ideologies that contributed to the formation of a new cleavage in Greek politics along pro- and anti-austerity political lines (Dinas and Rori 2013). Such a combination of political and discursive opportunities often serves as a springboard for far-right movement parties (see Chapter 2 in this volume). As such, the rise of ANEL is considered one of the most visible symptoms of the crisis of Greek representative democracy (Pappas 2014). However, ANEL was not the only actor which attempted to exploit the beneficial conditions. Between 2010 and 2014, over 30 new movements and parties were founded; 11 of these were situated on the (far) right, and all of them proved to have very limited political success (Aslanidis and Marantzidis 2016). So how did ANEL manage to take advantage of this situation to its benefit?

In answering this question, the present study focusses on the context in which ANEL emerged, its available resources, and the framing efforts taken by its leadership to mobilise 'national indignation'. Based on an actor-centric perspective, the study traces the political genesis of ANEL from a grassroots rebellion rooted in Greek conservatism and nationalism to a governing party and, subsequently, a declining political actor. This chapter pursues an analytical descriptive strategy based on party documents, newspaper coverage, and secondary literature.

In the first section, ANEL will be introduced as a prototype of far-right movement parties, with a focus on the connection between street mobilisation and party politics. The second section addresses the political and discursive context of the party's emergence. The chapter then moves on to discussing mobilising resources with regard to the party's origins in the reactionary segment of the *aganaktisme-noi* and nationalist opposition to austerity measures. The fourth section elaborates on how ANEL's leadership has attempted to conceal its far-right agenda and proclaim an inclusive model of politics. The final section scrutinises the limitations of ANEL's ambitions in the wake of declining poll ratings, situating ANEL within the broader picture of current Greek politics.

Introducing ANEL as a far-right movement party

Recent years have demonstrated an increasing conflation of street and institution-alised politics in the European far-right. On the one hand, far-right parties have been making increased use of movement tactics, and have harnessed their organisational resources to stage extra-parliamentary opposition with a strong focus on enhanced media coverage (Art 2011). On the other hand, far-right parties and movements are creating common ground between discourse and action: with one foot inside and one outside representative politics, movements and parties form a 'middle ground which is composed of actors that want parties and movements to work together' (Heaney and Rojas 2015: 22). Another pattern of the conflation of street and institutionalised politics is represented in the present case study of ANEL. Here, the actor emerges as a party political umbrella that comes to represent disparate constituencies by absorbing the energies of numerous movements. This approximates the concept of movement parties, understood as: 'coalitions of activists who emanate from social movements and try to apply the organizational and strategic practices of social movements in the electoral arena of party competition' (Kitschelt 2006: 280). Scholars have highlighted the transitional character of movement parties as 'emerging parties prior to their institutionalization' with 'fluid organizational characteristics' (Gunter and Diamond 2003: 188) and little investment 'in the process of solving problems of social choice' (Kitschelt 2006: 280). Hence, far-right movement parties proved to flourish under conditions of economic crisis, exploit social unrest with ethno-national agendas, and pursue a populist agenda that sets a 'pure people' in contrast to a 'corrupt elite' (see Chapter 2 in this volume).

Politics in transition: ANEL as a prototype of a far-right movement party

Studying the far right always entails a hunt for a moving target. Its agendas and personnel change over time, the way that these actors frame issues is strategic and adapts to changing political conditions, and, moreover, conflict and secession constantly characterise the heterogeneous field of the far right. The transitionary character of the concept of movement parties accounts for this fact. The analytical value offered by the movement party approach in the context of studying the far right, in general, and ANEL as a prototype, in particular, not only contributes to a better understanding of the conditions from which they emerge, but it likewise brings three aspects to the fore:

First, this approach does not consider the fusion of street and routine politics to be exceptional, but rather one of the very principles of far-right politics. Speaking of movement parties underlines the deliberate combination of various modes of politics, emphasising the agency of actors who manoeuvre among different strategies, and react to changing cultural and structural contexts (see Minkenberg 2003). In the case of ANEL, this means harmonising a statesmanlike attitude with a low threshold for engaging in grassroots participation – one of the keys to understanding its efficacy in the early stages of political action.

Second, the movement party approach contextualises the actions of political parties vis-à-vis other related movements. In this vein, the process of far-right party formation is often inextricably linked to the proximate social movements from which they originated (Kitschelt 1989). Likewise, the biographies of the members and leaders were strongly intertwined with movements that served as entry points into politics (ibid.). ANEL could always make reference to the heterogeneous *aganaktismenoi* in order to gain legitimacy beyond fixed party ranks in the nationalist movement (Karamichas 2012).

Third, the movement party concept provides a time-diagnostic component by insinuating a common context of emergence that is open to trans-national and cross-type comparison. The multiple crisis diagnoses in European countries serve as common research umbrella for investigating far-right reactions to similar institutional contexts, political and discursive opportunities, and threats. Hence, ANEL is part of a larger European party family that emerged in the context of political and economic crisis. It comes as no surprise that ANEL is in touch with Eurosceptics such as Nigel Farage,[4] and that it applauded the election of Donald Trump, as its chairman Kammenos intensified the connections to Trump's (former) controversial consultant George Papadopoulos.[5]

In sum, the hybrid nature of movement parties as 'fuzzy and transitional organizational arrangements, whose configuration depends on investments in formal party structures, aggregation of interests, and forms of external mobilization' (Pirro 2016: 5), strongly correlates to diversification processes in the far right and its reorientation in the wake of new windows of opportunity, with the economic crisis and the so-called refugee crisis serving as common gateways.

Contextual factors for the rapid rise of ANEL

In the Greek context, intense street mobilisation affected institutional politics during the crisis (Aslanidis and Marantzidis 2016). Greek cities – and especially its capital, Athens – witnessed a surge of contentious demands, as people felt that they were not being represented by the coalition of the major parties PASOK and ND, and they refused to comply with the country's bailout (Karyotis and Gerodimos 2015). The economic crisis and the lack of coherent alternatives clearly led to a political crisis that found its expression in the decline, and eventually cessation, of the traditional bipartisan constellation that dominated the post-dictatorial era, and brought about deep mistrust in political institutions (Muro and Vidal 2016; Simiti 2015). The emergence of new political actors, and a boost for fringe movements and parties were an inevitable consequence of this. While a plethora of studies has addressed left-wing movements which organise against the status quo of austerity and crisis (Sepheriades, 2016; Stavrakakis 2014), opportunities for right-wing contenders are largely researched in the framework of party politics.

This section aims to interrelate right-wing responses from both institutional and non-institutional positions by discussing two interrelated causes. The first relates to foreign interference and the undermining of national sovereignty that played into the hands of the protectionist right-wing agenda. The second is that the dilution of political boundaries boosted the reputation of the right, as nationalist discourse was also utilised by left-wing movements and parties.

Economic crisis, foreign interference and the end of bipartism

After the outbreak of the economic crisis, Greek party and movement politics witnessed the most fundamental changes since the end of the military junta in 1974. Up until 2009, the country's party system had been characterised by immense stability in terms of governmental alteration of the two major parties, ND and PASOK. When the elected PASOK retreated from office in 2010, after agreeing to the first Memorandum of Understanding with the international lenders of the troika (i.e. the International Monetary Fund, the European Central Bank, and the European Commission), institutions and democratic representation plunged into severe crisis. Under the leadership of former ECB vice-president Loukas Papadimos, the two opposing parties participated in a 'government of unity' supported by the far-right party LAOS. The non-democratic installation of this government was broadly conceived as an instrument to enforce the international demands of Greece (Fragoudaki 2013). Lacking serious parliamentary opposition, protests formed on the streets to a greater extent than ever before, and radicalised the political discourse. While the ruling government set the stakes for the austerity programmes that would follow, they paved the way for a multifaceted movement to come into existence, with new forms of coalition building (Kanellopoulos et al. 2016). Different societal forces united under the umbrella of anti-austerity and cultivated a new cleavage structure: pro- vs. anti-memorandum (Della Porta 2015: 37–38). As a consequence of this, movements on the radical left, as well as on the far right gained momentum.

On the far right, the nation was presented as being under attack by foreign investors in relation to its economy, and by 'mass migration' in relation to national identity. Economic misery was strongly ethnicised, as migrants were blamed for the situation of Greece. The intermingling narratives of saving the nation, and returning to protectionist, nativist visions played into the hands of radical nationalist forces.

The steady dilution of political boundaries as a favourable context

At the same time, the anti-memorandum front led to a steady dilution of political differences in the constellation of the protests. While left-wing and right-wing protests were traditionally spatially and politically divided, they both appeared together at the large-scale protests on the streets against the crisis governance (Kousis 2016: 161). The consensual refusal of all political parties coalesced with anti-political sentiments that invigorated narratives of national salvation (Fragoudaki 2013: 213). In popular protests, national symbols soon became commonplace, and Greece was presented as a victim of an international conspiracy. Public figures such as musician Mikis Theodorakis played a key role in transforming political dissent into national identification. His self-described 'non-political' Movement of Independent Citizens aimed at overcoming political divides and 'the creation of a patriotic/democratic front beyond the closed containers of 'left'/'right''.[6] Theodorakis, as a symbol of resistance against the Regime of the Colonels, identified a 'new Junta' in the crisis management pursued by the troika, thereby relativising right-wing political oppression, and fostering a resurgence of Greek nationalism. Traditionally left-wing narratives of liberation and independence were appropriated by nationalist forces, while the vocabulary of treason and betrayal envisaged a common destiny for the Greek people beyond any political divide.

This gradual dilution of political boundaries was a gateway for ANEL to harness the rather diffuse dismissal of the status quo. As Kitschelt observed: 'the electoral rise of radical rightist parties presupposed the presence of salient issue positions that remained unrepresented by existing conventional political parties and thereby made possible the entry of ambitious political entrepreneurs into the arena of party competition' (Kitschelt 2006: 286). The salient issues of independence and liberation could easily be integrated within a far-right agenda, representing an ostensibly non-political form.

Mobilising from the margins and the centre

In March 2012, the official foundation congress of ANEL took place at the historically significant site of Distomo, a village whose population had fallen victim to a German massacre as alleged retaliation against partisan attacks in 1944. The location was strategically chosen, as the ANEL leader Kammenos repeatedly compared the German role in the austerity programmes to the extermination policy of the Nazi Germany. In this vein, Greece was presented as a vulnerable victim of international interests, and ANEL as the saviour of national independence.[7] It soon became clear that one cornerstone in the formation of the movement was the absorption of the opposition against the bailout agreements of the Greek government with international lenders dominated by Germany.

This opposition was mobilised for the first time in the context of the Indignant People's Movement in 2011. While most scholars emphasise the emancipatory character of this movement, its nationalist and protectionist side has long been ignored. To understand the ambivalence that marks the genesis of ANEL (and the subsequently formed SYRIZA-ANEL government), it is vital to look into its roots: the concurrency of left- and right-wing anti-austerity mobilisation that rallied around the common umbrella of national sovereignty and the expulsion of foreign lenders.

An additional aspect to consider were the favourable conditions for a new force on the right: its political milieu was in decline after the far-right LAOS lost credibility among nationalist circles, and ND had reinforced a neoliberal agenda.

Absorbing the indignant spirit of the aganaktismenoi

In May 2011, the wave of protest initiated by the Spanish *indignados* reached Greek urban centres, and spurred a new cycle of austerity protests along with appropriations of public space. The month-long occupation of Syntagma Square in the heart of Athens became a symbol of a developing grassroots movement that struggled with peaceful means for achieving 'real democracy'. The assembled individuals and collectives adopted the indignant wording of their Spanish counterparts, and called themselves *aganaktismenoi*. For the time being, hundreds of citizens, the majority of whom lacked political experience (see Sotirakopoulos and Sotiropoulos 2013), collectively organised improvised camps and exchanged ideas for a social transformation horizontally among their ranks. Up until the camp was later violently dispersed by riot police in late June 2011, they marched in full force in front of the parliament to protest against the measures imposed by the troika (Simiti 2015). Those protests were warmly welcomed by leftist parties and activist scholars as the resistance they embodied against crisis governance proved that there *is* an alternative to capitalist crisis management and its disastrous consequences (Douzinas 2013; Thomassen 2012).

As the new government, the Indignant People's Movement did, however, consist of two opposing camps that were bound together by their rejection of the first Memorandum of Understanding with the troika, the dismissal of the social democrat government, and the demand for public referenda as a form of political participation. Spatially separated in the upper and lower side of the square, the progressive forces sided with an assortment of convicted nationalists and conspiracy theorists. Patriotic symbols, chauvinist displays , and even neo-Nazi salutes dominated the upper side directly in front of the parliament (Karamichas 2012). References to the Battle of Thermopylae were paired with wild theories presenting Greece as the victim of an international conspiracy. The anti-Semitic connotation strongly referred to nationalist discourse and it gave rise to a new wave of far-right mobilisation, as well as attempts to institutionalise the nationalist indignation of the square occupation movement.

The impact of the *aganaktismenoi* on Greek politics was tremendous. Around two dozen new parties emerged in the period following the decline of mobilisation (Aslanidis and Marantzidis 2016). Moreover, after the dispersal of the Indignant People's Movement, discussions continued in online forums. The nationalist segment, in particular, engaged in creating blogs that contributed to a heterogeneous far-right online network (Smyrnaios 2013). Lacking a party-political platform to express their disenchantment with the political situation, core members of the later ANEL attempted to give the indignation a direction. ANEL adopted the language and symbols of groups that participated in the square occupation movement and tried to integrate movement figures by offering candidacies for elections, which caused serious conflict among the respective groups.[8] Eventually, the nationalist segment of the Indignant People's Movement found its expression through the formation of ANEL, and dispersed on the street. On the first anniversary of the *aganaktismenoi* movement, ANEL called for a return to the squares. Interestingly, they retrospectively present themselves as the driving force behind mobilisation; however, the vanguard motive was strongly criticised by other movement organisations.

The legitimation crisis of the centre right and the far-right void

When scrutinising the origins, mobilisation, and consequences of movement parties such as ANEL, it is essential to tackle the history, peculiarity, and conflicts of the milieu from which it emerges and recruits its members. ANEL is neither the sole heir of a long tradition of nationalist mobilisation in Greece, nor the only challenger on the far right. However, there are two developments that contributed to the gap that ANEL subsequently filled. On the one hand, the far-right LAOS party, the party political anchor for Greece's far right, was being discredited in nationalist circles after participating in the 'government of unity', and for its ambivalent role in implementing preparations for the Memorandum.[9] On the other hand, conservatism lost its monopoly on representing mainstream nationalism, as ND's compliance with austerity was framed as a surrender of national(ist) positions. Representatives of ND were publicly attacked as 'traitors of the nation' and, as Takis Pappas concludes, 'ND's 'betrayed' constituents did not follow along, turning their backs on their party in search of something more radical' (Pappas 2014: 190). ANEL's chairperson Kammenos was able to profit from dissatisfaction with the Conservatives. Accordingly, he filled the space between conservatism and the far right based on his personal reputation.

Inclusive and directly democratic: the framing of ANEL's far-right agenda

In the context of political mobilisation, ANEL had to walk a thin line between not being identified as part of the political system and, at the same time, attracting mainstream constituencies. This manoeuvring was reflected in contradictory statements, and a general flexibility in the basic orientation of the movement. This rather arbitrary prioritization was basically framed by two principles that dominated the public presentation of ANEL: that of an inclusive movement open to all, and that of a new form of direct democracy that emanated from the Indignant People's Movement. However, these two premises are quickly debunked; quite on the contrary, while articulating an inclusive character, an exclusivist agenda of nativism followed, drawing on the narratives of Greek nationalists. And similarly, while lauding democratic bottom-up procedures, a fixed top-down hierarchy is implemented with an undisputed leader at the top. The next section will elaborate on these two misleading interpretations.

The elephant in the room: ANEL's nativist agenda

While most movement parties vehemently deny being grouped along with established left–right categorisations in terms of their political programme (see Della Porta et al. 2017), ANEL reversed this trend. By repeatedly stressing that 'we are right, centric and left but beyond all we are Greeks',[10] Kammenos is rhetorically open to various political schemes. This catch-all approach to politics is well-known among far-right parties during their early stages (Art 2011). However, behind the inclusive rhetoric lies a far-right agenda. Examining ANEL's programme, and how it is framed in public statements, the topics of mobilisation coalesce with those of the post-dictatorial far right in Greece. Three factors obviate this trend in particular.

A concentration on *national issues* is certainly the most appealing for Greek nationalists.[11] Party officials repeatedly questioned the existing borders and reinvigorated conflicts related to territory disputes.[12] Kammenos' provokative visits to remote islands signal the old narrative of leaving no Greek citizen behind, given the ostensible Turkish threat. Among these public interventions, ANEL officials are present at nationalist ceremonies and rituals which also host extremist groups. It is, consequently, no coincidence that Kammenos assumed the position of Minister of National Defence, a prestigious post within far-right circles. After the fall of the Regime of the Colonels in 1974, the military has never been purged of dictatorial influences, nor has there been a full account as to the role of the military in torture and human rights violations (Christopoulos 2014). Quite on the contrary, authoritarian patterns continue to exist, and anti-Turkish along with anti-Albanian slogans are common during parades.

Additionally, ANEL took ownership of the xenophobic anti-memorandum front on the right wing. In far-right circles, the installation of an international crisis regime was strongly tied to *anti-migration resentments* among the population. According to this discourse, national sovereignty was under siege, both by international lenders, and by arriving migrants that threatened Greek self-determination in financial and ethnic terms. ANEL profited from this discourse, and concurrently fuelled it. Conspiracy theories with strong anti-Semitic connotations are part and parcel of this worldview, and conducive to an exclusionist understanding of nationhood (Antoniou et al. 2017: 14).

Another clear far-right approach to politics is unquestionable ties to the Orthodox Church and a stance on protecting the traditional, heterosexual family. The Orthodox Church has always been a central political player in Greece that allegedly preserves the traditional Greek way of life, one presumably threatened by foreign forces. In this context, homosexuality and multi-culturalism are often presented as part of a decadent lifestyle that harms the traditional way of life in Greece. Being Greek for ANEL is inseparable from being an Orthodox Christian. From the very onset, ANEL attempted to maintain a close relationship with central church representatives. As Greek nationalism is historically inseparable from Orthodoxy (Georgiadou 1995), ANEL is a stalwart for the interests of the church in the parliament, and has gained further legitimacy by forging relations with church officials (Martino and Papastathis 2018). This is particularly reflected in a unanimous rejection of the construction of a mosque in a suburb of Athens.[13]

Taking these insights together, ANEL clearly pursues a far-right agenda. The appeal to national independence serves as the overarching framing for ANEL's mobilisations and connects all the above-mentioned issues together. Under this umbrella, the party leadership incorporates a refusal to allow international actors to intervene in the national economy, a contempt for western consumption culture that is perceived to be imperial and anti-traditional, sovereignty in military matters, and, not least, a rejection of immigration as an instrument that harms the homogeneous composition of the Greek *ethnos*. Given these dimensions of independence, the renunciation of a clear right-wing agenda is more of a tactical tool for pandering to disenchanted citizens than a free-floating ideological composition, as it is often presented. Taken from a broader perspective, the issues discussed here have been the cornerstones of the Greek far right for decades (Georgiadou 2013). The national-populist logic set against the alleged globalism of a new world order goes hand in hand with conspiracy theories, ethno-nationalist rhetoric, and an authoritarian transformation of society (Tsatsanis 2011). Hence, even though ANEL made appeals to different political orientations, they had a specific agenda in mind when running for elections (see also Georgiadou and Rori 2015).

The myth of a direct democratic mass movement

Every political movement has its own foundational myth, and also cultivates guiding narratives. In the case of ANEL, everything began with a latent online formation that presumably gave rise to a new 'direct democratic' movement. ANEL's founding statement describes the process of the movement's (or party's) formation as a collective decision following two years of meetings and online discussions between 'Greek citizens' in an aim to resist the 'new order of the memorandum, the national humiliation and the violent economic attack on the Greek family.'[14]

Referring to the alleged democratic nature of online formation, chairperson Panos Kammenos presented the movement as a grassroots initiative, without a leader, and without programmatic determination. The myth of a procedural, democratic foundation is, however, as misleading as its claim to be a leaderless, horizontal organisation based on a non-ideological orientation. In contrast to this self-representation, ANEL recruits from patriotic segments of Greek society, cultivates core issues of right-wing mobilisation and nationalist ideology, and orients itself towards models of far-right party formations in Greece. Moreover, it revolves around one leader who deviates from mainstream politics, and is marked by an unbalanced power distribution, as well as the personalisation of leadership. Kammenos is present in virtually every public appearance of ANEL: he is (with few exceptions) the only party spokesperson whose videos appear on the official ANEL website, he is the sole party representative in TV election spots and campaigning posters, and he holds the only ministry post of the left–right government.

As such, is it fair to speak of a personalistic party whose '*only* rationale is to provide a vehicle for the leader to win an election and exercise power' (Gunter and Diamond 2003: 187)? Kammenos himself strongly denies the accusation that the party is oriented around his person:

> The political parties of post-dictatorial Greece were launched from above. There was a leader who gathered some staff members and built a pyramid, saying to the Greek people: 'Join us!' This [model] is finished. [...] We began from below. We haven't been at the forefront, but we have all been together. Now, the citizens will launch this constellation.[15]

However, the invisible processes from below manifest in the person of Kammenos the leader. The internet is sketched as a form of legitimisation for these participatory claims. From its very onset, the steering committee of ANEL relied on social media, and strong visibility on internet sites. At a time when more established parties were (still) highly cautious about online mobilisation and social media representation, ANEL primarily campaigned using websites and social media channels. Similar to comparable formation processes such as the *Five Star Movement* in Italy, the internet has likewise been used as 'a tool for organization, decision-making, communication and identity building' (Mosca et al. 2015: 217). However, with the first party congress in 2012, institutionalised structures became established, and online approaches lost ground.

Furthermore, ANEL's process of movement formation resembles the pattern of a deviant formation amid conservatism and extreme right in Greece. Kammenos himself held central positions in the ranks of ND. He was vice minister in the cabinet of former conservative prime minister Kostas Karamanlis, and he was known to be a hardliner and publicist of patriotic literature. Similarly, former prime minister Antonis Samaras founded his movement *Political Spring* in the early 1990s following a naming dispute with the Republic of Macedonia. Later, Giorgos Karatzaferis established the far-right party LAOS after he had been expelled from the conservative Nea Dimokratia (Psarras 2010). Similar to Samaras, Kammenos eventually blamed the party from which he came as being the main culprit of national decay; he played the outsider card to craft his own organisation and agenda (see Barr 2009).

What's left? The declining life-cycle of ANEL and its position in Greek politics

In political party research, the formation of new political parties has received far greater attention than the reasons for their persistence (or failure). While the emergence of new challengers is mostly explained through socio-economic and institutional factors, their persistence is discussed in terms of the 'ability to navigate successive developmental stages in their political life cycle' (Art 2011: 7; see Pedersen 1982). The development of a party base, a political programme that contrasts with other competitors, and the accumulation of (financial) resources are just as important as filling the gap when political opportunities present themselves (Lucardie 2000). 'Flash parties' – those which suddenly ascend the political ladder only to decline as quickly as they appeared (Art 2011) – are seen as failing to achieve these thresholds. They vanish due to a lack of resources and experience as well as because their ranks are dominated by opportunists who 'were soon exposed as empty shells' (Art 2011: 43). Hence, flash parties pass through an accelerated life cycle of rising and falling, leaving hardly any political footprint behind. But has this been the case for ANEL? It would be too early to make a definite judgement. ANEL still holds the ranks of the government; however, its good fortune in the polls recently shrank to less than 2 per cent of the votes. We can, however, identify some underlying reasons for this, as well as for the tentative position assumed by ANEL in modern Greek politics.

One reason for the lack of a programme was the inexperienced and overly heterogeneous staff that could not forge consensus beyond a basic nativist orientation. ANEL was unable or unwilling to draft a coherent programme that it could be held accountable for. This, of course, backfired; as Kitschelt puts it: 'Once a party has gained electoral momentum [...] its internal ability to develop a viable organization, a substantive political program, and effective strategies become equally decisive for its success' (Kitschelt 1989: 41). Without a competent organisational corpus, ANEL has not been able to stage its own campaigns, or to sustain a competent image in public. Consequently, the party is almost non-existent in public discourse. At the beginning, this was part of the aim to integrate as many constituencies as possible. But even when in government, the party still cultivates the image of a movement without political distinction.

Second, the lack of a strategy while in governmental office contributed to the demise of ANEL. Joining the ranks of SYRIZA, ANEL never formulated a modus for how to deal with its coalition partner, beyond setting red lines for a national agenda that should not be crossed.[16] Its only interest was to denounce the austerity measures imposed by the troika. It did not enter the coalition negotiations with its own constructive ideas for the legislative term, and was instead quickly satisfied with assuming control of the Ministry of Defence and becoming the junior partner in the coalition.

Third, without a clear profile, the decisions taken by ANEL were unpredictable for voters and sympathisers. The lack of coherence in their positioning was a logical consequence that sparked strong criticism from multiple sides. In relation to central initiatives, such as a bill for granting citizenship to second-generation immigrants, and a bill on changing gender identity, ANEL made contradictory statements and reversed its initial refusal.[17] Torn between a basic conservative/far-right orientation and the will to avoid a disintegration of the government, the party leadership failed to fill their overarching framework of 'national independence' through a coherent policy.

Taken together, ANEL may leave a small footprint on Greek politics in the near future. However, the populist modus operandi exemplified in a policy orientation without liability has aggravated the critical condition of the political system 'defined by political polarization and adversarial politics expressed through a confrontational rhetoric premised on populist blame-shifting' (Vasilopoulou 2014: 400). This condition was not only formed by the SYRIZA–ANEL coalition, but it is one that has pervaded Greek politics for decades. And even though the left–right government is considered a novelty in Greek politics, it actually continues the left-right coalitioning between the centre-right and centre-left of the prior government as well as the disappearance of clear political lines. The politics of ANEL are rather a symptom of an underlying problem in Greek politics: the flawed institutionalisation of political conflict and the clientelist, short-sighted vision that political parties offer. Overall, ANEL exemplifies an acceleration of politics in terms of a changing political landscape as well as the mainstreaming of nationalist forces beyond the conservative ND. It demonstrates how national grassroots indignation can transform political power structures, while also showing that indignation is clearly a sustainable mode of politics.

Conclusion

'Don't wake up the Greeks' was a central parole of the Spanish *indignados* that provoked the formation of the Indignant People's Movement in Greece, and the mobilisation of citizens with little prior political experience (Rüdig and Karyotis 2013; Kousis 2016). While most of the participants followed a progressive, emancipatory agenda with demands for real democracy and egalitarian counter visions, the mobilisation also summoned a new nationalist movement whose institutional guise, the ANEL, soon entered the political stage. As this chapter has demonstrated, ANEL was capable of absorbing reactionary indignation and channelled it into a party platform that would soon participate in the national government. Despite its rapid rise to power, ANEL received surprisingly little scholarly attention. While the bulk of literature categorised the rise of deviationist parties as populist phenomena related to the representation crisis, this chapter took an actor-centric perspective to uncover the origins, strategies, and fortunes of this very specific movement party in the favourable conditions of economic depression, political reconfiguration, and shifting cleavage structures.

The analysis has demonstrated the necessity of connecting the study of movement parties to the transformation of party *and* street politics. The rise of ANEL is symptomatic of prior shifts in the political landscape, and the restructuring of the milieu it gave rise to. It built on protectionist sentiments that were widely spread across all political spectra and cultivated the overarching framework of 'national independence' that especially resonated among dissatisfied layers of the population which had lost faith in conservative politics. The communication strategy of denying allegiance to any political camp worked well at the beginning, but this approach was unable to ensure sustainable development, as a definite political base never emerged. Taking the convergence of movement and party politics as a given, the SYRIZA-ANEL government illustrates that the path from the squares to the parliament has shrunk. From today's perspective, it would hardly be an exaggeration to say that the Indignant People's Movement paved the way for the left–right government which took power in 2015.

The concept of movement parties is therefore a convenient tool as it accounts for the interwoven dynamics of street mobilisation and party formation, and also scrutinises the transitionary character of politics in times of political restructuration. It likewise shows that strategies depend on the respective stage of development: while the catch-all approach seems to resonate in times of party formation, it turns out to be unfavourable for office. Moreover, this chapter revealed that hidden agendas might stand behind the 'charm of anti-politics' (Mosca 2014: 46). ANEL follows a straightforward agenda of far-right patterns in Greece, even though it has pledged non-alignment within the established political realms. However, this cannot hide the fact that Hellenic nationalism remains a central force in Greek politics. The strong ideological salience of national themes in public along with the constant agitation created by charismatic movement entrepreneurs in an organisationally diversified milieu make it plausible for new parties and movements to emerge when others fail. LAOS was a case in point here, and ANEL may rewrite this history of far-right decline after entering the country's government. At the same time, while ANEL has obviously lost support, other formations such as Golden Dawn persist, despite stronger opposition from political parties and civil society. Hence, further research from a comparative angle is needed to identify the dynamics of the conditions informing the far right's rise and decline. For now, the genesis of ANEL may help shed light on how quickly new actors can rise from the protest scene to official politics. In the truest sense of the phrase, the Hellenic parliament is only a stone's throw away from Syntagma Square.

Notes

1 Panos Kammenos (24 February 2017) https://twitter.com/panoskammenos/status/172907485773045760, accessed 15 December 2017. Author's translation.
2 ANEL (2012) 'Founding Statement' http://anexartitoiellines.gr/diak.php, accessed: 15 December 2017.
3 Quote by Panos Kammenos, explaining himself to private TV channel. Antenna TV (24 February 2012) 'P Kammenos Independent Greek 24-2-2012' https://www.youtube.com/watch?v=DVJIbCXLt5g, accessed 15 December 2017. Author's translation.
4 ANEL (2014). Press Release from 15 April 2014. http://www.anexartitoiellines.gr/post.php?post_id=4383, accessed 15 December 2017.
5 Washington Post (10 December 2017) 'Trump adviser at center of Russia probe, a rapid rise and dramatic fall in his ancestral land' https://www.washingtonpost.com/world/europe/for-trump-adviser-at-center-of-russia-probe-a-rapid-rise-and-dramatic-fall-in-his-ancestral-land/2017/12/10/91bb696a-d390-11e7-9ad9-ca0619edfa05_story.html?utm_term=.ec9d921e402a, accessed 15 December 2017.
6 Movement of Independent Citizens (2015) 'Spark' http://www.mikis-theodorakis-kinisi-anexartiton-politon.gr/spitha, accessed 15 December 2017.
7 ANEL (2012) Founding Statement.

8 As ANEL called for a gathering at Syntagma Square on the first anniversary of the beginning of the square movement, some groups distanced themselves from this kind of institutionalisation of their movement.

9 LAOS later left the government, but the party could not regain its credibility.

10 Antenna TV (2012) 'Kammenos: We are right, left, center' https://www.youtube.com/watch?v=Pubo8xd3xm0, accessed 15 December 2017.

11 In the Greek context, these mainly include territorial conflicts such as open border conflicts with Turkey and Albania as well as the naming of the Republic of Macedonia. Speaking about national issues in Greece also includes the national question of Cyprus and the Muslim minority in Thrace. It implies a nationalist position that promotes the rights of ethnic Greeks.

12 The Guardian (30 January 2015) 'New Greek nationalist defence minister resurrects old tensions with Turkey' https://www.theguardian.com/world/2015/jan/30/greece-turkey-imia-kardak-tensions-fighter-jets, accessed 15 December 2017.

13 Kathimerini (04 August 2016) 'Mosque bill approved with support of all parties, bar ANEL, Golden Dawn' http://www.ekathimerini.com/211020/article/ekathimerini/news/mosque-bill-approved-with-support-of-all-parties-bar-anel-golden-dawn, accessed 15 December 2017.

14 ANEL (2012) 'The presentation of the party Independent Greeks by Panos Kammenos in Distomo' https://anexartitoiellines.gr/files/parousiasi.pdf, accessed 15 December 2017.

15 Quote by Panos Kammenos, explaining himself to the private TV channel. See Footnote 3.

16 ANEL draws red lines with regard to the national issues, especially the question of Macedonia. See ANEL (10 January 2015) 'Press release: The pre-election speech of the president of the Independent Greeks Panos Kammenos in Patras' http://www.anex-artitoiellines.gr/post.php?post_id=5495, accessed 15 December 2017.

17 Kathimerini (27 September 2017) 'ANEL make U-turn on gender identity bill' http://www.ekathimerini.com/221980/article/ekathimerini/news/anel-make-u-turn-on-gender-identity-bill, accessed 15 December 2017.

References

Antoniou, G., Kosmidis, S., and Dinas, E. (2017) *Antisemitism in Greece Today*, Thessaloniki: Heinrich Böll Foundation – Greece.

Art, D. (2011) *Inside the Radical Right: The Development of Anti-Immigrant Parties in Western Europe*, Cambridge: Cambridge University Press.

Aslanidis, P. and Marantzidis, N. (2016) 'The Impact of the Greek Indignados on Greek Politics', *Southeastern Europe*, 40(2): 125–157.

Aslanidis, P. and Rovira Kaltwasser, C. (2016) 'Dealing with Populists in Government: The SYRIZA-ANEL Coalition in Greece', *Democratization*, 236: 1–17.

Barr, R.R. (2009) 'Populists, Outsiders and Anti-Establishment Politics', *Party Politics*, 15(1): 29–48.

Christopoulos, D. (2014) *Mapping Ultra-Right Extremism, Xenophobia and Racism within the Greek State Apparatus*, Berlin: Rosa Luxemburg Foundation.

Della Porta, D. (2015) *Social Movements in Times of Austerity: Bringing Capitalism Back Into Protest Analysis*, New York: John Wiley & Sons.

Della Porta, D., Fernández, J., Kouki, H. and Mosca, L. (2017) *Movement Parties against Austerity*, Cambridge: Polity.

Dinas, E. and Rori, L. (2013) 'The 2012 Greek Parliamentary Elections: Fear and Loathing in the Polls', *West European Politics*, 36(1): 270–282.

Douzinas, C. (2013) *Philosophy and Resistance in the Crisis: Greece and the Future of Europe*, New York: John Wiley & Sons.

Fragoudaki, A. (2013) *Nationalism and the Rise of the Radical Right [Ο εθνικισμός και η άνοδος της ακροδεξιάς]*, Athens: Alexandreia.

Georgiadou, V. (1995) 'Greek Orthodoxy and the Politics of Nationalism', *International Journal of Politics, Culture and Society*, 9(2): 295–315.

Georgiadou, V. and Rori, L. (2015) 'The Right beyond ND: ANEL and Golden Dawn [Η Δεξιά πέραν της ΝΔ: ΑΝΕΛ και Χρυσή Αυγή]', *ToVima*, 8 March [Online]. Available at: http://www.tovima.gr/opinions/article/?aid=683498.

Gunter, R. and Diamond, L. (2003) 'Species of Political Parties: A New Typology', *Party Politics*, 9(2): 167–199.

Heaney, M.T. and Rojas, F. (2015) *Party in the Street: The Antiwar Movement and the Democratic Party after 9/11* [Online], Cambridge: Cambridge University Press.

Kanellopoulos, K., Kostopoulos, K., Papanikolopoulos, D., and Rongas, V. (2016) 'Competing Modes of Coordination in the Greek Anti-Austerity Campaign, 2010–2012', *Social Movement Studies*, 16(1): 101–118.

Karamichas, J. (2012) *Square Politics Key Characteristics of the Indignant Mobilizations in Greece* [Online]. Paper prepared for the 62th PSA Annual International Conference.

Karyotis, G. and Gerodimos, R. (eds) (2015) *Politics of Extreme Austerity: Greece in the Eurozone Crisis*, Basingstoke, Hampshire: Palgrave Macmillan.

Kitschelt, H. (1989) *The Logics of Party Formation: Ecological Politics in Belgium and West Germany*, Ithaca, NY: Cornell University Press.

Kitschelt, H. (2006) 'Movement Parties', in Katz, R.S. (ed) *Handbook of Party Politics*, London: Sage, 278–290.

Kousis, M. (2016) 'The Spatial Dimensions of the Greek Protest Campaign against the Troika's Memoranda and Austerity, 2010-2013', in Nez, H., Angelovici, M., and Dufour, P. (eds) *Street politics in the age of austerity: From the Indignados to Occupy* [Online], Amsterdam: Amsterdam Univ. Pr., 147–173.

Lucardie, P. (2000) 'Prophets, Purifiers and Prolocutors', *Party Politics*, 6(2): 175–185.

Martino, M.G. and Papastathis, K. (2018) 'The Radical Right and Religious Discourse', in Zapf, H., Hidalgo, O., and Hildmann, P. W. (eds) *Das Narrativ von der Wiederkehr der Religion*, Wiesbaden: Springer Fachmedien Wiesbaden, 261–287.

Miconi, A. (2015) 'Italy's Five Stars movement and the role of a leader: Or, how charismatic power can resurface through the web', *New Media & Society*, 17(7): 1043–1058.

Minkenberg, M. (2003) 'The West European Radical Right as a Collective Actor: Modeling theImpact of Cultural and StructuralVariables on Party Formation and Movement Mobilization', *Comparative European Politics*, 1: 149–170.

Mosca, L. (2014) 'The Five Star Movement: Exception or Vanguard in Europe?', *The International Spectator*, 49(1): 36–52.

Mosca, L., Vaccari, C. and Valeriani, A. (2015) 'An Internet-Fulled Party?: The Movimento 5 Stelle and the Web', in Tronconi, F. (ed) *Beppe Grillo's Five Star Movement: Organisation, Communication and Ideology* [Online], Farnham: Ashgate Publishing Ltd, 127–152.

Muro, D. and Vidal, G. (2016) 'Political mistrust in southern Europe since the Great Recession', *Mediterranean Politics*, 22(2): 197–217.

Pappas, T.S. (2014) *Populism and Crisis Politics in Greece*, Basingstoke: Palgrave Macmillan.

Pedersen, M.N. (1982) 'Towards a New Typology of Party Lifespans and Minor Parties', *Scandinavian Political Studies*, 5(1): 1–16.

Pirro, A.L. (2016) *The Hungarian Jobbik as 'Movement Party': A Theoretical and Empirical Assessment* (Paper Prepared for the 10th ECPR General Conference), Prague.

Psarras, D. (2010) *The Hidden Hand of Karatzaferis [Το κρυφό χέρι του Καρατζαφέρη]*, Athens, Alexandreia.

Sepheriades, S. and Johnston, H. (eds) (2012) *Violent protest, contentious politics, and the neoliberal state*, London: Routledge.

Simiti, M. (2016) 'Rage and Protest: The Case of the Greek Indignant Movement', *Contention*, 3(2): 33–50.

Sotirakopoulos, N. and Sotiropoulos, G. (2013) "Direct Democracy Now!': The Greek Indignados and the Present Cycle of Struggles', *Current Sociology*, 61(4): 443–456.

Stavrakakis, Y. (2014) 'The Return of 'the People': Populism and Anti-Populism in the Shadow of the European Crisis', *Constellations*, 21(4): 505–517.

Thomassen, L. (2012) *Political Theory in the Square: Protest, Representation and Subjectification*, APSA 2012 Annual Meeting Paper.

Tsatsanis, E. (2011) 'Hellenism under Siege: The National-Populist Logic of Antiglobalization Rhetoric in Greece', *Journal of Political Ideologies*, 16(1): 11–31.

Vasilopoulou, S., Halikiopoulou, D. and Exadaktylos, T. (2014) 'Greece in Crisis: Austerity, Populism and the Politics of Blame', *JCMS: Journal of Common Market Studies*, 52(2): 388–402.

Verney, S. (2014) "Broken and Can't Be Fixed': The Impact of the Economic Crisis on the Greek Party System', *The International Spectator*, 49(1): 18–35.

8

REMAINING ON THE STREETS

Anti-Islamic PEGIDA mobilization and its relationship to far-right party politics

Manès Weisskircher and Lars Erik Berntzen

Introduction[1]

The concept of movement parties (Kitschelt 2006) represents one of the latest attempts to connect the study of social movements and political parties (see Chapter 2). The growing academic attention to the links between movement activism and party politics reflects the empirical importance of this relationship. While the close connection between movements and parties for the political left is well established (e.g. Almeida 2010; Kitschelt 1989), we know little about its relevance for the right, especially for the radical right – which is the strongest challenger of mainstream politics in contemporary Western Europe (Kriesi et al. 2012).[2]

Academic research on the far right was for a long time restricted to the study of party politics (e.g. Mudde 2007; Rydgren 2007). Recently, scholars have begun investigating the growing relevance of far-right social movements (e.g. Blee and Creasap 2010; Caiani et al. 2012; Berntzen 2018). This specialized literature on far-right activism has, however, neglected the *relationship* between far-right movement activism *and* far-right party politics (with notable exceptions e.g. Art 2011; Giugni et al. 2005; Hutter 2014; Minkenberg 2003; and Pirro and Castelli 2018).

This chapter adds to the literature that assesses the importance of far-right party politics for far-right social movement activism by analysing PEGIDA, the Patriotic Europeans against the Islamization of the Occident (*Patriotische Europäer gegen die Islamisierung des Abendlandes*). PEGIDA rapidly became the largest recent instance of far-right street mobilization in Western Europe. Originating in the eastern German city of Dresden, Saxony, PEGIDA activists started their mobilization effort in October 2014 – almost one year *before* the 'refugee crisis'. At their peak in December 2014 and January 2015, around

20,000 supporters attended PEGIDA's weekly marches through the streets of Dresden. Given their mobilization success, it does not come as a surprise that PEGIDA was quickly studied by German political scientists (for example, Daphi et al. 2015; Decker 2015; Dostal 2015; Geiges et al. 2015; Patzelt and Klose 2015; Vorländer et al. 2016; and in English: Virchow 2016; Vorländer et al. 2018).

While Dresden was, and continues to be, the epicentre of PEGIDA protests, it is not their only location. In many other German cities, and in some other countries – such as Austria, Belgium, Denmark, the Netherlands, Norway, Sweden, Switzerland, and the United Kingdom – far-right activists have tried to mobilize under the 'banner' of PEGIDA. Despite representing widely-covered cases of far-right street activism in countries such as Austria and Norway, none of these offshoots managed to mobilize anywhere close to the initial PEGIDA group in Dresden (Berntzen and Weisskircher 2016). This chapter also contextualizes PEGIDA involvement in the far-right mobilization in the Saxon city of Chemnitz in late summer 2018. These protest events made international headlines as some involved participants showed the Nazi salute or violently attacked, in their perception, 'foreigners'.

The exceptional development of PEGIDA was also shaped by its relationship with far-right party politics, and this was especially so in Dresden. We demonstrate this important relationship in four different ways. First, we show that large-N findings which underline that nationally established radical right parties hamper far-right movement activism have less power to explain cross-national differences in PEGIDA mobilization than often assumed. Second, we discuss the importance of party activists in the early stages of PEGIDA mobilization. Third, we elaborate on how and why PEGIDA never became a movement party, despite attempts to enter party politics. Fourth, we show that PEGIDA in Dresden and the AfD (Alternative for Germany: *Alternative für Deutschland*) have grown closer together over time up until late summer 2018, and discuss how this came about while PEGIDA was overshadowed by this new radical right party. Overall, taking far-right party politics into account adds to the understanding of important dimensions of PEGIDA, especially its emergence and its dynamics over time.

Apart from making the theoretical point to emphasize the significance of party politics for understanding far-right social movement mobilization, we also discuss how social movement concepts such as political opportunity structures, resources, social networks, and coalition building explain these movement-party relations.

Methodologically, our chapter presents an analysis of the crucial case study of PEGIDA in Dresden, with references to many other attempts of PEGIDA protests in Germany and beyond, which are taken into account as 'shadow cases', providing non-formal reference points for a better understanding of our main case (e.g. Gerring 2017: 139; for another PEGIDA study explicitly using shadow cases, see Hafez 2016). We primarily draw on the sizeable scholarly literature on the German case as well as our previous protest event analysis and study of online sources on PEGIDA in Austria, Norway, Sweden, and Switzerland (Berntzen and Weisskircher 2016). Interviews with leading PEGIDA activists would have certainly shed light on some of the issues discussed in this chapter; for example, on their efforts to enter party politics. However, beyond the general methodological difficulties in studying far-right activism (e.g. Blee 2009), interview access to PEGIDA activists has proved to be particularly difficult (e.g. Daphi et al. 2015: 4).

The chapter proceeds as follows. First, we introduce the case of PEGIDA, describing the history, ideology, activists, supporters, and diffusion of PEGIDA protest. Afterwards, we discuss the above-mentioned key dimensions of the relationship between PEGIDA and far-right party politics. In the conclusion, we discuss our findings in the broader context of contemporary far-right politics.

PEGIDA in Dresden and beyond

Since the summer months of 2015, the intensification of the 'refugee crisis' has shaped German politics. Much as in other European countries of destination for asylum seekers, immigration and integration turned into two of the most salient political issues, shaping how people talk about politics (Weisskircher and Hutter 2019). However, almost a year before the summer of 2015, during the last months of 2014, an anti-Islamic far-right protest group had already entered the German political stage: PEGIDA started to mobilize in the city of Dresden, the capital of Saxony, a region in the east of Germany. What was only the idea of a dozen people or so at the beginning quickly morphed from a Facebook group into a protest wave with two defining features: first, the number of participants was unprecedented for far-right protest in the Federal Republic. Although estimates vary, at its peak, in December 2014 and January 2015, up to 20,000 individuals attended some of the PEGIDA events. Second, the endurance of PEGIDA activists has been unusual. By the end of 2018, PEGIDA still regularly organized its protest events in Dresden, mobilizing more than 1,000 people on a regular basis. This is substantially lower than the peak, but still significant.

The many speeches at PEGIDA protests and the few PEGIDA 'position papers' shed some light on the ideology of the organizers. PEGIDA groups are primarily opposed to Muslim immigration, although many of their written demands did not explicitly include a rejection of all immigration to Germany. In addition, PEGIDA has also regularly criticised the political establishment as well as mainstream media, giving prominence to the term 'lying press' (*Lügenpresse*). Calls for more direct democracy have been another important part of PEGIDA ideology (Berntzen and Weisskircher 2016: 559). An official PEGIDA logo represented a person dropping four symbols into a dustbin: an Antifa movement symbol, icons of the PKK and of ISIS, but also the Swastika (Dostal 2015: 524). At the same time, key figures within PEGIDA posted discriminatory comments on Facebook. In 2016, Lutz Bachmann was fined €9,600 for incitement after calling immigrants 'rubbish' (*Gelumpe*) and 'dirty pack' (*Dreckspack*). Siegfried Däbritz, another key PEGIDA activist, used even worse language against Muslims and Kurdish.

Beyond the inner circle of PEGIDA, collecting information on the participants of PEGIDA protests has proved to be methodologically difficult, as many followers refused to engage with researchers. Therefore, the number of those that responded to survey questions has regularly been rather low (e.g. Daphi et al. 2015; Vorländer et al. 2016). Those PEGIDA supporters who responded to survey questions were probably the ideologically more 'moderate' individuals. According to one survey, 89 percent of respondents would have voted for the AfD at the next German election, while 5 percent preferred the extreme right NPD. Only 6 percent of those who responded had other preferences. At the same time, interestingly, only 33.3 percent of respondents self-identified as 'right' and hardly anyone – merely 1.7 percent – self-reported as 'extreme right'. A plurality of respondents, 48.7 percent, regarded themselves as part of the political 'centre' (Daphi et al. 2015).

As large-scale PEGIDA mobilization was a Dresden phenomenon, the context of Saxony is crucial for our understanding. Saxony is a region of the former German Democratic Republic, where many have faced difficulties and disappointments since the *Wende*, related to economic and cultural deprivation in the east (Vorländer et al. 2016: 142). The political culture of Saxony is more conservative than in many other *neue Länder* (Dostal 2015), and it includes a strong sense of regional and local identity (Vorländer et al. 2016: 144f). This is not only reflected in the strong regional CDU (*Christlich Demokratische Union*), a particularly conservative branch of the party. Saxony has also been a traditional stronghold of the extreme right NPD (*Nationaldemokratische Partei*: National Democratic Party). While less than two months before the start of the PEGIDA protests, in August 2014, the extreme right NPD was voted out of the Saxon parliament, it gained 4.9 percent of the vote, and was therefore barely below the required 5 percent threshold needed to gain legislative representation. Simultaneously, the AfD entered the Saxon parliament. With 9.7 percent of the vote, it was less than three percent behind the SPD (*Sozialdemokratische Partei Deutschlands*: Social Democratic Party of Germany). The PEGIDA protests also alluded to important elements of local protest culture. Similar to the Monday demonstrations at the end of the German Democratic Republic, the PEGIDA *Abenspaziergänge* ('evening walks') took place every Monday evening. The slogan '*Wir sind das Volk*' ('We are the people') has also been used both in 1989, and during the PEGIDA protests. In addition, before PEGIDA existed, major far-right protests had already occurred annually – on February 13, the first day of bombing raids of US and British air forces in 1945, destroying the city of Dresden (Vorländer et al. 2016: 144).

All over Germany, many attempts were made to organize local protest under the banner of PEGIDA. However, these groups never managed to mobilize large numbers of supporters. LEGIDA (*Leipziger Europäer gegen die Islamisierung des Abendlandes*: Leipzig's Europeans against the Islamization of the Occident), the PEGIDA spin-off in Leipzig, the most populous city in Saxony, belonged to the more successful mobilization attempts outside of Dresden. According to Dostal (2015: 524), 'only in Munich, Suhl, Leipzig and Dippoldiswalde did the number of participants rise above 1000, and these rallies all fizzled out quickly'. The contrast to the 'original' PEGIDA protest in Dresden is stark.

Local and national concerns have been important for PEGIDA protests, but PEGIDA's identity also relates to Europe. It is not the self-ascribed patriotic 'Germans', but the patriotic 'Europeans' that have staged these protest events. Accordingly, far-right activists have mobilized under the banner of PEGIDA outside of Germany (for more on the European dimension of far-right activism such as PEGIDA see Caiani and Weisskircher forthcoming). These efforts were similarly small-scale as the German attempts outside of Saxony, although there were some important differences between weak mobilization in countries such as Austria and Norway, and the failure to mobilize even modest support in countries such as Sweden and Switzerland. State bans were a significant factor in preventing some activists from marching under the PEGIDA banner, for example, in Switzerland, to a lesser extent in Austria (Berntzen and Weisskircher 2016), and also in Belgium (Geiges et al. 2016: 165). Despite low levels of street mobilization, public attention for PEGIDA was considerable outside of Germany too, making the far-right protests also publicly salient there (Berntzen and Weisskircher 2016).

By the end of 2018, PEGIDA mobilization in Dresden was not over yet. While the first wave of PEGIDA faded away over the course of the first half of 2015 as the number of participants declined, at the end of 2015, when the 'refugee crisis' intensified, PEGIDA mobilization attracted more participants again; it experienced a second wave. At its one-year anniversary, on October 19, 2015, up to 20,000 people attended the PEGIDA protest. Although support faded away for a second time soon afterwards, PEGIDA has remained on the streets of Dresden. There, PEGIDA celebrated its fourth anniversary in October 2018 with an attendance of 3,000 to 4,000 supporters. This number was higher than in the year before. As of 2018, weekly Monday protests are still continuing, regularly attracting more than 1,000 participants.

Even outside of Saxony, German far-right activists still try to mobilize under the banner of PEGIDA. For example, PEGIDA Munich has mobilized up to 2018. In 2016 and/or 2017, some groups outside of Germany also still tried to march under the banner of PEGIDA, such as in Denmark, France, and the Netherlands.[3]

The emergence of PEGIDA and the importance of established radical right parties

Why did PEGIDA only really take off in Dresden, and not in other regions and countries where activists also tried to make use of the PEGIDA label? Various scholars point to the lack of an established radical right party that would channel far-right attitudes in the German political system, underlining the importance of far-right party politics for the presence or absence of protest (Geiges et al. 2016: 163–164; Hafez 2016; Opratko 2015). As parties such as the NPD, the *Republikaner*, or the DVU were unable to establish themselves in the German political system (Art 2006), individuals with far-right stances needed to look for means beyond electoral politics to articulate their political views.

This reasoning corresponds to the notion of the importance of political opportunity structure in the political process model. Large-N studies show that far-right political parties do have an impact on far-right movement mobilization. Based on a protest event analysis in six Western European countries, Hutter (2014: 138) demonstrates that far-right protest is particularly weak when radical right parties are established political players in the respective political system: 'the *more* salient [radical right parties] are in electoral politics, the *less* often they give rise to protest mobilization'. Hutter (2014: 139) then theorizes that one reason for this pattern might be that strong radical right parties do not have an interest in public showings with extreme right activists. The assumption is that associations with groups such as skinheads, or actions such as violent protests would hurt political parties that try to present themselves as credible opposition or even governing party. Other research provides similar findings. Giugni et al. (2005) indicate that the emergence of strong radical right parties shrinks the political space for extra-parliamentary far-right mobilization. According to them, party politics and movement activism 'are two strategic options available to extreme-right actors to make their claims to the political authorities', but '[i]f one option can be adopted, the other becomes less viable and therefore is less often used' (Giugni et al. 2005: 148). Also, Minkenberg (2003: 165) finds 'a rather clear pattern of countries with strong radical right-wing parties and a weak movement sector and those with weak radical right-wing parties and a strong movement sector'.

When PEGIDA emerged in October 2014, there was indeed no radical right party in the German Bundestag. In contrast to Germany, in countries such as Austria, Denmark, Norway, and the Netherlands, where PEGIDA mobilization was modest, radical right parties had already been established players in the national parliaments. In countries such as France and the United Kingdom, where PEGIDA was also unsuccessful, radical right parties had also performed well in European Parliament elections held under proportional voting rules.

Nevertheless, the relevance of the negative relationship between the electoral strength of radical right parties and the mobilization of far-right street protest needs to be qualified for the case of PEGIDA in Dresden. While not being in the German *Bundestag* at the time of the emergence of PEGIDA, the AfD had already entered the European Parliament, becoming the fifth-strongest German party at the EP election in May 2014. In Saxony, the AfD received 10.1 percent of the vote at the EP election, a result which was substantially stronger than its overall support in Germany (7.1 percent). At that point, however, the anti-Islamic, radical right faction was not yet dominant in the AfD, which was led by neoliberal politicians – at least on the national level (Arzheimer 2015). The extreme right NPD benefited from the lack of an electoral threshold at the EP election in Germany – one percent of the overall vote was enough to gain one seat. The NPD also received substantially stronger support in Saxony (3.6 percent) than in the whole of the country. Two months before the first PEGIDA protest, in August 2014, the AfD managed to enter its first regional legislature – the *Landtag* of Saxony. The regional branch of the party was dominated by individuals that were significantly to the right of the then national leadership. At this election, the NPD missed legislative representation by a mere 0.1 percent. Therefore, pointing only to the absence of an established radical right party in the German parliament during the peak of PEGIDA mobilization would miss that Saxon voters participated in two other elections in 2014, where they could, and did, articulate their support for far-right parties. On the regional level of Saxony, the strength of the AfD and the NPD actually correlates with PEGIDA mobilization success.

Outside Germany, there have also been differences in PEGIDA mobilization across countries. While PEGIDA managed to mobilize some support on the streets in Austria, Denmark, the Netherlands and Norway, it failed completely to do so in Sweden and Switzerland. In all these countries, however, radical right parties are established players in the national parliament. In Norway and Switzerland, they have even been members of government in 2015, when activists tried to march under the banner of PEGIDA there. The small but significant cross-country differences in PEGIDA mobilization outside of Germany cannot be explained by the presence or absence of the radical right in the respective parliaments. Instead, the agency of the activists, especially their insertion into pre-existing far-right networks, and the response of the state, which banned mobilization efforts in some instances, were important factors in explaining PEGIDA mobilization outside of Germany (Berntzen and Weisskircher 2016).

These patterns point to the limits of explanations focusing on the relationship between the national party arena and the protest arena when explaining street mobilization, especially those with a local stronghold such as PEGIDA. However, this should not be misunderstood as a rejection of the empirical pattern found in the literature. To be sure, the relationship between radical right party success and far-right mobilization only describes probabilities and does not aim to explain every single case. Also, it still seems like an important part of the puzzle to maintain that PEGIDA took off in a city in one of the few Western European countries without an established radical right party at that point in time.

Still, the qualifications mentioned above point to the importance of other factors in explaining the emergence of PEGIDA protest, and why precisely it took off in Dresden. These are the agency of its activists, and the local context (Dostal 2015). Political opportunities as conceived in the political process model, such as the presence or absence of a radical right party in national parliament, are insufficient, and too structural for a comprehensive explanation. The importance of agency instead of structural variables has been emphasized both in the literature on the radical right (e.g. Art 2011; Berntzen and Weisskircher 2016), in social movement studies (e.g. Jasper 2006), and in party politics (e.g. de Lange and Art 2011; Weisskircher 2017).

Party politics as a resource pool for PEGIDA street mobilization

According to the standard formulation of the political process model, 'indigenous organizational strength' is a crucial factor facilitating the mobilization of social movement activism (McAdam 1982: 43). The concept is defined as 'the resources of the minority community that enable insurgent groups to exploit these opportunities', which includes 'members', the 'established structure of solidarity incentives', the 'communication network', and 'leaders' (McAdam 1982: 45–48). To what extent did pre-existing organizations matter for the street mobilization of PEGIDA in Dresden and beyond? How did political parties and their activists provide a resource pool for PEGIDA mobilization?

In Dresden, from its very beginning, PEGIDA included a small number of (former) party members in its inner circle. Siegfried Däbritz, a key activist of PEGIDA, was previously active for the FDP, Thomas Tallacker was a local politician for the CDU, and Achim Exner was a member of the AfD. Tatjana Festerling, who joined PEGIDA only after a few months, had previously been involved in a local AfD branch. Therefore, some PEGIDA activists had experience of being lower-rank members of political parties. However, many other of PEGIDA's leading organizers, such as Lutz Bachmann, were never involved in party politics. In general, much more relevant than previous involvement in party politics of individual activists were their common friendship networks, related to the local sports and party scene (Vorländer et al. 2016: 10–11).

Still, from the very beginning, PEGIDA and the AfD had an important, but complicated relationship – a combination of competition and cooperation. Some AfD politicians, such as the leader of the party's group in the city council, publicly stated their support for PEGIDA. Others, especially politicians in the west of Germany, and related to the neoliberal wing of the AfD, were more reserved, sometimes even hostile to PEGIDA. While the Saxon AfD party leader Frauke Petry, later national party leader and key figure of the party's turn to the radical right in 2015 (Franzmann 2017), became distant after personally meeting with Bachmann, many of her regional party's members attended PEGIDA events. Crucially, some of them were also important in supporting the organization of PEGIDA in its early weeks, for example by helping to equip the PEGIDA security staff and providing a proper stage with sound system – in the first weeks of PEGIDA mobilization, Bachmann had only talked with a megaphone to his followers (Vorländer et al. 2016: 39–43). After PEGIDA had taken off, some important AfD politicians, such as Alexander Gauland and Björn Höcke, both from the 'nationalist' wing, made public statements of support for the protests (Gabrow 2016: 174).

In December 2015, the extreme-right NPD called its supporters to attend PEGIDA events. Nevertheless, while the NPD tried to connect to PEGIDA, PEGIDA activists rather tried to keep their distance, as they did not want to be associated with the extreme right party (Vorländer et al. 2016: 43–46).

On April 13 2015, PPV party leader Geert Wilders became the most promi-nent guest speaker at a PEGIDA event, pointing to further connections between PEGIDA and a political party, even one that is based abroad. Nevertheless, while PEGIDA protest in Dresden was related to subcultural milieus that included polit-ical parties and party activists, the latter played only a modest part in the story of PEGIDA. A closer association with the AfD occurred mainly later, and did not remain uncontested within the party (see below).

Outside of Dresden, ties to political parties proved to be important to some extent. For example, in Switzerland, key supporters of local attempts to stage PEGIDA protests were involved in minor political parties, espe-cially in the DPS (*Direktdemokratische Partei Schweiz*: Direct Democratic Party of Switzerland) of Ignaz Bearth, a former SVP member, and one of the best-known figures of the Swiss far right. Outside of Switzerland, Bearth also became a guest speaker at several PEGIDA rallies. In Austria, some low-ranked FPÖ members as well as individuals close to the party became highly involved in PEGIDA. Georg Immanuel Nagel, a journalist writing for a weekly edited by a former MEP of the FPÖ, became the first spokesperson of PEGIDA in Vienna. Another low-rank FPÖ member publicly appeared as a key figure behind PEGIDA protests in the western part of the country. Some of the party's politicians, including MPs, attended PEGIDA protest events, and leading FPÖ members made positive remarks about PEGIDA at the beginning of its mobilization efforts in Germany and Austria (Berntzen and Weisskircher 2016: 565–568).

Therefore, political parties provide resources in the early phase of PEGIDA, but only to a limited extent. In Dresden, these 'resources' were party activists themselves, some of what neoliberal jargon has come to call 'human resources', but also material resources, for example, a stage, were provided through them. In Switzerland, PEGIDA could draw on the activists and resources of pre-existing fringe parties, as they and PEGIDA were more or less identical there. In Austria, some FPÖ members or individuals close to the party have had influential roles within PEGIDA. However, apart from political parties, other pre-existing far-right organizations were often important for the emer-gence of PEGIDA, especially outside of Saxony. These were groups such as the Identitarians, student fraternities, skinheads, football hooligans, or Defence League groups.

All these organizational linkages can be regarded as 'indigenous organiza-tional strength', in the language of the political process model. Without them, much fewer activists outside of Saxony would have attempted to copy the PEGIDA mobilization success in Saxony. Understanding social movements as networks (Diani 1992) also highlights the importance of resources from other organizations, such as other far-right groups and parties. A network approach, going beyond the political process model, highlights organizational overlap as political normalcy in movement activism.

Attempts to form a party

As stated, PEGIDA never turned into a movement party. What comes closest are the efforts by PEGIDA activists in Saxony to enter party politics. Tatjana Festerling ran for mayor of Dresden, and Lutz Bachmann announced the formation of his own political party. However, their efforts were unsuccessful – an outcome that underlines the difficulty of establishing themselves in party politics, given that the political space on the far right was already covered by the AfD. The party had already entered the *Landtag* in Saxony and quickly built structures in the rest of the country. It did not seem to be their lack of will that prevented Festerling and Bachmann from getting involved into party politics. Rather, their room to manoeuvre in party politics was very limited.

Tatjana Festerling had been one of the key PEGIDA activists in Dresden after she intensified her engagement in the winter months of 2014 and 2015. She did not come to PEGIDA without political experience, as she previously had been involved in a local branch of the AfD. In June 2015, at a time when the first wave of PEGIDA protest had already faded away, Festerling ran for mayor of Dresden. She managed to gain 9.6 percent of the vote, and became the fourth strongest candidate. What was particularly interesting was that her result was substantially better than that of her AfD competitor Stefan Vogel (4.8 percent) – back then, '[t]he relationship between the two organisations was close to a complete breakdown' (Grabow 2016: 174). While Festerling did not compete in the second run, she publicly stated her support for the incumbent mayor Dirk Hilbert, close to the liberal FDP, in order to prevent his left-wing competitor from winning. In the second round, Hilbert was re-elected. After the mayoral race, Festerling continued to take part in far-right activism, also outside of Germany. Amongst others, she set up the 'Fortress Europa' initiative alongside other anti-Islamic organizations (Berntzen 2018) and traveled to Bulgaria in order to 'defend' the European Union's external border with Turkey, together with local Bulgarian far-right paramilitaries (Rone and Weisskircher 2016).

While Festerling's result in the mayor election was solid, it did not leave her or PEGIDA with any institutionalized voice in local politics: The election for the local legislature of Dresden had already taken place in May 2014, almost half a year before the emergence of PEGIDA. The next election was due only in 2019. Timing prevented PEGIDA from gaining representation in the Dresden legislature.

Going beyond merely an individual candidacy, in July 2016 Lutz Bachman reported the formation of his own political party. He announced its name as *Freiheitliche Direktdemokratische Volkspartei* (FDDV: 'Liberal Direct-Democratic People's Party). According to Bachmann, he himself would abstain from holding an official position within the party. The party's stated scope was modest – it wanted to participate in a limited number of electoral districts at the national election 2017. No German-wide candidature was planned and competition with the AfD was not an aim. However, Bachmann's announcement turned out to be an empty one. The responsible administrative bodies in the German political system, the *Bundeswahlleiter*, never received the documents which are required to officially register the party.[4] Correspondingly, the FDDV did not actually contest the German federal election of 2017.

While the candidacy of Festerling for mayor of Dresden and the public announcements of Bachmann point to the political will of some leading PEGIDA figures to enter the arena of party politics, their efforts did not prove to be successful. In other countries, PEGIDA was not relevant enough in the first place to make any credible claim of forming a party – even more so in contexts where there were established radical right parties. Nevertheless, in Austria, a PEGIDA party was registered in March 2015. While the motivations are not completely known, observers assume that it was done to secure the right to use the PEGIDA label.[5]

Despite the degree to which their claims resonate with popular attitudes, anti-Islamic initiatives such as PEGIDA are also perceived as being broadly illegitimate by many (Berntzen, Bjånesøy, and Ivarsflaten 2017). They have consequently been met with large-scale counter-mobilization, as well as police and state interventions (Berntzen and Weisskircher 2016). Besides hampering accumulation of necessary financial resources and patronage (Edwards and McCarthy 2008: 135), this kind of state and non-state response hinders the recruitment of skilled personnel necessary for forming an electorally successful party (Art 2011). In sum, whilst there were efforts to enter into party politics, opportunities were limited.

Coalition building and remaining on the streets

As previously discussed, while radical right presence in party politics may reduce the potential scale and duration of far-right street mobilization and limit activists' ability to enter into party politics themselves, radical right parties can also be a beneficial resource. Earlier, we showed to what extent people with a background in party politics were important in the initial PEGIDA mobilization in various places. Political process scholars have emphasized the importance of coalition building in order to sustain movements (e.g. Tarrow 2005), and radical right parties can serve as natural coalition partners due to their ideological proximity. Such coalitions may be understood as 'collaborative, means-oriented arrangements that permit distinct organizational entities to pool resources in order to effect change' (Levi and Murphy 2006: 654).

PEGIDA benefited from some resources of individual AfD members at its start (see above), but its relationship with the party was far from easy. At the beginning of the PEGIDA protests, when the neoliberal wing was still in charge of the AfD at the national level, many of its representatives criticized PEGIDA. Also, Frauke Petry, then leader of the Saxon AfD, after some initial attempts of outreach to Bachmann, has repeatedly denounced the idea of cooperating with PEGIDA, and refused to speak at PEGIDA demonstrations, despite invitations by Lutz Bachmann. When Bachmann faced widespread criticism after particularly discriminatory remarks, and a selfie posing as Adolf Hitler, Petry demanded his resignation. Similarly, Bachmann sharply criticized the AfD, accusing leading party figures of careerism, for example (Grabow 2016: 174). At the same time, several major and minor AfD politicians praised PEGIDA at some point or another, and also participated in PEGIDA events. Still, driven by Petry, in May 2016 the national executive of the AfD spoke out against its members appearing at PEGIDA events – a decision that remained contested within the party. At that time, the relationship between PEGIDA and parts of the AfD became openly closer, reflected in the presence of guest speakers at each other's events (Grabow 2016: 178f): Prominently, PEGIDA activist Däbritz had given a speech at an AfD rally in Erfurt, the capital of the eastern German region of Thuringia, on the border to Saxony. The leader of the AfD group in the regional legislature of Thuringia is Björn Höcke, a politician at the right-wing end of the political spectrum, even within the AfD.

Especially from May 2017 onwards, PEGIDA and the AfD cooperated more and more. On May 8, both political players staged a demonstration at the *Neumarkt* next to the *Frauenkirche* in Dresden, with two different stages, and formally at different times. Various forms of cooperation have continued throughout the year 2017. For example, on July 17 PEGIDA cancelled its regular Monday *Abendspaziergang*, and told its members to join a demonstration of the AfD in front of a hall where Germany's Minister of Justice Heiko Maas gave a speech on hate speech and the internet. When Petry left the party after the federal election of 2017, some AfD members, mainly from the west of Germany, continued to reject cooperation with PEGIDA. Nevertheless, in March 2018 the party's leadership explicitly asserted that its members could indeed appear at PEGIDA events in Dresden. Only two months later, a high-profile public rapprochement took place: Björn Höcke, AfD party leader in Thuringia, gave a speech at a PEGIDA demonstration in Dresden, with the AfD regional party leaders of Brandenburg and Saxony present.

In late summer of 2018, PEGIDA and AfD cooperated in a most controversial setting: They staged a common demonstration during the far-right mobilization in Chemnitz. Triggering these events was the killing of a German-Cuban man on August 26, the suspects coming from Syria and Iraq. Multiple demonstrations followed – far-right players, including activists from groups in Chemnitz, Saxony, and elsewhere, used the killing to target liberal immigration policies. What made international headlines was that several far-right activists showed the Nazi salute or violently attacked individuals that were regarded as 'foreign' by the violators. Moreover, the arrest warrant against one of the suspects was leaked and then published, among others by PEGIDA founder Bachmann. Ultimately, three regional organizations of the AfD, again the ones from Brandenburg, Saxony, and Thuringia, announced a joint 'silent protest' with PEGIDA: On September 1, some high-profile AfD members and Bachmann marched together on the streets of Chemnitz. While some AfD politicians have continued to speak out against cooperation with PEGIDA, and in particular with Bachmann, their influence over the course of events seems limited.

Not surprisingly, this rapprochement and coalition-building has developed after PEGIDA's failed attempts at entering into local party politics, which have reduced the potential threat and competition between the two players. By remaining on the streets, PEGIDA can potentially enter into a more symbiotic relationship with the AfD. In turn, the strengthening of the bond between PEGIDA and AfD reduces the chances of PEGIDA activists making new attempts at forming a movement party, as activist perceptions of political parties not being efficient allies is precisely one of the reasons why they themselves want to form their own parties in the first place (Kitschelt 1989). However, the future relationship between PEGIDA and AfD will depend on the interest of the latter in investing energy in cooperation with what is now a small, but persistent, local protest group. Some AfD members certainly have such an interest, while others have remained sceptical. In 2019, the AfD aims to play a key role as challenger of the CDU at the regional election in Saxony. The vote will be a testing ground for the potential of future cooperation. It will also be of importance whether Germany's Federal Office for the Protection of the Constitution starts observations on the AfD – a scenario that has been part of Germany's political debate since the Chemnitz protests. Should such an observation occur, key AfD figures might prefer to keep distance from radical street demonstrators.

Conclusion

This chapter has underlined the importance of taking far-right party politics into account when analysing far-right social movement mobilization. Even though PEGIDA is not a movement party, analysing their activism through this lens adds to the understanding of the emergence and development of PEGIDA, the most important far-right mobilization effort in recent Western European politics. More precisely, we analysed four different dimensions of PEGIDA: first, we showed how large-N findings which indicate that established far-right parties hamper the mobilization of far-right street protest provides some, but limited, explanatory power for explaining cross-national differences in and the local emergence of PEGIDA mobilization. Second, we discussed the relevance of party activists in the early stages of PEGIDA mobilization. Third, we pointed to the failed efforts of PEGIDA activists to enter the arena of party politics. Fourth, we showed that PEGIDA and parts of the AfD have started to openly cooperate as they organize common protest events, among others. So far, this cooperation peaked in a particular controversial setting, when both staged common protest during the far-right mobilization of Chemnitz in late summer 2018.

In addition, we also demonstrated that social movement concepts shed light on the relationship between PEGIDA and party politics – such as political opportunity structures, resources, social networks, and coalition building.

Counterfactually, for the case of Germany, it would be tempting to think about the possible trajectory of PEGIDA if the AfD had not been already on the political stage, ready to develop into an electorally successful radical right party. How would PEGIDA mobilization and its diffusion have been different? Where would PEGIDA have been now? Alternatively, what if the AfD had managed to enter the Bundestag already in 2013, when the party barely missed the five percent threshold. How would this have affected the trajectory of PEGIDA, which emerged only a year later? While it is impossible to find satisfying answers to these questions, posing them points to the element of contingency in politics, including far-right politics, and how the room for manoeuvre of one player, such as a far-right social movement organization, is related to the trajectory of another player, such as a radical right political party.

In Germany, as well as in other Western European countries, far-right social movement activism seems to be at its strongest point in recent decades. Still, left-wing protest activity is much more widespread (Hutter 2014). In addition, far-right street activism pales in comparison to the strength of many radical right parties. Nevertheless, not only the electoral support of these parties, but also public surveys on specific issues might indicate potential for a further growth of far-right movement activism. A survey by the London-based think tank Chatham House (Goodwin et al. 2017) conducted in December 2016 and January 2017 found strong support for the statement that '[a]ll further migration from mainly Muslim countries should be stopped', a call more radical than the Islamophobic 'Muslim Ban' of the Trump administration. A majority of respondents in eight of the ten countries studied approved of the demand. Poland was leading the list, with 71 percent of support for the statement. The survey included only four countries where PEGIDA mobilized: in Austria, 65 percent of the respondents agreed with the statement, while the numbers in Belgium (64 percent) and France (61 percent) were similar. Also in Germany, both the motherland of *Willkommenskultur* and of PEGIDA, 53 percent of respondents agreed with the above-mentioned statement. Therefore, a lack of support for anti-immigration demands hardly explains why far-right street activism is much more infrequent than left-wing activism.

This demonstrates that individuals' attitudes on political issues are not everything. Survey data shows that the propensity of individuals to attend demonstrations is significantly influenced by his or her position on the left–right political spectrum. Far-right individuals, and even more so centre-right ones, only rarely attend demonstrations, in comparison to left-wing individuals (Torcal et al. 2016). It remains to be seen whether PEGIDA and other contemporary far-right protests are a harbinger for a change of this pattern in political behaviour. As in the last decades 'unconventional strategies' have become widely accepted (e.g. Meyer and Tarrow 1998; van Aelst and Walgrave 2001), it seems at least possible that street activism becomes more frequent on the right side of the political spectrum too. If so, not only the relationship between far-right movement and party activism, but also the far-right challenge to liberalism (Albertazzi and Mueller 2013) would become even more complex than it already is today.

Notes

1 We especially thank Anders Ravik Jupskås, Maik Herold, Swen Hutter, Abby Peterson, Julia Rone, and the editors of this volume for valuable feedback and advice. An earlier version of this chapter was presented at the ECPR General Conference in Oslo 2017.
2 With the major exception of some Eurozone debtor states in Southern Europe.
3 In Denmark the PEGIDA off-shoot quickly changed their name to For Freedom (*For Frihed*).
4 We thank Juin-Chi Lin for information on this matter.
5 We thank Anita Nissen for information on this matter.

References

Albertazzi, D. and Mueller, S. (2013) 'Populism and Liberal Democracy: Populists and Government in Austria, Italy, Poland and Switzerland', *Government and Opposition*, 48(3): 343–371.

Almeida, P. (2010) 'Social Movement Partyism: Collective Action and Political Parties', in Van Dyke, N. and McCammon, H.J. (eds) *Strategic Alliances: Coalition Building and Social Movements*, Minneapolis, MN: University of Minnesota Press, 170–96.

Art, D. (2006) *The Politics of the Nazi Past in Germany and Austria*, Cambridge: Cambridge University Press.

Art, D. (2011) *Inside the Radical Right. The Development of Anti-Immigrant Parties in Western Europe*, Cambridge: Cambridge University Press.

Arzheimer, K. (2015) 'The AfD: Finally a Successful Right-Wing Populist Eurosceptic Party for Germany?', *West European Politics*, 38(3): 535–556.

Berntzen, L.E. (2018) 'The Anti-Islamic Movement: Far Right and Liberal?', PhD Thesis, European University Institute.

Berntzen, L.E. and Weisskircher, M. (2016) 'Anti-Islamic PEGIDA beyond Germany. Explaining Differences in Mobilisation', *Journal of Intercultural Studies*, 37(6): 556–573.

Berntzen, L.E., Bjånesøy, L., and Ivarsflaten, E. (2017) 'Patterns of Legitimacy on the Far Right. University of Bergen', DIGGSCORE Working Paper (4).

Blee, K. (2009) *Access and Methods in Research on Hidden Communities: Reflections on Studying U.S. Organized Racism*, eSharp: 10–27.

Blee, K. and Creasap, K.A. (2010) 'Conservative and Right-Wing Movements', *Annual Review of Sociology*, 36: 269–286.

Caiani, M., della Porta, D., and Wagemann, C. (2012) *Mobilizing on the Extreme Right. Germany, Italy, and the United States*, Oxford: Oxford University Press.

Caiani, M. and Weisskircher, M. (forthcoming) 'How Many 'Europes'? Social Movements and their Visions of Europe', in Flesher Fominaya, C. and Feenstra, R. (eds) *The Handbook of Contemporary European Social Movements*, London: Routledge.

Daphi, P., et al. (2015) 'Protestforschung am Limit. Eine soziologische Annäherung an PEGIDA'. Available at: www.wzb.eu/sites/default/files/u6/pegida-report_berlin_2015. pdf [Accessed July 1, 2017].

Decker, F. (2015) 'Alternative für Deutschland und Pegida: Die Ankunft des neuen Rechtspopulismus in der Bundesrepublik', in Decker F., Henningsen, B., and Jakobsen, K. (eds) *Rechtspopulismus und Rechtsextremismus in Europa. Die Herausforderung der Zivilgesellschaft durch alte Ideologien und neue Medien*, Baden-Baden: Nomos, 75–90.

de Lange, S. and Art, D. (2011) 'Fortuyn versus Wilders: An Agency-Based Approach to Radical Right Party Building', *West European Politics*, 34(6): 1229–1249.

Dostal, J.M. (2015) 'The Pegida Movement and German Political Culture: Is Right-Wing Populism Here to Stay?', *The Political Quarterly*, 86(4): 523–531.

Edwards, B. and McCarthy, J.D. (2008) 'Resources and Social Movement Mobilization', in Snow, D.A., A. Soule, S.A., and Kriesi, H. (eds) *The Blackwell Companion to Social Movements*, Malden, MA: Blackwell.

Franzmann, F. (2017) 'A Right-wing Populist Party Founded by Economists: The Strange Case of Germany's AfD'. LSE EUROPP Blog.

Geiges, L., Marg, S., and Walter, F. (2015) *Pegida. Die schmutzige Seite der Zivilgesellschaft?* Bielefeld: Transcript Verlag.

Gerring, J. (2017) *Case Study Research: Principles and Practices*, Cambridge: Cambridge University Press.

Giugni, M., Koopmans, R., Passy, F., and Statham, P. (2005) 'Institutional and Discursive Opportunities for Extreme-Right Mobilization in Five Countries', *Mobilization*, 10: 145–162.

Goodwin, M., Raines, T., and Cutts, D. (2017) 'What Do Europeans Think about Muslim Immigration?', Chatham House. Available at: www.chathamhouse.org/expert/comment/what-do-europeans-think-about-muslim-immigration.

Grabow, K. (2016) 'PEGIDA and the Alternative für Deutschland: Two Sides of the Same Coin?', *European View*, 15(2): 173–181.

Hafez, F. (2016) 'Pegida in Parliament? Explaining the Failure of Pegida in Austria', *German Politics and Society*, 34(4): 101–118.

Hutter, S. (2014) *Protesting Culture and Economics in Western Europe. New Cleavages in Left and Right Politics*, Minneapolis, MN: University of Minnesota Press.

Kitschelt, H. (1989) *The Logics of Party Formation: Ecological Politics in Belgium and West Germany*, New York: Cornell University Press.

Kitschelt, H. (2006) 'Movement Parties', in Katz, R. and Crotty, W. (eds) *Handbook of Party Politics*, London: Sage, 278–90.

Kriesi, H., et al. (eds) (2012) *Political Conflict in Western Europe*, Cambridge: Cambridge University Press.

Levi, M. and Murphy, G.H. (2006) 'Coalitions of Contention: The Case of the WTO protests in Seattle', *Political Studies*, 54(4): 651–670.

Luther, K.R. (2011) 'Of Goals and Own Goals: A Case Study of Right-Wing Populist Party Strategy For and During Incumbency', *Party Politics*, 17(4): 453–470.

McAdam, D. (1982) *Political Process and the Development of the Black Insurgency 1930–1970*, Chicago, IL: Chicago University Press.

Meyer, D. and Tarrow, S. (1998) *The Social Movement Society. Contentious Politics for a New Century*, Lanham, MD: Rowman & Littlefield.

Minkenberg, M. (2003) 'The West European Radical Right as Collective Actor: Modeling the Impact of Cultural and Structural Variables on Party Formation and Movement Mobilization', *Comparative European Politics*, 1: 149–170.

Mudde, C. (2007) *Populist Radical Right Parties in Europe*, Cambridge: Cambridge University Press.

Mudde, C. (2010) 'The Populist Radical Right: A Pathological Normalcy', *West European Politics*, 33(6).

Opratko, B. (2015) 'PEGIDA in Österreich: Eine Massenbewegung? Available at: http://sciencev2.orf.at/stories/1753092/index.html.

Patzelt, W. and Klose, J. (eds) (2015) *PEGIDA: Warnsignale aus Dresden*, Dresden: Thelem.

Pirro, A. and Castelli, P. (2018) 'Movement Parties of the Far Right: The Organization and Strategies of Nativist Collective Actors', Mobilization, 23(3): 367–383.

Rone, J. and Weisskircher, M. (2016) 'Unity makes strength? How the radical right could become kingmakers in Bulgaria', LSE EUROPP Blog.

Rydgren, J. (2007) 'The sociology of the radical right', *Annual Review of Sociology*, 33: 241–262.

Tarrow, S. (2005) *The New Transnational Activism*, Cambridge: Cambridge University Press.

Torcal, M. et al. (2016) 'Word on the Street: The Persistence of Leftist-dominated Protest in Europe', *West European Politics*, 39(2): 326–350.

van Aelst, P. and Walgrave, S. (2001) 'Who is that (Wo)man in the Street? From the Normalisation of Protest to the Normalisation of the Protester', *European Journal of Political Research*, 39(4): 461–486.

Virchow, F. (2016) 'PEGIDA: Understanding the Emergence and Essence of Nativist Protest in Dresden', *Journal of Intercultural Studies*, 37(6): 541–555.

Vorländer, H., Herold, M., and Schäller, S. (2016) *PEGIDA: Entwicklung, Zusammensetzung und Deutung einer Empörungsbewegung*, Wiesbaden: Springer.

Vorländer, H., Herold, M., and Schäller, S. (2018) *PEGIDA and New Right-Wing Populism in Germany*, New York: Palgrave Macmillan.

Weisskircher, M. (2017) 'The Electoral Success of the Radical Left: Explaining the Least Likely Case of the Communist Party in Graz', *Government and Opposition*, 1–22.

Weisskircher, M. and Hutter, S. (2019) 'Idle Democrats? Talking about Politics in Germany', in: Klandermans, B. and Saunders, C. (eds.) *When Citizens Talk Politics*, Abingdon: Routledge.

9

THE RELATIONSHIP BETWEEN A MOVEMENT PARTY AND ITS RADICAL FLANK

The Sweden Democrats and the militant factions within the Swedish neo-Nazi ultra nationalist movement[1]

Abby Peterson

Over the past twenty-odd years, the Sweden Democrats have experienced a miraculous metamorphosis from an obscure neo-Nazi sect to becoming a parliamentary party in 2010 (Peterson 2016). Enjoying rising support among the electorate in the 2018 parliamentary elections, the party garnered 17.53% of the vote making it the third largest party in Sweden, which led to the party wielding a controversial position in the parliamentary balance of power. Despite the spectacular success of the dominant party arm of the wider neo-Nazi ultra nationalist movement, the space for a 'radical'[2] flank, I argue, has not contracted.

The neo-Nazi ultra nationalist movement in Sweden, both its more moderate parliamentary party arm and its militant flank factions, share similar goals – the difference lies in their choice of tactics and rhetoric. The party 'make-over' process resulted in new additions to the fringe – two splinter parties, which were only ostensibly in competition with their 'mother party', but rather picked up the more 'untameable' supporters of the goals of the wider movement (Peterson 2016). Through the movement's Internet sites and social media, new, more informal militant action groups developed, as well as two consolidated 'alternative news media' joining the flank. The Sweden Democrats, in its search of parliamentary power, has been augmented by an array of militant movement factions that incorporate the more unruly supporters of the shared goals of the wider movement, thereby mirroring the heterogeneity of its potential supporters, and more or less defusing potential conflicts between the parliamentary party arm and its radical flank. As Garner and Zald (1987: 312) point out, parties and movements are closely intertwined, and in this chapter I will tease out the dialectical and multi-polar relationship between the Sweden Democrats and its radical flank. How does a radical flank impact upon the outcomes for a more moderate movement party? And vice versa, how does the success of a more moderate movement party impact upon the movement's radical flank.

The relationship between moderate and radical factions

For the first time in Swedish history a radical nationalist political party – the Sweden Democrats – has emerged from its roots in the Swedish neo-Nazi movement, to become a political force to be reckoned with on the national level. Alongside its now dominant political wing, the broader neo-Nazi ultra nationalist movement nonetheless appears to flourish (see also Chapter 13 regarding the reinforcing relationship between AfD and Pegida). While there is general agreement on the broad political objectives of the movement, the Sweden Democrats differ from the more militant factions in their strategy for achieving them. This may, or may not, cause uneasy tensions between the various militant factions, and between these factions and the dominant political wing in the movement. How, and in what ways, does a radical movement flank alter the context for a dominant movement party – and vice versa?

Hypothetical scenarios

In order to grasp the multi-polar relationship between the Sweden Democrats and its radical flank we can posit a number of possible scenarios. These scenarios are not necessarily mutually exclusive, but serve as ideal relational tools for the analysis. *Scenario One* suggests that the success of the Sweden Democrats has limited the 'organizational space' for other competing flank parties, organizations, and networks. The success of the Sweden Democrats has saturated the organizational space, leaving little room for competitors to attract the necessary resources to emerge, develop, or even survive. Scenario one has found solid empirical support by a number of scholars analysing the relations between dominant movement parties and radical flanks in Western Europe and Eastern-Central Europe (see Chapter 2, this volume). According to these scholars, if there is an established parliamentary party which articulates a similarly radical agenda, the space for a radical flank shrinks, since potential supporters and economic resources will be siphoned off to the established party. The movement party's gain is a loss for the radical flank.

Recognizing that social movements are very rarely homogeneous, but consisting of factions and flanks, some scholars have studied intra-movement relations in terms of 'radical flank effects' (Gupta 2007, 2013; Ellefsen, forthcoming). Herbert H. Haines (1984), the pioneer working within this conceptual framework, suggests two other possible scenarios.

The activities of radicals in a social movement can undermine the position of moderates by discrediting movement activities and goals, and by threatening the ability of moderates to take advantage of the resources available from supportive third parties. I refer to this general backlash as the *negative radical flank effect* (Haines 1984: 32, emphasis in original).

> Conversely, a *positive radical flank effect* can occur when the bargaining position of moderates is strengthened by the presence of more radical groups. [...] The radicals can provide a militant foil against which moderate strategies and demands are redefined and normalized — in other words, treated as 'reasonable'.

Hence we have *Scenario Two* in which the Sweden Democrats' electoral appeal has been weakened by the increasingly violent provocations on the part of the radical flank, as the party's coalitional potential has been weakened. *Scenario Three*, on the other hand, implies that the extremism of the neo-Nazi and ultra nationalist radical flank has worked to normalize the more moderate demands and rhetoric of the Sweden Democrats, increasing their electoral appeal as well as their coalitional potential. Zald and McCarthy (1979: 11–12) call this the function of the radical flank in the struggle of moderate organizations for legitimacy.

Lastly, a *Scenario Four* would suggest that the success of the Sweden Democrats has strengthened the neo-Nazi movement's radical flank and, in turn, the radical flank has enhanced the respectability of the Sweden Democrats thereby strengthening them; in short, a 'win-win' scenario. Before I return to an evaluation of these possible scenarios, I will address the Sweden Democrats' 'make-over process' and briefly map the disarrayed terrain of the wider neo-Nazi movement in Sweden.

The Sweden Democrats and their makeover process[3]

Formed in 1988, the Sweden Democrat Party (SD) elected Anders Klarström as its first president. Klarström and most of the first members of the party executive had backgrounds in the neo-Nazi movement, and some had backgrounds in the violent militant right at that time (Larsson and Ekman 2001: 126; Gestrin 2007: 153). During the 1990s, anti-racist activists persistently challenged Sweden Democrat manifestations; for the burgeoning anti-racist movement the Sweden Democrat Party was its focal opponent and the two sides in the 'drama of immigration in Sweden' were repeatedly embroiled in violent encounters (Peterson 1997). Despite these confrontations, the party began the laborious process of transformation to become a democratically legitimate party. This work began in 1995 when the newly elected party president Mikael Jansson prohibited Nazi salutes and the wearing of uniforms at party manifestations and renounced Nazism in 1999. Initially the party patterned itself after the British National Front and was at this time partially funded by the Front National, and joined the European nationalist network (Euro-Nat) (Hellström and Nilsson 2010: 58). It achieved its first electoral successes in 1998, gaining eight seats in municipal assemblies in southernmost Sweden. In 2005, the new party leader Jimmy Åkesson continued with even more vigour the efforts to reform the party along the lines of the more successful far-right parties in Western Europe (Rydgren and Ruth 2011: 4). Its first major electoral breakthrough came in 2006 when it secured 2.9% of the vote at the national level, and representation in approximately half of Sweden's municipalities. The success of the party in the 2006 elections had a springboard effect for their success in 2010 when the party entered parliament with 5.7% of the vote at the national level (Peterson and Mattsson-Wallinder 2012). Electoral support for the party increased dramatically in the 2014 parliamentary elections when they collected 12.9% of the vote and 17.53% in the 2018 elections.

The Sweden Democrats have evolved from a movement party firmly rooted in its neo-Nazi movement origins to a party with significant electoral appeal. This evolution has followed with organizational developments that have successfully distanced the party from its movement roots. In order to enhance the appeal of the party among the electorate, the party rid itself of its most radical militant elements (Peterson 2016). The Sweden Democrats have undergone many of the internal organizational strategies which are characteristic of movement parties during a process of reform. As Schwartz (2000: 460) points out, factionalism is a frequent characteristic of movement parties, the result of power struggles and ideological disputes. Factions have formed within the Sweden Democrats between 'hardliners' and a new generation of political entrepreneurs bent on transforming the party into a viable alternative in the electoral arena. Factionalism, as a result of internal power struggles, led to a split in the party in 2001 when hardliners founded the National Democrats. The factionalism has continued with purged and/or disgruntled members leaving to either join other more radical party alternatives or forming new political alternatives on the movement's radical flank. These purges or strategy of purification have been employed to weed out members that have been regarded as jeopardising the party's integrity. There have been ongoing purges when party officials have been expelled for public statements that have put in question the sincerity of the party's reform process, e.g. overt and offensive racist claims or support for Nazism (Hellström and Nilsson 2010: 69). I argue that the purges have revitalized the radical flank, a point I will return to in the next section.

One of the first measures in 2006 that the new leadership took was to replace the earlier party flag with a burning torch held in a clenched fist (modified from the British National Front symbol) to its new symbol, the hepatica flower (the established parties in Sweden traditionally have flowers as their party symbols). Jimmie Åkesson motivated this change in the following words:

> We have carried out profound changes to the better and we are not the same party we were ten or fifteen years ago. It is logical that these changes are also manifested in our outward symbols.
>
> *(cited in Palani 2011: 26)*[4]

The change of the party's symbol heralded the new leadership; it dramatically announced to the party's members that a new leadership with new goals for the party had taken the helm. The new leadership set out upon a strategy of moderation to convince the electorate that it has 'cleaned out its closet and should now be regarded as the most viable democratic alternative' (Hellström and Nilsson 2010: 66–67).

The primary adaption strategy undertaken by the Sweden Democrats leadership during the 2000s was a makeover of the party's ideological basis (Peterson 2016). While the movement party worked to tone down the party's connection to Nazism and the neo-Nazi movement in the 1990s, during the 2000s the party step-by-step toned down its racist and nationalist discourse, choosing a more general diluted rhetoric. This was not an uncontroversial course in their makeover process. The controversy came to its head during the debates over the new party programme during their congress in November 2011. The new party programme set in centre stage the new party ideology – 'social conservatism' – that would convince voters that they offered the 'third way' in Swedish politics. Jimmie Åkesson motivated the ideological turn in the following words:

> By calling us social conservative we secure our position in the middle by being both pragmatically left and right. We remind voters that we believe in the Swedish model of political consensus. Secondly, we confirm our role as a people's home party, that we reinstate the values of the people's home.[5]
> *(SVT, Jimmie Åkesson, 2011 party congress speech)*

Two major points were raised in the ensuing debate over the new party programme, which engaged 10 opponents and 13 supporters (Peterson 2016). Firstly, opponents of the programme were concerned that nationalism as the guiding ideological principle now took on a secondary position. 'Redefining our ideology from nationalism to social conservatism is not a broadening of our politics but a step to the side. We do not have the mandate to abandon nationalism' (SVT, Patrik Repo, 2011 party congress). Secondly, a major bone of contention was the process by which the programme had been formulated. 'A party with *movement traditions* should have had a longer period to discuss its contents. A political programme is not the work of one man' (SVT, Patrik Ehn, 2011 party congress; my emphasis).

> We need a vigorous debate. We need to be either 100% behind the programme or 100% opposed, but we do not have any leeway to come with suggestions for changes. We have not had an adequate democratic process so the programme does not have the full support of party members.
> *(SVT, Gustav Kasselstrand, 2011 party congress)*

Factionalism occurred again in 2017 as a result of a power struggle between the Sweden Democrats Youth organization (SDU) and the mother party. SDU's charismatic leader Gustav Kasselstrand, together with William Hahne, was purged from the party in 2015. In spring 2017, the Sweden Democrats took the radical step to disband its youth organization, purging a further six prominent members, and forming a new organization, Young Swedes. The party had rid itself from some critical voices, but it has also led to a new young generation re-entering the movement with the formation of a new party – Alternative for Sweden, modelled on Alternative for Germany (AfD). Kasselstrand emphasized that their exclusion was part of a power game, not the result of dissentient ideological positions. At the same time, he took the opportunity to condemn the 'radicalism' of Nordic Youth.[6] It appears as if this new party intends to lock heads with the Sweden Democrats with a similar ideology and electoral strategy. The question remains if this new party has the resources to compete with SD, and the research would indicate not.

Party discipline was used throughout the 2000s to discourage party members participating in the annual ritual demonstrations and manifestations staged by the movement: e.g. Charles XII commemorations and the so-called Salem marches that brought more than a thousand extremist participants each year (Lööw 2016a); these were marches that SD had taken part in as central actors in the 1990s. Since the mid-2000s, SD has been reluctant to run the risk of being equated with the movement's radical flank. An important strategy in the makeover process has been for party leadership to exercise discipline to maintain a relative autonomy to the wider movement and its radical fringe (see Haines 1998: 182). In short, party discipline, factional splits, and purges have left the party with relative decisional autonomy with respect to the wider neo-Nazi ultra nationalist movement from which it springs. However, this autonomy is relative and fragile. Despite the party leadership's efforts to distance themselves from the wider movement, the connections run deep. When *Expo* and the newspaper *Expressen* examined all of the 2014 SD candidates in the municipal, regional, and parliamentary elections who had a Facebook page, one out of three either liked or spread materials from the radical flank, unapproved by party leadership (Poohl 2014). Party discipline has proved difficult to enforce. A delegate to the party's national congress in November 2017, in direct TV transmission, claimed that Muslims on a scale of 'humanity' could be more or less placed as non-humans. The police were notified the same day, and SD's party leadership banned him from the congress venue, and subsequently purged the delegate from the party. Party leader Jimmie Åkesson is cited as claiming 'this is the worst I have heard' (*Aftonbladet* 25 November 2017). In the next section, I will map the wider movement.

The Swedish neo-Nazi ultra nationalist movement

The movement's political party arm(s)

As Heléne Lööw (2016a and 2016b) has pointed out, the neo-Nazi ultra nationalist movement has throughout its existence been deeply divided. The movement has historically organized around competing political parties, locked in power struggles, which was an obstacle for a parliamentary breakthrough during the interwar years when their combined numbers would have indicated otherwise (Lindström 1983). Many neo-Nazi and fascist parties have come and gone throughout the history of the movement. They have been in competition, small, and generally embroiled in power struggles (Lööw 2016b). It was first in 2010 that the movement acquired a dominant political party able to take the electoral step into parliament. However, that has not meant that the movement is united. Then, as now, the movement was split between factions supporting forming parties appealing (more or less) to the electorate, and a more radical flank seeking a revolutionary extra parliamentary political avenue of struggle, together with combinations of these two strategies.

As we saw above, factionalism has recently led to the formation of Alternative for Sweden. An earlier split within the Sweden Democrats led to the formation of the National Democrats, which assumed its place beside the Sweden Party, which had emerged out of 'Keep Sweden Swedish' and the Swede's Party, which had in turn emerged out of National Socialist Front in 2008 and disbanded 2015. Skåne Party, in existence since 1979, is a regional nationalist anti-immigration and anti-Islam party. The New Swedish Movement and Sweden's National Association were both Nazi organizations from the interwar period, and while they disbanded in the early 1990s, individuals from these organizations were influential in building both the Skåne Party and the Sweden Democrats (Lööw 2016a: 42). Forming competing parties remains popular within the wider neo-Nazi ultra nationalist movement. However, the National Democrats (disbanded 2014) and the Swedes' Party have only had local impact, gaining seats in scattered municipal governments (through SD mandates). The Skåne Party had been relatively successful in the region of Skåne, but in municipal elections since 2006 has lost votes to the Sweden Democrats. Skåne is the region where SD has garnered their most votes. Scenario one, where the organizational space for competing political parties is constricted by the success of a more moderate movement party, appears to find support; however, the movement has always had small competing parties, and as I have pointed out, SD is the first movement party to reach this level of dominance. However, the neo-Nazi ultra nationalist movement is not only its flora of parties, but also includes a militant revolutionary flank with a violent extra parliamentary agenda.

The radical revolutionary flank

Today's radical revolutionary flank in the Swedish neo-Nazi ultra nationalist movement has historically evolved from its Nazi roots to now also include ideas from the US white supremacy movement. During the 1980s and 1990s, movement activists began importing racialist ideas and organizational strategies from the US white supremacy milieu, blending with Sweden's heritage of fascist and Nazi ideas and parties. Alongside the political parties mentioned above, these new influences brought two new developments to the wider movement. Firstly, propaganda campaigns using local 'free' radio, and later the Internet, gained in intensity, and were even further fuelled by the spread and popularity of 'white power' music. This latter trend brought many new and younger supporters, what Lööw (2016a) calls sympathetic 'consumers'. Secondly, during the 1980s and 1990s, a wave of violence targeting immigrants and homosexuals appeared, spurred on by new paramilitary groups inspired by the US' The Order (Peterson 1997). While most of these groups, organizations and parties have largely come and gone, the individuals have remained, realigning in new power constellations. Both the political arm and the activist arm of the neo-Nazi ultra nationalist movement are fluid, inventing and reinventing themselves. Let us now turn to the organizations, networks, and social media outlets in the radical flank.

Together with Legion Wasa, a small paramilitary group, the Nordic Resistance Movement (NMR) founded in 1997, originally under the name the Swedish Resistance Movement, is today the most radical organization/network in the neo-Nazi ultra nationalist movement in Sweden, as well as in Denmark, Norway and Finland. A High Court decision on 30 November 2017 declared the organization illegal in Finland.

NMR, understood as a neo-sect (Peterson 2001), has favoured an image of a close community of 'elects', emphasizing purity rather than proselytization, exclusivity rather than expansion (also della Porta 1992). However, in the last few years they have staged a number of high-profile public actions, which have marked a shift in their strategy from being a relatively small covert sect of 'elects' to a strategy that opens up for recruits to join them in their demonstrations if they share NMR's ideology. NMR now has a multi-level system of membership, with the neophytes only loosely associated with the 'core' of the organization. Hence, the neophytes are closer to the status of non-participants, from which *testing and education* can eventually lead him to grasp the totality or core of the association, i.e. the secrets of the organization (Peterson 2001). NMR's core thus gains protection and isolation from the outside through the buffer of partially initiated. Consequently, NMR's core can retain its sense of purity and exclusivity, while opening its doors to neophytes to march in their demonstrations, and to participate in at least some of their more public actions, thereby expanding their numbers.

Between 2010 and 2014, NMR's actions increased by 30%. However, most of the actions were connected to spreading propaganda and internally orientated activities, e.g. combat training and educational meetings (Jakobsson 2014). After 2014 NMR has shifted its focus. Since 2015, the NMR has staged a significant number of large and smaller protest events. NMR has staged, now augmented by the organization's neophytes, highly publicized demonstrations during 1 May, in conjunction with the annual 'political week' *Almedalen* on the island of Gotland, violently intervened at Pride parades, together with a number of unregistered demonstrations with members dramatically marching in formation in uniforms with their shields, flags, and banners through central city streets.

These demonstrations have been highly provocative, for example, a demonstration staged on Yom Kippur in conjunction with the largest book fair in

Scandinavia in Gothenburg 2017. The demonstration, which was stopped by the police, brought tens of thousands of counterdemonstrators to the city, reminding us that since the early 1990s, immigration and ethnic relations constitute the most prominent and controversial field of protest contention in Sweden (Peterson 1997; also regarding Western Europe, see Koopmans et al. 2005: 3). Then as now, the number of neo-Nazi ultra nationalist participants does not match its prominence (Hutter and Kriesi 2013). Classical cultural liberal counter-protesters outnumbered the neo-Nazis more than 20 to 1 in the event above.

Three men connected to NMR were convicted for the bombing of a syndicalist locale in Gothenburg in November 2016 and the bombing and the attempted bombing of two asylum accommodations in January 2017 (*Göteborgs posten* 2017.02.04). The perpetrators were not leaders or 'core' members of NMR, and might have been acting on their own as an attempt to 'prove' themselves as 'worthy and dedicated' neo-Nazis (*Svenska dagbladet* 2017.02.10). We can only speculate. Nonetheless, neophytes and less connected members can act as rogues, undermining the control of the core over strategic decisions, which is an inevitable potential problem for neo-sects in general (Peterson 2001).

According to the Global Terrorism Data Base, the number of terror attacks in Sweden between 2010 and 2015 by right-wing extremists rose dramatically to peak in 2015, with 36 recorded arson attacks. Most of the attacks were directed towards asylum accommodations and care homes for adolescent refugees.[7] However, hidden among these statistics is a significant number of unrecorded attacks, and none of the attacks on Roma were included in the data. In general, the tone in social media was, and continues to be, highly aggressive (Gardell 2016). Five days before the attack on a school in a small city in west Sweden by a costumed extremist wielding a 'Viking sword', leaving three ethnic minority victims dead and one severely injured, the perpetrator logged into a site that distributed the speech made by Kent Ekeroth, member of parliament for the Sweden Democrats and then the party's representative in the Justice Committee, to a gathering of party members and assorted neo-Nazis in southern Sweden.

> The Swedish people have a long fuse. But when that fuse has burned out, then they explode. And we will show them: now it is going to explode! We don't have time to wait any more. You are the spearhead we need to take back our country. We are the resistance movement.
>
> *(cited in Gardell 2016)*

The response to the attack on social media was chilling, in which his actions were acclaimed for 'making our world a little safer for the rest of us', 'it's time to load rifles and sharpen knives', 'may Odin be with the person that freed Trollhättan from the scum', 'a big day for Sweden. Death to 'black heads'' (Gardell 2016). On the young perpetrator's computer, police uncovered a potpourri of violence, racism, and fascism, with films celebrating Hitler, Anders Behring Breivik, and Jimmy Åkesson, leader of the Sweden Democrats (Gardell 2016).

While police have cleared up relatively few arson attacks, the perpetrators that have been brought to prosecution are generally young local men and boys who are not, or are only loosely, connected to a neo-Nazi ultra nationalist organization or network. However, they have found their inspiration from social media and the Internet. The flora of neo-Nazi ultra nationalist alternative media in Sweden and Scandinavia is widespread and diverse. What had previously been an underground secret world is now digital, readily accessed by far more potential sympathizers. Primary outlets since 2015 are *Nya tider* (with links to SD) and *Nordfront* (Nordic Resistance Movement: NMR), and the site Avpixlat (with links to SD), but there are countless YouTube portals, and blog portals such as Motpol (Nordic AltRight), as well as Facebook pages, which attract supporters and which egg them on to acts of violence. 'Lone wolf' acts of terrorism are, of course, difficult to prevent (Gardell 2017).

Lööw (2016a: 78) emphasizes that alongside the organizations discussed here there are a myriad of different networks, such as Info-14, ideological 'producers', companies, and other small groups, such as Yellow Cross, making up the dense undergrowth of the radical flank of the Swedish neo-Nazi ultra nationalist movement. The latest addition to this undergrowth is Nordic AltRight, an Internet-based network with thousands listening to their podcasts. In May 2017, Christoffer Dulny left his top position in SD's central offices to lead a Swedish subsidiary to the US AltRight Corporation; while denied by SD leadership, Dulny's defection demonstrates the close ties between SD and the radical flank. In addition to Dulny, Nordic AltRight is led by Daniel Friberg, who heads up Arktos Publishing and Motpol, and organizes an annual AltRight conference in Sweden, together with Richard Spencer, the subsidiary's US 'strategic consultant'.[8] Nordic AltRight's ambition is to consolidate the radical flank and act as an umbrella movement for the flora of organizations, networks, and parties in the neo-Nazi ultra nationalist movement, including, unexpectedly, a close relationship with NMR. They hope to acquire the same political influence that Alt-Right exercised during Trump's US campaign and now during his presidency.[9]

In order to sum up this section, and further clarify the relationship between SD as a movement party and the movement's radical flank, we will return to the Nordic Resistance Movement (NMR). In 2015, NMR surprisingly opened a new branch after seeking the necessary 1,500 signatures to register as a political party. NMR's organizational strategy was now to combine two branches: the party and its network of what they call activist 'nests' spread throughout the country. Klas Lund, the leader of NMR, in a speech in Stockholm 2015, explained his organization's relationship with the Sweden Democrats. He saw SD's electoral success functioning as a trailblazer for more militant and radical forces. Lund maintained that even if SD could reach a position of power in the 'out-dated political system', the party's efforts to reach their goals would be doomed to failure, which in turn would lead their members and sympathizers to seek a more radical alternative (Lööw 2016a: 76–77). 'The Nordic Resistance Movement must be the revolutionary and radical force that takes over and which the Sweden Democrats have involuntarily cleared the way for' (cited in Lööw 2016a: 77). It is clear that NMR's political branch was not intended to be a party working within a representative democracy. And interestingly he sees the success of the Sweden Democrats as having cleared the way for more revolutionary forces. In the following pages, I will return to our questions: How does a radical flank impact upon the outcomes for a more moderate dominant movement party? And vice versa, how does the success of a more moderate movement party impact upon the movement's radical flank?

Same movement, different actors, different roles

In order to simplify the concluding discussion, I will limit my analysis to comparing the movement party, the Sweden Democrats (SD), and the Swedish movement's (at this time) most militant flank organization, the Nordic Resistance Movement (NMR). The most obvious difference is their strategic orientations, less so their goals. Firstly, SD has successively under their makeover process opted for a more moderate incremental strategy for social change, the depth of their challenge far more moderate than that of NMR, an organization which seeks fundamental revolutionary change. Secondly, in regards to their breadth of appeal, we have SD with a mass strategic orientation, and NMR with an insular strategic orientation. SD is seeking a wide social base, in the case of a movement party, maximising their appeal with the electorate. NMR, as we discussed above, has an entirely different organizational strategy, appealing to a relatively small core of dedicated, highly committed activists (see Downey and Rohlinger 2008). Same movement, different actors – a moderate movement party and a radical flank organization – how does this influence their interactions and the roles they play?

SD's electoral success has been dependent upon convincing the electorate that the party is a viable, legitimate choice, hence their makeover process that distances them from the more revolutionary actors in the wider movement (Peterson 2016). In response to NMR's disruptive participation during the annual 'politics week', *Almedalen*, in 2017, SD party leader Jimmie Åkesson is quoted as saying:

> NMR is a terrorist organization. If one uses political violence then one is in first hand a terrorist and not a politician and then one should be dealt with in another way than other political organisations.[10]

This is a clear example of what Haines (1984: 32) called the 'positive radical flank effect' in which 'the radicals can provide a militant foil against which moderate strategies and demands are redefined and normalized – in other words, treated as "reasonable"'. This is what Zald and McCarthy (1977) maintained was the function of a radical flank in a moderate flank's struggle for legitimacy. While the ultimate goals of SD and NMR may be very similar, Åkesson used the opportunity to assure the electorate that SD could not abide their use of political violence. Åkesson contrasted NMR's revolutionary tactics with their own political tactics, and so emphasized SD's legitimacy in the political system, a strategic articulation in relation to NMR by emphasising their differences (also Haines 1988: 182). The NMR, on the other hand, as discussed above, understands SD's role in the movement as 'clearing the way' for more revolutionary actors. Lund, the optimistic leader of NMR, speculated that SD would ultimately be unable to achieve their goals in the present political system, thereby opening the doors for his own organization's revolutionary and non-democratic strategy to be given a place in the struggle. Lund, speaking for NMR, the most radical flank actor, appeared to see SD and their electoral success, at this time, as a complement to his own organization's activities, not as a competitor. Both SD and NMR see their roles in the neo-Nazi ultra nationalist movement as distinctly separate. NMR, on the one hand, perceives SD as a complement to their struggle, and judging by the acceleration in their militant actions, they are feeling wind in their sails because of SD's electoral success. SD, on the other hand, appears to see NMR as neither a complement nor a competitor to the movement. SD, bent on maximising electoral votes, employs the function of the radical flank – NMR – as a foil to their own party to increase their legitimacy, which as Haines (1984 and 1988) points out can be a very valuable tool. SD's and NMR's strategic articulation of their interactions are different, but not necessarily exclusive for the wider movement.

Before we return to our hypothetical scenarios, it is important to keep in mind that my case study lacks the essential characteristics of a controlled investigation, in contrast to studies based on solid quantitative research, which suggest that the space for radical protest in Western Europe, in our case, on the part of the radical revolutionary flank of the neo-Nazi ultra nationalist movement, will contract or close with the emergence of a successful parliamentary movement party, in our case the Sweden Democrats (see Chapter 2, this volume). Their findings are difficult to refute. Nevertheless, the (at best) sketchy data available for my case study in Sweden, does not support Scenario One. If anything, the success of the Sweden Democrats appears to have emboldened and bolstered the radical flank. And even if we cannot measure with any accuracy the numbers of activists and supporters of the radical flank, we can state with some confidence that the radical flank has not shrunk, and its actions have both increased in numbers and taken on a new militant public face. On the one hand, the sheer numbers of participants in the neo-Nazi ultra nationalist flank have never been, historically or today, anything but marginal. I cannot provide data that indicates that the number of participants since the 1990s to the present has either increased or decreased. On the other hand, the number of the flank's actions fluctuates, and higher numbers and more intense periods have been observed in the late 1980s, late 1990s/early 2000s, and since 2015. Again, there is no reliable available data to suggest that the numbers of actions have decreased; only some of these organizations report their actions. During the high-profile periods listed above, they have assumed different characteristics. During the 2010s, when SD is enjoying its parliamentary success, reported terrorist actions by flank groups or non-affiliated groups/individuals, e.g. arson attacks, bombings, murders, have increased, peaking in 2015. The number of their manifestations, marches, and demonstrations has also increased, and these public actions have also become more provocative and confrontational, and have garnered intensive media coverage during 2016–2017. To be sure, the number of counterdemonstrators far out-numbers the neo-Nazi ultra nationalist activists on the streets, but that is to be expected: the same was true in the 1990s. My argument is that the radical space has not contracted, but opened for the role that the radical revolutionary flank plays for the wider neo-Nazi ultra nationalist movement, and for its dominant movement party SD. The number of radical revolutionary activists is not necessarily a key to understanding their impact. More important is their commitment and their ability to gain media attention. In this sense, the radical flank in the Swedish movement has been very successful – capturing, for example, widespread coverage weeks prior to and after their aborted demonstration in Gothenburg on 30 September 2017. The participation of *Nya Tider,* the SD linked periodical, with a booth at the Gothenburg Book Fair also resulted in massive media debate. The book fair's director faced severe criticism for allowing their participation, and a significant number of authors subsequently boycotted the fair, and alternative events were arranged across the city. The book fair lost more than a quarter of their visitors.[11] These examples remind us that it is not necessarily the number of participants, but the actions' level of provocation and the media attention these actions are awarded that determines their impact and subsequent success. Widespread media coverage means that the issue of immigration and integration dominates the public discourse, ultimately benefitting the parliamentary movement party – i.e. SD.

Scenario Two, Haines' (1984) 'negative flank effect', did not find any support in my study. SD has been very successful in distancing the party from both its relatively recent neo-Nazi roots, and the actions of the wider movement. While media, and the mainstream political parties, have emphasized this relationship, it has not won traction among the electorate. SD has not been affected by guilt by association, measured by the party's stable support in public opinion surveys, hovering around 15%. Rune Ellefsen (forthcoming) concludes that the negative radical flank effect is most common when moderate and radical flanks cooperate and coordinate their actions, which appears to be presently the case in Germany (Chapter 13). This was not the case in the Swedish neo-Nazi ultra nationalist movement.

Scenario Three, which suggests that the radical flank and their actions can provide a foil for a more moderate movement party to emphasize their strategic differences and thereby functions to enhance their political legitimacy, finds, I argue, strong support in my case study. The Sweden Democrats' strategic orientation is in stark contrast with that of the radical flank. This has had the result, I argue, that their goal for limiting immigration has won growing sympathy among the electorate, and increasingly among some parliamentarians – the new 'normal' in Europe. In contrast with the virulent rhetoric of the radical flank, SD's goals and rhetoric appear 'reasonable', and the discourse of anti-immigration has become more and more normalized, as witnessed in Sweden's drastic turnabout in its refugee policy, now amongst Europe's most restrictive – 'the death of the most generous country on earth' (Peterson 2017).[12]

Lastly, we have Scenario Four: a 'win-win' situation. The spectacular electoral successes of the Sweden Democrats have strengthened the radical flank, while the radical flank, in turn, has enhanced the respectability of the Sweden Democrats thereby normalising the party's rhetoric and political goals (Scenario Three). It is Scenario Four that I argue finds the most solid support in my case study. It appears that indeed in Sweden, the movement party has been able to employ the function of the radical flank as a foil to contrast their 'democratic' strategic orientation with the radical fringe's revolutionary and violent strategic orientation, which appears to have obscured for the voters the fact that their goals, if not their tactics or official rhetoric, are more or less the same. SD's demands have in contrast with the rhetoric from the revolutionary flank have become more or less normalized.[13] The radical flank, in turn, appears to thrive in the wake of the Sweden Democrats' electoral success. I have no firm data that the numbers of revolutionary radical activists have increased, or decreased, for that matter; nor do I have reliable data that the numbers of the flank's actions have increased or decreased, but they have become more provocative. Through the strategic targeting of their place and timing, their actions have become increasingly confrontational, and have hence acquired significant media attention. The Swedish neo-Nazi ultra nationalist movement, both its movement party and the wider movement's radical flank, and most of the established parliamentary parties (Peterson 2016), together with the Swedish anti-racist movement, have locked horns in an increasingly polarized climate around the issue of immigration and integration, which is thus effectually kept on the political agenda.

Conclusion

My study does not refute the work discussed in the introduction and that has not been the intention of the chapter. A dominant movement party, which achieves parliamentary status, may very well constrict the space for (some) other actors in the wider movement, particularly if the analysis focuses simple numbers. My point has been to emphasize, in a specific movement, the different roles a movement's actors play. A more moderate movement party and the wider movement's radical flank play *different* roles in the movement's struggle; not necessarily competing *or* cooperating, and not mutually exclusive, but, in some cases, mutually beneficial – same movement, different actors, different roles.

Notes

1 I have chosen to use throughout this chapter a descriptive term for the Swedish movement and not the generic term 'radical right movement'. The reason is perhaps specific to the Swedish case. Aside from the US inspired organisations/networks/groups, the Swedish movement is centre and centre-left on the left–right political dimension (Erlingsson et al. 2013), favouring a regulated market economy, economic redistribution, and in the case of the Sweden Democrats, a solidaristic (albeit chauvinistic)

welfare model (Erlingsson et al. 2013). The economic positioning of the Swedish movement reflects in part the entrenched ideology of a 'people's home' and the welfare model, and in part, the influence of the country's interwar Nazi movement upon the contemporary movement. National Socialism, and its anti-capitalism stance, lives on, particularly in the ideology of the Nordic Resistance Movement (NMR). In my descriptive term, neo-Nazism alludes to the movement's Nazi roots and continued ideological influence and ultra nationalism to the more recent ideological and organisational imports from the US white supremacy movement.

2 Again, throughout this chapter I am not using the adjective generically, but strictly descriptively. In this chapter 'radical' refers to actors whose rhetoric and tactics are generally perceived as illegitimate and threatening and whose goals call for fundamental social change.

3 This section has heavily drawn upon material from within: 'The Institutionalization processes of a neo-Nazi movement party: securing social movement outcomes' from Bosi, L., Giugni, M., Uba, K. (eds.) (2016) *The Consequences of Social Movements*, New York: Cambridge University Press, reproduced with permission.

4 All of the Swedish quotes have been translated by the author.

5 'People's home' in the Swedish political vernacular harks back to the origins of the Swedish welfare state in the 1930s. Åkesson is emphasising SD's commitment to the Swedish model and the values of welfare solidarity, positioning the party as centre-left on the left-right political dimension.

6 https://www.nordfront.se/Gustav-kasselstrand-och-william-hahne-bilder-ny-parti.se; accessed 2017 October 2008.

7 National Consortium for the Study of Terrorism and Responses to Terrorism (START). (2016). Global Terrorism Database [Data file]. Retrieved from https://www.start.umd.edu/gtd, 15 October 2017.

8 http//www.friatider.se/dulny-1-mnar-sd-f-f-alth-gern; accessed 25 October 2017; Richard B. Spencer is a prominent US white supremacist and president of the National Policy Institute, a white supremacist think-tank.

9 http://sverigesradio.se/sida/artikel.aspx?programid=83&artikel=6806378; accessed 25 October 2017.

10 HYPERLINK "https://www.aftonbladet.se/senastenytt/ttnyheter/inrikes-/article25292 069.ab" https://www.aftonbladet.se/senastenytt/ttnyheter/inrikes-/article25292069.ab; accessed 20 October 2017.

11 https://www.aftonbladet.se/kultur/a/3LVj9/bokmassans-vd-slutar; accessed 27 October 2017.

12 The title of James Traub's (2016) article.

13 Obviously it is not only the radical flank that has functioned to help 'normalize' SD's demands, but also the political context which emerged in the face of the so-called refugee crisis in autumn 2015, when under pressure from more and more voters in the electorate the main political parties have more or less abandoned their previous 'friendly' refugee policy (Peterson 2017).

References

della Porta, D. (1992) 'Political Socialization in Left-Wing Underground Organizations: Biographies of Italian and German Militants', *International Social Movement Research*, 4(1): 259–290.

Downey, D.J. and Rohlinger, D.A. (2008) 'Linking Strategic Choice with Macro-Organizational Dynamics: Strategy and Social Movement Articulation', *Research in Social Movements, Conflicts and Change*, 28: 3–38.

Ellefsen, R. (forthcoming) 'Deepening the Explanation of Radical Flank Effects: Tracing Contingent Outcomes of Destructive Capacity', *Qualitative Sociology*.

Erlingsson, G.Ó., Vernby, K. and Öhrvall, R. (2013) 'The Single-Issue Thesis and the Sweden Democrats', *Acta Politica*, 40(2): 196–216.

Gardell, M. (2016) 'Mördande propaganda', *Aftonbladet*. 22 October 2016.

Gardell, M. (2017) 'Lone-wolves: hatet från ensamagerande politisk våldsbrottslingar', in Dahlberg-Grundberg, H., Gardell, M., and Lööw, H. (eds) *Den ensamma terroristen? Om lone wolves, näthat och brinnande flyktingsförläggningar*, Stockholm: Ordfront.

Garner, R.A. and Zald, M.N. (1987) 'The Organisational Economy of Social Movement Sectors', in Zald, M.N. and McCarthy, J. (eds) *Social Movements in an Organisational Society*, New Brunswick, NJ: Transactions, 293–318.

Gestrin, H. (2007) *Högerextrema rörelser och deras symboler*, Stockholm: Natur och kultur.

Gupta, D. (2007) *Militant Flanks and Moderate Centers: The Struggle for Power and Influence in Nationalist Movements*. Phd. Dissertation presented to the Faculty of the Graduate School of Cornell University, Ithaca, New York.

Gupta, D. (2013) *The Strategic Logic of the Radical Flank Effect: Theorizing Power in Divided Social Movements*. Paper presented to the annual meeting of Midwest Political Science Association, Chicago, IL.

Haines, H.H. (1984) 'Black Radicalization and the Funding of Civil Rights: 1957–1970', *Social Problems*, 32(1): 31–42.

Haines, H.H. (1998) *Black Radicals and the Civil Rights Mainstream, 1954–1970*. Knoxville, TN: University of Tennessee Press.

Hellström, A. and Nilsson, T. (2010) "We Are the Good Guys': Ideological Positioning of the Nationalist Party Sverigedemokraterna in Contemporary Swedish Politics', *Ethnicities*, 10(1): 55–76.

Hutter, S. and Kriesi, H. (2013) 'Movements of the Left, Movements of the Right Reconsidered', in van Stekelenburg, J., Roggeband, C., and Klandermans, B. (eds) *The Future of Social Movement Research: Dynamics, Mechanisms, and Processes*, Minneapolis, MN: University of Minnesota Press, 281–298.

Jakobsson, J. (2014) 'SMR kapade SD-mandat', *Intolerans 14: En årsrapport från stiftelsen Expo*, Stockholm: Expo, 18–19.

Koopmans, R., Statham, P., Giugni, M. and Passy, F. (2005) *Contested Citizenship: Immigration and Cultural Diversity in Europe*, Minneapolis, MN: University of Minnesota Press.

Larsson, S., and Ekman, M. (2001) *Sverigedemokraterna: Den nationella rörelsen.* Stockholm: Ordfront.

Lindström, U. (1983) *Fascism in Scandinavia 1920–1940*. Doctoral thesis. Umeå: Department of History, Umeå University.

Lööw, H. (2016a) *Nazism i Sverige 2000–2014*, Stockholm: Ordfront.

Lööw, H. (2016b) *Nazism i Sverige 1924–1979*, Stockholm: Ordfront.

Palani, N. (2011) 'Sverigedemokraterna: Från högerextremister till radikala högerpopulister — En idealtypsanalys av partiets politiska program', Unpublished manuscript. Karlstad: Department of Political Science.

Peterson, A. (1997) *Neo-Sectarianism and Rainbow Coalitions. Youth and the Drama of Immigration in Contemporary Sweden*, Aldershot, UK: Ashgate.

Peterson, A. (2001) *Contemporary Political Protest: Essays on Political Militancy*, Aldershot, UK: Ashgate.

Peterson, A. (2016) 'The Institutionalisation Processes of a Neo-Nazi Movement Party Securing Social Movement Outcomes', in Bosi, L., Uba, K., and Guigni, M. (eds) *The Consequences of Social Movements: People, Policies and Institutions*, Cambridge, UK: Cambridge University Press, 314–337.

Peterson, A. (2017) 'Humanitarian Border Workers in Confrontation with the Swedish State's Border Making Practices: 'The Death of the Most Generous Country on Earth'', *Journal of Border Studies*: 1–17.

Peterson, A. and Mattsson-Wallinder, Y. (2012) 'An Explorative Study of the Impact of Local Political Opportunity: Structures on the Electoral Mobilisation of the Far-Right Movement in Sweden', *Moving the Social*, 48: 111–132.

Poohl, D. (2014) 'Nya tider för valets segrare', *Intolerans 14: En årsrapport från stiftelsen Expo*, Stockholm: Expo, 18–19.

Rydgren, J. and Ruth, P. (2011) 'Voting for the Radical Right in Swedish Municipalities: Social Marginality and Ethnic Competition?', *Scandinavian Political Studies*, 34(3): 1–24.

Schwartz, M.A. (2009) 'Continuity Strategies among Political Challengers: The Case of Social Credit', *American Review of Canadian Studies*, 30(4): 455–477.

Traub, J. (2016) 'The Death of the Most Generous Country on Earth', *Foreign Policy.* 2016 February 2010.

Zald, M.N. and McCarthy, J.D. (1979) Social Movement Industries: Competition and Cooperation Among Movement Organizations. CRSO Working Paper no. 201. University of Michigan, Ann Arbor: Center for Research on Social Organization.

PART III

Central and Eastern Europe

10

LO AND BEHOLD

Jobbik and the crafting of a new Hungarian far right

Andrea L.P. Pirro

Introduction

The far-right *Jobbik Magyarországért Mozgalom* (Movement for a Better Hungary: Jobbik) entered the realm of institutional politics after meteoric performances at the 2009 European Parliament and 2010 national elections (14.8 and 16.7 per cent, respectively). The different interpretations of these outcomes have predominantly focused on Jobbik's articulation of anti-Roma and anti-corruption issues within demand-side and supply-side interactions (e.g. Bíró-Nagy and Róna 2011; Pirro 2014a). *Prima facie*, these readings would give credence to the diffusion of a potent master frame combining ethno-nationalist xenophobia and anti-establishment populism for the success of the contemporary far right (Rydgren 2005). While valid in principle, existing electoralist accounts have neglected other, more sociologically oriented, aspects of far-right emergence. Above all, the qualification of Jobbik as a social movement, and the interpretation of its undertakings through social movement theory, have played only a marginal role in the literature (Pirro forthcoming). The chapter seeks to redress this oversight by tackling the evolution of the Hungarian far right in the political process. While highlighting elements of continuity and discontinuity within the far-right milieu, this contribution should also come across as an explicit plea for interdisciplinary dialogue.

The far right's ability to draw on 'resonant' – but previously unaddressed – ideas (Tarrow 1994: 122) has generally enhanced its electoral prospects. Jobbik has to be listed among those actors that successfully interacted with its environment by advancing new interpretive frames for particular issues. Looking at the ways post-communist political actors have set to 'transform' the transformation process (Minkenberg 2015), moreover, the far right has exerted influence through differentiated effects on national policy dimensions (Pirro 2015a). This notwithstanding, elements and preconditions going beyond far-right 'effects' or 'impact'

(Minkenberg 2001; Schain et al. 2002), and the party-political or institutional arenas (Williams 2006), have received remarkably little attention. As success entails continuous investments to attain sufficient political leverage (McAdam 1999: 37), the chapter relies on the heuristic potential offered by the political process model to assess the fortunes of Jobbik.

Besides the intrinsic value of analysing political actors located at the intersection of the protest and electoral arena through multidisciplinary lenses, the chapter calls attention to an outsider group's disrupting potential within a system that has substantially spawned it (e.g. Schwartz 1976). The value of focusing on Jobbik's disrupting potential is meant to reinstate the role of agency in the political process and, thus, the importance of organisational strength and new master frames for the far right. Indeed, while the political opportunity structure may bear limited explanatory power for the crafting of a 'new' Hungarian far right, this chapter specifically looks at the ways Jobbik has mobilised resources along its path to collective action.

The chapter is structured as follows. First, I set the theoretical starting points of discussion, by highlighting the advantages and limits of turning to social movement theory for the analysis of the far right in general, and Jobbik in particular. Drawing on the political process model, I move on to analyse those conditions underlying Jobbik's emergence and consolidation. Finally, I conclude by summarising the value of the analytical strategy adopted in this chapter.

Social movement theory and the far right

Social movement studies and the scholarship on party politics have only rarely crossed paths in the analysis of the far right. There could be at least two reasons behind this oversight. From the perspective of social movement scholars, the investments of movements have been primarily directed at stopping 'threatening developments', redressing 'instances of injustice', and promoting 'alternative options to the managing of social life and economic activity' (della Porta and Diani 2006: 3). As a result, *progressive* social movements have taken the lion's share in the debate – being interpreted as inherent expressions of the good side of politics, with altruistic motivations and a pluralistic worldview. This reading would evidently clash with the *illiberal values* the far right is seen to foster. With their ideological core of 'nativism', the far right would represent a threat to the liberal-democratic status quo. Indeed, the far right argues that 'states should be inhabited exclusively by members of the native group ('the nation') and that non-native elements (persons and ideas) are fundamentally threatening to the homogenous nation-state' (Mudde 2007: 19). From the perspective of party politics scholars, events unfolding inside the institutional arena had been long considered separate from those taking place at the extra-parliamentary level, or in the protest arena. While there are, of course, exceptions to note (e.g. Minkenberg 2003; Rydgren 2005; Caiani et al. 2012; Hutter 2014; Castelli Gattinara and Pirro 2018; Pirro and Castelli Gattinara 2018), the interpenetration of social movement theory and party-political perspectives in the study of the far right can turn out to be more than a didactical exercise.

Scholars that have deployed tools of social movement theory in the analysis of the far right, or that have moved beyond narrow interpretations of the far right 'as political party', have indeed referred to the far right as a *collective actor* (Minkenberg 2003). This notion stems from the idea that, regardless of the arena in which it operates (i.e. party-political, movement, or subcultural), the far right expresses a collective commitment to nativist principles and organised investments (e.g. Melucci 1995). This particular interpretation not only emphasises the cognitive aspect of collective action – for it crafts internal self-identification and belonging for activists inside of it, and external recognition from the outside – but also hands-on agentic aspects.

Far-right collective actors may additionally take movement party clothes. As collective actors may operate in multiple arenas under the banner of a shared ideology, and yet remain substantially distinct in their quality or character, movement parties denote 'coalitions of political activists who emanate from social movements and try to apply the organizational and strategic practices of social movements in the arena of party competition' (Kitschelt 2006: 280). While a movement party is primarily defined as a hybrid and transitional organisation type along a trajectory of institutionalisation – i.e. the final stage of transition to the party form, when the organisation eventually 'solidifies' (Panebianco 1988: 49) – it may characterise the several activities of a single far-right organisation in the multi-organisational field. As I will argue further below, this connotation aptly resonates with the Hungarian Jobbik, which formed as a network of Christian right-wing students (*Jobboldali Ifjúsági Közösség*, Right-Wing Youth Association) in 1999 and transitioned to the party form in 2003.

Focusing on the contentious politics of nativism also increases the leverage of this analysis, not least by integrating demand-side and supply-side perspectives in a dynamic fashion. To be sure, far-right studies had already embarked on a similar endeavour (e.g. Eatwell 2003; Carter 2005; Pirro 2014a). Yet, they have by and large considered the institutional sphere as all-encompassing, thus neglecting grassroots aspects of mobilisation. Addressing those developments unfolding outside the institutional arena seems even more compelling in the face of collective actors in transition from the protest to the electoral arena (McAdam and Tarrow 2010; Pirro forthcoming).[1]

Possibly the most encompassing theory elaborated within the context of social movement studies is the 'political process model' (McAdam 1999). Aimed at redressing the irrational aspects of social strain subsumed in the classical model (e.g. Durkheim 1964), and the overly structuralist focus of the resource mobilisation approach (McCarthy and Zald 1977; Tilly 1978), the political process model moved to consider the level of organisation within the aggrieved group, and contributed to bring the political context of social movements and the transformation of consciousness into the equation (McAdam 1999; McAdam et al. 1996). While certainly not immune from criticism (e.g. Gamson and Meyer 1996; Goodwin and Jasper 1999), the political process approach has nevertheless helped tackling interactions between newer and older actors, and between unconventional forms of action and institution-alised interest representation (della Porta and Diani 2006: 17).

In analysing developments within the Hungarian far right, I will look at a particular 'tipping point' of accelerated change, consider the resources available to nativist collective actors, the evolution of far-right frames in the country, and the formal political opportunity structure. In reference to the political opportunity structure, it is worth noting that the concept has been stretched to the point that its expounding potential has been reduced to one of "dustbin' for any and every variable relevant to the development of social movements' (della Porta and Diani 2006: 17). In address-ing elements that might encourage or discourage movements to use their internal resources to take action (Tarrow 1996), I will thus focus on four elements in particu-lar: the openness or closure of formal political access; the prevailing strategies of political parties; the shifting of political alignments; and the constellation of oppo-nents and allies. The combination of these elements is claimed to grant activists more (or less) access to policy-making and, in general, participation and influence in the political sphere (e.g. Gamson 1990; Tarrow 1989).

The value of taking a social movement perspective and investigating these dimensions rests, above all, in Jobbik's emergence from, and substantial con-tinuity with, the Hungarian movement sector (Pirro and Róna 2018; Pirro and Castelli Gattinara 2018). The following section turns the attention to the broad socioeconomic processes, organisational strength, cognitive liberation, and politi-cal opportunities underlying the crafting of a new far right in Hungary.

Long time in the making or long overdue?

Germane to our discussion, Jobbik qualifies as a movement party essentially for two reasons; the way it aggregates interests, and the way it engages in extra-parliamentary activities (Kitschelt 2006). While numerous changes occurred in the internal organisation of the movement party after the 2018 elections,[2] Jobbik presents a rather diffuse leadership with one president, one deputy president, six vice-presidents, an articulate cabinet system, and, additionally, it relies on the input of local branches and grassroots members in its decision-making. Yet, most visibly, Jobbik retains a social movement profile for the significant emphasis it places on 'protest events' such as public rallies, demonstrations, and confron-tational activities. Despite its decision to take the electoral option, entering the party-political arena may have been dictated by the ambition to change the system from within, and may not necessarily have compelled the organisation to give up its movement principles and tactics (Pirro and Castelli Gattinara 2018).

The Hungarian far right in transition

As previously argued, Jobbik can be interpreted as a by-product of the Hungar-ian system. During its 'social movement phase' (1999–2003), Jobbik openly endorsed the activity of the mainstream party of the right, *Fidesz – Magyar Polgári Szövetség* (Hungarian Civic Alliance: Fidesz), seeking its re-election in 2002. After the *Magyar Szocialista Párt* (Hungarian Socialist Party: MSZP) gained power in 2002, however, the relationship between the youth organisation and Fidesz started to grow sour. At first, Viktor Orbán's party failed to support a demonstration organised by Jobbik (July 2002), which sought to have the ballots from the recent elections recounted (Bíró-Nagy and Róna 2013).

In the face of defeat, then, Fidesz turned to civil society to regain lost ground, on the premise that: 'Even if our parties and elected representatives might be in opposition in the parliament, we … will not and cannot be in opposition, because it is impossible for the nation to be in opposition' (Viktor Orbán, 7 May 2002). The *Polgári Körök* (Civic Circles) initiative, launched by Fidesz in the wake of the lost elections, was met with enthusiasm by Jobbik future leaders. However, the Civic Circles swiftly exhausted their political potential (Molnár 2016; but see Greskovits 2017 for a different, longer-term assessment), prompting Jobbik to take the electoral option in 2003 amid growing disenchantment with the state of the national right (Jobbik 2008).

Interpreting Jobbik's disruptive potential exclusively through its initial association with Fidesz and other nationalist milieus would be obviously reductive. Yet reference to an endogenous origin from the Hungarian system itself is quite compelling. The emergence and consolidation of a strong far-right contender has been a latent prospect ever since Hungary's transition to democracy. For one, the communist regime had proven little effective in curbing those nationalistic tendencies widespread among society. Upon transition, the nation's typified space (homeland), time (history), and agency (compatriots) had been swiftly re-established by means of ideal continuity with the pre-communist past (Csepeli 1991).

> [I]n the vacuum of post-communist politics, the recourse of most self-acclaimed conservatives was to the past, to political traditions with "Hungarian roots," to a policy of national and historical restoration. … [T]he vision of many of Eastern Europe's national conservatives is regressive, harking back to a folkloric utopia that they claim existed sometime, somewhere in their country's noble and glorious past. While even the radical restorationists pragmatically acknowledge that a return to the last century is neither feasible nor wholly desirable, they romantically seek to revive the values and traditions that had flourished in Hungary before the rude interruption of communism and other "foreign" ideologies, such as liberalism.
>
> *(Hockenos 1993: 112)*

The *Magyar Igazság és Élet Pártja* (Hungarian Justice and Life Party: MIÉP) set out to respond to these concerns in the early 1990s. Expelled from the then-ruling *Magyar Demokrata Fórum* (Hungarian Democratic Forum: MDF) for the publication of an essay with anti-Semitic and nativist contents (Csurka 1992), István Csurka first founded the *Magyar Út* (Hungarian Way) movement in January 1993, and then the MIÉP in July 1993. The party eventually made it to the Hungarian Assembly in 1998 with 5.47 per cent of the votes. At the height of success, the MIÉP managed to attract the urban lower middle class, the *déclassés* of rural areas, and the unemployed or pensioners part of the 'Christian middle class' – i.e. those portions of society that, 'by virtue of their social status, are incapable of keeping the pace with the socio-economic changes that the post-communist transition and the concomitant transfer to a market economy involve' (Szőcs 1998: 1101). This outlook might give weight to a socioeconomic grievance underlying the breakthrough of a well-organised movement with an 8,000-strong membership and some 300 grassroots organisations spread across the country (Bernáth et al. 2005: 82). Still, the *interaction context* should also be taken into account.

By the 1998 elections, Fidesz had already completed its ideological transformation into a mainstream conservative force (Kiss 2002). During its first term in government (1998–2002), Orbán's party had been preoccupied with attracting MIÉP voters; he occasionally flaunted a nativist discourse in order to build a 'united party comprising a united right wing' (*RFE/RL Newsline*, 23 September 2002). Fidesz's effort paid off, for it concomitantly succeeded in cementing its status of key player of the Hungarian right and 'cannibalising' the party of the far right. Even so, Fidesz could not take advantage of its improved performance in the 2002 elections, and was relegated in opposition due to increased voter turnout. Due to the last reason, the MIÉP failed to meet the 5 per cent threshold or, for that matter, ever enter parliament again.

The 2006 tipping point: condensed timing and reactive mobilisation

Appraising movement emergence 'over a long period of time in response to broad social, economic, and political processes' (McAdam 1999: 60) might justify the emergence of an aggrieved group like the MIÉP (or, better, the convergence of its support base at a particular point in time), though – by itself – not its swift decline. At the same time, the emergence of Jobbik, though linked to the MIÉP for their joint electoral alliance in 2006 (the *MIÉP-Jobbik – A Harmadik Út* split ticket), cannot be straightforwardly interpreted in terms of continuity of far-right grievances. To be sure, Jobbik reaped electoral fruits at a time of economic downturn, eventually entering the Hungarian Assembly in 2010. Yet, its rise had commenced before the breakout of the financial crisis that hit Hungary in 2008–2009, indicating that the economic crisis has been actually preceded and overshadowed by a crisis of political kind (e.g. Enyedi 2015). Unlike the MIÉP, moreover, Jobbik voters cannot be defined as losers of transition in a strict sociological sense (Krekó and Mayer 2015). As we will get to see, the crafting of a new Hungarian far right might have been long overdue, but not necessarily long in the making.

Moving beyond standalone macro-level accounts, it may be then worth focusing on the far right's *own* agency and disruptive potential amid the particular circumstances preceding Hungary's economic downturn. The year 2006 has been defined as a turning point for the fate of Hungarian civil society (Molnár 2016: 171), and its magnitude also resonated with the far right. In the wake of the 2006 elections, the recently re-elected MSZP might have suffered the biggest blow in its history. On 17 September 2006, *Magyar Rádió* broadcasted a private speech originally delivered by PM Ferenc Gyurcsány at a meeting held with MSZP MPs on 26 May. In the 'Őszöd speech', Gyurcsány admitted to having lied extensively in order to win another mandate at the elections held in April.

> There is not much choice. There is not, because we have fucked it up. Not a little but a lot. No European country has done something as boneheaded as we have. It can be explained. We have obviously lied throughout the past one and a half-two years. It was perfectly clear that what we were saying was not true. We are beyond the country's possibilities to such an extent that we could not conceive earlier that a joint government of the Hungarian Socialist Party and the liberals would ever do. And in the meantime, by the way, we did not do anything for four years. Nothing.
>
> *(Ferenc Gyurcsány, 26 May 2006)*

The leak led to grand scale upheavals in major Hungarian cities – particularly in Budapest, where protests erupted in full-blown riots and violence. Unrest lasted over a month, involving several thousands of protesters. The alleged cases of police brutality against demonstrators additionally presented the police as an instrument of political repression, thus further eroding the Socialist government's legitimacy (Molnár 2016: 172). Amid this rather exceptional occurrence, far-right activists spearheaded anti-government protests, *de facto* giving these 'reactive' mobilisations (McAdam and Tarrow 2010: 533) a strong nationalist imprint (e.g. Spiegel 2006; Pirro forthcoming). A good portion of the 'new radicals' involved in these demonstrations were either already part, or would later join, Jobbik's ranks (Mikecz 2015), helping shape what has been identified as the 'second generation' of the Hungarian far right (Kovács 2013).

Until that point, the far-right subculture consisted of many sparse groups attracting thousands of young activists, generally constrained by poor organisational skills and bound to political marginality (Pirro and Róna 2018). Hence, it is through a *snap reaction* in the midst of the 2006 protests that Jobbik managed to take advantage of a catalysing event and condense the timing usually required to transform a potentially explosive situation. As Vona himself stated, 'we actually needed the Autumn of 2006 – many of us woke up because of that' (Jobbik 2010). Partly counter to widespread views among political process scholars, who compel longer-term perspectives for the emergence of movements (McAdam et al. 2001: 147), the far right's re-emergence may have been sparked by a rather accidental event, and also come across as the primordial starting point for Hungary's oscillation of electoral regime, not to mention the 'illiberal turn' to be witnessed in subsequent years.

Mobilising human and financial resources

Within this context, the relevance of resource mobilisation and far-right agency cannot be neglected. Agency-oriented paradigms have played a marginal role in accounts on far-right parties (e.g. de Lange and Art 2011). Social movement studies, on the other hand, often stressed the tight link between mobilising public support and the maintenance of a semi- or quasi-professional organisation (della Porta and Diani 2006: 141). In the Hungarian case, Jobbik could rely on a group of committed activists, successfully expanding on this initial pool of human resources. Drawing from a sizeable membership of 1,500 towards the end of its social movement phase, Jobbik essentially preserved this figure intact upon registration as a party in 2003. Membership figures and member organisations grew steadily across time (Table 10.1), clearly providing a significant backbone of activists to transform grievances into successful collective action – and sustain them over time.

Besides the sheer number of members, another aspect may have proven relevant for organisational purposes – i.e. financial resources. In April 2006, Jobbik had contested elections in alliance with the MIÉP on their joint ticket, receiving 2.2 per cent of the votes nationwide. By no means an exceptional result, the outcome allowed Jobbik to access electoral reimbursements, as with any party crossing the 1 per cent threshold in Hungary. These resources were estimated at about 26 million forints – moneys transferred to the party through the donations of the *Új Radikalizmusért Alapítványa* (New Radicalism Foundation), i.e. Jobbik's principal funding body, established by Jobbik's then-president Gábor Vona (HVG 2010).

The combination of human and financial resources notably rendered possible the establishment of the *Magyar Gárda* (Hungarian Guard) in August 2007. The *Magyar Gárda* was founded and led by Vona, and has served as the non-armed paramilitary-like arm of Jobbik. Its creation can be interpreted as a response to yet another tipping point, i.e. the increased importance of the 'Roma issue' after the Olaszliszka assassination, whereby a teacher was murdered by a group of local Roma (Karácsony and Róna 2011). The organisation, which held a number of protest events across the country, set out to restore 'law and order' in rural areas with a high concentration of Roma minorities – areas where the presence of the state has steadily retrenched over the years. After its activities were held in breach of human rights, the organisation was disbanded by court ruling in July 2009. For the record, the *Magyar Gárda* has since continued its activities through different

TABLE 10.1 Jobbik membership figures and member organisations, 2003–2016

	2003	*2007*	*2008*	*2009*	*2010*	*2011*	*2013*	*2016*
Members	1,200	n/a	3,000	5,000	11,000	12,430	14,000	17,943
Organisations	n/a	80	249	387	750	800	n/a	n/a

Sources: MTI (2011); Új Szó (2011); Bíró Nagy and Róna (2013); Tóth and Grajczjár (2015); Pirro and Róna (2018); self-declared figures from personal interviews.

associations (e.g. *Új Magyar Gárda*, *Szebb Jövőért Magyar Önvédelem*, etc.), which are now only informally linked to Jobbik.

The successful mobilisation of resources has projected Jobbik into a self-sustaining circle. The activities of its non-armed militia received enormous media exposure – a form of publicity that concomitantly put Jobbik on the mainstream political map, and elevated it to viable electoral option. Estimates suggested that Jobbik's eventual entry to parliament in 2010 (16.7 per cent of the votes) granted it access to some 260 million forints of state funding on a yearly basis (HVG 2010) – a large capital to be reinvested in the growth of the organisation and the differentiation of its political supply, in both the protest and the electoral arena.

The new master frame

Jobbik has skilfully mobilised resources at a relatively early stage in its lifecycle. Generally interpreted as key in the consolidation phase of far-right organisations (Mudde 2007), Jobbik actually used its presence at the grassroots level to *break through* the Hungarian political system. As some observers argued, Jobbik had swiftly evolved from a marginal extremist party to 'a freedom-fighting force against its morally broken left-liberal opponent' (Tóth and Grajczjár 2015: 137). After initial exposure in the 2006 protests, Jobbik was thus charged with the elaboration of a new potent master frame to break from electoral marginalisation. In this respect, the typical ideology–organisation nexus according to which it is first important to mobilise on an issue, and then organise to preserve status, seems reversed in the specific case at hand.

The movement party first and foremost presented itself a populist anti-establishment actor. This attribute is engrained in its own genetic makeup, for Jobbik rose as an anti-corruption 'generational organisation' (Kovács 2013) – a definition which I hereby use to describe both its predominantly young support base (i.e. below 30 years of age) and its overall extraneousness to pre-1989 politics. At the time of the 2006 elections and protests, however, Jobbik had not yet elaborated on the issue of 'Roma criminality' that would grant it a following on its way to the 2009 European elections. Only with Vona's designation to presidency (November 2006) and through (his personal) investments in the *Magyar Gárda*, has Jobbik overtly defined its anti-Roma agenda.

By combining its anti-establishment profile with the issue of relationships between Roma and non-Roma in Hungary, Jobbik has, in turn, provided impetus to the process of cognitive liberation of a large group of disenchanted, but theoretically connected people (e.g. Piven and Cloward 1979: 3–4); and ultimately delivered a new far-right master frame, combining ethno-nationalist xenophobia with anti-political-establishment populism (Rydgren 2005). Disenchantment with established politics and negative attitudes towards ethnic minorities in Hungary have long offered a breeding ground for large-scale far-right mobilisations (Pirro 2014a). Therefore, the new master frame advanced by Jobbik seemed to resonate with the lived experiences, attitudes, and preconceptions of many people (Snow and Benford 1992).

Although the MIÉP had already tried to catalyse anti-Roma sentiments, its failure to capitalise on the issue arguably rested on its inability to frame aversion to ethnic minorities in cultural, rather than biological terms. Two interview excerpts may serve explicative purposes in this regard, and help differentiate between framings of the Roma issue, from a biologically based notion of racism (MIÉP), and an ethno-pluralist perspective (Jobbik), respectively.

> We can no longer recoil from the fact that there are also genetic reasons behind degeneration. We must acknowledge that disadvantaged strata and groups of our society have been with us for too long, groups where the severity of natural selection has not worked.
>
> *(István Csurka, quoted in Hockenos 1993: 160)*

> The Gypsy minority represents a national threat to public security. This issue has escalated into a problem that affects the majority of the Gypsy community – masses that have fallen out of education, the labour force, and that, in a time of crisis with cuts on social expenses, has resulted into crime.
>
> *(Márton Gyöngyösi, quoted in Pirro 2015b: 80)*

At a time of non-politicisation of a highly salient issue, Jobbik has been capable of beating the drum of 'Roma criminality', framing minority issues not necessarily in terms of biological inferiority, but in terms of security threats and cultural incompatibility (e.g. Betz and Johnson 2004).

Having profited from a rewarding discursive strategy, the movement party persuasively expanded its agenda to other issues related to its ideological core of nativism, authoritarianism, and populism. These included issues that romanticise the pre-communist past and help revive old myths, such as clericalism and irredentism; a 'social national' economic agenda; and a range of issues – including relations with ethnic minorities, corruption, and Euroscepticism – articulated in response to treacherous post-1989 developments (Pirro 2014b).

Political opportunities: whither closure?

Turning our gaze to the external supply side, social movement scholars have elaborated on how the political context may favour or hinder prospects for emergence, mobilisation, and success (e.g. McAdam 1999; Kriesi et al. 1995; Rucht 1996). In identifying dimensions relevant to the relationship between social movements and the institutional system, the elements outlined in the theoretical framework are evidence that the political context may overall have delivered discouraging signals to far-right activists, again reinstating the value of far-right agency in crafting its own regeneration and eventual fortunes amid unfavourable political opportunities. I elaborate on these external supply-side factors, from the most favourable and open, to the least.

For one, formal political access has been severely limited by the traditional closure of the Hungarian party system, hereby particularly referring to elements of structural competition (see Casal Bértoa and Enyedi 2016). In addition, the shifting of political alignments, eventually culminating in the outcome of the 2010 elections (Enyedi and Benoit 2011), suggests that any opening has, at best, been circumscribed. Before the 2006 tipping point, the prospect of an opening of political opportunities may have simply seemed non-viable. As elaborated above, however, the Hungarian left was projected into a deep crisis of legitimacy throughout the 2006–2010 mandate, ostensibly offering the possibility of oscillation of electoral regime as well as access for new political actors (Pirro forthcoming). While the realignment brought about by the 2010 elections granted both the far-right Jobbik and the Green/libertarian *Lehet Más a Politika* (Politics Can Be Different: LMP) access to parliament, Fidesz's rise to power immediately appeared to veer towards substantial system closure. In fact, Orbán's party's 'constitutional revolution' and continued dominance since 2010 may have posed serious challenges, not only to political competitors, but also to democracy as such (Herman 2016).

Most importantly, both before and after parliamentary representation, Jobbik could not rely on institutional allies, nor on a favourable set of strategies adopted by other political parties. Although not formally subject to a *cordon sanitaire*, Jobbik had been long ostracised from the Hungarian media, and excluded from cooperation with the other parties sitting in parliament. In order to overcome this first hurdle, the movement party made skilful use of the resources available; for instance, turning the internet into an indispensable outreach tool. Jobbik's popularity on Facebook and the dense far-right online networks have at least in part contributed to craft and sustain its relevance throughout (see e.g. Karl 2017). Only after the 2014 elections has Jobbik seen an increase its levels of coverage in the national media (NMHH 2017). In relation to institutional allies, however, the movement party had to go it alone through most of its political activity.[3]

In relation to the prevailing strategies adopted by political parties, Jobbik has additionally faced significant obstacles. As noted, Jobbik has consistently mobilised on a nativist and populist platform. Unlike the majority of far-right parties in Europe, however, Jobbik presents a rather broad palette of issues; the issues articulated range from the economy to foreign affairs, through to info-communication technologies (e.g. Jobbik 2014). The closure of this dimension would practically derive from the nativist route taken by Fidesz. Since 2010, Orbán's party has explicitly embarked on an illiberal trajectory, not least aimed at wooing far-right voters. This strategy has largely materialised by enhancing policies originally proposed by its far-right competitor, Jobbik. Original reference to Jobbik's diversified political platform is compelling, for Fidesz's co-optation extended beyond predictable nativist issues, such as ethnic minorities, or minorities abroad. In fact, it included social and economic policies, and clerical and moral issues, in addition to an ever-confrontational stance towards the EU (e.g. Pirro 2015a, 2015b, 2017). Amid the 'radicalisation of the mainstream' witnessed in Central and Eastern Europe (Minkenberg 2013), commentators have indeed wondered whether Fidesz should be deemed as radical as the far right (Mudde 2015; Pirro 2016).

A cursory look at Jobbik's electoral performance in 2014 would suggest that, despite the formal closure of opportunities, cannibalisation from Fidesz has not taken place. On the contrary, Jobbik has improved its scores and – at the time of writing – comes across as the biggest and most immediate electoral threat to Orbán's regime. This may as well depend on voters' preference for untried alternatives (e.g. Pop-Eleches 2010), or the legitimation of the far right conceded by Fidesz's implementation of Jobbik's policy proposals (e.g. Arzheimer and Carter 2006). Therefore, in the face of an ongoing strategy of rhetorical moderation on the part of Jobbik, the ability to sustain its profile of genuine nativist supplier currently – or, better, *once more* – seems to rest in its own hands.

Conclusions

Advocates of the political process approach have argued that the emergence of social movements depends upon a series of contingent factors. In this sense, developments within far-right milieus are by no means exceptional, as 'each community evolves according to its own inner rhythms and … its self-expressions and destinies are radically different, even unique' (Smith 1986: 138). Precisely for this reason, this chapter sought to treat the far right as a *normal* movement actor. The opportunity to draw on social movement theory for the study of the far right proves even more fitting in the Hungarian case, as the rejuvenation of nativist politics witnessed over the past decade indeed started *from below*. A precious toolkit for the analysis of far-right collective actors operating in multiple arenas, the application of the political process model also highlighted that not all the dimensions addressed played an equally relevant role in the fortunes of the far-right Jobbik.

In answering whether the crafting of a new Hungarian far right has been long in the making or long overdue, it is possible to argue that the success of Jobbik epitomises a skilful response to a demand for nativist issues at the time only partly satiated by the MIÉP. While a latent potential for the far right has been long out there, it is probably more appropriate to define the rise of a new Hungarian far right as long overdue, for Jobbik and the MIÉP bore distinguishing traits throughout.

Jobbik emerged from the 2006 protest season as a credible anti-establishment grassroots actor and subsequently thrived on the politicisation of 'Roma criminality' on its way to the Hungarian parliament. While certainly a by-product of its own system, the crafting of a new far right enacted by Jobbik presented both elements of continuity and discontinuity. Certain elements of continuity can be traced at the organisational level through the links that Jobbik sustained with pre-existing far-right networks; after 2006, then, Jobbik surged to become a far-right trailblazer, aggregating multiple instances that had remained disaggregated until that point. Discontinuity mostly relates to discursive innovation. By coupling populist anti-establishment frames with ethno-pluralism, Jobbik has substantially contributed to the rejuvenation of the nativist discourse in Hungary, and to enhance its own electoral prospects.

These elements, occurring at a time of accelerated political change, largely reinstate the value of agency-oriented foci in the study of the far right, and contentious politics at large. Indeed, both the mobilisation of resources and the elaboration of a new master frame pertain to the internal supply side of politics – and, thus, the sphere of agency of collective actors. Conversely, other structural elements, usually deemed crucial to mobilise aggrieved groups, convey only limited illustrative potential. Remarkably, a structural account exclusively based on the political opportunities available might dictate Jobbik's failure. Apart from a temporary opening of the electoral regime amid MSZP's collapse, Jobbik has been confronted with significant closure, both as an extra-parliamentary (2003–2010) and a parliamentary force (since 2010).

One may certainly argue that there is just not one way to interpret what movements and movement parties can make out of the opportunities available to them. As a case in point, Jobbik seems to have insisted on its outsider profile, and successfully turned formally closed opportunity structures to its own advantage. This confirms that it is not possible to neglect the agency of the far right in crafting its own fortunes. By taking a more sociological route, this chapter prompted us to look beyond the institutional arena, suggesting that the far right's success does not come from nowhere. With the specific case at hand, a significant portion of its mobilising potential had indeed been crafted at the grassroots level.

Notes

1 Within the context of this discussion, the adoption of the movement party concept entails an ongoing transition from the social movement to the party-political form. The trajectory upon which these organisations are set is one of partial or incomplete institutionalisation; hence, they should be deemed as 'collective actors in transition'.

2 The results scored by Jobbik at the 2018 general elections (19.1 per cent) prompted much internal debate on the strategy of moderation undertaken since late 2013 (Bíró-Nagy and Boros 2016). Gábor Vona, chairman since 2006, stepped down in May 2018. He was succeeded by Tamás Sneider, who won over the more radical Lászlo Toroczkai. The latter was eventually expelled from Jobbik for challenging the leadership on programmatic grounds and went on to establish the *Mi Hazánk Mozgalom* (Our Home Movement) with other outgoing members of Jobbik.

3 A significant change has occurred after the 2014 elections. After a fall-out with PM Viktor Orbán in 2015, businessman Lajos Simicska expressed public endorsment for Jobbik. Simicska is owner of a media empire that includes the daily *Magyar Nemzet* and news TV channel *Hir TV* (Reuters 2017).

References

Art, D. (2011) *Inside the Radical Right: The Development of Anti-Immigrant Parties in Western Europe*, Cambridge: Cambridge University Press.

Arzheimer, K. and Carter, E. (2006) 'Political opportunity structures and right-wing extremist party success', *European Journal of Political Research*, 45(3): 419–443.

Bernáth, G., Miklósi, G., and Mudde, C. (2005) 'Hungary', in C. Mudde (ed) *Racist Extremism in Central and Eastern Europe*, London: Routledge, 80–100.

Betz, H.G. and Johnson, C. (2004) 'Against the current – stemming the tide: The nostalgic ideology of the contemporary radical populist right', *Journal of Political Ideology*, 9(3): 311–327.

Bíró-Nagy, A. and Róna, D. (2011) 'Rational radicalism. Jobbik's road to the Hungarian Parliament', in G. Mesežnikov, O. Gyárfášová, and Z. Bútorová (eds) *Alternative Politics? The Rise of New Political Parties in Central Europe*. Bratislava: Institute for Public Affairs, 149–184.

Bíró-Nagy, A. and Boros, T. (2016) 'Jobbik going mainstream. Strategy shift of the far-right in Hungary', in J. Jamin (ed) *Extreme Right in Europe*. Brussels: Bruylant, 243–263.

Caiani, M., della Porta, D., and Wagemann, C. (2012) *Mobilizing on the Extreme Right: Germany, Italy, and the United States*, Oxford: Oxford University Press.

Carter, E. (2005) *The Extreme Right in Western Europe: Success or Failure?*, Manchester: Manchester University Press.

Casal Bértoa, F. and Enyedi, Z. (2016) 'Party system closure and openness: Conceptualization, operationalization and validation', *Party Politics*, 22(3): 265–277.

Castelli Gattinara, P. and Pirro A.L.P. (2018) 'The far right as social movement', *European Societies*, doi: 10.1080/14616696.2018.1494301.

Csepeli, G. (1991) 'Competing patterns of national identity in post-communist Hungary', *Media, Culture & Society*, 13(3): 325–339.

Csurka, I. (1992) 'Néhány gondolat a rendszerváltozás két esztendeje és az MDF új programja kapcsán', *Magyar Fórum*, 20 August.

de Lange, S.L. and Art, D. (2011) 'Fortuyn versus Wilders: An agency-based approach to radical right party building', *West European Politics*, 34(6): 1229–1249.

della Porta, D. and Diani, M. (2006) *Social Movements: An Introduction*. 2nd ed. Oxford: Blackwell.

Durkheim, É. (1964) [1893] *The Division of Labor in* Society, New York: Free Press.

Eatwell, R. (2003) 'Ten theories of the extreme right', in P.H. Merkl and L. Weinberg (eds) *Right-Wing Extremism in the Twenty-First Century*, London: Frank Cass, 45–70.

Enyedi, Z. (2015) 'Plebeians, citoyens and aristocrats, or where is the bottom of the bottom-up? The case of Hungary', in H. Kriesi and T.S. Pappas (eds) *European Populism in the Shadow of the Great Recession*. Colchester: ECPR Press, 235–250.

Enyedi, Z. and Benoit, K. (2011) 'Kritikus választás 2010. A Magyar pártrendszer á trendeződése a bal-jobb dimenzióban', in Z. Enyedi, R. Tardos, and A. Szabó (eds) *Új Képlet: A 2010-es Választások Magyarországon*, Budapest: DKMKA, 17–42.

Gamson, W. (1990) *The Strategy of Social Protest*, 2nd ed, Belmont: Wadsworth.

Gamson, W. and Meyer, D.S. (1996) 'Framing political opportunity', in McAdam, D., McCarthy, J.D., and Zald, M.N. (eds) *Comparative Perspectives on Social Movements: Political Opportunities, Mobilizing Structures, and Cultural Framings*. Cambridge: Cambridge University Press, 275–290.

Goodwin, J. and Jasper, J.M. (1999) 'Caught in a winding, snarling vine: The structural bias of political process theory', *American Sociological Forum*, 14(1): 27–54.

Greskovits, B. (2017) 'Rebuilding the Hungarian Right through civil organization and contention: The Civic Circles movement', EUI Working Papers, RSCAS 2017/37.

Herman, L.E. (2016) 'Re-evaluating the post-communist success story: party elite loyalty, citizen mobilization and the erosion of Hungarian democracy', *European Political Science Review*, 8(2): 251–284.

Hockenos, P. (1993) *Free to Hate: The Rise of the Right in Post-Communist Eastern Europe*, London: Routledge.

Hutter, S. (2014) *Protesting Culture and Economics in Western Europe: New Cleavages in Left and Right Politics*, Minneapolis, MN: University of Minnesota Press.

HVG (2010) 'A Jobbik titokzatos milliói'. Available at: http://hvg.hu/itthon/2010 0425_jobbik_milliok.

Jobbik (2008) 'Miért alakult meg a Jobbik Magyarországért Mozgalom-Párt'. Available at: http://zuglo.jobbik.hu/miert_alakult_meg_a_jobbik_magyarorszagert_mozgalom_part.

Jobbik (2010) 'A Jobbik nemzedék (teljes)'. Documentary. Available at: http://www.youtube.com/watch?v=R30fmLzFslY.

Jobbik (2014) *Kimondjuk. Megoldjuk. Választási Program* 2014. Party manifesto. Available at: http://www.jobbik.hu/sites/default/files/cikkcsatolmany/kimondjukmegoldjuk 2014_netre.pdf.

Karl, P. (2017) 'Hungary's radical right 2.0', *Nationalities Papers*, 45(3): 345–355.

Karácsony, G. and Róna, D. (2011) 'The secret of Jobbik: Reasons behind the rise of the Hungarian radical right', *Journal of East European and Central Asian Studies*, 2(1): 61–92.

Kiss, C. (2002) 'From liberalism to conservatism: The Federation of Young Democrats in post-communist Hungary', *East European Politics and Societies*, 16(3): 739–763.

Kitschelt, H. (2006) 'Movement parties', *in R.S. Katz and W. Crotty (eds) Handbook of Party Politics*, Thousand Oaks, CA: SAGE.

Kovács, A. (2013) 'The post-communist extreme right: The Jobbik party in Hungary', in R. Wodak, M. Khosravinik, and B. Mral (eds) *Right-Wing Populism in Europe: Politics and Discourse*, London: Bloomsbury Publishing, 223–234.

Krekó, P. and Mayer, G. (2015) 'Transforming Hungary – Together?', in Minkenberg M. (ed) *Transforming the Transformation? The East European Radical Right in the Political Process*, London: Routledge, 183–205.

Kriesi, H., Duyvendak, J.W., Giugni, M. and Koopmans, R. (1995) *The Politics of New Social Movements in Western Europe*, Minneapolis: University of Minnesota Press.

McAdam, D. (1999) *Political Process and the Development of Black Insurgency, 1930–1970*. 2nd ed. Chicago, IL: University of Chicago Press.

McAdam, D., McCarthy, J.D. and Zald, M.N. (eds) (1996) *Comparative Perspectives on Social Movements: Political Opportunities, Mobilizing Structures, and Cultural Framings*, Cambridge: Cambridge University Press.

McCarthy, J.D. and Zald, M.N. (1977) 'Resource mobilization and social movements: A partial theory', *American Journal of Sociology*, 82(6): 1212–1241.

Melucci, A. (1995) 'The process of collective identity', in H. Johnston and B. Klandermans (eds) *Social Movements and Culture*, London: Routledge.

Mikecz, D. (2015) 'Changing movements, evolving parties: The party-oriented structure of the Hungarian radical right and alternative movement', *Intersections: East European Journal of Society and Politics*, 1(3): 101–119.

Minkenberg, M. (2001) 'The radical right in public office: Agenda-setting and policy effects', *West European Politics*, 24(4): 1–21.

Minkenberg, M. (2003) 'The West European radical right as a collective actor: Modeling the impact of cultural and structural variables on party formation and movement mobilization', *Comparative European Politics*, 1(2): 149–170.

Minkenberg, M. (2013) 'From pariah to policy-maker? The radical right in Europe, West and East: Between margin and mainstream', *Journal of Contemporary European Studies*, 21(1): 5–24.

Minkenberg, M. (ed) (2015) *Transforming the Transformation? The East European Radical Right in the Political Process*, London: Routledge.

Molnár, V. (2016) 'Civil society, radicalism and the rediscovery of mythic nationalism', *Nations and Nationalism*, 22(1): 165–185.

MTI (2011) 'Tiny fraction of Hungarians members of political party', *Politics.hu.* Available at: http://www.politics.hu/20110516/tiny-fraction-of-hungarians-members-of-political-party/.

Mudde, C. (2007) *Populist Radical Right Parties in Europe*, Cambridge: Cambridge University Press.

Mudde, C. (2015) 'Is Hungary run by the radical right?'. Available at: https://www.washingtonpost.com/news/monkey-cage/wp/2015/08/10/is-hungary-run-by-the-radical-right.

NMHH (2017) 'Politikai szereplők médiahasználata'. Available at: http://nmhh.hu/szakmai-erdekeltek/mediafelugyelet/politikai-szereplok-mediahasznalata.

Panebianco, A. (1988) *Political Parties: Organization and Power*, Cambridge: Cambridge University Press.

Pirro, A.L.P. (2014a) 'Digging into the breeding ground: Insights into the electoral performance of populist radical right parties in Central and Eastern Europe', *East European Politics*, 30(2): 246–270.

Pirro, A.L.P. (2014b) 'Populist radical right parties in Central and Eastern Europe: The different context and issues of the prophets of the patria', *Government and Opposition*, 49(4): 599–628.

Pirro, A.L.P. (2015a) 'The populist radical right in the political process: Assessing party impact in Central and Eastern Europe', in M. Minkenberg (ed) *Transforming the Transformation? The East European Radical Right in the Political Process*, London: Routledge, 80–104.

Pirro, A.L.P. (2015b) *The Populist Radical Right in Central and Eastern Europe: Ideology, Impact, and Electoral Performance*, London: Routledge.

Pirro, A.L.P. (2016) 'Illiberal tangos in central and eastern Europe'. Available at: https://www.opendemocracy.net/can-europe-make-it/andrea-l-p-pirro/illiberal-tangos-in-central-and-eastern-europe.

Pirro, A.L.P. (2017) 'Hardly ever relevant? An appraisal of nativist economics through the Hungarian case', *Acta Politica*, 52(3): 339–360.

Pirro, A.L.P. (forthcoming) 'Ballots and barricades enhanced: Far-right "movement parties" and movement-electoral interactions', *Nations and Nationalism*.

Pirro, A.L.P. and Castelli Gattinara, P. (2018) 'Movement parties of the far right: The organization and strategies of nativist collective actors', *Mobilization: An International Quarterly*, 23(3): 367–383.

Pirro, A.L.P. and Róna, D. (2018) 'Far-right activism in Hungary: Youth participation in Jobbik and its network', *European Societies*, doi: 10.1080/14616696.2018.1494292.

Piven, F.F. and Cloward, R.A. (1979) *Poor People's Movements*, New York: Vintage Books.

Pop-Eleches, G. (2010) 'Throwing out the bums: Protest voting and unorthodox parties after communism', *World Politics*, 62(2): 221–260.

Reuters (2017) 'Hungary's top news portal passed to entities close to PM Orban's adversary'. Available at: https://www.reuters.com/article/us-hungary-media-politics/hungarys-top-news-portal-passed-to-entities-close-to-pm-orbans-adversary-idUSKBN17M2FL.

Rucht, D. (1996) 'The impact of national contexts on social movement structures: A cross-movement and cross-national comparison', in McAdam, D., McCarthy, J.D., and Zald, M.N. (eds) *Comparative Perspectives on Social Movements: Political Opportunities, Mobilizing Structures, and Cultural Framings*, Cambridge: Cambridge University Press, 185–204.

Rydgren, J. (2005) 'Is extreme right-wing populism contagious? Explaining the emergence of a new party family', *European Journal of Political Research*, 44(3): 413–437.

Schain, M., Zolberg, A., and Hossay, P. (eds) (2002) *Shadows over Europe: The Development and Impact of the Extreme Right in Western Europe*, New York: Palgrave Macmillan.

Schwartz, M. (1976) *Radical Protest and Social Structure*, New York: Academic Press.

Smith, A.D. (1986) *The Ethnic Origins of Nations*, Oxford: Blackwell.

Snow, D.A. and Benford, R.D. (1992) 'Master frames and cycles of protest', in Morris, A.D. and Mueller, C.M. (eds) *Frontiers in Social Movement Theory*, New Haven, CT: Yale University Press, 133–155.

Spiegel (2006) 'Hungary Prepares for Renewed Unrest'. Available at: http://www.spiegel. de/international/riots-in-hungary-hungary-prepares-for-renewed-unrest-a-437991. html.

Szőcs, L. (1998) 'A tale of the unexpected: The extreme right *vis-à-vis* democracy in post-communist Hungary', *Ethnic and Racial Studies*, 21(6): 1096–1115.

Tarrow, S. (1989) *Democracy and Disorder: Protest and Politics in Italy, 1965-1975*, Oxford: Oxford University Press.

Tarrow, S. (1994) *Power in Movement: Social Movements and Contentious Politics*, Cambridge: Cambridge University Press.

Tarrow, S. (1996) 'States and opportunities. The political structure of social movements', in Adam, D., McCarthy, J.D. and Zald, M.N. (eds) *Comparative Perspectives on Social Movements: Political Opportunities, Mobilizing Structures, and Cultural Framings*, Cambridge: Cambridge University Press, 41–61.

Tilly, C. (1978) *From Modernization to Revolution*, New York: Random House.

Tóth, A. and Grajczjár, I. (2015) 'The rise of the radical right in Hungary', in P. Krasztev, P. and van Til, J. (eds) *The Hungarian Patient: Social Opposition to an Illiberal Democracy*, Budapest: CEU Press, 133–163.

Új Szó (2011) 'Egy százalék körüli a párttagság aránya Magyarországon'. Available at: http://www.ujszo.com/online/kulfold/2011/05/14/egy-szazalek-koruli-a-parttagsag-aranyamagyarorszagon.

Williams, M.H. (2006) *The Impact of Radical Right-Wing Parties in West European Democracies*, New York: Palgrave Macmillan.

11

WORKING IN THE GAPS LEFT BEHIND

Radical right movement parties in a consolidating party system

Ben Stanley

Introduction

A plethora of radical right movements and parties emerged during the first 25 years of post-communist Polish democracy. However, only in 2015 did a radical right movement party experience electoral success, and even then, it was not formally a political party. This chapter explains why it has been so difficult for these parties to establish themselves in the Polish party system.

The argument rests on a distinction between three types of actors: radical right *parties*, radical right *movement parties*, and radical right *party movements*. Where movement parties shift from the streets to the institutions of state, party movements head in the other direction, leveraging visibility and resources to operate as patrons and organizers of protests, happenings, and other extra-parliamentary events that go beyond the typical scope of political party engagement with the street. By operating as a traditional political party that appeals primarily to moderate mainstream voters, and as a party movement that appeals primarily to those with more radical views, the governing Law and Justice party reduces the scope for radical right movement parties to maintain a distinct position in the party system, forcing them to work in the gaps it leaves behind.

I apply the descriptive research strategy outlined by Caiani and Císař in Chapter 1 of this volume to four distinct phases: the 1990s, in which neither radical right parties nor movement parties achieved conspicuous success; the electoral breakthrough of the radical right in 2001; the 'populist coalition' of 2005–2007 and the emergence of the 'party movement' strategy of Law and Justice in its aftermath; and the rise of the radical right movement party Kukiz'15 in 2015 and after.

Radical right movements, parties, movement parties, and party movements: conceptual distinctions

First, it is necessary to clarify the key conceptual terms. In Mudde's (2007: 26) influential definition, the politics of the radical right consists in 'opposition to fundamental values of liberal democracy' and 'belief in a natural order with inequalities'. Such movements go beyond conservatism and nationalism, espousing a xenophobic and exclusionist nativism and the authoritarian principle of subservience to in-group authorities. However, radical right organizations do not follow anti-democratic 'far' or 'extreme' right organizations in rejecting democracy itself.

The concept of movement parties implies an overlap of its constituent elements. Kitschelt (2006: 280) defines them as 'coalitions of political activists who emanate from social movements and try to apply the organizational and strategic practices of social movements in the arena of party competition'. While they have shifted the focus of their activities from 'the street' to the electoral and legislative arenas, they have not adapted their organizational structures or systems of interest aggregation and articulation to those typical of political parties.

When confronted by the appeals of movement parties, traditional parties may move in the other direction, becoming 'party movements' which remain focused on operating in the traditional spheres of party politics, but which also form links with and capitalize on the resources of social movements, and make consistent and systematic use of 'non-institutionalized means' to express their message (Schwartz 2016).

Parties without movements and movements without parties: 1989–2001

The first decade of post-communist democracy in Poland might have provided a fertile opportunity structure for the emergence of radical right movement parties. A citizenry socialized by the authoritarian interwar regime or the communist regime suddenly faced very different economic, political, and cultural norms, while political elites had the chance to create political parties largely from scratch.

Social acceptance of the need for difficult decisions swiftly gave way to anger at the inflation, unemployment, and shortages that ensued (Dudek 2017: 82–3). Negative views of the state of the economy and standard of living far outweighed positive views during the first five years of transition (CBOS 2018). An electoral system designed to encourage pluralism led to fragmented parliaments, with a multitude of weak and quarrelsome parties forming unstable coalition governments (Millard 1999: 84–7). Rapid Westernization promoted a sense of cultural estrangement among those attached to traditional identities and values.

The early emergence of extremist and radical right movements prompted fears about the susceptibility of sections of Polish society to a backlash against liberal-democratic transition (Hockenos 1993: 265–7). However, in spite of these conditions, the anticipated wave of support for parties and movements of the radical right did not materialize.

The 'post-communist divide' as a structural constraint

The scope for radical right movements and parties to achieve significant electoral successes during the 1990s was significantly reduced by the persistence of a 'post-communist divide' between the successors to the communist-era Polish United Workers' Party (*Polska Zjednoczona Partia Robotnicza*: PZPR) and a variety of parties with roots in the Solidarity movement. At the elite level, there was a taboo against formal cooperation across the divide, while at the popular level, it was decisive in determining voting behavior between 1989 and 2001 (Grabowska 2004: 358).

The persistence of the post-communist divide greatly reduced the intensity of party competition over the politics of transition, as it cut across ideological differences on major areas of policy. The post-communist left supported civic rights and socio-economic rights, but the post-Solidarity side was split, with liberal parties favoring civic rights and rejecting socio-economic rights, while conservative and Catholic-nationalist parties supported socio-economic rights, but rejected an overly individualistic conception of civic rights (Kurczewski 2009: 85–8).

Radicalism at the margins

Constrained by the pre-eminence of this divide, neither parties nor social movements were able to translate public fears about the politics of transition into strong and consistent electoral support. Parties of the radical right were at the fringes, or were members of broad, amorphous coalitions centered on moderate ideological positions.

Radical right parties and movements built organizational structures and engaged in cultural mobilization, but failed to appeal to a broader constituency. The nationalist music scene was instrumental in the spread of radical right views among young people during the 1990s (Pankowski 2011: 94), but this movement's restricted milieu and associations with extreme-right, anti-democratic organizations meant that it had limited appeal as a basis for a broader radical right movement that could fully engage on the terrain of democratic politics.

Even those movements which attempted to contest elections were unsuccessful. During the first two decades of post-communist transition, the organization that most clearly fitted the definition of a movement party was the populist Self-Defence (*Samoobrona*: SRP) party, which emerged from an agrarian social movement and trade union. Yet while SRP cooperated with parties of the right as a junior coalition partner in 2006–2007, it lacked their nativist rhetoric and policies, prioritizing economic issues instead, and is better understood as a 'social populist' party (Mudde 2007: 48). Despite the publicity and notoriety it gained from protests and instances of direct action, SRP repeatedly failed to achieve an electoral breakthrough during the 1990s.

The rise of the Radio Maryja movement

By far the most successful organization of the radical right to emerge during the 1990s was the Radio Maryja social movement. In 1991, Redemptorist priest Father Tadeusz Rydzyk set up a radio station under concessions for 'social broadcasters'. The station rapidly became an important and influential locus of political discussion and agitation on the right.

The success of the radio station led to the establishment of a media conglomerate. This currently comprises a set of foundations headed by Father Rydzyk that supervise the 'Our Daily' (*Nasz Dziennik*) newspaper, the 'I Abide' (*TRWAM*) television station, a School of Social and Media Culture, the 'In The Family' (*wRodzinie*) mobile telephone service, the 'Our Future' (*Nasza Przyszłość*) publishing house, and the *Servire Veritati* Institute of National Education, which organizes teacher training and the production of educational materials (Krzemiński 2016: 87–9).

The growth of Radio Maryja's media organization also helped it generate financial resources through the solicitation of donations from its listeners, and to broaden its political influence by providing politicians of the radical right with access to media outlets of national reach.

Radio Maryja also provided inspiration for the creation of so-called 'Radio Maryja families': the spontaneous, grassroots initiatives of circles of Radio Maryja listeners, such as local prayer circles, protests, and pilgrimages to holy sites (Burdziej 2008: 28; Zuba 2017a: 90). In this, it was aided by the existence of a nationwide organizational structure in the form of Church parishes, whose physical resources it co-opted to expand the network of families.

For many of its socially and economically isolated listeners, the Radio Maryja conglomerate offered a point of spiritual commonality and solace, a trusted alternative to the mainstream news media, and a world-view that provided a simple and internally logical framing of complex trends and developments. This worldview is grounded in a tradition of thought associated with the pre-war intellectual and politician Roman Dmowski, for whom nation-states were the sole legitimate political collectivity, and Catholic principles the only legitimate set of values on which to base the Polish state (Dmowski 2000: 26–7). Drawing on these principles, Radio Maryja produced a Catholic-nationalist counter-ideology to the emerging liberal-democratic constitutional order (Krzemiński 2016: 94).

Parties serving movements: the radical right breakthrough in 2001

After a decade of underperformance, the radical right experienced a significant breakthrough at the 'earthquake' election of 2001 (Szczerbiak 2002). These elections ushered in a new phase in party-system development in Poland after the 'false start' of the post-communist divide. This phase reflected the emergence of a new political agenda based on appealing to the 'anxieties of transition' (Millard 2006: 107). For the first time, the ideological concerns and priorities of the radical right were articulated by a single party.

The anxieties of transition: a new ideological divide

By the end of the 1990s, Poland had implemented many of the key institutional reforms of democratization, and was regarded as one of the more successful examples of economic transition. However, attitudes to the new regime belied the picture of a civilizational leap: the average Pole was 'richer, but unhappy' (Otto 2006). The profound material and psychological impact of transition produced a multiple and overlapping set of anxieties, resentments, and insecurities among those in Polish society.

The emergence of radical anti-establishment parties was also facilitated by the fact that both sides of the 'regime divide' had now rotated in power. Although the 2001 election brought the post-communist coalition of the Democratic Left Alliance (*Sojusz Lewicy Demokratycznej*: SLD) and the Polish Peasant Party (*Polskie Stronnictwo Ludowe*: PSL) to power, the new 'transition divide' provided a more legible basis for the stabilization of the party system around ideological issues.

Parties which did not belong to either side of the regime divide, and which openly contested the validity of the constitutional settlement of the Third Republic, now comprised a significant element of the Polish party system. The largest of these was the aforementioned SRP, which gained 10.2% of the vote, while a new radical right party, the League of Polish Families (*Liga Polskich Rodzin*: LPR), gained 7.87%.

The League of Polish Families

The emergence of the LPR was only in a superficial sense a victory for a radical right *party*. LPR came into being in May 2001, just prior to the election campaign, when members of the National Party (*Stronnictwo Narodowe*: SN) renamed the moribund National-Democratic Party (*Stronnictwo Narodowo-Demokratyczny*: SND), and entered into an electoral alliance with several minor clerical and nationalist parties (Zuba 2017b: 159).

Formally a party, LPR was in practice a coalition engineered to surmount the 5% threshold for representation. It was clearly a product of the extra-parliamentary radical right, and owed its origins to the patronage of the Radio Maryja movement. Yet it did not constitute a movement party in the sense of being the parliamentary wing of an established social movement.

The relationship between Radio Maryja and LPR was symbiotic. LPR gave institutional articulation to the media empire's ideological discourse and policy priorities, fusing a fundamentalist Catholic approach to social values with a strong emphasis on nationalism, and appealing to a 'Pole-Catholic' (*Polak-katolik*) conception of national identity (Zubrzycki 2006: 56). Programmatically, it espoused hard Euroscepticism, the protection of traditional values, the inculcation of patriotic attitudes, and an economic model based on self-sufficiency and restrictions on foreign competition and capital (Liga Polskich Rodzin 2006: 5–6). In return, Radio Maryja gave LPR access to a disciplined constituency of clerically-oriented voters and a friendly – although not always uncritical – set of media outlets with national reach.

Both prior to and after the 2001 elections, radical right parties and social movements benefited from the new opportunity structure created by the rise in transition anxieties and disenchantment with established parties. As the only party opposed on principle to accession, LPR was able to exploit growing concern at the potential effects and costs of accession, and peaked electorally with 15.92% of the vote in the 2004 European Parliament elections.

LPR joined the radical SRP in bringing elements of the radical social movement repertoire into the arena of party politics, using sit-ins and blockades to disrupt the work of parliament. However, it remained dependent on the patronage of a social movement it could not control, and attempts by the party leadership to assert independence from Radio Maryja was ultimately to contribute to the downfall of the party.

LPR had some resources of its own: one of the reasons for Giertych's rise to pre-eminence in the party was his association with the All-Polish Youth (*Młodzież Wszechpolska*: MW), a youth movement which originated in a pre-war movement of the same name, and which Giertych had been instrumental in reviving. MW played an important role in promoting LPR's Catholic-nationalist values and opposition to European integration among young supporters of the radical right, and provided a mechanism for recruiting and socializing future members of the party (Pankowski 2011: 112). Yet it lacked Radio Maryja's capacity to frame the politics of the radical right in more broadly palatable terms. Although it engaged in social activities, such as promoting Polish products and encouraging patriotic education of the young, MW was known mostly for organizing protest marches and gatherings that were reminiscent of extremist rallies, and often deployed many of the same slogans and imagery.

The growth of the party movement: the populist coalition of 2005–2007 and its aftermath

The 2001–2005 parliamentary term appeared conducive to the growth of the radical right, with the post-communist coalition government struggling to cope with economic turbulence, corruption allegations, and the challenging tasks of accession to the European Union (Millard 2006: 1011). Yet at first, the chief beneficiaries appeared to be more moderate parties of the centre right: the conservative and anti-communist Law and Justice (*Prawo i Sprawiedliwość*: PiS), and the liberal-conservative Civic Platform (*Platforma Obywatelska*: PO).

PiS first entered parliament during the earthquake election of 2001. The continuation of a dissident element of Solidarity which felt sidelined by a liberal establishment, it initially emphasized the objectives of tackling corruption and decommunizing the state, and otherwise espoused a relatively moderate conservatism. By the time of the dual parliamentary and presidential elections of September–October 2005, PiS and PO were widely expected to be in line to form the next government. However, the decline of the left was so precipitous that these two parties ended up competing against each other.

PiS emerged victorious in both elections by reframing the contest as a choice between 'solidaristic' and 'liberal' visions of Poland (Szczerbiak 2007: 204). Two long and acrimonious election campaigns poisoned relationships between the PiS and PO leaderships, ensuring the failure of coalition negotiations. Reluctant to risk sacrificing its slim advantage in new elections but unable to govern as a minority, Law and Justice reluctantly entered into a coalition with SRP and LPR in May 2006.

The populist coalition: the framing and performance of crisis

PiS's decision to form a coalition with SRP and LPR was greeted with widespread shock at the time, yet its short, turbulent period in office demonstrated that its constituent parties had much in common. The political appeals of each party reflected the greater salience of the 'anxieties of transition', with the old, rurally resident, low-educated, low-earning, and welfare-dependent increasingly more likely to express negative views of post-1989 reforms and disenchantment with Polish democracy (Czapiński 2006: 184; Paczynska 2005: 598–600).

The coalition's agenda emphasized thorough reform of the state and public institutions, an assertive and unilateral approach to foreign policy, moral and cultural renewal, and a more socially sensitive economy. Stymied by internal instability and the opposition of liberal-democratic institutions, the major opposition parties, and the European Union, the coalition achieved few of its legislative objectives during its short period in office. Its political impact was far more significant.

Moffitt's (2014: 198) conceptualization of the populist 'performance' of crisis provides a useful framework to understand how PiS captured the radical narrative. PiS began by 'identifying failure' in a political sense (corruption and state capture), an economic sense (the exclusion of social groups from experiencing the fruits of growth), and a cultural sense (the threat of cosmopolitanism to 'authentic' Polish identity and values), and elevated these discrete areas of failure to the level of a systemic crisis by attributing them to a broader narrative of 'transition gone wrong' which they had cultivated since the early 1990s. They then framed the crisis as a Manichean conflict between the 'mendacious elites' (*lże-elity*) of Poland's Third Republic and 'ordinary people, ordinary Poles' (Jarosław Kaczyński, cited in Sejm Rzeczypospolitej Polskiej (2007), session 10, day 3, 12 May 2006).

Having created this ideological narrative of crisis, PiS then set about implanting it in the public imagination. By purging public media outlets and populating them with loyalists, and subjecting flagship news programming to the editorial ministrations of a 'political commissariat' (Kublik 2007), PiS gained the resources it needed to frame the thwarting of its legislative program as a perpetual crisis. PiS's message was designed to construe the party as the loser, rather than the winner, of political battles, in order to maintain a constant aura of threat.

The fostering of crisis politics was facilitated by the significant growth in extra-parliamentary forms of expression on the part of the coalition and opposition alike, with competing marches and rallies in support of – or in opposition to – the government a particularly potent form of mobilization (Grzymski 2008: 28). The use of marches and rallies also enabled PiS to frame their leader Jarosław Kaczyński as a strong leader who could cut through the 'impossibilism' of institutional checks and balances.

Eating the starters: Law and Justice's radical shift

PiS's populist performance of crisis had two consequences for Polish politics. First, it reoriented the fundamental line of political competition away from the post-communist divide to one between complacent, cosmopolitan, and elitist liberals on the one hand, and a 'solidaristic' body of 'ordinary Poles' who were alert to the threats posed to their authentic identities and values. Second, and most significantly for the radical right in Poland, PiS mainstreamed the radicalism of LPR and SRP into a discourse of much broader appeal.

By turning sharply toward clericalism and nationalism when in office, PiS supplanted LPR as the natural voice of the radical right. By emphasizing the need for social sensitivity, it outflanked the scandal-hit SRP. In its radicalism, it transcended the rhetoric of both parties. By the early election of 2007, PiS was left as the only credible voice of radical opposition to the transition elite. This election, essentially a plebiscite on radicalism (Szczerbiak 2008: 27), confirmed the reshaping of the key line of competition. PO won convincingly, but PiS increased its vote share and share of seats, while LPR and SRP failed to return to parliament.

As exit poll data from the 2005, 2007, and 2011 elections show, while PiS did not attract all those who had previously voted for LPR and SRP, after 2007 the profile of its core electorate shifted to incorporate social groups which had previously favored those parties: the religiously devout, those with strongly right-wing views, rural dwellers, and the less well-educated. By contrast, PO disproportionally attracted support from those with liberal views, those living in urban areas, and those with higher education (Gazeta.pl 2011; Markowski 2006: 826, 2008: 1064).

PiS's radical shift was a conscious strategy, summarized by Jarosław Kaczyński as 'nothing to the right of us except the wall' (Lichocka 2008). In capturing and maintaining that position, PiS benefited from the patronage of Radio Maryja, which transferred its favour from LPR as soon as the advantages of associating with a larger, more effective party became evident. This enabled PiS to draw on the substantial organizational and ideological resources of Poland's most significant radical right social movement, while maintaining its appeal to more moderate voters through its own channels of communication and mobilization.

Law and Justice as party movement

After 2007, the new competitive structure persisted. The awkward cohabitation of a PO-led government with the presidency of Lech Kaczyński kept PiS's populist discourse in the public eye, even if the parliamentary party initially struggled to make headway against PO's pragmatic and explicitly anti-radical political program. By 2009, Bustikova and Kitschelt (2009: 471) classified PiS as a party 'nearby' the radical right, a term which usefully captures PiS's ideological adjacency to the extreme end of the spectrum, while acknowledging its capacity to project a more conventional right-wing conservative image. PiS's ability to move between these two categories is crucial to the party-system dynamics that have shaped the sphere of action enjoyed by radical right movement parties.

The death of President Kaczyński in the Smoleńsk air crash of April 2010 further consolidated this competitive structure, becoming a focal point for angry public exchanges over political loyalties and religious values. Crucially, the aftermath of the Smoleńsk disaster also prompted a shift in political strategy on the part of PiS, which increasingly embraced extra-parliamentary forums as an arena of mobilization. PiS initially distanced itself from conspiracy-theory explanations of the disaster which blamed it on the Russian government, the Polish government, or both. However, after the defeat of Jarosław Kaczyński in the presidential election that followed the death of his brother, the party began to forge more significant links with the social movements that had emerged in protest at the government's handling of the aftermath of the disaster, in particular the Solidarni 2010 association. May 2010 saw the first of the cyclical monthly Smoleńsk gatherings outside the presidential palace. While these gatherings were initially religious in character, with time the event became increasingly political, particularly following the publication of the official report into the Smoleńsk crash, and the subsequent pursuit of the 'truth about Smoleńsk' among those who declared the report a whitewash.

The Smoleńsk gatherings, which typically culminated with a speech by Jarosław Kaczyński, became a focal point for PiS to disseminate its message and mobilize support at a time when it was deprived of the communicative resources it had enjoyed as a party of power. From 2010 onward, PiS increasingly functioned as a party movement: while remaining the major opposition force in a party system that was consolidating around the 'solidaristic-liberal' divide, it used an extra-parliamentary repertoire of cyclical protest to articulate a radical populist narrative that was more effectively conveyed on the street than in institutions of power.

The rise of the radical right movement party: 2015 and after

In 2015, the opportunity structure might have seemed less than favorable to the emergence of radical right parties and movement parties. If in 2001 Poles were richer, but less happy, in 2015 they were richer *and* happier: just prior to the 2015 election, over half (56%) said they were content with their family's standard of living, compared with only just over a fifth (22%) at the same point in 2001 (CBOS 2018).

The United Poland (*Solidarna Polska*: SP) party, formed in 2012 following the departure of a faction on the right of PiS, failed to prove viable as a challenger party on the right. It eventually opted to run candidates on the victorious PiS electoral list in 2015, and after entering government, became increasingly indistinguishable from its former mother party.

Attempts to revive radical right social movements also met with mixed fortunes. The MW movement faded from prominence after its abandonment by the LPR, but remained active, entering into cooperation with a number of other social movements to form the National Movement (*Ruch Narodowy*: RN). The National-Radical Camp (*Obóz Narodowo-Radykalny*: ONR) remained marginal due to its extremism, but cooperated with the MW and RN in the organization of demonstrations and parades.

Yet the Polish party system, while consolidating at the center, still remained open to challengers who exploited the 'politics of newness' (Sikk 2012) and an anti-establishment rhetoric, or targeted a particular niche electorate which was poorly served by established parties.

The Kukiz'15 movement

In 2015, the Kukiz'15 social movement emerged from a campaign for electoral reform pursued by its leader, rock singer Paweł Kukiz. This campaign achieved national prominence in the months prior to the presidential election of May 2015, in which Kukiz came an unexpected third. This result encouraged Kukiz to create a citizens' movement, and register electoral lists for the October 2015 parliamentary elections, where it gained 8.81% of the vote. This was the first time a radical right movement party had entered parliament on its own electoral lists.

Kukiz'15 refuses to register itself as a political party, to take subventions from the state budget, or to enforce party discipline when voting in the legislature. However, it is more than a social movement; it functions as a coherent force within the legislature, participating fully in plenary and committee work as a distinct parliamentary club, and submitting bills and resolutions to parliament. While the parliamentary club has experienced several defections, this is typical for parliamentary clubs of minor opposition parties.

The movement defines itself as non-ideological, and has refused to publish a manifesto, asserting that empty statements of programmatic intent are a symptom of what is wrong with the 'partiocracy'. However, its ideological positions can be reconstructed on the basis of its 'Strategy For Change' (Kukiz'15 2015), and through observation of its actions and rhetoric. The most clearly expressed element of the movement's political appeal is its opposition to the institutional settlement of Poland's Third Republic and its political elite, which it describes as 'a cancer on the healthy tissue of our Nation' (Kukiz'15 2015: 3).

The ideological priorities and preferences of Kukiz'15 are consistent with those of parties which explicitly identify with the radical right. As Mudde (2007: 137) has observed, populist radical right parties typically instrumentalize economic policy in the pursuit of their 'primary ideological agenda' of nativism, authoritarianism, and populism. In common with a number of radical right parties, Kukiz'15's economic policy contains an eclectic mixture of libertarian and interventionist elements, calling for the liquidation of personal income tax and dramatic lowering of corporate income tax, but also for 'solidarity levies' on bank transactions, property taxes on large supermarkets, and value-added tax exemptions on a state-defined basket of 'primary-needs goods'. The main purpose of this policy is to put an end to Poland's status as the 'neo-colony of foreign governments and international corporations' (Kukiz'15 2015: 17).

The emphasis on protecting the nation from external predation extends beyond economic policy. A significant element of Kukiz'15's appeal in the 2015 elections was its opposition to the relocation of Syrian refugees. This stance was expressed in a nativist, exclusionary discourse, which emphasized the protection of Poland's Catholic identity and the threat of Islamic terrorism.

Re-energizing the right: the interaction of Kukiz'15 and social movements

The clearest indicator of Kukiz'15's socio-cultural orientation lies in the links of the movement with a number of organizations of radical right ideological provenance. The most significant of these is the National Movement (*Ruch Narodowy*: RN).

The RN was set up on 11 November 2012 following the National Independence Day march on the same day, which is a focal point of radical right agitation. Through the pooling of the resources of several organizations of the radical right, the most important of which were the aforementioned MW and ONR, the formation of RN was designed to re-energize a radical right movement whose influence had waned since 2007 (Kasprowicz 2015: 175).

At the beginning, RN deliberately adopted a social movement strategy rather than a party-political strategy, aiming to mobilize the nation against the establishment from the bottom up. Using the existing organizations and networks established by ONR and MW, RN focused on disseminating radical right messages through a variety of channels, organizing meetings, rallies, and marches of local sympathizers in towns and cities across Poland, engaging with right-wing think-tanks and academics, and making particularly adroit use of social media to cultivate support among young people, the socio-demographic group least likely to be mobilized by political parties. Appeals to the young were facilitated by an emerging trend for symbolic displays of pride in nationalist attitudes, such as the 'patriotic leisurewear' sold by several clothing firms.

The groundwork undertaken by the RN provided the underdeveloped Kukiz'15 movement with access to a burgeoning organizational structure. In return Kukiz'15 gave RN, which had registered as a political party in 2014 and unsuccessfully competed in that year's European Parliament and local elections, the opportunity to place its candidates on electoral lists that appealed to a broader constituency of voters. Five RN members gained seats in parliament from the Kukiz'15 list, along with five other candidates endorsed by the party.

After RN leader Robert Winnicki failed to engineer a split in the Kukiz'15 parliamentary club during April 2016, he remained the only RN deputy in parliament, the others joining Kukiz'15. Shortly afterward, several members of Kukiz'15 co-founded the *Endecja* association, an organization of activists whose views echo the National Democratic movement of Roman Dmowski, and created a National-Democratic Parliamentary Committee for the cultivation of these ideological traditions.

While Kukiz'15 remained internally heterogeneous, the radical right platform of the RN became a major element of the movement's appeal. In its focus on protecting the sovereign Polish nation from the depredations of liberal cosmopolitanism, this program echoed the Catholic-nationalist appeal of LPR, but was updated to address new issues such immigration, the relocation of refugees, and the threat of terrorism (Ruch Narodowy 2016). Kukiz'15 also sought to co-opt RN's appeal to young right-wing voters by setting up 'Kukiz'15 Youth Clubs', grassroots organizations intended to spread the movement's ideas of direct democracy, self-governance, and institutional reform (Kukiz'15 2017).

Movement party meets party movement: the interaction of Kukiz'15 and PiS

While the 2015 election saw a breakthrough for a movement party, it also saw PiS gain an overall majority.[1] PiS soon embarked on a controversial program of radical reform, establishing political control of the Constitutional Tribunal, the judiciary, and the media (Kelemen 2017: 227–229).

Kukiz'15 survived initial predictions that it would rapidly unravel. However, it was unable to build on its electoral breakthrough and become a movement that monopolized support on the radical right. This was partly attributable to the indiscipline of the movement and its ideological heterogeneity. However, the more significant bulwark to the future prospects of Kukiz'15 and other movement parties such as RN was the party movement strategy deployed by PiS.

Although PiS governed as a traditional political party, its interaction with other parties was increasingly unconventional. PiS's ruthless control of parliamentary procedure restricted genuine scrutiny of and debate over many aspects of its legislative program, and the parliamentary opposition was largely ineffectual. More consequential opposition to the PiS government occurred in the extra-parliamentary sphere, with rallies and protests becoming the idiom in which politics was conducted. This dovetailed well with the party-movement strategy that PiS had been developing since the Smoleńsk disaster, with counter-protests to anti-government demonstrations, and the monthly Smoleńsk rallies becoming focal points of political conflict. Although this was an arena in which RN had particular experience, PiS's ability to control the news cycle via its domination of public media enabled it to hegemonize street politics as efficiently as it had established domination over parliament.

In a similar manner, PiS was able to control the framing of key issues. The refugee issue offered an exemplar case of the asymmetry of resources and capacities party movements and movement parties enjoy. While Kukiz'15 derived much of its initial success from exploiting the refugee crisis, after the election PiS quickly established ownership of the issue by refusing to fulfil Poland's commitment to take in the quota of refugees it had been allocated under the EU's relocation program. They then re-framed this issue in broader terms by linking it to their ongoing clash with the European Union over the rule of law: refusing to admit refugees was not simply about 'protecting ordinary Poles from terrorism', but also an expression of sovereign defiance of overbearing institutions which were alleged to be exceeding their mandate.

Kukiz'15's breakthrough owed more to a temporary opportunity structure in the shape of a semi-open party system than it did to the movement's capacity to command significant resources and frame issues. By contrast, as a consolidated element of that party system, PiS could draw on the resources of a stable electoral base, substantial legislative, and executive experience, the support of a key radical right social movement in the form of Radio Maryja, and the compliance of a captive public media. Finally, PiS's legislative supremacy also gave it access to instruments through which it could discipline competitors. On several occasions, PiS raised the prospect of changing the electoral law to ensure that only political parties could put up candidates for election. Such a change would force Kukiz'15 to register as a party, undercutting its credibility as a social movement, which was founded on its refusal to submit to the formal structures of party politics.

Conclusions

The combination of radical right ideology, social movement mobilization, and traditional party politics is not new to Polish politics. However, only a quarter of a century after Poland's transition to democracy did a radical right movement party make an independent electoral breakthrough, and even then, it faced considerable obstacles to establishing itself as a distinct and significant element of Poland's semi-consolidated party system.

The preceding discussion has identified four distinct phases, characterized by distinct dynamics with respect to the interaction of radical right ideology, social movements, and political parties. Each of these phases differed in terms of prevailing contextual factors, access to resources, and deployment of cultural resources.

In the 1990s, radical right parties and movements were marginal phenomena, with the legacies of the past much more salient than contemporary economic and social crises. Deprived of the resources enjoyed by mainstream post-communist and post-Solidarity political parties, radical right parties and movements were compelled to generate their own, with the Radio Maryja movement proving the most capable at this task. The dominance of the regime divide also restricted the extent to which parties and movements of the radical right could deploy the cultural resources they possessed in order to frame political realities. At the elite and popular level, the identities and narratives of the post-communist divide structured all consequential political debate and action.

After 2001, the decline of the post-communist divide made it possible for the radical right to exploit the political, economic and cultural dislocations of transition to mobilize 'transition losers'. However, this was not a movement party breakthrough. LPR had links with social movements, but was a relatively orthodox radical right political party that served the interests of a powerful social-movement patron. Although LPR enjoyed a degree of financial independence from Radio Maryja thanks to state subventions, it remained dependent on it for access to and communication with a disciplined electoral base.

From 2005 onward, the party movement came to the fore, with PiS shifting the contours of Polish politics into a new alignment. Initially, PiS benefited from Radio Maryja's transfer of patronage, but over its period in opposition, the party developed significant resources of its own, particularly in the shape of the collective action frames generated in the aftermath of the Smoleńsk disaster and the social movement activities that emerged around them. By the time PiS regained power in 2015, it remained a traditional political party, but it had also developed the capacity to communicate and reproduce its discourse as a distinct social movement.

As a result of PiS's party movement strategy, when radical right movement parties eventually emerged in Poland, they emerged into a constrained context. The increased salience of the politics of the radical right created opportunities for movements like Kukiz'15 and RN to exploit events like the refugee crisis, but PiS's structural advantages allowed it to co-opt the resources generated by these movements. When Kukiz'15 framed the refugee crisis as a clash between Pole-Catholic and Muslim identities and values, PiS appropriated this frame and transformed it into a discourse of sovereignty and resistance to an over-aggrandizing EU. When RN co-organized the nationalist Independence March of November 2017, PiS deployed its media resources to re-frame it as an expression of patriotic virtues, leaving radical right organizations to carry the blame for xenophobic and racist excesses.

An important element of Polish politics over the first quarter century of post-communist Polish democracy, in recent years the ideology of the radical right has moved closer to the mainstream. It is possible to envisage a counterfactual scenario in which, after 2001, a dominant radical right social movement such as Radio Maryja made a decisive entry into party politics in its own right. However, the recent experience of Kukiz'15 suggests that the critical juncture for radical right movement parties to establish themselves as permanent features of the Polish party system has passed. The success of PiS in establishing itself as a hegemonic traditional party with significant social movement features leaves radical right movement parties with very little room to move in.

Note

1 Technically, this was a majority for PiS's electoral list, on which two minor parties also ran, rather than a majority for PiS, but in practice it functioned as a party majority.

References

Burdziej, S. (2008) 'Radio Maryja a społeczeństwo obywatelskie', *Znak*, 640: 17–28.
Bustikova, L. and Kitschelt, H. (2009) 'The radical right in post-communist Europe. Comparative perspectives on legacies and party competition', *Communist and Post-Communist Studies*, 42(4): 459–483.
CBOS. (2018) 'Trends'. Available at: http://www.cbos.pl/EN/trends/trends.php.
Czapiński, J. (2006) 'Stosunek do przemian systemowych i ocena ich wpływu na życie badanych', in Czapiński, J. and Panek, T. (eds) *Diagnoza Społeczna 2005: Warunki i jakość życia Polaków*, Warsaw: Wyższa Szkoła Finansów i Zarządzania w Warszawie, 182–189.
Dmowski, R. (2000) *Kościół, naród i państwo*, Warsaw: Wydawnictwo NORTOM.
Dudek, A. (2017) *Historia polityczna Polski 1989-2015*, Kraków: Znak.
Gazeta.pl. (2011) 'Wyborcza demografia. Którą partię wolą kobiety, a na kogo zagłosowali mieszkańcy wsi?'. Available at: http://wiadomosci.gazeta.pl/wiadomosci/1,114873,10 440924,Wyborcza_demografia__Ktora_partie_wola_kobiety__a.html.
Grabowska, M. (2004) *Podział postkomunistyczny: społeczne podstawy polityki w Polsce po 1989 roku*, Warsaw: Scholar.
Grzymski, J. (2008) *Rozmowa czy konfrontacja? Protesty pisane, marsze i strajki w Polsce 2005–2007*, Warsaw: Instytut Spraw Publicznych.
Hockenos, P. (1993) *Free to Hate: The Rise of the Right in Post-Communist Eastern Europe*, London: Routledge.
Kasprowicz, D. (2015) 'The radical right in Poland – from the mainstream to the margins: a case of interconnectivity', in Minkenberg, M. (ed.) *Transforming the Transformation?: The East European radical right in the political process*, London: Routledge, 157–182.
Kelemen, R.D. (2017) 'Europe's Other Democratic Deficit: National Authoritarianism in Europe's Democratic Union', *Government and Opposition*, 52(02): 211–238.
Kitschelt, H. (2006) 'Movement Parties', in Katz, R.S. and Crotty, W.J. (eds) *Handbook of Party Politics*, London: Sage Publications Ltd, 278–290.
Krzemiński, I. (2016) 'Radio Maryja and Fr. Rydzyk as a Creator of the National-Catholic Ideology', in Ramet, S.P. and Borowik, I. (eds) *Religion, Politics, and Values in Poland*, New York: Palgrave Macmillan, 85–112.
Kublik, A. (2007) 'Pytania do prezesa TVP', *Gazeta Wyborcza* 5 December.
Kukiz'15 (2015) 'Strategia zmiany' Available at: http://ruchkukiza.pl/klub-poselski/strategia-zmiany/#page/1.
Kukiz'15, Kluby Młodych (2017) 'Kluby Młodych Kukiz'15.' https://klubymlodych.pl.
Kurczewski, J. (2009) *Ścieżki emancypacji: osobista teoria transformacji ustrojowej*, Warsaw: Trio.
Lichocka, J. (2008) 'Na prawo od nas tylko ściana [interview with Jarosław Kaczyński]', *Rzeczpospolita* 20 November.
Liga Polskich Rodzin (2006) 'Skrót programu gospodarczego', in Inka Słodkowska and Magdalena Dolbakowska (eds) *Wybory 2005: Partie i ich programy*, Warsaw.
Markowski, R. (2008) 'The 2007 Polish Parliamentary Election: Some Structuring, Still a Lot of Chaos', *West European Politics*, 31(5): 1055–1068.
Markowski, R. (2006) 'The Polish elections of 2005: Pure chaos or a restructuring of the party system?', *West European Politics*, 29(4): 814–832. https://doi.org/10.1080/01402380600842452.
Millard, F. (2006) 'Poland's politics and the travails of transition after 2001: The 2005 elections', *Europe-Asia Studies* 58(7): 1007–1031. https://doi.org/10.1080/09668 130600926215.

Millard, F. (1999) *Polish Politics and Society*, London; New York: Routledge.

Moffitt, B. (2014) 'How to Perform Crisis: A Model for Understanding the Key Role of Crisis in Contemporary Populism', *Government and Opposition*, 50(2): 189–217.

Mudde, C. (2007) *Populist Radical Right Parties in Europe*, Cambridge: Cambridge University Press.

Otto, J. G. (2006) 'Polak bogatszy, ale nieszczęśliwy – portret obywatela RP po 16 latach transformacji', *Studia Politologiczne*, 10: 233–251.

Paczynska, A. (2005) 'Inequality, Political Participation, and Democratic Deepening in Poland', *East European Politics & Societies*, 19(4): 573–613.

Pankowski, R. (2011) *The Populist Radical Right in Poland: The Patriots*, London: Routledge.

Ruch Narodowy (2016) *Suwerenny naród w XXI wieku*, Warsaw: Kongres Programowy Ruchu Narodowego.

Schwartz, Mildred A (2016) 'Party Movements.' *Oxford Research Encyclopaedia of Politics*. http://politics.oxfordre.com/view/10.1093/acrefore/9780190228637.001.0001/acrefore-9780190228637-e-18.

Sejm Rzeczypospolitej Polskiej (2007) 'Sprawozdanie stenograficzne z posiedzeń Sejmu RP V kadencji'. Available at: http://orka2.sejm.gov.pl/Debata5.nsf.

Sikk, A. (2012) 'Newness as a winning formula for new political parties', *Party Politics* 18(4): 465–486.

Szczerbiak, A. (2002) 'Poland's Unexpected Political Earthquake: The September 2001 Parliamentary Election', *Journal of Communist Studies and Transition Politics*, 18(3): 41–76. https://doi.org/10.1080/714003608.

Szczerbiak, A. (2007) '"Social Poland' Defeats 'Liberal Poland'? The September–October 2005 Polish Parliamentary and Presidential Elections', *Journal of Communist Studies and Transition Politics*, 23(2): 203–232. https://doi.org/10.1080/13523270701317463.

Szczerbiak, A. (2008) 'The Birth of a Bipolar Party System or a Referendum on a Polarizing Government? The October 2007 Polish Parliamentary Election', *Journal of Communist Studies and Transition Politics*, 24(3): 415–443.

Wawrzyńczak, A. (2017) 'Red Is Bad: Jak patriotyczna odzież podbiła serca i kieszenie Polaków', *Rzeczpospolita*, 9 November.

Zuba, K. (2017a) 'From fringe to fringe: the shift from the clericalist League of Polish Families to the anticlericalist Palikot Movement 2001–2015', *Religion, State and Society*, 45(2): 87–105.

Zuba, K. (2017b) 'Liga Polskich Rodzin (LPR)', in Glajcar, R., Turska-Kawa, A., and Wojtasik, W. (eds) *Leksykon polskich partii politycznych*, Toruń: Wydawnictwo Adam Marszałek, 159–164.

Zubrzycki, G. (2006) *The Crosses of Auschwitz*, Chicago, IL: University of Chicago Press.

12

FOR THE PEOPLE, BY THE PEOPLE?

The Czech radical and populist right after the refugee crisis[1]

Ondřej Císař and Jiří Navrátil

Introduction

The concept of movement parties is one of the current innovations in the study of political mobilisation and this includes mobilisation by the radical right (see Chapter 2). The radical right represents one example of movement parties in Kitchelt's (2006) original sense, although it does not seem to neatly fit the version of the model as it was put forth (see below). In general, the relationship between movements and parties on the (far) right is less researched than the relationship between parties and movements on the left (however, there are exceptions, such as Minkenberg 2003; Giugni et al. 2005; Kriesi at al. 2012; Hutter 2014). This chapter contributes to this literature by analysing the mobilisation of the radical right in the Czech Republic, and its consequences during and after the 2015 'refugee crisis'. We look at both the protest and electoral arenas and strive to see whether the concept of a movement party can bring a better understanding of their interactions.

Before proceeding to a more conceptual discussion, we seek to analyze the processes and actors of the populist and radical right scene in the Czech Republic between the 2013 and 2017 election years. This period was selected because it represents the most likely timeframe in which the field of the radical right could undergo the organisational shift from movement(s) to party(ies). The reasons for this can be found in the political context (political opportunity structure; see Chapter 2). First, there were major changes in the institutional context, and more precisely in the context of interaction between political actors (Kriesi 2004). Czech party politics has undergone a major realignment in the studied period. A new political organisation called ANO (defining itself as a movement) that was founded in 2011 was successful in the 2013 parliamentary elections, and became part of the governing coalition (see below). A previously dominant right-wing party was almost erased in the elections, as ANO won support not only from the right, but also from voters previously on the left. These elections signified a major reshuffling of the seemingly consolidated party system and also created room for the success of a more radical right-wing party (Dawn of Direct Democracy), which also entered parliament. Second, the 2015 'refugee crisis' seemed to open up the discursive context for the country's radical right to enter the political stage. Even if the actual number of refugees coming to the country was very low, the issue preoccupied most of the political elites and the media (Navrátil and Hrubeš 2016), who converged on a rather restrictive stance towards refugees.

In this chapter, we focus on the interactions of party and movement-based organisations in the studied period. Therefore, we seek not only to map empirically the strategies and activities in the organisational field of the radical right, but also to explore the theoretical aspects of their organisational trajectories. Here we draw on the concept of movement parties to refer to actors that are in transition from extra-institutional movements to the partisan electoral competition 'as their primary vehicle to bring societal interests to bear on policy-making' (Kitschelt 2006: 278). Therefore, we also try to assess the processes of change in relation to the shifts of various actors between the field of political protest and electoral politics.

Data

Here we include only parties that have had some type of parliamentary representation, either in the European or the national parliament, at some point in time. By this decision, we exclude minor players in the field of radical right politics in the Czech Republic (for a description of them, see, for example, Mareš at al. 2015). Our data come from multiple sources. We use all publicly available information on the political actors that fit our definition (such as public statements, web presentations). The chapter also draws on three datasets.

First, we conducted an analysis of protest events that raised pro-/anti-refugee claims in 2015 (see Navrátil and Kluknavská 2017). The unit of analysis was a collective protest action in the public space where at least three persons convened. Protest event data were generated from searches of digital media databases using keywords (the electronic archives of two Czech newspapers – *MF Dnes* and *Haló noviny* – were selected), and the triangulation of other electronic resources (activist websites, Internet-based media, etc.) was applied in order to complete and contextualise the information on protest. The selected protest events concerning refugees (N=61) were further coded for date, place, duration, organisers, number of participants, the presence of foreign actors, repertoire, and the existence of counter-events.

Second, a claim analysis of Czech refugee crisis was conducted (see Navrátil and Hrubeš 2016), in which we collected and analysed all public claims related to refugees during the three selected months (see below). The unit of analysis is a political claim on refugees: 'the expression of a political opinion by physical or verbal action related to refugees in the public sphere'. We used the digital media database Anopress using keywords. Two key nationwide Czech newspapers were selected for the search for articles – *Právo* and *Hospodářské noviny*. Three months were selected for the article search, January 2015, October 2015, and June 2016, as these represent the beginning, the peak, and the aftermath of the heated public discourse on refugees in the Czech Republic. There were 77 claims identified in January 2015, 216 claims in October 2015, and 58 claims in June 2016. The selected claims were coded for source (newspapers), type of article (article, opinion, interview), author of the claim, type of activity (event, claim), and polarity towards refugees (positive, negative, neutral).

Third, we conducted an organisational survey of ten radical and Islamophobic civic associations, which were selected according to local protest activities in four large Czech cities (Survey 2016). The representatives of the organisations were invited to take part in a semi-structured interview focusing on various organisational and strategic aspects of their groups. The survey took place during the second half of 2016.

The Czech radical right: introducing party actors[2]

A key feature of the contemporary Czech radical right is that the parties/organisations established in the 1990s are vanishing, and new projects are emerging that have succeeded in utilizing new types of political and discursive opportunities, and have thus become much more visible and politically successful. In the past, there was the far-right party Coalition for the Republic–Republican Party of Czechoslovakia (SPR-RSČ), which reached the peak of its popularity in the mid-1990s (Hanley 2012a). After some time, elements of that old political programme started to re-emerge before the 2010 elections in the programme of right-wing populists in the Public Affairs party (Věci Veřejné: VV), which managed to get a place in parliament in 2010. VV's discourse was centred on anti-corruption, direct democracy, and social renewal (Hanley 2012b; Havlík and Hloušek 2014; Linek 2012: 170–172). It simultaneously took direct aim at the political elite at the time, which, according to the party, consisted of 'dinosaurs', whom this new project sought to replace (Sikk 2010). Zero tolerance for those deemed unable to 'fit' into society (the unemployed, drug addicts, etc.) became part of the party's discourse, and mirrored the population's fears and sentiments, which were then fully expressed by the radical parties that followed the mobilisation of VV later on. The party completely disintegrated during its first term in parliament (and as a minority coalition partner in the right-wing government of the Civic Democratic Party) after a series of internal scandals and fights. However, some of its founders have remained active in the background of other current projects (for more, see below).

The 2013 elections brought a new radical right project with the emergence of the Dawn of Direct Democracy party (Úsvit přímé demokracie: ÚPD; it won 6.88 per cent of the vote, and is the direct predecessor of what is currently the most important radical right project, Freedom and Direct Democracy/Svoboda a přímá demokracie: SPD). The Dawn of Direct Democracy party was founded by Tomio Okamura, a businessman and, until March 2015, the party leader. Okamura was vocal in the public arena before he established his party; he published books on governance, and promoted direct democracy as a corrective to the country's corrupted system of representative democracy. His programme focused (discursively) on the part of the population it defined as hard-working and who were also defined in cultural or ethnic terms. In this respect, he drew on, and further radicalised, a framework that resonated at that time, which led to a gradual reshuffling of Czech party politics (on the political opportunity structure and ANO, see below). As a result, his public discourse was aimed against foreign elements in the Czech state, against immigration in general, and expressed the ideology of nativism that is common for this type of political party (see Mudde 2007). Okamura in particular was able to skilfully exploit an important political narrative that had defined individual success as the defining moment in a person's general worth (see another version of the same trope in the discourse of the Free Citizens' Party below). Under this viewpoint, if people are in difficult socio-economic circumstances, they have only themselves to blame, and their lack of success is the ultimate proof that they are unable to adapt. In other words, they are 'unadaptable'—a label applied generally to the unemployed, the poor, and the socially excluded, and often ethnicised to refer to the Roma community and, later on, migrants.

According to Okamura and his ÚPD, which disintegrated during the first term in Parliament, the time has come for the 'adaptable' people (the Czech nation) to rise up against the unadaptable (who are not deemed part of the nation). This is why the ÚPD promoted the tools of direct democracy, since such tools would make it possible for the nation to bypass professional politicians. In this view, politicians are not only corrupt, they also coddle the unadaptable (in cooperation with the EU and its programmes), and Okamura is here not only to expose them, but also to make them pay their dues. In its programme, the ÚPD underscored that

> it is intolerable to support a system in which a stratum of people is forming who have no interest in work, who do not know the meaning of words such as duty, and who terrorise those around them with their criminal activity … We are against affirmative action. We will make access to social benefits more restrictive. Only those people who live proper lives and raise their children properly deserve support.
>
> *(ÚPD, Party Programme)*

This is where the programme of Okamura's current party project, the SPD, originated. Before we come to that, we need to mention one more small but persistent player in the field of the radical right.

Very similar rhetoric – though with an even bigger emphasis on formally defining liberty in the terms of private property – can be found in the programme of the Free Citizens' Party (Strana svobodných občanů: SSO). This party (which has no seats in the national parliament, but had one member in the European Parliament in 2014–2017) is not usually classed as part of the radical right, but it fits the criteria applied here. The party takes formal liberty as the only value worth pursuing, without any regard for the potential real-world consequences of this. In its political vision, a paradise of liberty would exist if there were as few rules as possible at the state level and, especially, at the EU level. The party strongly supports a traditional conception of sovereignty and the Czech Republic's departure from the European Union. In this sense, it is anti-elitist and pits the Czech nation against the EU's supposedly coercive powers. The existing political structures and their excessive regulations constrain people's freedom, and almost turn them into serfs since they are forced to pay taxes, contribute to public budgets (even at the EU level), and behave according to an ever-increasing number of rules regulating human affairs. In fact, the SSO favours a Hobbesian state of nature, where the will of the strongest is the only rule that must be obeyed.

Freedom and Direct Democracy (Svoboda a přímá demokracie: SPD) was established in May 2015 after T. Okamura and R. Fiala were expelled from their original party (ÚPD). The conflict in the ÚPD, largely over funding and influence, lasted for several months and the party still existed for the rest of the electoral term (unlike the newly established SPD with Okamura at the helm, the ÚPD did not run in the 2017 elections). The SPD's programme builds on the ÚPD's programme. The party wants to radically transform the political system by introducing mechanisms of direct democracy, such as general referenda on fundamental political issues and political mandates that can be directly revoked by the public. Regarding referenda, the SPD would first of all like to call a referendum on leaving the European Union. The party also targets non-governmental organisations, which it views as a danger to democratic governance; it would cut off public funding to them. The programme includes additional populist demands targeting the political class, such as the close monitoring of its property, and at the same time, promises the electorate almost everything, such as lower taxes, new jobs, an effective state, and welfare provisions – but only to those who deserve it (see also ÚPD above). However, the party's rallying cry in the elections was anti-Islamism, and it made radical demands aimed against Islam. In fact, the party has promised to ban Islam in the Czech Republic, alleging that the religion is a threat to national security and culture, and that it creates conditions for terrorism. On the international level, the SPD actively cooperates with far-right populists in other countries. In Fall 2017, Okamura hosted a meeting of the European radical right in Prague at which the main stars were Marine Le Pen and Geert Wilders.

Analytical framework

Drawing on the framework introduced in Chapter 2, we first analytically describe the dimensions of the current wave of radical right mobilisation, looking at the context, resource mobilisation strategies, and cultural framing. With this analysis, we seek to contribute to the conceptual debate on movement parties of the radical right. The mobilisation pathway of these actors seems to be distinct in the CR, which sets it apart from other Eastern European countries, especially Hungary. Whereas in Hungary, radical right parties mobilised from the bottom up (see Chapter 10 on Hungary in this volume; Mikécz 2015; and Greskovits 2017), in the CR, the radical right mobilisation seems to have been disconnected from social movement mobilisation and rooted more in private business than in civil society. In other words, we can see some important overlaps between business activism and the radical right in the Czech Republic. Can the concept of a move-ment party still be used to categorise such parties?

Political and discursive opportunities: contextual change after 2013

Party Politics Realignment: After the elections in 2010, the centre-right govern-ment was in power. For the first time since 1993, a newly emerged political party became a part of the cabinet (Public Affairs party: VV). There were several politi-cal controversies surrounding the appointment of ultra-conservatives to high pub-lic positions (e.g. at the Ministry of Education, Office of the Government), which sparked public debates on the legitimacy of xenophobic claims and opinions in the country. These claims came from both the mainstream parties and the new business party VV. It was founded in 2001, but was later taken over by one of the largest Czech private security companies that was well connected with the police and state security agencies and was headed by V. Bárta (Klíma 2016: 553). The emergence and success of VV was generally interpreted as an indicator of the end of the domination of the party system by two big parties on the right and the left that characterised the period up to 2010 (Hanley 2014). This deconsolidation of the party system has continued ever since.

In 2013, the government was replaced by an interim cabinet after a series of political scandals, which engulfed the (until then) hegemon of the right, the Civic Democratic Party (Občanská demokratická strana: ODS), and its prime minister, P. Nečas. This led to a major political crisis and further weakened the already low level of citizens' trust in the government and other democratic political institu-tions. The legitimacy of democracy has been decreasing, and a growing number of people support alternatives to it in the form of some authoritarian system (Linek at al. 2018). Indeed, the current proliferation of protest parties, which resulted in a complete realignment of Czech party politics that was then further deepened by the 2017 elections, is generally attributed to the population's growing dissatisfac-tion with post-1989 party politics and particularly with the corruption scandals associated with the traditional parties (Linek 2010; Hanley 2014).

After the elections in 2013, the Czech political and party landscape started to change significantly. Two new protest parties entered Parliament, with the runner-up party, the Action of Dissatisfied Citizens 2011 (Akce nespokojených občanů or ANO 2011) becoming a part of the coalition government (with close to 19 per cent of votes (2013); it is currently the most popular party in the Czech Republic and it actually won the 2017 parliamentary elections). ANO 2011 was founded in 2011 by Andrej Babiš, the second-richest Czech entrepreneur and the owner of the country's largest agricultural and food-processing holding company, Agrofert (which is also active in multiple other business sectors, including the news media). The core of ANO 2011's programme has so far been to substitute management for politics—literally, to 'manage the state as a firm', which the leader repeatedly stresses. According to Babiš, no suitable political solution can be found on either the left or the right; what is needed is a rational managerial approach, a technocratic formula that will streamline the functioning of public administration (Císař and Štětka 2016). The success of ANO has been a real game changer in Czech (party) politics. In addition to the electorally strong ANO 2011 party, other protest parties included the ÚPD (which got almost 7 per cent of the vote in the 2013 elections). Its candidate list included some former members of VV, including its former chairman, V. Bárta, of the SSO, and some former ODS members (R. Fiala, today vice-chairman of the SPD).

The Refugee Crisis: In 2015, the political landscape received a blow from the outside: the so-called 'refugee crisis' hit Europe, and started to polarise political discourse and political activities in the Czech Republic as well. Even though nothing much happened in the country in terms of the number of asylum-seekers and in terms of the number of people granted asylum, migration became high on the domestic political agenda. Some established political elites embraced xenophobic discourse and claims – President Zeman openly condemned migrants as 'connected to terrorism', and some heads of established parties represented in Parliament actively supported erecting fences, and applying other restrictive measures against asylum-seekers. The entry of the migration crisis into the Czech political agenda sparked a series of protest mobilisations against receiving refugees, but also gave rise to counter-mobilisations against xenophobia and supportive of refugees. Generally, most of the public political claims made about the refugee crisis came from members of the government and two-thirds of them were negative (Navrátil and Hrubeš 2016). In almost half of these claims, migration/migrants were framed as a threat. The discourse on the refugee crisis also had a profound impact on public opinion, which was generally opposed to allowing any immigrants into the country – even if they were coming from countries affected by war (62 per cent of citizens; Navrátil and Hrubeš 2016).

Both civil society actors in the protest arena and established political parties have joined in the public debate on refugees. New civil society initiatives emerged that sought explicitly to mobilise citizens against Islam ('We Do Not Want Islam in the CR'/Islám v ČR nechceme: IVČRN), while relying heavily on various online platforms and social media. Also, the new agenda caught the interest of political parties on the extreme right (such as Dawn and Freedom and Direct Democracy). The new conflict transcended the socio-economic left-right divide and included Communists, a portion of Social Democrats, and liberal-conservatives in the anti-refugee camp, with Greens, liberals, and (a rather minor) portion of Social Democrats on the other side.

In the Czech context, the issue of Islam has been connected to the issue of immigration since the very beginning, as the debate over the refugees started soon after the Paris attacks in January 2015. Symbols of Islam, such as mosques and headscarves, became important symbols in the debate, and multiculturalism became one of the targets of the recently formed and mobilised anti-refugee camp. Soon after the 2015 Paris attacks in January, the anti-refugee campaign intensified and became intertwined with the anti-Islamic rhetoric.

Some officials in the country, like President Zeman, tried to establish symbolic links between Islam and terrorism (thus linking terrorism to refugees), and to recast the refugee crisis as 'an invasion organised by the Muslim Brotherhood'. This link was also utilised by various civil society actors in the streets. The issue of EU involvement in the crisis resonated especially after the debate on quotas for EU member states, which were meant to establish the number of refugees each member country would be obliged to accept. This fed the widespread Euroscepticism of Czech citizens (Caiani and Kluknavská 2017).

Resource mobilisation

The newly formed political parties that combined populism and radical right rhetoric were often described as business-firm parties, and they employed a significant amount of private commercial resources. VV were closely affiliated with the security agency ABL and its majority owner, Vít Bárta, and some of the party's prominent supporters helped the party with their own investments, which were the source of most of the party's funding (Seznam 2018). In 2012, the party also received significant funding from anonymous companies registered in tax havens. Later on, the party benefited from state subsidies for votes obtained in the elections. Initially the party attracted 1700 members, but their number decreased significantly after 2010 (to 700 members, Aktuálně.cz 2010).

However, one of the main purposes of the party, which was managed as a firm itself, was to help the security business of Vít Bárta; in other words, there was no significant difference between the interests and functioning of the party and those of Bárta's firm (Havlík and Hloušek 2014: 560–564). Because of its success in the elections, the party was entitled to a substantial subsidy from the state budget as part of the state funding scheme. According to some interpretations, this was the primary purpose of the party's existence.

The very same model, and probably connected to many of the same people, was repeated in the case of the ÚPD in 2013 (Seznam 2018). After its electoral success in 2013, the party was entitled to a multimillion-crown sum, and that money was transferred to firms with ties to the party's leaders (Pšenička 2017). Later on, conflicts over this money led to the party's breakup (see above). In terms of resource mobilisation strategies, the ÚPD seems like the continuation of VV's project both in terms of people (V. Bárta was a ÚPD candidate in the parliamentary elections in 2013), and financial resources (Bastlová 2017). In addition, the SPD also seems to be yet another incarnation of the same network of business interests (Pšenička 2017; Seznam 2018).

Radical right organisations in the civic sphere/protest arena do not usually rely on employees, but rather on active volunteers (typically a few dozen of them).

Unlike the radical right parties, they rely on active membership, and do not restrict it to a narrow group of people. The typical number of members is several dozen per organisation. The role of commercial subjects, such as firms and entrepreneurs, is much less important than in political parties. As a result, these organisations often have very limited resources, which prevent them from maintaining a continuous political existence (Survey 2016).

In 2015, as a follow-up to some joint campaigns, there was an attempt to establish electoral cooperation between at that time most visible anti-Islamic initiative, the Block against Islam, and a new version of the ÚPD (after the departure of Okamura and Fiala from the party), but it was not successful. The Block left the coalition, because its partner, according to the Block's leaders, was not trustworthy. In fact, resources were the main problem, since the ÚPD was supposed to contribute money to the Senate campaign of one of the Block's main activists. As he himself put it: 'The main problem is that I have nothing to fund my election campaign with. We started cooperation with the ÚPD on the condition that it would put 60 million crowns into the campaign, but it turned out to be much more complicated.' (iDnes 2016)

Cultural and symbolic tools (framing)

There is a feature common to all populist actors, and that is criticism of the contemporary political establishment. According to VV representatives, the existing political elite were formed by 'political dinosaurs', and the party started its electoral campaign in 2010 by symbolically shooting a cannon in the direction of the Office of the Government. The party relied on the instruments of direct democracy, and combined them with a technocratic and neoliberal vision of the government: they promoted universal extra payments in education and healthcare, anti-corruption policies, pro-business measures, and lowering direct taxation. Generally, the redistribution of taxes was labelled 'inefficient', the system of taxation 'enormously complicated', and the level of direct taxation 'demotivating'. The party representatives spoke of 'parasites', and of the need to enable municipalities to cut social benefits under certain circumstances. They also called for the implementation of 'public benefit work' among the unemployed as a condition for their receiving social benefits (Věci veřejné 2010).

The ÚPD advocated much harsher symbolic strategies towards refugees, mixing nativism and welfare chauvinism. Except for its agenda combining direct democracy with criticism of existing political elites ('mafia'), since 2014 it has explicitly combined an anti-Islamic framing with an anti-refugee one:

> The ongoing Islamisation of European countries is incompatible with these [our] values .... Ongoing illegal immigration is the first phase of a conflict that in its consequences will threaten freedom, democracy and the very existence of the Czech Republic and our nation.

The party started to frame the issues in economic terms ('No to immigrants! Let's give jobs to our citizens'), but also used claims that implicitly draw on negative images that had so far been associated with the Czech Roma minority: 'Social benefits cannot let lazy people live better lives than those who work.' Similarly, refugees were rejected as social benefit tourists who will steal resources from the Czech population (Mareš at al. 2015: 138).

As is clear by now, the SPD is a continuation of the ÚPD by almost the same means, even in terms of its framing and discursive strategies. The party relies on the same images as the ÚPD did, and presents itself as the main defender of the Czechs against the looming Islamisation of the country. Immigrants and 'local unadaptable people' are portrayed as parasites who should not have any rights. The party would like to support 'Czech working families with children' to boost the future development of the country (SPD 2017).

Extra-institutional mobilisation: the refugee 'crisis' of 2015

Since 2015, various organised actors have started to mobilise and raise claims in relation to the refugee crisis. First, we look at public protest events and at the public debate that went on during the crisis. In terms of pro-refugee events, these were often organised as counter-events against the rallies of Islamophobic groups, but there were also projects and activities organised to help refugees (e.g. medical students travelled to refugee camps abroad, or a project was founded to help the children of refugees). Anti-refugee events were mostly rallies by Islamophobic groups, demonstrations 'against illegal immigration', or protests of local inhabitants against the opening of detention centres in their towns.

As far as the claims and framing are concerned, the pro-refugee camp used the argument of the low number of refugees planning to stay in the country, equal rights, or directly labelled the other side as the 'Nazi' camp. There was also strong criticism of the media and politicians and their negative framing of the situation, but also of the police and the 'inhuman' treatment of refugees in the country's detention centres. There were only a few claims made about the situation in war-torn Syria or Afghanistan. All in all, the dominant framing used was mostly the notions of solidarity, humanity, and labelling the anti-refugee camp as Nazis. On the other side, the anti-refugee camp was producing claims of maintaining national control over immigration (in response to EU and German pressure on national politics), and increasing both physical and 'cultural' security. The most important framing used here was generally the anti-elitist one – the politicians (especially those in Brussels) were deemed responsible for the crisis situation. Also, frames stressing both Islamic and economic threats to the Czech/European culture and economy were employed.

In 2015, 61 protest events took place in the country. There were both mobilisations against accepting refugees and against Islam, and mobilisations supporting asylum-seekers. Only a small portion of the events were in support of welcoming refugees or expressing sympathy with them. A large number of anti-refugee mobilisations took place in Prague (37 per cent) and small cities (24 per cent), and most of them were public demonstrations (76 per cent). Most of the counter-mobilisations took place in Prague (57 per cent).

The key actors in the anti-refugee mobilisations can be divided into several groups according to the type of actor involved. First, some of the mobilisations were organised by local inhabitants and usually focused on (proposed) measures to expand detention centres, or the plans of ministries to dedicate some of the existing centres to migrants from non-Western countries. Some of the citizens involved in these mobilisations even became professional leaders and travelled to various demonstrations, while (unsuccessfully) trying to build mobilisation networks against immigration from below. Most of these events were framed as 'acting against the threat of an increase in crime in the locality and of encounters with dramatically different culture and religion'.

The second group of organisations comprises recently established civic anti-Islamic initiatives that were explicitly linking the migration crisis with the 'threat of Islam' and 'cultural wars', and warned against the 'Islamisation of the country and Europe as such'. One of the most important anti-Islamic civic initiatives was founded back in 2009 (We Do Not Want Islam in the Czech Republic: IVNČR), so it easily gained momentum when the 'crisis' arrived in Europe. The initiative attempted to turn itself into a political movement in 2015 (The Block against Islam/Blok proti Islámu: BPI), and for some time formed a coalition with the ÚPD for the regional/Senate elections in 2016 (see above). After internal struggles, the coalition broke up. A new political party without connections to any former founding subject, but with connections to the ÚPD, emerged ('The Block against Islamisation"). There was also an attempt to establish the Czech version of the German political network PEGIDA, but it failed to get wider support.

The third group consists of radical right parties and movements. There is the ÚPD (see above), which succeeded in pushing out other and older radical right parties that traditionally targeted Roma and Jewish minorities and were not quick enough to pick up the issue of immigration (such as the Worker's Party of Social Justice and its youth organisation National Democracy and others; for more on these marginal parties, see Mareš at al. 2015: 81–97). The protest events of these organisations were typically supported by neo-Nazi subcultures and football hooligans. Next, there was the SSO (see above) and the former president of the country, V. Klaus, who participated in the campaign. Klaus publicly introduced the initiative 'Against Immigration', which appealed to the government not to receive any refugees, to secure the national borders, and to refuse the EU refugee real-location quota system. One of the interesting features of the mobilisations against the refugees was the cooperation of the Czech organisers with their foreign counterparts – this was one of the differences from the mobilisations of the supporters of the refugees. Most remarkably, Slovak radical nationalists and extremists came and supported the protests of the Czech radical right (Slovak Community, Action Resistance Kysuce, Kotleba/People's Party Our Slovakia; see also Chapter 13 on Slovakia in this volume).

Even if there were various types of actors engaged in the protests, some clearly visible patterns of cooperation appeared during the protests. Typically, while traditional radical right organisations such as the SPR-RSČ or National Democracy sponsored their own not very well-attended rallies, 'new' actors such as the ÚPD/SPD co-organised protest events in cooperation with civic initiatives (IVNČR, BPI) in order to boost attendance and get media attention, and to compensate for the lack of their own members.

In terms of public claims made via media, the most active and visible were the representatives of executive power – the prime minister, cabinet, and ministers. This is mostly due to the fact that it is the Ministry of Interior that is technically responsible for the issue of immigration, and that the heads of the coalition parties, who often expressed their political views on the refugees, were the heads of ministries (Deputy Prime Minister and the Finance Minister). The representatives of the executive were followed by the representatives of domestic legislative power who usually used the opportunity to clarify the position of their parties on the refugee crisis. Organised civil society groups and citizens occupied the third most active position in claims production, and were even more active than the media, the President, and the police. It is interesting that even if the President is often cited as one of the most important actors in the debate, his activity was not that frequent (Navrátil and Hrubeš 2016). However, it was his institutional and symbolic status that brought his statements relatively considerable attention. The general polarity of the claims on refugees in the public sphere was negative, even if it was not as dominant as one might expect from the unsystematic observation of public discourse on the issue. What is more striking, however, was the rise of the negative polarity of claims in time.

Discussion and conclusions

While there was relatively visible extra-parliamentary mobilisation on cultural issues such as sovereignty and especially against migration, during the 2015 crisis, this mobilisation did not turn into a new party or a political movement in the electoral arena. Despite episodic protest alliances that sought to utilise the momentum of the refugee crisis, the protest and electoral arenas remained unaligned in terms of institutional or coalitional relations and the past and current party projects of the radical right lacked any roots in civil society or networks of social movements. If we look at the most visible and successful party projects in the Czech Republic in recent years, they all are related more to business interests than grassroots. Although the demonstrations of 2015 indicated a demand for representatives of these issues in politics, the supply of political parties did not come from these mobilisations themselves. Rather, it has been served by skilful leaders and their marketing strategists, who created a resonating mix of slogans targeting migration and Islam. At the same time, the Czech radical right was not born from the migration crisis, since it existed even before that and was represented in parliament. In fact, it even retained its main structural target, which is minorities, but replaced internal minorities, such as the Roma, with external ones, namely refugees. This is in line with a general trend in the region, which is this shift in focus from an internal minority to an external one (see Buštíková 2018).

However, in its mobilisation and target shift, the radical right in the Czech Republic took a different path from the movement-based mobilisation that occurred in some other Eastern European countries. Except for the issues, episodic encounters at demonstrations, and one cursory and unsuccessful attempt to cooperate, radical right actors in the two political arenas each followed their own separate logic. The pre-crisis distance between the fields of party politics and extra-parliamentary activism remained the same after the crisis. The most important reason seems to be the fact that the Czech radical right has not even tried to mobilise a movement. On the contrary, it mobilises on the basis of a business model, in which the tools of political marketing and charismatic leadership help maximise votes in exchange for state subsidies.

When looked at from the perspective of Kitchelt's original concept, the path of the Czech radical right seems to defy the model of a movement party, which rests on movement mobilisation and strategies: 'Movement parties are coalitions of political activists who emanate from social movements and try to apply the organizational and strategic practices of social movements in the arena of party competition' (Kitchelt 2006: 280). The Czech radical right, in its established form at least, does not employ protest or disruptive strategies often, nor is it based on mass mobilisation. On the other hand, this is exactly how Kitchelt views the Western radical right, which, according to him, lacks movement support and its distinctive characteristics, such as informality and fluidity, do not 'primarily derive from bottom-up participatory politics promoted by rank-and-file activists, but from the dominance of a single or of a handful of rival charismatic political leaders' (Kitchelt 2006: 287). At the same time, Western radical right parties still initiate protest events, and in this respect, they are movement parties 'only in the sense that they create or displace social movement practices' (Kitchelt 2006: 286). Although Czech radical right parties organised some protest events during the refugee crisis, they do not use this strategy on a regular basis. Clearly, they prefer institutional strategies (on preferred strategies and arenas of action, see Hutter 2014 for differences between the left and the right in Western Europe; Hutter points in the same direction as our chapter). Therefore, it is harder to class them as movement parties than their West European counterparts.

When there is no crisis, it seems that for the radical right, there is no lasting institutional connection between the electoral arena and the social movement/ protest arena. However, this connection can be reconfigured by external developments; a major crisis. In such moments, the party and protest fields may become aligned, such as during the migration crisis of 2015. If we look at the ability of general protest actors to get their issues on the political agenda, Jack Goldstone (2004) shows that it is triggered by crises (see Chapter 2). According to him (1980: 1041), a protest group has 'excellent chances of eventually attaining its aims, provided it maintains its challenge until a crisis arises that makes success likely'. This could probably help explain the speed with which the anti-refugee agenda became a new political mainstream in Czech politics, as well as the success of a new party project (the SPD) that based itself on the cultural issues of sovereignty, migration, and Islam.

Notes

1 This chapter was prepared as part of work on the research project 'Activism in Hard Times' funded by the Czech Science Foundation (no. 16-10163S).
2 With the exception of the SPD, the description of parties in this section utilises revised parts of the text from Císař and Štětka 2016).

References

Aktuálně.cz (2010) 'Věci Veřejné'. Available at: https://www.aktualne.cz/wiki/politika/ politicke-strany/veci-verejne/r~i:wiki:631/.

Bastlová, M. (2017) 'Kam zmizel superguru V.B.'. Available at: http://neovlivni.cz/ kam-zmizel-superguru-v-b/.

Buštíková, L. (2018) 'The radical right in Eastern Europe', in Rydgren, J. (ed.) *The Oxford Handbook of the Radical Right*, New York: Oxford University Press.

Caiani, M. and Kluknavská, A. (2017) 'Extreme right, the Internet and European politics in CEE countries: The cases of Slovakia and the Czech Republic', in Barisione, M. and Michailidou, A. (eds) *Social Media and European Politics: Rethinking Power and Legitimacy in the Digital Era*. London: Palgrave Macmillan UK.

Císař, O. and Štětka, V. (2016) 'Czech Republic: The rise of populism from the fringes to the mainstream', in: Aalberg, T., Esser, F., Reinemann, C., Stromback, J., and De Vreese, C. (eds) *Populist Political Communication in Europe*, eds. London: Routledge.

Giugni, M., Koopmans, R., Passy, F. and Statham, P. (2005) 'Institutional and discursive opportunities for extreme-right mobilization in five countries', *Mobilization: An International Quarterly*, 10(1): 145–162.

Goldstone, J. (1980) 'The weakness of organization: A new look at Gamson's *The Strategy of Social Protest*', *American Journal of Sociology*, 85(5): 1017–1042.

Goldstone, J. (2004) 'More social movements or fewer? Beyond political opportunity structures to relational fields', *Theory and Society*, 33(3/4): 333–365.

Greskovits, B. (2017) 'Rebuilding the Hungarian Right through civil organization and contention: The Civic Circles movement', EUI Working Papers, RSCAS 2017/37.

Hanley, S. (2012a) 'The Czech Republicans 1990–8: A populist outsider in a consolidating democracy', in Mudde, C. and Kaltwasser, R.C. (eds) *Populism in Europe and the Americas: Threat or Corrective for Democracy*, Cambridge and New York: Cambridge University Press.

Hanley, S. (2012b) 'Dynamics of new party formation in the Czech Republic 1996–2010: Looking for the origins of a political earthquake', *East European Politics*, 28(2): 119–143.

Hanley, S. 2014. 'Two cheers for Czech democracy', *Politologický časopis-Czech Journal of Political Science*, 3: 161–176.

Havlík, V. and Hloušek, V. (2014) 'Dr Jekyll and Mr Hyde: The story of the populist Public Affairs party in the Czech Republic', *Perspectives on European Politics & Society*, 15(4): 552–570.

Hutter, S. (2014) Protesting Culture and Economics in Western Europe: New Cleavages in Left and Right Politics, Minneapolis, MN: University of Minnesota Press.

iDnes (2016) 'Blok proti islámu se rozešel s Úsvitem. Nejsou slíbené desítky milionů'. Available at: https://zpravy.idnes.cz/blok-proti-islamu-vypovedel-smlouvu-s-usvitem-flr-/domaci.aspx?c=A160425_074507_domaci_hro.

Kitschelt, H. (2006) 'Movement parties', in Katz, R.S. and W. Crotty, W. (eds) *Handbook of Party Politics*, Thousand Oaks, CA: SAGE.

Klíma, M. (2016) 'The Czech Republic', in Viola, D. (ed) *Routledge Handbook of European Elections*, London: Routledge.

Kriesi, H. (2004) 'Political context and opportunity', in Snow, D., Soule, S., and Kriesi, H. (eds) *The Blackwell Companion to Social Movements*, Malden, MA: Blackwell.

Kriesi, H., Grande, E., Dolezal, M., Helbling, M., Höglinger, D., Hutter, S. and Wüest, B. (2012) *Political Conflict in Western Europe*, Cambridge: Cambridge University Press.

Linek, L. (2010) *Zrazení snů? Struktura a dynamika postojů k politickému režimu a jeho institucím a jeho důsledky*, Prague: SLON.

Linek, L., Císař, O., Petrůšek, I. and Vráblíková, K. (2018) *Občanství a politická participace v České republice*, Prague: SLON.

Mareš, M. at al. (2015) *Stop islámu! Protiislámská politika v České republice*, Brno: CDK.

Mikecz, D. (2015) 'Changing movements, evolving parties: The party-oriented structure of the Hungarian radical right and alternative movement', *Intersections: East European Journal of Society and Politics*, 1(3): 101–119.

Mudde, C. (2007) *Populist Radical Right Parties in Europe*, Cambridge: Cambridge University Press.

Navrátil, J. and Hrubeš, M. (2016) 'Fear and loathing in the Czech Republic: Analysis of the role of civil society in the public discourse on the refugee crisis', paper presented at ECPR General Conference, Prague, 7–10 September 2016.

Navrátil, J. and Kluknavská, A. (2017) 'Counter/mobilizing on the migration crisis in the Czech Republic and Slovakia', paper presented at Czech Sociological Association Conference, Prague, February 1–3, 2017.

Seznam. (2018) 'Pro Topolánka kmotr, pro Babiše zločinec. Zpověď velkého zákulisního hráče, který dnes radí SPD'. Available at: https://www.seznamzpravy.cz/clanek/pro-topolanka-kmotr-pro-babise-zlocinec-zpoved-velkeho-zakulisniho-hrace-ktery-dnes-radi-spd-44244?seq-no=1&dop-ab-variant=&source=clanky-home.

Sikk, A. (2010) 'Newness as a winning formula for new political parties', *Party Politics*, 18(4): 465–486.

SPD (2017) 'Politický program SPD'. Available at: http://www.spd.cz/program.

Věci Veřejné (2010) 'Politický program'. Available at: http://www.olympic.cz/finan covani/docs/VV.pdf.

13

RADICALIZATION OF RADICAL RIGHT

Nativist movements and parties in
the Slovak political process[1]

Oľga Gyárfášová

Introduction

Post-1989 development in Slovakia attracted a lot of academic attention, mostly due to a more complicated path to consolidated democracy than that of its neighbours. The country represented a post-communist "show-case" of nationalism accompanied with clearly identified semi-authoritarian populist politics and radical-right nationalistic appeals. Foreign scholars (Deegan-Krause 2004; Haughton 2005; Henderson 2002; Deegan-Krause and Haughton 2009; Mareš 2009; and others), as well as the domestic ones (Učeň 2004; Mesežnikov and Gyárfášová 2008; Mesežnikov 2009; Nociar 2012) concentrated on identifying the causes and consequences of these developments, focusing mostly on the first and second decades of transformation.

As for the third decade of consolidating democracy in Central Eastern European countries (CEEC), not only post-communist democracies, but also most Western ones face the challenge of radical right-wing movements' electoral fortune, rising xenophobia, populism, and Euroscepticism. The electoral success of parties based on such appeals is often explained by the 'mobilization of losers'. The worldwide economic crises along with global and national turbulences have brought new populist impetus for democratic societies – be it post-communist, or established traditional democracies. In early years of the post-1989 transformation, the term 'losers' was defined vis-à-vis accelerated economic changes, the radical shift from the state-controlled economy based on state paternalistic care – at least, that was the narrative – to a free market economy with higher individual responsibility.[2] Later on, the EU accession countries were challenged by polarization between winners and losers of the EU integration. A new societal cleavage, which has recently emerged as a consequence of globalization, political trans-nationalization and manifold crises, has less social and economic character;

instead, cultural, identitarian dividing lines are in the foreground (cf. Inglehart and Norris 2017). Furthermore, in several EU countries, including the CEEC, the current migration crises accelerated the shifts in saliency of political issues, and have made the changes in their reconfiguration manifest. These developments are to be observed across the liberal democracies; where, of course, the country context is extremely important.

Nationalist movements and right-wing national and populist political parties in Slovakia have been an integral part of politics since the very early years of democratic transition. However, the phenomenon went through several metamorphoses in terms of actors/organizations, discourse, appeals, and electoral success/failure. The key player within this type of agenda used to be the *Slovak National Party* (Slovenská národná strana: SNS) (Gyárfášová and Mesežnikov 2015; Nociar 2012; Pytlas 2016). In the early 1990s, it became the leading representative of the country's nationalist forces, and since then it has acted as the main driver for nationalist socio-political discourse, influencing policies in selected areas of public life, either in the position of a parliamentary opposition or a co-ruling party. However, in approximately the last five years, SNS became more moderate, which eased its nationalistic profile and statements. The nationalist agenda has been taken over by the more radical movement party – *Kotleba – People's Party Our Slovakia* (Ľudová strana-Naše Slovensko: ĽSNS) which surprisingly received eight per cent of votes in the 2016 general election and is represented in the National Parliament by 14 out of 150 MPs. Nevertheless, the first electoral breakthrough of the party was the 2013 regional election, when its leader Marian Kotleba has been elected a governor in one of Slovakia's eight administrative regional units.

The ĽSNS is a radical, extreme right-wing protest party that bears clear signs of anti-systemness. Above all, the party completely denies the entire concept of human and minority rights, making dehumanizing proclamations about the Roma and other minorities (ethnic, racial, religious, sexual, and similar). As far as Slovakia's core pro-Western geopolitical orientation is concerned, the ĽSNS endorses Slovakia's withdrawal from the Eurozone, the EU, and NATO. Furthermore, the party refuses to acknowledge the democratic historical tradition of the Slovak Republic represented by the Slovak National Uprising against the Slovak state in 1944, and instead praises the Slovak wartime fascist state. In May 2017, the anti-systemness of the party, and its threat to Slovakia's democracy, was recognized by the Prosecutor General of the Slovak Republic when he asked the Supreme Court to ban the party as an extremist group whose activities violate the country's constitution. The court hearing is pending.

With the ĽSNS in the national parliament, Slovakia is confronted by even more radicalized right-wing party whose profile and agenda go further right than that of the "traditional" representative of the radical right. This fact demonstrates the process of radicalization of the far-right agenda, at least for the current legislation period (2016–2020).

The key objective of this study is not only to capture the rise of the radical right-wing People's Party Our Slovakia (ĽSNS) but also to identify and discuss possible key factors of this rise. Furthermore, the paper concentrates on the context of this development in terms of political and discursive opportunity structures as well as cultural and symbolic tools (framing) of cultural resources and symbols which are employed by the movement party. The detailed focus on this actor includes the resource mobilization for electoral success, but discusses also its political defeat in 2017 regional election. The concluding part discusses the consequences of radical right for political discourse and political process in Slovakia.

I. Radical far-right: general and country specific perspective

In the academic literature, there are different categories, names, and labels used for radical right, right-wing populism, and far-right, extreme right, etc. (cf. Caiani 2017). However, we can rely on and work with common denominators of all of them – ideological features as they are clearly summarized by Cas Mudde. These are: nationalism (internal homogenization, external exclusiveness, ethnic nationalism, and state nationalism), exclusionism (ethnopluralism, Anti-Semitism), xenophobia, the quest for a strong state (law and order, militarism), welfare chauvinism, traditional ethics, and revisionism. (Mudde 2007: 21).

Radical right is most commonly related to nationalism; they are close 'bedfellows', and following Mudde's conceptualization, populist radical right parties can be seen as a specific form of nationalism (Mudde 2007: 30–31). Following this line, the concept of *nativism* is very useful for further elaboration because:

> Nativism entails a combination of nationalism and xenophobia, i.e. an ideology that holds that states should be inhabited exclusively by members of the native group ('the nation') and that non-native (or 'alien') elements whether persons or ideas, are fundamentally threatening to the homogeneous nation-state.
>
> *(Mudde 2011: 12)*

In radical right-wing agenda, 'others' means an external threat to cultural homogeneity, to cultural and national identity. In 2007, Mudde wondered 'if the concept of nativism is to "travel" to the Eastern part of the European continent, since in post-communist Europe mass immigration has so far remained a fairly marginal concern...' (Mudde 2007: 31). After the 2015 refugee crises, it is evident that the answer is 'yes'; nativism is also an applicable and useful concept in CEEC – it conceptualizes the xenophobic stances which go beyond the traditional animosity towards the autochthonous minorities. That is true despite the fact that some countries, like Slovakia, for example, experienced the immigrants and refugees only virtually, in the speeches and fear appeals of politicians. Slovakia, similarly to other Visegrad Four countries, did not accept any refugees and did not accept the relocation scheme of the European Commission.

Radical right political parties and nationalism as such did not emerge in CEE countries 'from scratch'. There are deep-rooted legacies, historical backgrounds, and structural conditions which drove and formed the post-communist radical right. Bustikova and Kitschelt made a complex comparative analysis of legacies which are 'deep durable causes that affect the potential for radical right-wing politics across the post-communist region' (Bustikova and Kitschelt 2010: 29). They believe that legacies create the baseline for patterns of party competition, shape partisan politics, and thus mould a proximate cause of radical right mobilization (Bustikova and Kitschelt 2010: 29–30). In the same line, Bartek Pytlas points out: 'Historical narratives of collective identity become particularly important blueprints of radical right political agency if one recalls that a mythic, romanticized vision of a nation lies at the core of this ideology' (Pytlas 2016: 50). Looking for 'usable past' after the communist regimes broke down was a vital and relevant process – especially in the countries which split shortly after the previous regimes collapsed, and they were confronted with the process of state-hood and nation-state building. This was the case in Slovakia with all the complications of the 'triple transition' (Offe 1991) which accompanied the process of building up and consolidating democracy.

Consequently, when examining the radical right in Slovakia, we have to bear in mind historical legacies and socio-political structural factors. Primarily, it was the long-term effect of these factors that formed the socio-cultural environment in which nationalists and national right-wing radicals spread and capitalized on their agenda. Slovakia is a country with a dominant titular ethnic entity (i.e. the Slovak nation) and religion (i.e. Catholicism) and simultaneously with a relatively high degree of ethnic and denominational diversity that is represented by ethnic minorities and groups (above all, Hungarians and Roma minorities), as well as smaller religious communities. Secondly, in the course of the twentieth century, the Slovaks were part of five constitutional entities (i.e. the Austro–Hungarian Empire, the first Czechoslovak Republic, the wartime Slovak State, the renewed Czechoslovak Republic and an independent Slovak Republic since 1993). During this period, the Slovak ethnic entity gradually went through various stages of its national development that were affected by mutual interactions with other ethnic groups. Upon the establishment of the first Czechoslovak Republic in 1918, it became the object of practical enforcement of political and ideological construct of the single Czechoslovak nation that, on the one hand, granted it the status of statehood nation, but, on the other hand, neglected or directly questioned its ethnic and linguistic independence. During World War II, it existed as a semi-sovereign, ethnically defined national state that came to be known as the wartime Slovak State. Still, ideology of Slovak extreme right and ultranationalists is connected to the legacy of that wartime clero-fascist state which put pseudo national independence over the political freedom. After the end of World War II, it was part of a two-nation partnership that recognized its ethnic and linguistic independence (post-war Czechoslovakia). Since the establishment of the Slovak Republic on 1 January 1993, following the split of Czechoslovakia, it has existed as a sovereign and prevailingly civic national state. The discontinuities in the twentieth century resulted in the fact that Slovakia was ruled by a great variety of political regimes, ranging from monarchist semi-authoritarianism to pluralistic democracy, fascist totalitarianism, limited 'national' democracy, communist totalitarianism, and turbulent developments after 1989 (cf. Gyárfášová and Mesežnikov 2015). Frequent changes (or even 'changes of changes') of social orders and political regimes over a relatively short period of time led to various degree of particular population groups' self-identification; these groups demonstrated their loyalty to different types of political culture (e.g. democratic or authoritarian), which affected their political behavior as well as political actors' strategies of appealing to them. This development was accompanied by increasing national self-awareness of the Slovaks as well as equally strong ethnic self-identification of members of principal autochthones ethnic minorities, particularly ethnic Hungarians.

II. Movement parties as political actors

Movement parties represent a new hybrid form of political organizations. The literature sees them as transition mode of social movements into political parties (Kitschelt 2006; Chapter 2 in this book). They became political actors which successfully mobilized voters above all in times of crises and in the situation when traditional parties are not able – or are perceived as unable – to tackle key social issues. Movement parties are characterized mostly by their anti-establishment, anti-elite appeals: they claim to be an alternative to mainstream parties. They do this not only by their profile and their way of addressing voters, but also by their organizational structure. They want to demonstrate 'alternativeness': they intentionally do not aim at mass membership, they avoid calling themselves a 'party' and have not built an organizational network, being usually centred on their (charismatic) leader. During the mobilization phase, they portray themselves as new actors that came from outside the established political elite. In addition, they used to present themselves as non-political or anti-politics, appealing to the frustrated and alienated voter (cf. Havelka 2016).

As Caiani and Císař argued in Chapter 2, so far, the academic focus has mostly been limited to left-wing and ideologically hybrid organizations, thus neglecting developments on the (far) right. However, the far-right – in its populist, radical, and extreme variants – is one of the most successful objects of inquiry in the social sciences and seemingly shares organizational features with other movement parties. Further on, they underline, that recently – with the economic crisis and the following refugee emergency – there are favourable conditions for the emergence and consolidation of populist parties (either on the right and on the left) (Caiani and Císař 2018). In Slovakia, the far-right nationalist profile is – so far – the dominant or even exclusive background of the movement parties.

II.1. Radical nationalist movements in Slovakia

Radical rights groupings, associations, and initiatives have existed in Slovakia since 1989. The milieu has never been fully united, it was rather a conglomerate of partially cooperative, partially competing bodies. In 2009, at the eve of 20th anniversary of the Velvet Revolution, there was an attempt to postulate the platform in a more coherent way. The program manifesto got a tempting title *Memorandum of the first post-November young generation* (Memorandum…, 2009). The text is quite indicative – it is expressing the frustration of young far-right nationalists of the post-1989 political and economic development. It is characterized by a clear rejection of the liberal democratic regime, the questioning of the basic principles of the market economy, historical revisionism, anti-Atlanticism and anti-Americanism, anti-minority settings, anti-Semitism, anti-Romani racism, demonstrative pan-Slavism, and declaratory signing to the Christian roots and traditional family values (2009).

It can be evidently documented that the key actor of radical right – ĽSNS – did not come out of nothing. In Slovakia the extreme right scene is quite 'populated'. Since the early 1990s, there were several, politically relatively marginalized formations representing the radical nationalist milieu. Among them were the Slovak People's Party (SĽS) and Slovak National Unity (SNJ), which had been running in the elections, although with very weak results, which never exceeded 1 per cent of the votes (Gyárfášová and Mesežnikov 2015: 236). Recently, in addition to the ĽSNS, there are two relevant radical right movement parties – Slovak Togetherness (Slovenská pospolitosť: SP) and the ultranationalist Slovak Revival Movement (Slovenské hnutie obrody: SHO).

Slovak Togetherness was formed in 1995 as a civic association. Recently, it claims to be the only genuine and authentic bearer of 'thousands of years of Slovak and Slavic traditions' and of the 'spirit of Ľudovít Štúr'[3] and the only uncompromising advocate of Slovak national interests (Mesežnikov and Gyárfášová 2017). The positions of SP were characterized by open opposition to parliamentary democracy as a form of political organization, radical nationalism, strong anti-Hungarian rhetoric, and antisemitism. The association was built on a strictly centralized and hierarchical 'leadership' principle. The activities of SP contributed significantly to the constitution of the current form of the right-wing extremist movement. For almost two decades, this association was considered to be a symbol of Slovak right-wing extremism, especially in terms of its activity, program, rhetoric, organizational base, and, to some extent, also the visual appearance of members who used uniforms on public events, calling to mind the domestic pattern of fascist politics from the Slovak wartime state (1939-45).

In 2003, Marian Kotleba, a young man with political ambitions, joined the SP and became the leader of the organization. After his entry, SP activities and visibility accelerated; it expanded its work on party policy and submitted a request to the Ministry of Interior for registration as a political party. In January 2005, the Ministry of the Interior registered a political party under the name Slovak Togetherness – the National Party (Slovenská pospolitosť – Národná strana: SP-NS). Representatives of the new political party stated that its establishment was a response to the long-term failure of the Slovak National Party's policy, especially during its participation in the government, and that the new party would be working to point at the danger of Slovakia's dominance by foreign groups and supranational institutions. During 2005, the SP-NS organized several public events, where its representatives spread racist messages and provoked conflicts with the police. In response to the situation, the Prosecutor General submitted a proposal to the Supreme Court for the dissolution of SP-NS in October 2005 and in March 2006, the SP-NS was dissolved. The Court concluded that the Party's activities were inconsistent with the law, and its program could violate democratic principles, and could eliminate democracy in the country. Representatives of the dissolved party continued in public activities under the SP's name as a civic association, they distanced themselves from Marian Kotleba and keep a profile of a movement without political ambitions (Vyhlásenie Slovenskej Pospolitosti,.., 2016).

Another important player in the ultranationalist scene is the Slovak Revival Movement (Slovenské hnutie obrody: SHO), which has existed since 2004. Formally, until June 2016, SHO was a civic association; in June 2016, it decided to register for a political movement with the intention to participate in the election. Wider political ambitions were identified in the SHO earlier. The very definition of the organization in its name (the 'movement', not the 'association', the 'union', or the 'association') suggested that it is an activity that goes beyond the interests of its formal members. The political ambitions of the SHO were represented by the participation of its representatives in events with clear political content, taking positions on political issues (domestic as well as foreign policy) (Programové tézy …, 2017).

SHO emphasizes that it promotes 'traditional values (family, culture, honour, and faith),' 'a healthy view of the world and patriotic sentiment', fighting the 'moral decay of society' (ibid.). Slovak analysts warn that in the future SHO could be replaced and become more sophisticated but not less radical alternative (Mesežnikov and Gyárfášová 2017).

The ĽSNS is an organization which embodied the political ambitions of the Slovak right-wing movements. The process of transformation from a movement to a party[4] under the recent name and with today's leader was completed in 2010, when the ĽSNS entered the political arena, although with a very insignificant electoral results – 1.33 per cent of valid votes in 2010, and 1.58 per cent in 2012. The rise was still to come.

III. Identifying the opportunity structure for radical right

What were the structural opportunities for radicalization of radical right? At the general level, the factors of emergence and success of radical right could be clustered into several categories according to different criteria. Some analyses distinguish between macro-, meso- and micro-level explanations and corresponding variables. These categories could be combined with individual, organizational, and structural factors. Other approaches work with the demand and supply side (cf. Caiani 2017).

In the following analysis of the context and political and discursive opportunities, I will combine and complement two key dimension: (a) party competition and the profiling of the political scene and other relevant actors as the political opportunity structure; (b) based on long time sociological surveys, I will identify deep-rooted values and attitudes of the Slovak public which – together with the political and public discourse – represent a discursive opportunity structure for nationalistic/nativist appeals. There are many areas that can be examined and highlighted; however, I only focus on three of them – attitudes towards the 'others'; features of historical memory; and 'geopolitical mentality', which means foreign policy orientations and international relations' public perception.

II.1 Political opportunity structure: party competition, or what's right to the right?

The basic indicators of political opportunities structures according to Sidney Tarrow are openness/closeness of the political institutions, presence/absence of influential allies within the political system, and the conflicts (or their absence) among the elite actors which increase (or decrease) the chances of political activists to get access to political decision making (Tarrow 2011). Along the same lines is the conceptualization by Ciaini and Císař. In Chapter 2 of this book they argue:

> The basic idea of the approach based on political opportunity structure is that open political institutions facilitate mobilization, and closed institutions impede it. The level of their openness or closedness is a function of the number of access points available to social movement organizations and other non-state actors in a political system at a given point in time.

Paul Lucardie also highlights the fact that apart from formal institutional barriers like registration procedures and electoral thresholds, new parties have to deal with informal procedures and cultural barriers. Another important aspect of the opportunity structure concerns salient cleavages in society (Lucardie 2000: 180–1).

Now let's examine the political opportunity structure of the ĽSNS. As has been mentioned already, during the 1990s and 2000s, the traditional 'issue and frame owner' of nationalistic agenda was the Slovak National Party (SNS). However, in 2012 election the party failed to come above the 5 per cent threshold and became an extra-parliamentary party with relatively limited impact on political and public discourse. There are many circumstances explaining this development. Above all, around 2010, there was a strong competition for radical right agenda from two sides: 'nationalism light' represented by Smer-SD, a strong party with highly appreciated competence in social and economic issues; and extreme radical parties and groupings, notably the ĽSNS. Secondly, the salience of the nationalistic agenda in the political competition as well as in the public discourse declined. This could be traced back to the split of the ethnically based Party of Hungarian Coalition (SMK) in 2009, and the foundation of the electorally more successful party Most-Híd (Bridge) which tries to address not only Hungarian, but also Slovak voters and which is less vocal in defending the rights of Hungarian minority living in Slovakia. It also partially smoothed the bilateral relation between Slovakia and Hungary, as the ruling Fidesz was fostering relations with the SMK and not Most-Híd that became represented in the national parliament. Consequently, lowering the salience of national agenda forced SNS to 're-brand' and search new issues. It tried to address its voters with Euroscepticism, but it did not work as efficiently as may be expected because the electorate has shown the pro-EU bias. Last but not least, the party has been weakened by internal quarrels and tensions, which led to splits and the replacement of long-serving chairman Jan Slota who was well-known for his vulgar statement and behaviour.

Nevertheless, after the four year 'parliamentary break', in 2016 the SNS could celebrate its comeback to national politics; it even became the junior party in the coalition government led by left-leaning Smer-SD. The third ruling partner is the above-mentioned Most-Híd, a bi-ethnic party whose mission is to build a bridge between the Slovaks and the Hungarians. This partnership with the 'eternal enemy' definitely made SNS a traitor in the eyes of its hardcore nationalist electorate. Without any doubt, it turned into a mainstream right-wing with very moderate nationalistic appeal looking for its position within the existing political competition.

II.2 Discursive opportunity structure: public receptivity for radical appeals?

Based on dozens of public opinion surveys conducted over the last three decades, three clusters of public attitudes can be identified as those making the public more receptive to nationalist appeals – perception of the 'others'; historical memory; and phenomena which I have called 'geopolitical mentality'.

The Slovak society is characterized by a distinct and long-lasting social distance to national minorities, foreigners and, in general, to any 'otherness'. In first two decades after 1989, the distance has been mostly articulated (and politically mobilized) towards traditional autochthonous minorities, especially the Hungarian and Roma (cf. Vašečka 2009; Gallová Kriglerová and Kadlečíková 2012). The mobilization of intolerance and questioning the need to respect the rights of national minorities became an important political issue and a key dividing line of political competition. Nationalism and national populism represented an obstacle to the consolidation of liberal democracy and Slovakia's integration to EU and NATO. The weakening of ethnic mobilization took place only after 2010. It was a combination of several factors, including the founding of the Most-Híd Party whose ambition was to act as a civic, political-minded force, and the withdrawal of SNS and SMK from parliamentary politics. In addition, an external factor was also involved – the combination of the non-nationalist, pro-reform government coalition in Slovakia in 2010–2011 and the government of Viktor Orbán in Hungary was not a suitable cooperation of Slovak and Hungarian nationalism for the dissemination of nationalist themes. 'Complementarities of nationalisms' (Slovak and Hungarian ones), which had worked before the 2010 elections, was lost, but it did not resume after the inauguration of the second government of Robert Fico in 2012. However, it was already clear that the weakening of the national agenda does not mean its retreat from Slovak politics; it remained a 'sleeping potentiality' which has been mobilized again. The prejudices against the 'others', the intolerance go hand in hand with social chauvinism (Bustikova 2014).

Furthermore, the surveys repeatedly identify (via different indicators) that Slovak public perceives their country ethnocentrically.[5] Such a public view undoubtedly reflects the overall set of political elites that live ethnocentric perceptions either by symbolic steps or by real policies.

The migration crises of 2015, which brought the 'xenophobization' of political and public discourse definitely created a situational discursive opportunity during the migration inflow in summer 2015, and has been politically utilized by all parties, above all by the ruling Smer-SD, before the 2016 general election. The politicians 'surfed' on the wave of majority opinion, while strengthening xenophobic and rejecting attitudes. The overall discourse was extremely polarized and emotional. Surveys conducted in the early September signalled that the willingness to accept refugees has been marginal in Slovakia.[6] The same was true of the relocation scheme suggested by the EU. Social climate has been clearly influenced by declining trust towards political parties and political class.

As for the historical consciousness, the surveys have revealed insufficiencies in knowledge and awareness. The activation of revisionists among historians finding support for a part of the political establishment led to the relativistic interpretations of many historical events and the dulling of the critical perception of the most problematic themes. Above all, young people and high school students know very little about the Holocaust, atrocities of the Slovak war-state, and forty years of the communist regime. Weak historical awareness provides fertile soil for extremism (Gyárfášová 2015).

Regarding the views of Slovak public of the overall geopolitical and civilization inclusion of the country, even more than decade after joining the European Union and NATO, about half of the population would want Slovakia to stand somewhere between the West and the East.[7] That points to the persistence of reservation over the unambiguous formal anchor of the country in the western clusters, and the major inclination to an ambivalent middle position. It is also related to the fact that political and military neutrality is still a fabled central alternative, reflecting the notion that for 'small' Slovakia it is best to be with everyone, not to stand out, to remain neutral even in case of conflicts. Such geopolitical 'science fiction' in-between, neutral positioning is a fertile soil for radical-right stances on the foreign policy issues. Certain susceptibility of some groups of citizens to isolationism, anti-Americanism, EU-phobia and anti-Western moods has been identified repeatedly. In its programme, the LSNS clearly declares critical and hateful attitudes towards integration groupings, like the EU and NATO, which Slovakia joined in 2004.

> We put Slovak interests above the dictate of Brussels and therefore refuse to restrict the sovereignty of member states of the European Union We will not allow any violation of Slovakian territorial integrity and we will strengthen the defense of the country. We will leave the NATO terrorist pact and our troops will no longer participate in occupation of foreign countries.
>
> *(Program ..., 2016)*

II.3 Symbols and framing

For the Slovak nationalists, the Slovak wartime state represents the most relevant historical frame. Contrary to the generally accepted view that the state was allied with Nazi Germany, and as such sent tens of thousands of its citizens to concentration camps and certain death, Kotleba and his party praise the state as the first-ever independent state of Slovaks. The 'independent' Slovak state's totalitarian regime that adopted racial legislation inspired by 'Nuremberg' laws, and actively collaborated with Hitler's Germany in the implementation of the Holocaust (i.e. 'Aryanizing' Jewish property, depriving Jews of their civil rights, and subsequently deporting them to Nazi extermination camps outside Slovakia's territory). The official state doctrine of the Slovak Republic is based on the anti-fascist tradition embodied by the Slovak National Uprising of 1944. Therefore, the modern Slovak Republic is considered a successor to the Czechoslovak federation, and neither a legal nor political successor to the wartime Slovak state proclaimed in March 1939; however, a revisionist perception of the period of 1939–1945 has become part of the country's public and political discourse regarding the issue of national history since 1989.

ĽSNS use the frame of the Slovak wartime state as the first-ever independent state of Slovaks and glorifies his hero Andrej Hlinka and the president Jozef Tiso.[8] The party's historical reference and the narrative is reflected on a symbolical level – its logo copies the one of the authoritarian party which embodied the war Slovak state in 1939–45; the party also applies the slogan of that party 'For God and For the Nation'. Moreover, ĽSNS MPs requested a minute of silence in memory of Jozef Tiso, and on its webpage party proudly rank Jozef Tiso among national heroes.[9] Of course, the party denies any connection to fascism.

Another strongly symbolic act has been conducted in 2015, at the day of the state holiday marking the anniversary of the Slovak National Uprising – then-governor Marian Kotleba hung two black flags on the regional authority building demonstrating a clear preference in history's interpretation.

III. Mobilization for electoral success – party and voters

III.1 Two steps of the electoral rise

Until 2013, the LSNS electoral popularity has been rather marginalized. The electoral breakthrough came initially at the regional level in fall 2013 by winning the seat of regional governor in Central Slovakia. The electoral success continued: in 2016 ĽSNS has been elected by 8 per cent of votes into the national parliament and the party got a new impetus.

The victory of Marian Kotleba in the second round of the regional election was an unexpected surprise. It went against the standard rule, according to which it is a moderate candidate who usually wins in a run-off. Nevertheless, the vote showed a pattern of mobilization that has also been repeated in the general election. In his sophisticated analysis of voters in the region of Banská Bystrica, Kamil Gregor examined voters' transitions in seven different votes around 2013 (2009 – 2014) and found out that: 'A crucial difference between the voters bases of Kotleba and Maňka is the fact that Kotleba was much more successful in attracting people that did not participate in other types of elections than Maňka' (Gregor 2015: 247). The analysis revealed that voters who did cast the vote for Marian Kotleba did not vote either in the two rounds of next presidential (March 2014) or EP elections (May 2014) either. That means that persistent continuous non-voters stand up and cast their vote for the radical right-wing candidate.

The same pattern has been proved for the 2016 general election. Based on exit-poll data, we have discovered that there is a specific segment of the electorate – the mobilized voters who abstained in 2012 but have been mobilized for the 2016 election. Large portion of these voters decided for the parties We are a family[10] and ĽSNS, which means that they have been effectively addressed by protest, anti-establishment alternatives. The study argues that the abstention in 2012 general election (excluding first-time voters) is the strongest predictor for vote choice for these two protest parties (Gyárfášová et al. 2017).

Both findings illustrate that the persistent non-voters who feel alienated from the politics and are mistrustful towards the traditional mainstream parties – that is why they usually abstain – are addressed and mobilized by far-right radical alternatives.

Who are the voters of radical right movement parties? It has been documented by many surveys, and for most countries that certain socio-demographic groups are more likely to vote radical right parties. A typical median voter of radical right-wing parties in Western Europe is described as a young male with lower education and lower social status, who often perceives social deprivation and feels diffuse social threats, mostly coming from the 'foreigners' (Arzheimer and Carter, 2006; de Lange et al., 2011; and others). It has been partially verified in Slovakia as well. The ĽSNS has been doing well in attracting young voters, above all the first-time voters. According to the exit poll, the ĽSNS has been the most successful party among first time voters (18–22), receiving 23 per cent of all their votes. Male voters were more likely to vote for the radical right – 2/3 of the ĽSNS voters were men. The well-known gender gap has been more significant among young men first-time voters – almost one third of them (which means twice as many as women) voted for the ĽSNS. Education as voting predictor does not show any significant differences. The same is true of contextual social variables – the analysis of contextual variables did not confirm unemployment as a clear predictor of the ĽSNS choice (Bahna and Zagrapan 2017). It partially verifies the hypothesis that it is not predominantly social economic factors that motivate radical right-wing voting choice. Similarly, Arzheimer and Carter concluded some years after examining the vote for extreme right in several west-European democracies: '… our findings suggest that the right-wing extremist vote will not be curbed by simply looking after economic conditions' (2006: 439). About a decade later, the same statement is well founded for the post-communist world.

III.2 The electoral decline: political loss in 2017 regional election

After the 2016 general election, the extreme radical right party started to be perceived as a problem.[11] The regional election which took place in Fall 2017 was seen as the opportunity to defeat Marian Kotleba. The mobilization took place at the level of challengers as well as civil society. At first, the opposition candidates agreed that they would coordinate and before the election they would step back in favor of that one who has greatest chance to win.[12] Finally, a unified political support of the government coalition (Smer-SD, SNS and Most-Híd), parliamentary democratic opposition as well as other parties was given to the independent candidate – Kotleba's challenger – Jan Lunter. In addition, non-governmental organizations and various civic initiatives made remarkable efforts to increase electoral participation within the anti-Kotleba camp. The result was clear – Mr Lunter won with 48 per cent of votes; the incumbent got 23 per cent. The new regional governor won the seat also due to increased electoral mobilization – the turnout in this region reached 40 percent, which was the record for the regional elections in the Slovak Republic since 2001, when the regional elections took place for the first time, and in this region was much higher than the nationwide average, which reached 30 per cent. Moreover, the ĽSNS failed to penetrate the regional parliaments: only two were elected by the 335 candidate members of the ĽSNS, including M. Kotleba himself.

However, the political defeat of the extreme right had one worrying moment, to which many analysts have immediately pointed out – measured by the number of votes, not taking into account the specificity of majoritarian electoral law for regional elections, which favours the candidates from larger parties or wider coalition, the electoral support of the ĽSNS did not decrease, compared to the 2016 general election. On contrary, in some parts of the country, it even increased slightly. Nevertheless, the intense political and civic mobilization against the extreme right was signal that extremists do not need to remain in politics for ever.

Concluding remarks

The chapter has brought three key arguments: (a) Slovakia is challenged by radicalization of the radical right-wing agenda which found its political and discursive opportunity structure; (b) the radicalized party ĽSNS, which came out of the far-right movement, broke the 'smoke screen' and after the success in regional election entered the national politics; (c) this party with its agenda is able to mobilize specific subsets of electorates who used to be alienated from the political processes and did not vote for the mainstream political actors.

Electoral fortune of the far-right party ĽSNS opened a new chapter of how such a party acts in Slovakia's social and political environment. In today's Europe, there are not many countries where the parties as ĽSNS managed to get into the centre of the political scene. The parties with a similar profile are usually on the margin. However, the ĽSNS with its 8 per cent electoral gain is currently too weak to change the character of the political regime. It is isolated in the parliament, its coalition potential is zero; all parties formed a *cordon sanitaire* around it. Moreover, the coalition parties declared themselves to be a barrier against extremism, which they made the raison d'être of their existence and a guarantee of stability. On the other hand, the ĽSNS is ready to barter on single issues, and it has been approached by other parties, both coalition and opposition ones, to bargain on issues such as the vote on increasing the number of members required for the registration of minority religions, when the ĽSNS deputies voted with the government, or the investigation of allegations of corruption at the Ministry of Foreign Affairs, when they voted with the opposition. Anyway, the impact of the ĽSNS on political processes is limited. However, the 'virus' of extremism is dangerous by its devastating effect on the social atmosphere, especially when it has acquired a parliamentary platform. On the socio-cultural level, the radical far-right is able to capitalize on the inherited and persisting patterns of the population's political culture and value orientations (nationalism, paternalism, and distrust of ethnic, religious and cultural diversity). This Slovak phenomenon could be a short-lived occurrence which will fade away with the next general election. Even if the ĽSNS as the current key actor of radical right movement party will not be represented in the national parliament, it does not mean that the potential, the 'dreaming potentiality' for its ideas, positions, program etc. would fade away.

Notes

1 The author wish to acknowledge that this work has been conducted within a research project supported by the Slovak Research and Development Agency under the contract APVV-14-0527).

2 In the 1990s the voters of nationalist-authoritarian Movement for a Democratic Slovakia (HZDS) were typical frustrated 'transition losers' (the elderly, rural dwellers, those with low education, with lower cultural and social capital). They also viewed the past nostalgically and regarded the previous regime as a better than the post-1989 one and tended to value the firm hand of authority, and were rather narrow-minded, relying on the protective hand of the state.

3 L'udovít Štúr (1815–1856), the leader of the Slovak national revival in the 19th century, and the author of the Slovak language standard. He was an organizer of the Slovak volunteer campaigns during the Hungarian Revolution of 1848 on the side of the Habsburg's Vienna. Štúr represents a nationalistic symbolical hero, perceived mostly positively, his panslavism and antisemitism is often overseen and underestimated, his life and political impact glamorized, above all by the Slovak nationalists. He was also a politician, poet, journalist, publisher, teacher, philosopher, linguist, and member of the Hungarian Parliament.

4 Interestingly enough, among a number of newly established political actors, the L'SNS is the only one to proudly use the word 'party' in its name. Following the general mistrust of the public towards political parties and political class in general, newly established protest parties try intentionally to avoid using the word 'party' in their names.

5 The statement that 'Slovakia is a country of the Slovaks and so should stay' was agreed by 68% of the respondents (Gallová Kriglerová and Kadlečíková 2012: 10).

6 According to a survey conducted by the 2Muse for the Citizens' Initiative Call for humanity, only 18 per cent of respondents said that Slovakia would become a new home country for refugees. Available at: http://www.pluska.sk/spravy/z-domova/prieskum-prijmeme-utecencov-za-svojich-takyto-je-postoj-slovakov.html.

7 Up to 52 per cent of respondents responded to the CEPI survey. About the quarter saw Slovakia in the West, 12 per cent saw it as part of the East. The survey was conducted by the Central European Policy Institute in February 2016.

8 Andrej Hlinka (1864–1938) was a Slovak Catholic priest, journalist, banker and politician, one of the most important Slovak public activists in Czechoslovakia before Second World War. As a politician he was the leader of the Slovak People's Party, later renamed to Hlinka´s Slovak People's Party, the totalitarian force of the wartime state which considered him as a national hero. Jozef Tiso (1887–1947) politician and Roman Catholic priest who governed the Slovak Republic from 1939 to 1945. In 1947 he was executed for war crimes and crimes against humanity. The Slovak nationalists see him as a martyr.

9 'The People's Party Our Slovakia continues in the legacy of our national heroes – L'udovít Štúr, Dr. Andrej Hlinka and Dr. Jozef Tiso'. http://www.naseslovensko.net/en/about-us/.

10 The party Sme rodina (We are a Family) has been founded by a controversial businessman Boris Kollár who 'purchased' and renamed a small regional party shortly before the 2016 election, thereby circumventing the time-consuming process of collecting supporters' signatures and applying to become legally registered. Surprisingly, the party got 6.6 per cent of votes and mandates in the National parliament. The party represents the phenomenon of non-political politics or "entrepreneurial populism": it has a very unclear ideological profile. Its agenda includes fight against corruption and it also uses radical anti-migration and eurosceptical rhetoric.

11 In summer 2017 about half of Slovakia's citizens would agree with dissolving the L'SNS by the Supreme Court, while 38 per cent would not approve such a decision, and 12 per cent would not take a stand (https://dennikn.sk/819428/rozpustit-ls-ns-kto-je-za-a-kto-proti/)

12 It should be noted that in 2017 the elections of the regional governors were for the first time held as one-round vote.

References

Arzheimer, K. and Carter, E. (2006) 'Political opportunity structures and right-wing extremist party success', *European Journal of Political Research*, 45(3): 419–443.

Bahna, M. and Zagrapan, J. (2017) 'Volia voliči v obciach s rómskou populáciou L'SNS častejšie? Analýza individuálnych a kontextuálnych faktorov volebných rozhodnutí v parlamentných voľbách 2016'. [Do voters in communities with Roma population more frequently vote for the ĽSNS? Analyses of individual and contextual factors of voting decisions in 2016 election] *Working Papers in Sociology* 1/2017. Available at: http://www.sociologia.sav.sk/pdf/Working_Papers_in_Sociology_012017.pdf.

Bustikova, L. and Kitschelt, H. (2010) 'The radical right in post-communist Europe: Comparative perspectives on legacies and party competition', in Minkenberg, M. (ed) *Historical Legacies and the Radical Right in Post-Cold War Central and Central and Eastern Europe*, Stuttgart: ibidem –Verlag, 29–61.

Bustikova, L. (2014) 'Revenge of the Radical Right', *Comparative Political Studies*, 47(12): 1738–1765.

Caiani, M. (2017) 'Radical Right-Wing movements: Who, When, How, and Why?', ISA (Editorial Arrangement of Sociopedia.isa). Available at:. http://www.sagepub.net/isa/resources/pdf/RadicalRightMovements.pdf. Accessed 07/09/2017.

de Lange, S.L., van der Brug, W. and Inger Baller, I. (2011) 'Adversaries or Competitors? The Rise of Green and Radical Right-Wing Populist Parties', in Meijers, E. (ed) *Populism in Europe*, planet Verlag. Green Europe Foundation, 47–66.

Deegan-Krause, K. (2004) 'Uniting the Enemy: Politics and the Convergence of Nationalisms in Slovakia', *East European Politics and Societies*, 8(4) Fall: 651–696.

Deegan-Krause, K. and Haughton, T. (2009) 'Toward a More Useful Conceptualization of Populism: Types and Degrees of Populist Appeals in the Case of Slovakia', *Politics & Policy*, 37(4): 821–841.

Gallová Kriglerová, E. and Kadlečiková, J. (2012) *Verejná mienka v oblasti pravicového extrémizmu.* [Public opinion in the sphere of right-wing extremism]. Výskumná správa. Nadácia otvorenej spoločnosti – Open Society Foundation, Bratislava 2012.

Gregor, K. (2015) 'Who are Kotleba's Voters? Voters' Transitions in the Banská Bystrica Region in 2009-2014', *Sociológia*, 47(3): 235–252.

Gyárfášová, O. (2015) 'Sonda do historickej pamäti slovenskej spoločnosti zaostrená na mladých' [Probe into the historical memory of Slovak society focused on youth], *Annales scientia politica*, online, 4(1): 23–33. Available at: http://www.unipo.sk/public/media/21957/04%20Gyarfasova.pdf. Accessed 07/09/2017.

Gyárfášová, O. and Mesežnikov, G. (2015) 'Actors, Agenda, and Appeals of Radical Nationalist Right in Slovakia', in Minkenberg, M. (ed) *Transforming the Transformation? The East European radical right in the political process*, London: Routledge, 224–248.

Gyárfášová, O., Bahna, M. and Slosiarik, M. (2017) 'Sila nestálosti: volatilita voličov na Slovensku vo voľbách 2016' [The Strength of Instability: Voters' Volatility in the Slovak General Election, 2016], *Central European Political Studies Review*, 18(1). Available at: https://journals.muni.cz/cepsr/article/view/6861 - Accessed 07/09/2017.

Haughton, T. (2005) 'Constraints and Opportunities of Leadership in Post-Communist Europe', Aldershot UK: Ashgate Publishing.

Havelka, M. (2016) '"Apolitics", "Anti-politics", "Non-political Politics" and "Sub-politics" as Threats and Challenges', *Sociální studia / Social Studies*, 13(1): 9–22. ISSN 1214-813X

Henderson, K. (2002) *Slovakia: The Escape from Invisibility*, London: Routledge Publisher.

Inglehart, R. and Norris, P. (2017) 'Trump and the Populist Authoritarian Parties: The Silent Revolution in Reverse', *Perspectives on Politics*, 15(2): 443–454.

Lucardie, P. (2000) 'Prophets, Purifiers and Prolocutors: Towards a Theory on the Emergence of New Parties', *Party Politics*, 6(2): 175–185.

Mareš, M. (2009) 'The Extreme Right in Eastern Europe and Territorial Issues', *Středoevropské politické studie*, 11(2–3): 82–106. Available at: https://journals.muni.cz/cepsr/article/view/4446 Accessed 03 January 2018.

Mesežnikov, G. and Gyárfášová, O. (2008) *National Populism in Slovakia*, Bratislava: Institute for Public Affairs.

Mesežnikov, G. and Gyárfášová, O. (2017) 'Heutiger Rechtsextremismus und Ultranationalismus in der Slowakei: Stand, Trends, Unterstützung', Inštitút pre verejné otázky - Hanns-Seidel-Stiftung. Bratislava.

Memorandum prvej ponovembrovej generácie slovenskej mládeže (2009). [Memorandum of the first post-November young Slovak generation]. Available at: https://sites.google.com/site/memorandumppgsm/. Accessed 10 January 2018.

Mudde, C. (2007) *Populist Radical Right Parties in Europe*, Cambridge: Cambridge University Press.

Mudde, C. (2011) 'Radical right parties in Europe: What, who, why?', *Participation*, 34(3): 12–15.

Nociar, T. (2012) 'Right-Wing Extremism in Slovakia', *Friedrich-Ebert-Stiftung International Policy Analysis*, 5–6.

Offe, C. (1991) "Capitalism by Democratic Design?', Democratic Theory Facing the Triple Transition in East Central Europe', *Social Research*, 58(4): 865–881.

Program – Desatoro ĽS - Naše Slovensko (2016). [Programme – Ten Commandments of People's Party Our Slovakia]. Available at: http://www.naseslovensko.net/wp-contentuploads201501volebny-program-2016-pdf/ Accessed 03 January 2018.

Programové tézy Slovenského Hnutia Obrody (2017). [Program Theses of the Slovak Revival Movement]. Available at: http://www.sho.sk/programove-tezy. Accessed 10 January 2018.

Pytlas, B. (2016) Radical Right Parties in Central and Eastern Europe: Mainstream party competition and electoral fortune, London and New York: Routledge.

Tarrow, S. (2011) *Power in Movement. Social Movements and Contentious Politics, 3nd edition*, Cambridge: Cambridge University Press.

Učeň, P. (2004) 'Centrist Populism as a New Competitive and Mobilization Strategy in Slovak Politics', in Mesežnikov, G. and Gyárfášová, O. (eds) *Party Government in Slovakia: Experiences and Perspectives*, Bratislava: Institute for Public Affairs, 45–73.

Vyhlásenie SP – My nie sme kotlebovci! (2016). [Declaration of the Slovak Togetherness - We are not Kotleba`s guys]. Available at: https://pospolitost.wordpress.com/2016/01/30/vyhlasenie-sp-my-nie-sme-kotlebovci/. Accessed 10 January 2018.

Vašečka, M. (2009) *Postoje verejnosti k cudzincom a zahraničnej migrácii v Slovenskej republike* [Public views on foreigners and international migration in Slovak Republic], Bratislava: IOM.

14

FROM STREETS TO SEATS?

Comparing movement-parties in southeast Europe: The cases of Kosovo and Macedonia

Alma Vardari and Ivan Stefanovski

Introduction

The aftermath of the Yugoslav wars and its relationship with the movement dynamics is yet to be explored by the contention politics' scholars. While the intervention of international actors has been crucial for conflict resolution and peacekeeping in the region, it has been neglected as a conceptual factor for the analysis of social movements. It is time to explore how the international state-building encompassing the Western Balkan countries have impacted the recent social resistances.

Kosovo's autonomy (granted by Tito in 1974) was abruptly abolished by the nationalist politics of Slobodan Milosevic in 1989, ensuing in the policy of ethnic cleansing in 1998–1999. In spite of many international attempts to resolve the conflict, Milosevic refused to accede to the Western terms, putting the international powers on trial. NATO's airstrike on Serbia led eventually to the end of war in June 1999, the withdrawal of the Serbian army from the province, and the installation of the international security forces. Kosovo was placed under the international authority of UNMIK, whose mandate was to secure its stability, to rehabilitate the domestic social structure, and to rebuild the political and economic system.

However, the West was not done. Following the Yugoslav breakup, Macedonia had her own conflict to deal with, resulting in the Ohrid Agreement (August 2001). This tenuous peace arrangement also needed Western supervision, especially given the fragile position of the Macedonian state at the time.[1] Adding to that later on the corrupted politics of the Gruevski's governments, has meant that the statebuilding process in Macedonia has since been heavily overseen by the political, military, and economic institutions, designed and sponsored by the international powers.

Hence, it seems obvious that these political transformations and many others in the region have had a crucial impact on the contention politics evolving in the Western Balkans. However, the protest movements taking thousands to the streets of Belgrade, Zagreb, Prishtina, Sarajevo, and Skopje seem to have fallen under the radars of the scholarly attention. Citizens from all walks of lives in the post-socialist Balkans, demanding political, economic, and social changes, are still missing from the study of collective action and contention politics.

In an attempt to address this scholarly gap, this chapter aims to understand the politics of contention in post-independence Kosovo (2011–2016) and Macedonia (2014–2017), focusing on the shifting matrix of the movements into right-wing (the former) and left-wing (the latter) registered political parties. Hence, the question that guides this study is: *how does the political context of the international statebuilding shape the emergence of movement-parties?*

The materials presented in this work explore the political contexts within which the Levizja Vetevendosje! (hereto LV), Albanian for the Movement for Self-determination[2], and Levica movement in Macedonia (hereto Levica)[3] act. Using the theoretical lenses of political opportunity structure, this chapter will analyse and compare the similar socio-political configurations that enabled the emergence of these two social movements into political parties located differently on the left/right-wing axis. In addition, through the comparative analysis, we aim to trace the emergence and transformation of these local actors into movement-parties, and to identify their particularities as featured in these two cases of South-Eastern Europe. Based on our findings and analysis, we argue that the dual presence of VV and Levica in streets and parliamentary seats is a consequence of the political context impacted by the creation of alliances between national governments and international actors, which in turn contribute to the establishment of inaccessible political structures.

This work starts with a theoretical framework, consisting of the theory of political opportunity structure and the need to identify the emergence of a new analytical yet neglected factor, i.e. the creation of a domestic–foreign alliance. The second part traces the development of the VV movement in Kosovo, while the third one explores the Levica movement in Macedonia. The fourth part presents a joint analysis of the organizations' political marginalization and their response to the domestic–foreign alliance resulting in their transformation into movement-parties. The concluding section indicates the similarities as well as the differences between the two cases, raising new questions for further research in the region.

(1) The theoretical lenses of this study

The political context within which collective action takes shape has long been recognized for its impact and studied thoroughly in the approach known as Political Opportunity Structure (POS). Every event or process that contests the existing political structure creates an opportunity for political change (McAdam, 1983; Eisinger, 1973). POS stands for a set of constraints and opportunities present in the socio-political environment that can encourage or suppress social action, thus shaping both strategy and structure (Tarrow, 1998; Crossely 2002).

Therefore, to identify when changes are interpreted as opportunities for mobilization and action, the political environment is conceptualized as consisting of four "visible factors: (1) opening of access to participation for new actors; (2) evidence of political realignment within the polity; (3) availability of influential allies; and (4) emerging splits within the elite" (Tarrow 2011: 165). Despite the usefulness of the POS model, it still applies mainly to the western societies, and as such it raises questions regarding its validity in other social and political contexts which are not built around western realities (elections, political parties, professional associations, media, etc).

In addition, the populist right is very frequently associated with the opposition to social and cultural forms of competition and the potential threat they pose to national identities (Wodak 2015). Although the emergence of the far right is justifiably connected to the questions of culture (Kriesi 2008 and Caiani 2017), and in the Western world is considered successful in its, so-called 'mobilization of the losers', this story takes a quite different turn when the Balkan realities are in question. Building on arguments from the recent history of the region, one can argue that the far right in Southeastern Europe derives from the enrooted nationalism which had been 'mainstream' for decades in the region.

The post-Yugoslav sentiments of Milošević's Serbia and Tudjman's Croatia, modified in the contemporary 'Gruevism' in Macedonia, 'Thacism' in Kosovo and 'Dodik-ism' in Republica Srpska, point to the direction that right-wing sentiments have been almost ever-present in the region. Even in times of communism, under Tito's ruling in former SFRJ, the 'non-existence' of nationalism and nationalist movements was just a smokescreen created by the regime.

Thus, given the international interventions in former Yugoslavia wars, and later on the establishment of many international institutions designed either to govern the region temporarily (UNMIK, KFOR), or to supervise the transition to democratic rule (ICO, EULEX), in this chapter we aim to locate two main conceptual differences between the Western tradition and the region under study: the contested statehood factor, and the configuration of alliances between national government and international actors. The identification of these two distinctions highlights the analytical shift needed to understand the dynamics of movement-parties emerging in the Western Balkans.

(2) The mobilization roots of Vetevendosje! in Kosovo

The origins of *the Vetevendosje! Movement* (hereto VV) are to be found in the Kosova Action Network (KAN), established in 1997 by a group of international activists led by the American writer Alice Mead, to support citizen's initiatives against Serbia's occupation and aggression in Kosovo. In July 2003, KAN decided to create a network in Kosovo, in order to foster a dynamic and representative society. In June 2004, a protest against UNMIK[4] Resolution 1244 was organized on its fifth anniversary. The protesters gathered around the UNMIK's building and pronounced themselves Citizens[5] by reading the Declaration of Citizen and promised to struggle against the anti-democratic regime of UNMIK (VV website, History of the movement). As recognized by the movement itself, it was this protest that constituted the genesis of VV, formally established in 2005. The following illustrates how the VV's activists define their organization:

> A people in movement. A generation with new conviction
> A community that refuses to submit. For self-determination
>   and until self-determination
>
> *(VV website, Who are we)*

The declared goal of VV is: "Self-determination, because it is something natural; it makes sense that *we* make the decisions about *our* own future much more effectively than anyone and everyone else who wants to decide on *our* behalf" (VV website, Movements' Manifesto, *italics mine*). It seems safe to maintain that action based on this contentious and shared identity, along with the continuous dominant presence in the national political arena, has turned VV into an essential collective actor, critical of the international agenda of Kosovo's statebuilding.

The metamorphosis of VV into a movement party

Since its establishment in 2005, VV's structure has changed from a grassroots core to a movement-party organization. Two years after the Kosovo's declaration of independence, the leadership of the movement initiated the parliamentary group of VV, which emerged in the elections of 2010 and has since maintained a fierce and persistent opposition in the Kuvend (Albanian for the National Assembly).[6]

According to the information provided by the spokesperson of VV, there are nearly 3,000 registered members, eligible to be elected for different positions within the organization,[7] thousands of activists regularly involved in VV's collective actions, and an unlisted number of volunteers, participating randomly in VV's activities. The members' ages range from early 20's to early 40's (women and men). They come from different regions within Kosovo, cities and rural areas. With some exceptions of Catholic background, all the rest come from Muslim families, although they display no religious attachment whatsoever. The leadership is comprised of members who have obtained their higher education either at the University of Prishtina or abroad (Europe and USA) in various disciplines.[8] Those in their late 30s and early 40s have spent time in jail, either in the time of the Milosevic regime or during the time of UNMIK, or both. As for the activists and volunteers of VV, they come from all walks of life: students, former KLA soldiers, peasants, workers, and intelligentsia. The membership fees, donations and contributions from individuals and businesses (in Kosovo and abroad) comprise the main financial base of VV. Besides the headquarters office located in Prishtina, the VV has founded 14 area offices spread all over Kosovo,[9] and eight offices in Europe, in the countries[10] in which reside the biggest communities of Kosovo's diaspora.

In June 2010, VV declared that it would run as an electoral group for the 2011 elections, which were held eventually on 12 December 2010,[11] due to the political crisis caused by the resignation of the former President Fatmir Sejdiu. Following the dual dominance of the two main parties in LDK and PDK supported by the international supervision, we read the VV's decision to expand their civic resistance to the realm of the political instrumental practices, as a response shaped by the closure of the dual governmental structure (domestic and foreign). The movement has repeatedly tended to confront its marginalization and radicalization (Vardari 2012), as well as the need to translate its growing popular support into political power by attempting to penetrate the institutional arena, as many VV members openly expressed.

Although publicly banned by the-then US Ambassador to Kosovo, Christopher Dell,[12] receiving 12.2% of the votes in their first electoral campaign[13] clearly indicated that the movement was perceived by the domestic society as trustworthy in matters involving statebuilding and policy-making. Looking at the latest electoral results (June 2017), in which VV received 27.49% of the overall votes and doubled the number of its representatives in the parliament,[14] and in light of the daily economic and political struggle (Vardari 2017), one might even argue that VV has transformed into a legitimate political actor, grounded heavily upon the national identity and statebuilding agendas.

(3) The mobilization roots of Levica in Macedonia

The logic and actions of the Levica movement

Levica finds its roots in two complementary leftist movements, *Lenka*[15] and *Solidarity*,[16] mainly dedicated to reintroducing social justice in Macedonia. Both movements are still registered and active. Solidarity was formed in May 2012 as a leftist activist organization which stands for humanization of all societal spheres, social justice, and enhancement of workers' rights, as well as preservation and enhancement of democracy. The movement mainly unites people fighting against authoritarian forms of ruling, and their forms of exploitation, but also against nationalism, militarism and clerisy.[17] On the other hand, Lenka dates to several years earlier, being formed as a movement of citizens advocating for social justice, solidarity, freedom, and equality. Very complementary with the prior organization, the latter mainly stands for social justice, antimilitarism, antinationalism, anti-capitalism, students' rights, and women's' rights.[18]

Based on the previous values, at the end of 2015, during the extended political crisis in Macedonia which began around 2012, a group of individuals originating from the two organizations registered the political party based on several ideological pillars: social justice; just redistribution and responsible usage of material goods and services which are produced; responsible practice of governing; equality and solidarity; opposing divisions following ethnic lines and opposing nationalism regardless of its ethnic frame; anticonservatism and secularism; and anti-imperialism.[19]

The membership of the party is regulated in the party Statute, and every person who accepts the main pillars of the party platform can freely join. The party regularly updates the membership registry, although this document is not available on the party website.[20] The main duties and obligations of the members are generally similar to the mainstream parties, with the partisan solidarity being highlighted.

The organizational characteristics of the party resemble old communist parties, having adopted both the organizational structure and the terminology of the former communist parties.[21] The political and electoral financing of the party is also regulated in the party Statute.[22] Being a movement-party, the grassroots of the party are considered to be its biggest strength. The Levica has local branches in 21 cities/municipalities and according to the Statute, a local branch must have at least three members.[23]

Levica's emergence can be clearly traced as a response to the neoliberal and internationally subordinated mainstream Macedonian parties – the SDSM and the VMRO-DPMNE. Although nominally Levica wanted to challenge the 'non-leftist policies of the declarative leftist SDSM', it also aimed at providing an alternative to the firm Euro-Atlantic positions of the two largest mainstream Macedonian political parties, the VMRO-DPMNE and the SDSM, continuously challenging issues like the NATO membership, and loans taken from the IMF and the World Bank, as well as a very firm position against the resolution of the years-long name dispute between Macedonia and Greece, a topic which has recently been reintroduced. Regarding the name dispute, Levica holds a very strong, at times nationalist and rightist position, claiming that "the change of the name will produce subordinated people and a country without a future" (Levica website).[24]

(4) Domestic-foreign alliance and marginalization of local movements

This section aims to link the political structure of opportunities with the transformation of VV into a right-wing movement-party, and Levica into a left-wing one, by tracing: (1) the opening access for participation of foreign actors; and (2) the formation of the power relationship between the local government and the international institutions, perceived as a threat by local actors.

Kosovo's international statebuilding and the entrance of foreign actors

Given the recognized impact of the external context (mainly state institutions, political elites, changing alliances etc.) on the emergence and development of social movements (Tilly 1978; McAdam 1982; Tarrow 1998), it is essential to identify the dual power structures emerging in Kosovo during the international intervention for the examination of its contention politics. What started as a dual polity of Albanian and Serbian institutions before the war (Kostovicova 2008) was replaced after the war by the dual polity of domestic and foreign political structures.

The establishment of the UNMIK administration, brought in 2001 the formation of the local government – Provisional Institutions of Self-Government (PISG); however, it was designed as an institution entirely dependent on UNMIK for every decision. Lacking any legislative and executive authority, Kosovo Albanians, although finally liberated of the Serbian oppression, found themselves totally subordinated to the Western powers. From 2001–2004, the international community undertook many attempts to solve the issue of Kosovo's status. The violent events sweeping Kosovo on March 2004 put pressure on the Western powers to come to a resolution. Eventually, Martti Ahtisaari[25] recommended that: 'Kosovo's status should be independence supervised by the international community', advocating essentially the transfer of the UNMIK's competencies to the civilian and political missions of the European Union to oversee the newborn state of Kosovo.

Consequently, the duality of the governmental authorities (national and international) has become in time an encumbering political system for the implementation of accountability by increasing the chances that each authority might shirk its responsibility while casting blame on the opponent (Belloni 2001; Gheciu 2005). Hence, it is the co-existence of the domestic and foreign political systems which has contributed to the array of constraints acting as a threat, and repressing local mobilization and collective actions (Vardari 2015).

Declaration of independence as a threat for local actors

This section further traces the development of the political events that have interjected with local actors, and have acted as a suppressing factor for their contentious activities. The declaration of independence (DoI) in February 2008, by the-then Kosovo PM Hashim Thaci, is a case in point. Following Ahtissari's vision, immediately after the DoI, the government invited two international agencies to monitor Kosovo's statebuilding. The first was the European Union Rule of Law Mission in Kosovo (EULEX)[26], and the defunct International Civilian Office (ICO)[27]. The succession of UNMIK's authorities by EULEX clearly illustrates the split of Kosovo's sovereignty between the internal and external actors (Krasner 2004), pinpointing the new international practices of statebuilding, and the translation of sovereignty as mere capacity for good governance (Chandler 2010). While Kosovo's government and Assembly are to this day in charge of the domestic management of the population, they are heavily monitored by the EU power holders and the international diplomats residing in Prishtina. Also, the police structure and the custom authorities are closely monitored by the EULEX, while NATO's forces are still present in the country.[28]

As Goldstone and Tilly point out in their joint work, "threat' has not been explored as extensively as 'opportunity" ... threat is an independent factor whose dynamics greatly influence how popular groups and the state act in a variety of conflict situations' (2001: 181). When conceptualized as a threat, the DoI has played an enormous impact on the contentious actions of the VV. On one hand, it has embodied the legal recognition of Kosovo institutions as sovereign, and of the entailing rights of its citizens. But, on the other hand, the DoI has cemented the regime of supervision endorsed by the international presence and authority, suspending thus the pragmatic realization of Kosovo's sovereignty. The 'imported' institutional structure and the creation of divided communities along ethnic lines has become a target of the VV's contentious politics.

The configuration of domestic–foreign alliance as a closed political structure

This part of the chapter addresses the marginalization of the local challengers, or social movements from the political decision-making process, leading to the decision to expand their protests politics and add that of the party politics.

The identification of the international statebuilders' role established in contemporary Kosovo calls for a new conceptualization of the political opportunities structure. The ongoing contestation of Kosovo's statehood, indicates that the state performs as a fragmented manifestation of institutions, its legitimacy is not anchored in the nation's will, and the temporal and spatial premises of sovereignty are contested (Lemay-Hebert 2012; Visoka and Bolton 2011; Chandler 2010). This has led to the continuous interdependence of the domestic government on the foreign institutions (EULEX, EU, NATO, UN, etc.) and vice versa. While the national governments depend on the international actors for political recognition and financial support, the later relies on the former's cooperation in order to maintain its democratic image and advance the Western agenda of statebuilding.

The detachment of local governing responsibilities thus from the state sovereignty rights and the lack of accountability, facilitate a space which carries significant implications for social organization, political legitimacy and collective action. The price of preserving this domestic–foreign alliance is the exclusion of the local society from the political decision-making process. To start with, a strong demonstration for this is Kosovo' constitution, a text which represents a replication of the Ahtisaari's proposal (Tomson 2012; Tunheim 2009), and went through an internationally supervised drafting process, completely sidelining the local society.

Other significant evidences for this marginalization are the recent EU-led agreement ensuing in the establishment of the association of the Serbian municipalities[29] and the foundation of the special court for war crimes.[30] In spite of the ongoing massive protests in the streets of Kosovo as well as in the Assembly's debates, organized by the VV and other opposing actors, Kosovo's government basically ignored the public voice and complied with the EU expectations (Vardari 2017).

Lastly, looking at the time of the VV's shift into a movement-party, one might argue that the marginalization of key local actors is just a reflection of the local society's exclusion from the political decision-making processes. Ample support for the citizens' marginalization and the consequential decline of the public trust can be found in the UNDP survey 'Public Pulse' and the Forum for Civic Initiative

(FCI) report named 'A Matter of Trust'.[31] The reports of Public Pulse, based on the surveys conducted twice in 2012, show that the level of public satisfaction with the work of Kosovo's key, executive, legislative and judicial institutions has constantly dropped. The political index at the time indicates a decrease of confidence on government from 46.9% on May 2008 to 21.2% on April 2012, and from 54% to 23.7% in regards with the prime minister (USAID and UNDP report 4). The Kosovo Government and the judiciary are the least trusted Kosovo institutions, with 22.8% and 22.3% respectively, stating 'not at all' when asked if they trust each institution (ibid., 15–16).

All the above-mentioned cases clearly illustrate the ongoing fragmentation of the political and judicial system in Kosovo by external supervision, further undermining the *de jure* sovereignty it purports to bolster. In our account thus, moving from streets to seats has been the VV's answer to the threat of confronting this closed political structure imposed by the national–international political configuration. The shift of the VV into a movement-party, and its adoption of a right-wing discourse goes hand-in-hand with the marginalization of local society from the decision-making process and the perceived national threat, instigated by the domestic–foreign alliance.

The international and national context as a threat to the Levica

One of the main programmatic characteristics of the Levica is the anti-imperialism. This is one of the main reasons why the party opposed the Przhino[32] negotiations, as well as the Citizens for Macedonia protest platform,[33] and was also skeptical towards the 'Colorful Revolution'.[34] Although a strong opponent to the regime of former PM Gruevski, the Levica had an almost equally strong criticism towards the SDSM, the main opposition social democratic party, whose place and role they intended to occupy. Still, this opposition to the international facilitation of the re-democratization process, which was publicly opposed by the Levica, limited their political maneuvering space.

Bad timing – from streets to (no) seats – the transformation

Following the Przhino negotiations and the signing of the political Agreement, the stage for the early parliamentary elections was set. The highly polarized Macedonian society had to promptly decide between the continuation of Gruevski's regime, which would have been reflected with slightly pro-Russian sentiments and incremental distancing from the Euro–Atlantic integration, and a pro-Western, pro-democratic, multiethnic, and multi-confessional platform proposed by the opposition led by the SDSM. The initiators of Levica decided that these elections were the best moment to promote themselves as a truly leftist "third" option. Several political analysts commented on the 'bad timing' by the Levica founders. In times of high polarization and politicization of Macedonian society, the Lenka and the Solidarnost members had to wait just one more electoral cycle in order to make a real statement. To the contrary, the newly established anti-establishment party was found between 'two giants' and was crushed by the big hopes and a strong will for immediate change. One renowned political analyst commented on these occurrences:

> The leftist were supposed to wait just one to one and a half year. Everything would have been different. Even from this perspective, a lot of the disappointed SDSM voters would have now, in the wake of the local elections, given the vote to the Levica. Conversely, now, being labeled as 'absolute losers', and ever-present criticizers, their chances are much lower.[35]

The 2016 electoral results have been more than disappointing for the newly established movement party. Just 12,120 votes were obtained, equaling 1.02% of the total votes.[36] This was very far from the number of votes needed to have secured a seat. Furthermore, failing to field a candidate list in all the six electoral units, sent a message that the dominantly Albanian inhabited regions are not interesting for the party. This was perceived as very unusual for a leftist party which nominally doesn't differ between citizens and potential voters, and should tend towards all nationalities and confessional groups.

The exclusion of local society can be traced in Macedonia as well. The roots of this process date back from the post-conflict 2001, when international representatives sponsored and fostered the Ohrid Framework Agreement (OFA 2001) which was later incorporated into the Macedonian constitution. Furthermore, following Gruevski's authoritarian ruling, since 2014, both the USA and the EU have had a strong saying in shaping Macedonian politics and its institutions. Since its very beginning, the Levica tried to oppose this international intervention treating it like colonialism, imperialism and interference in the national sovereignty. This is mainly expressed through the negative sentiments regarding the Przhino negotiations, the very rigid stance towards the name dispute with Greece,[37] as well as the public sanctioning of party members who took positions in the newly appointed reformist government led by the SDSM.[38]

Conclusions: parallels and divergences between VV and Levica

This chapter seeks to offer a new analytical factor in the analysis of right-wing movement-party development in contemporary Kosovo and Macedonia, perceiving it as an elaborate account of a domestic–foreign alliance leading to an inaccessible political system. As such, the chapter has shown that both VV and Levica share many similarities, mainly in their structure, the key reasons for their emergence and mobilization, as well as their similar thinking and agenda-setting. Both parties have built their party structures from numerous grassroots moving bottom-up, following some general principles resembling former communist and socialist political parties typical for the region where they operate.

In the case of the VV, the operationalization of both UNMIK's and EULEX authorities clearly illustrates the lack of traditional sovereignty, indicating the intersection of internal and external power structures, as envisioned by the international practices of statebuilding. The political opportunity structure approach indicates that the configuration of the political environment, and the actors and structures within the state boundaries may create, encourage, or restrain the opportunities for collective action (Koopmans 1999; Mayer 2004). Given the porous state boundaries of Kosovo, the movement seems to overcome this barrier in terms of the structure of political opportunities by expanding their politics of protest to an additional sphere, that of formal politics, thus transforming into a movement-party.

In the case of Levica as well, the state consolidation and the constant international involvement have introduced an array of governmental, constitutional, and diplomatic developments, resulting in a closed political structure sidelining the local voice and presence in the policy-making process. Furthermore, as a relatively new political subject in the electoral arena, Levica has a lot of work to do, especially at grassroots level and within its ideological matrix in order to reach the level and influence of VV.

Furthermore, the line of reasoning and acting of both VV and Levica follows a similar anti-NATO and anti-EU agenda, contesting the neoliberal statebuilding pillars on which international powers and the national governments of Kosovo and Macedonia base their entire years-long strategy in the region. In fact, the emergence of both entities is enrooted in the political marginalization imposed by the largest mainstream political parties in both respective countries.

It can also be easily concluded that both movement parties operate in similar political environments, especially with regard to the role of the international statebuilders and the traditional political parties. The VV and the Levica have faced relatively closed political opportunities, although the former has managed to "break the ice" using the "power in numbers" (DeNardo 1985) and applying a slightly more radical and nationalist discourse in comparison to later. This has contributed to its large electoral success in the general elections.

In regards to the political opportunity structure, the two cases differ in the 'presence' of the international actors. While in Kosovo, the EU is the strongest international actor which largely dictates the political developments in the framework of the statebuilding agenda, Macedonia faces a dichotomous partnership both with the USA and the EU, where the first actor throughout the years had shown stronger and more organized presence and influence. We strongly believe that it is the combination of the origins along with the state status differences that accounts for the right versus left divergence between the two movements.

Because in Kosovo the state status is still contested by Serbia, Russia and other EU member states, this enables the EU to fully interfere and dictate the statebuilding agenda and directly shape the national politics. This in turn threatens the national mindset of local actors, which feel threatened and tend to mobilize the right-wing discourses, the VV being a case in point. In contrast to Kosovo, the state status of Macedonia is not contested (except for the name dispute), therefore the US and the EU involvement are consistently structured as more diplomatic and advising, thus inciting the local actors to adopt a rather more left-wing discourse.

Notes

1 For more read about the Ohrid Agreement and its implementation at: http://www.esi-web.org/index.php?lang=en&id=563.
2 For more details see the website of the movement: http://www.vetevendosje.org/en/.
3 For more details see the website of the movement party https://levica.mk/.
4 See the framework of UN Resolution 1244 (10/06/1999).
5 People in Kosovo, until the declaration of independence (February 2008) were considered residents as opposed to citizens, a status that usually refugees enjoy.
6 For an extensive documentation of activities in the Kuvend see: http://www.vetevendosje.org/aktivitetet-ne-kuvend/. The entrance of the movement in the formal political sphere is perceived by its members as a spatial move which enhances and complements their existing contention in the informal space, ensuing merely in a spinoff of their conceptual work and action strategies.
7 Interview with Dardan Molliqi, February 2013, in Prishtina.
8 Political studies, philosophy, economics, journalism, education, literature, sociology, architecture, engineering, etc.
9 The centres of VV in Kosovo are: Burim, Decan, Drenas, Gjakove, Gjilan, Kacanik, Kline, Lypjane, Mitrovice, Peje, Prizren, Sharr, Viti and Vushtrri.
10 The centres of VV in Europe are: U.K, Denmark, Germany, Ireland, Norwegian, Sweden, Switzerland and Turkey.
11 According to the CEC (http://www.kqz-ks.org/SKQZ-WEB/en/shv/ovpp/zotesiju-ridike.html), PM Hashim Thaci's Democratic Party of Kosovo (PDK) received 33.5% of the vote, Democratic League of Kosovo (LDK) 22.6%, Vetevendosje 12.2%, Alliance for the Future of Kosovo (AAK) 10.8%, New Kosovo Alliance 7.1%, Democratic League of Dardania 3.% and Fryma e Re 2.2%.
12 See: Koha Ditore, 19 November 2010, *Dell: Vetevendosje Doesn't Deserve my Visit* (my translation).
13 See: BBC, 12 December 2010, *Kosovo PM Hashim Thaci Claims Election Victory*, at http://www.bbc.co.uk/news/world-europe-11978021.
14 http://kosovotwopointzero.com/en/kosovo_official_election_results_announced/.
15 See more about Lenka at http://lenka.mk/.
16 See more about Solidarnost at http://solidarnost.mk/.
17 See http://solidarnost.mk/za-nas.
18 See http://lenka.mk/za-nas/#.WcwDdMgjE2w.
19 https://levica.mk/makedonski/.
20 Statute of Levica, articles 15–18 https://levica.mk/statut/.
21 Statute of Levica, Articles 19 and 24–39: The four central organs of Levica are the Plenum, the Central Committee, the Presidium and the Tribunal. The Plenum is the highest organ of the party, comprised of all the members of the central organs, all the party officials which hold public office and the party delegates from the local branches. The main competences of the Plenum are the definition of the partisan course and the strategic directions, enacting main internal party documents, and appointing of the Central Committee of the party. The Central Committee is the highest authority between two plenums. It has a mandate of three years and decides on the crucial partisan issues.
22 The party is financed through membership fees and donations, as well as state financing if the party acquires a certain electoral result. One provision which attracts the

attention is the legitimacy of the spending, something which is difficult to find in the statues of the mainstream parties. Glancing at the financial reports, one can be persuaded in the very modest financial resources of Levica. https://levica.mk/wp-content/uploads/2017/02/Registar-na-donacii-2017-1.pdf.

23 See https://levica.mk/lokalni-ogranoci/ The local branches are: Gazi Baba, Butel, Gjorche Petrov, Karposh, Centar, Aerodrom, Kisela Voda, Bitola, Kumanovo, Strumica, Prilep, Tetovo, Kratovo, Gevgelija, Struga, Kavadarci, Kriva Palanka, Kochani, Shtip and Veles.

24 https://levica.mk/2018/01/22/promena-na-ime-pokorni-lugje/.

25 United Nations Special envoy for Kosovo, and former Finnish President, Martti Ahtisaari presented his plan to the U.N. secretary-general in March 2007, known as the Comprehensive Proposal for the Kosovo Status Settlement.

26 EULEX – European Union Rule of Law Mission in Kosovo, established by the EU Council Joint Action (12.2.08) and EU Council Joint Action appointing the EUSR (4.2.08).

27 ICO – International Civilian Office, established by the International Steering Group (28.2.08).

28 For more info see: https://www.nato.int/cps/en/natolive/topics_48818.htm.

29 For more information see: http://eeas.europa.eu/archives/docs/statements-eeas/docs/150825_02_association-community-of-serb-majority-municipalities-in-kosovo-general-principles-main-elements_en.pdf.

30 See: https://www.scp-ks.org/en.

31 See the Public Pulse Report No. 4, at: http://www.ks.undp.org/content/kosovo/en/home.html, and the joint report of Forum for Civic Initiatives and Safeworlds: "A Matter of Trust", Nov. 2010, at: http://www.saferworld.org.uk/downloads/pubdocs/A%20matter%20of%20trust_ENG_WEB.pdf.

32 The Przhino negotiations were a set of political negotiations by the four largest political parties in Macedonia: the VMRO-DPMNE, the SDSM, the DUI and the DPA. The negotiations were fostered by the EU and the USA, and a political agreement was reached after almost two years of political crisis and several months of political negotiations. See more about the Przhino agreement http://europa.eu/rapid/press-release_STATEMENT-15-5372_en.htm.

33 See more about the "Citizens for Macedonia" in Stefanovski (2015) http://isppi.ukim.edu.mk/images/387685annual-2015-5-ivan-stefanovski.pdf.

34 See more about the "Colorful Revolution" in http://www.dw.com/en/macedonia-colorful-revolution-paints-raucous-rainbow/a-19203365.

35 See interview with Sasho Ordanoski.

36 See https://drive.google.com/file/d/0B8ZpCwro9h-zWndudTFnSnpYdk0/view.

37 https://levica.mk/2018/02/04/pismo-do-siriza/.

38 https://levica.mk/2018/01/28/zamrznuvanje-chlenstvo-branimir-jovanovikj/.

References

Aminzade, R., et al. (2001) *Silence and Voice in the Study of Contention Politics*, Cambridge: Cambridge University Press.

Chandler, D. (2006) *Empire in Denial: The Politics of State-building*, London: Pluto Press.

Chandler, D. (2010) *International Statebuilding: The Rise of Post-liberal Governance*, New York: Routledge.

Della Porta, D. and Mattoni, A. (2014) *Spreading Protest: Social Movements in Times of Crisis*, Colchester: ECPR Press.

Diani, M. (1996) 'Linking Mobilization Frames and Political Opportunities: Insights from Regional Populism in Italy', *American Sociology Review*, 61: 1053–69.

Gamson. A.W., Fireman, B. and Rytina, S. (1982) *Encounters with Unjust Authority*, Homewood, IL: Dorsey Press.

Godwin, J. and Jasper, J.J. (eds) (2004) *Rethinking Social Movements: Structure, Meaning and Emotions*, Lanham, MD: Rowman and Littlefield.

Ignatieff, M. (2003) *Empire lite: Nation-building in* Bosnia, Kosovo *and Afghanistan*, London: Vintage.

Johnston, H. (2011) State and Social Movements, Cambridge: UK, Polity Press.

Lemay-Heberst, N. (2009) 'State-Building from the Outside-in: UNMIK and its Paradox', *Journal of Public and International* Affairs, 20: 65–86.

Lemay-Heberst, N. (2009) 'Coerced Transition in Timor-Leste and Kosovo: managing competing objectives of institution-building and local empowerment', *Democratization*, 19(3): 465-485.

Marks, G. and McAdam, D. (1996) 'Social Movement and changing Structure of Political Opportunities in the European Union', *West European Politics*, 19(2): 249–278.

McAdam, D. (1982) 'The Classical Model of Social Movements Examined in Buechler and Cylke, (1997) *Social Movements: Perspectives and Issues*, California & London & Toronto: Mayfield Publishing Company.

McAdam, D., Tarrow, S. and Tilly, C. (2001) *Dynamics of Contention*, Cambridge: Cambridge University Press.

McAdam, D. (2003) 'Beyond Structural Analysis: Toward a More Dynamic Understanding of Social Movements', in Diani, M. and McAdam, D. (eds) *Social Movements and Networks*, Oxford/New York: Oxford University Press, 281–98.

Polleta, F. (2004) 'Culture is not Just in Your Head', in Godwin, J. and Jasper, J.J. (eds) *Rethinking Social Movements: Structure, Meaning and Emotions*, Lanham, Rowman and Littlefield, 97–110.

Pond, E. (2008) 'The EU's Test in Kosovo', *The Washington Quarterly*, 31(4): 97–112.

Tansey, O. (2009) 'Kosovo: Independence and Tutelage', *Journal of Democracy*, 20(2): 153–166.

Tarrow, S. (1998) *Power in Movement:* Social Movements, Collective Action and *Politics*, 2nd ed, New York/Cambridge: Cambridge University Press.

Tilly, C. (1978) *From Mobilization to Revolution*, Reading, MA: Addison-Wesley.

Tilly, C. (1982) *Warmaking and Statemaking as Organized Crime*, Center for Research in Social Organization, Working papers No. 256, Ann Arbor, Michigan.

Tilly, C. (2005) *Trust and Rule*, Cambridge: Cambridge University Press.

Vardari, A. (2012) 'Politics of Protest in Supervised Statehood: Co-Shared Governance and Erosion of Citizenship', *Journal of Southeast Europe*, 36(2).

Vardari, A. (2015) 'Statehood without Sovereignty! Negotiations and Statebuilding in Kosovo', in Papakostas, N. and Passamitros, N. (eds) *An Agenda for the Western Balkans: From Elite Politics to Social Sustainability*, Stuttgart: Ibidem-Verlag.

Vardari, A. (2017) 'People's Power Hits Glass Ceiling? Statebuilding and Contention in Contemporary Kosovo', in Armakolas, I. et al. (eds) *State-building in Postindependence Kosovo: Policy Challenges and Societal Considerations*, Kosovo Foundation for Open Society, Pristina.

Visoka, G. and Bolton, G. (2011) 'The Complex Nature and Implications of International Engagement after Kosovo's Independence', *Civil Wars*, 13(2): 189–214.

Zaum, D. (2007) *The Sovereignty Paradox*, Oxford: Oxford University Press.

15

CONCLUSION

Movements vs. parties, movements and parties, movements or parties? Types of interactions within the radical right[1]

Manuela Caiani and Ondřej Císař

Introduction

In the view of some groups of voters, the establishment's political response to the crises of Europe has been too muted. This viewpoint, which the radical right movement parties analysed in this volume also embrace, sees the EU and the national political establishment as another problem, and not a solution to the current crises. In fact, recent developments in Europe, starting with the economic crisis and followed by the refugee crisis, seem to have created favourable conditions for the consolidation of right-wing (populist) parties and movements (Kriesi and Pappas 2015; Inglehart and Norris 2017). This process can be observed in both Western and Central and Eastern Europe, and both inside and outside the electoral arena. For instance, in the West, Alternative for Germany (AfD) entered the German Bundestag after winning almost 13% of the votes in the 2017 federal elections, after their successes in previous elections and 'remarkable mobilisation' (Arzheimer, 2015: 552) and in 2018 it obtained 10,2% of the vote in the regional elections in Bavaria and 13,1% in Hessen; the Danish People's Party placed second (21%) in the 2015 Parliamentary elections in Denmark, becoming the second largest party in the country for the first time amid a plurality for the centre-right parties. In the East, Kotleba-People's Party Our Slovakia (ĽSNS) secured 14 seats in Parliament (8%) in the 2016 Slovak Parliamentary elections, and Jobbik received 20% of the votes in both the 2014 and 2018 Hungarian national elections. In sum, as Cas Mudde (2016) points out, around 6.8% of Europeans voted for radical right parties within the context of a challenging economic situation.

The shockwaves these various crises caused were accompanied by the resurgence of the radical populist right in the electoral arena, but, as this book demonstrates, also by its mobilisation in the protest arena (see also Kriesi 2013). Most of these protests have taken place in higher-income countries where dissatisfaction with the impact and with the perceived mismanagement of the economic crisis is strong. Economic justice, austerity, the failure of elected representatives, global justice, and the rights of the people were the dominant issues at these demonstrations (Ortiz et al. 2013). The wave of anti-austerity demonstrations has been followed in recent years by protests centred on the migrant crisis. Among the factors that have been suggested as lying behind the recent mobilisation and success of the (populist) radical right, some of the most significant are institutional allies (Jackman and Volpert 1996), the legacy of the authoritarian past (Bustikova and Kitschelt 2009), low trust and confidence in democratic institutions (Lubbers, Gijsberts, and Scheepers 2002), youth sub-cultures and hooliganism and the diffusion of xenophobic values in society (Caiani 2017a), and immigration and anti-establishment sentiment (Caiani 2017b). In many countries, migration has been a recurring issue at street demonstrations since 2015. The issue of migration has also been successfully picked up by political parties in order to win the support of discontented voters.

Most studies have focused either on political parties and political elites on the one hand, or on social movements and civil society groups and their protests on the other. Although there are exceptions, relatively few studies have tried to take in the interactions of both parties and movements/protest groups. While left-leaning movements and groups have primarily focused on the economic crisis, the radical right was mobilised in response to the perceived migration crisis (Inglehart and Norris 2017). In fact, right-wing parties and movements are mostly associated with the cultural dimension of crisis (Mudde and Kaltwasser 2013). These movements went a step further in their political articulation and interpreted the economic and cultural crises as a symptom of a flawed democracy (Cavero 2015; Kaldor and Selchow 2012; Della Porta 2012):

> The multiple crises that began in 2008 have caused and strengthened the feeling that [citizens] have no influence over decision made regarding their lives, that they are not heard or taken into account in any way by those making the decisions, and that these 'representatives' do not act in the people's interest.
>
> *(Sitrin and Azzellini 2014: 40)*

The corruption of political parties has been linked to the corruption of representative democracy in general (Della Porta 2012: 275). Left- and right-wing movements both claim to be the true representatives of the needs of the population and emphasise the genuinely democratic character of their groups.

Against this backdrop, in our concluding chapter we look at the different forms that the interactions between political parties and movements can take, with a special focus on the radical right, proposing a typology to interpret them. The goal is to explore how political parties are challenged and/or supported by other forms of political actors, such as social movements and informal groups, which are increasingly challenging political parties in this arena and/or providing established parties with support in their claims to be the true 'representatives of the will of the people' (Mudde 2007). In this respect, we build on the study of the particular type of actor that this volume has been organised around, the movement party, which usually captures only one possible type of mobilisation and political articulation, which is the transition from movements to parties.

There are, on the one hand, studies that have been done on political parties and elections by party scholars who focus on party change and the current and increasing weaknesses of parties (e.g. their difficulties recruiting and mobilising people). On the other hand, social movement literature has recently devoted attention to the waves of social mobilisation that have occurred in the context of the economic and migrant crises, and they have mainly focused on the internal characteristics of the organisations as potential sources of explanations for their emergence and action strategies, characteristics such as organisational resources, issues, and targets. Only a small number of studies have focused on the relationship between parties and social movements and the forms this relationship can take. This concluding chapter seeks to answer the following question: What are the different forms that interaction between political parties and movements can take?

The challenges to traditional actors: political parties

To start with the theoretical debate around the question of what challenges parties and traditional actors and institutions are facing today, we can identify three types of crises that also constitute the sources of strength of the new political actors and their mobilisation (Cavero 2015). First, the current crisis of parties can be seen as a crisis of representative democracy. More specifically, there has been a weakening of traditional party identities and changing party functions in Europe over the past decades (Mair 2002: 5). It is said that political parties have lost many of their traditional functions, and this has provided growing space for the emergence of representative parties that were not governing parties – this has for many years been the case of European right-wing populist parties (Kaltwasser and Taggart 2016). What's more, as Colin Crouch (2004) has stressed, a 'post-democracy' era has emerged. This means a minimalist version of liberal visions of democracy that limits citizens' political participation to the sphere of electoral politics, reduces the state's role in the market, and leaves power to economic interests (see also Streeck 2014). For many European countries post-democracy has also meant a crisis of responsibility, that is, a drastic drop in the capacity of governments to respond to citizens' demands (della Porta 2014).

Second, the crisis of Western political parties can also be interpreted as a crisis of legitimacy, which, more specifically, means a crisis of the traditional concept of representation where elections are equated with good and fair representation. Indeed, new forms of representation and a new generation of non-elected actors claiming to be representative (Castiglione and Warren 2006), are increasingly being heard and 'legitimised' by public consensus (within and outside the electoral arena), and, ultimately, representation has come to signify 'the complex set of relationships that result in activating the "sovereign people" well beyond the formal act of electoral authorization' (Urbinati and Warren 2008).

The third type of crisis of traditional political parties today relates to the internal long-term transformation of these actors, which was more recently accelerated by the economic and financial collapse. Indeed, party politics has long been in the process of a profound transformation. More specifically, over the past decades there has been a weakening of party identities and changing party functions. As regards the former, voters have begun to view the programmes of previously ideologically different parties as increasingly alike and this has given rise to the idea that 'because of the changing relations between parties, as well as changes in the way the present themselves, voters seem to find it less and less easy to see them as representative as such' (Mair 2002: 5). The task of interest articulation and aggregation traditionally performed by parties has become more difficult. Parties are no longer the main channel of political intermediation (Del Aguila 1994). Their depoliticisation and tendency towards cartelisation (Katz and Mair 2009) have paralleled their increasing power of patronage (Ignazi 2004). In sum, as party scholars point out, (traditional) political parties have more and more become bureaucratic-electoral machines, in contrast to the flexibility of other types of (political) groups. However, new market-like flexible solutions have also emerged in the party field in the form of memberless parties and/or business parties. On the radical right, examples of this include the Freedom Party in the Netherlands and the SPD in the Czech Republic (see Mazzoleni and Voerman 2017 and Chapter 12 on the Czech Republic in this book).

All these transformations have empirical consequences that are similar in many Western European democracies: low electoral turnout, electoral volatility, declining party membership and party identification, and the emergence of anti-party sentiments (Zsolt Enyedi 2014; see also Katz and Mair 1995). The parties are unable to cope with voters' expectations and therefore 'have become more remote from the citizenry' (Mair 2003: 5). Parties are increasingly unable to read public opinion, and survey findings indicate that distrust in political parties and representative institutions has been rising since the 1990s (Mair 2009).

Movements vs. parties?

However, beyond the above-mentioned long-term transformations of traditional political parties, one of the most important challenges to political parties in recent years has been the emergence of informal groups and social movements (on the left, various anti-austerity movements; on the right organisations such as Jobbik and PEGIDA) claiming to be the true representatives of the needs of the population. Movements 'have become vessels for articulating and enacting a critique of conventional, representative politics' (Cox and Szolucha 2013: 61). These movements allegedly seek to empower the masses 'bearing the brunt of economic strains. (…) Protesters do not consider themselves to be represented by any traditional party, either on the Left or Right' (Tejerina, et al. 2013). During the great recession, new political actors and social movements have been challenging austerity measures and playing an oppositional role to the traditional political parties (Wainwright 2013). The same happened on the radical right in relation to the 2015 migrant crisis, which gave rise to new political actors and empowered old ones.

While mainstream political parties are facing a deep crisis owing to their association with a political system that does not address the conditions citizens live in, social movements have emerged and reshaped the political process (Cavero 2015), and in some countries have even become an elected political party (for example, PODEMOS in Spain, M5Stelle in Italy, Jobbik in Hungary). In other cases, these movements have not (or not yet) been electorally successful; however, they have been able to shift the political agenda from the outside by introducing new issues such as the problem of corrupt governments and migration. In some cases, the protests that emerged were not able to produce durable movements, and were not met with any overt reaction on the side of political parties. In all cases, the recent mobilisations required that political parties prepare certain strategies to deal with the emergence and growth of these informal political actors, and there have been certain patterns to and different outcomes from the interactions between them.

In this respect, we can see that scholars (focusing on the Left) were already noting decades ago that social movements go through 'life cycles' which determine changes in their organisational structure, goals, strategies, and identities. Rucht (2018), summarising the main approaches to movements cycles, points out that: (i) movements can institutionalise themselves (this stage marks the end of the movement: Rammstedt 1978; Alberoni 1984); (ii) they can go through four different stages, namely emergence, coalescence, bureaucratisation, and finally decline; (iii) they can initially emerge out of a social crisis and then, after going through several changes, come to an end (Rammstedt 1978). Rucht (2018: 4) writes:

> according to Rammstedt, the underlying condition of a social movement is a social crisis. Yet not every crisis is triggering a movement. The latter only takes off when individual reactions to the crisis are overcome so that those who are negatively affected become aware of its negative consequences and start to propagate these effects. Like his forerunners, Rammstedt argued that the step of institutionalization marks the ideal-typical end of a movement.
>
> *(Rammstedt 1978: 146)*

However, in the form of movement party, the movement survives its institutionalisation.

There is an established argument on the relationship between an institutionalised radical right party in Parliament and protest politics. As argued by, in most cases, comparative studies based on protest event data (Giugni 2005; Hutter 2014; see also Chapter 2 of this book; see Minkenberg 2018 for a somewhat different view), if there is a radical right party in Parliament, it should have an eliminatory effect on street protests by radical right organisations. Interestingly, several chapters in our book (especially see Chapter 3 on Germany/PEGIDA and Chapter 9 on Sweden/Sweden Democrats) challenge this expectation in the framework of their respective case studies. A possible explanation for this contradiction may be the nature of political conflict in the countries studied, where the political conflict is not defined by sociocultural issues articulated primarily by the radical right. As demonstrated by our research findings on the general logic of party movement interactions (see Císař and Vráblíková 2019), the presence of a political party in Parliament only has a substitutive or eliminatory effect if the party articulates the main conflict line in a given society. In other words, we can expect the elimination of protest only if a party is a mainstream party that articulates the main conflict line in party politics. Since neither the Sweden Democrats nor the AfD can be viewed as mainstream political parties and, on the contrary, have remained radical right niche parties – outliers on the left-right continuum of their societies – they cannot be expected to have an eliminatory effect on protest. On the other hand, we should be able to observe this effect in societies where sociocultural content defines political party conflict, as in Hungary. Although available data are limited, there does indeed seem to have been a decrease in radical right protest in Hungary since the landslide victory of Viktor Orbán in 2010 (see Císař and Navrátil 2017).

A typology of interactions

David Bailey (2017) has divided the potential responses social democratic parties can have to emerging social movements associated with the crises into seven main categories: alliance, substantive advocacy, reformulated representation, superficial advocacy, non-reaction, dismissal, and repression. In another example, Stefano Bartolini and Peter Mair (2001: 334–335), focusing more on the mechanisms of interaction than on its possible forms, argue that social movements may be expanding their activities, and could even form an important mode of communication between citizens and parties, but that they are not an alternative to parties. However, they also claim that movements are challenging parties' monopoly on communicating the public's interests to the state, and that this also benefits parties because they have an extra source of information on citizens' interests. In sum, political parties are likely to cultivate relationships with social movements, when links to social movements can strengthen the political party's social base, and when connecting with social movements' claims provides parties with information about citizens' interests.

Finally, Rucht, identified four ideal types of possible interactions between (mainly left-wing) social movements and political parties (2018): (a) a symmetric/symbiotic relationship, which is a 'win–win' situation where both sides need each other; (b) a 'movement-powered' situation, where the movement has more power than the party; (c) the opposite 'party-power' situation, where the social movement is not so important, but the party becomes more creative; and finally (d) the movement party type. In the latter situation, both elements (movement and party) become enmeshed, and you have one internally cohesive party that merges the advantages of both structures. According to Rucht, such a model can be also applied to the radical right, or at least to some empirical cases of interactions between a radical right movement and a radical right party (see the case of the AfD and PEGIDA in Germany). Based on this literature, the few previous models of party movements interactions (e.g. Cavero 2015), and the contents of this book, we have formulated a new typology (see Table 15.1).

As some of the chapters in this book have shown, movement parties, the book's primary focus, can hardly be seen as a result of movement party interactions, which are understood as the interactions of two different types of actors. For example, as summarised by Jeanne Hanna and Joel Busher for this Conclusion, British UKIP could be said to be acting as a political party or as a social movement. UKIP arguably works as both of these and as neither, often at the same time – this is evidence of the value of the movement party concept, which makes it possible to analyse UKIP as a genuinely hybrid political actor. At the same time, where our typology might offer purchase for analysing UKIP would be in shedding light on how UKIP's internal components interacted with one another as the more social movement-oriented actors at various points in time cooperated, clashed, and sought to appropriate attention or resources from those more intent on formalising and expanding the party structures and vice versa.

However, other chapters distinguished between the various action logics of radical right parties and movements. Therefore, it is possible to think of possible combinations of strategic interactions, as summarised in Table 15.1. The typology does not differentiate between possible levels of interactions, which can be issues/ideologies, action/strategy, resource exchange, and membership.[2] The interactions can occur on different levels and to differing degrees. Also, as illustrated by the case of UKIP, social movements and movement parties are often diverse, and do not have a common position or strategy regarding their relationship to (other) political parties. However, as the same case demonstrates, it is possible to focus on the interactions among different components of movement parties (see also the case of PEGIDA below)

TABLE 15.1 A typology of party–movement interactions

		Social movements/protest groups		
		Open to cooperation with parties	*Closed to cooperation with parties*	*Indifferent to parties*
Political parties	*Open to cooperation with social movements*	Cooperation	Agenda appropriation	Co-optation/ penetration
	Closed to cooperation with social movements	Rejection	Competition	Exclusion
	Indifferent to social movements	Agenda setting	Attack	No interaction

Cooperation

Social movements and political parties may share some goals. Through a voluntary agreement, parties and movements may define a common strategy to protest against government measures or may decide to jointly fund political campaigns or organise demonstrations or strikes in order to achieve a common goal. In this case, as expressed by Kitschelt and other social movement scholars, social movements complement the representative role traditionally played by political parties, providing an alternative mode of political participation.

Jobbik in Hungary represents a clear example of cooperation between the fields of movements and parties. As summarised by Andrea Pirro for this Conclusion, at least until recently, at the heart of Jobbik's success has been its cooperation with the movement behind it. However, as Rucht (2018) pointed out about the relationship of cooperation between (left-wing) movements and parties: the relationship is precarious. It is uncertain whether in Hungary, in the face of Jobbik's increasingly moderate stance in recent years, the balance of this relationship can be sustained.

In relation to cooperation, scholars have highlighted the role of social movements as a necessary and supplementary institution in modern democracy, rather than as an alternative to political parties. In this case social movements become an alternative mode of political participation, where a functional distinction is made between social movements, as actors driving the political agenda, and political parties, focused usually on constraining or promoting those agendas.

Agenda appropriation

Social movements have been identified as political actors that are able to put new issues on the political agenda, often against the will of, or in direct conflict with, established political parties. As such, new issues originally not recognised by the political elite start spreading on the basis of bottom-up mobilisation, such as the mobilisation of the environmental, feminist, and anti-globalisation movements on the progressive side, and the anti-abortion movement on the conservative side.

One way to neutralise such movements has traditionally been cherry-picking by parties that might want to overtake or appropriate parts of a newly politicised agenda. This is what happened, to different degrees, in all the case studies in this volume. Movements can actively resist appropriation of their agenda by playing a militant role at least for some time. This is exactly the situation this interaction type captures. As summarised by Gilles Ivaldi for our Conclusion, interactions between the French FN as an institutionalised party, and the broader and more informal cultural movement within which it functions mainly fall into the agenda-appropriation category. Both party and movement are developing relatively independently of one another, and the reactionary movement, because of its heterogeneity, has as yet failed to form a united political force to support the party. The FN is essentially seeking to appropriate the cultural resources and issues provided by the movement while not formally cooperating with it.

Co-optation/penetration

Co-optation or penetration is understood in the traditional sense to refer to a situation where the institutionalised group subsumes or assimilates a smaller group (usually a non-institutionalised group). The activists who join the party use their formal position to voice claims that originally emerged out of a social movement. However, here movement organisations have no intention of engaging in formal cooperation with parties. As a result, the political parties introduce into their agenda new claims, interests, and ideals that were not present before.

As summarised by Maik Fielitz for this Conclusion, the case of Greece's ANEL is an illustration of the co-opting dynamics of a movement in decay. The *aganaktismenoi* had long since disappeared from the political stage, but it moved to online spheres and continued its conversation. ANEL tried to become an umbrella for political discontent by presenting itself as an open platform that would abandon ideological divides. The movement party cherry-picked popular demands from the *aganaktismenoi*, such as national sovereignty, direct democratic procedures, and anti-elitist rhetoric, and combined them with a traditional radical right agenda. ANEL thereby seized the ideas that were cultivated by the right-wing part of the *aganaktismenoi* and tried to transform the indignation on the streets into electoral gains.

Rejection

When the claims raised by a movement directly clash with the interests or the agendas of the political parties, it is possible to observe their rejection by a political party. This reaction can serve as a trigger for the rejected movement to form a (movement) party to directly challenge the established political parties in the electoral arena. As summarised by Abby Peterson for this Conclusion, this was the case of the Sweden Democrats, in that the traditional political parties did not have an anti-immigrant agenda, and the SD were excluded from the parliamentary arena.

There are numerous examples of claims being rejected by political parties. However, given the characteristics of the issues articulated by the radical right and their current resonance, such as migration and cultural identity, it has become difficult to simply reject these claims. As several chapters in this book show, (traditional) parties tend to try to eliminate their radical right competitors using the alternative strategies of co-optation and agenda appropriation. There may also be different types of interactions taking place at the same time at different levels.

As summarised by Manès Weisskircher and Lars Erik Berntzen for this Conclusion, PEGIDA in Dresden had complicated relationships with other German parties – most parties had a negative opinion of PEGIDA, while the AfD was ambivalent about the protests going on. This ambivalence was due not only to changes in their interactions over time, but also to the heterogeneity of the AfD, in which there were many different views on how to deal with PEGIDA. While some AfD figures have called for cooperation with PEGIDA, and in some instances have also actually cooperated, other AfD politicians, especially from West Germany, rejected the protest claims in Dresden. However, PEGIDA and the AfD also competed in Dresden, even electorally, when both of them nominated a candidate to run for mayor in the 2015 election. In the same year, the AfD changed leadership at the national level: Dresden-born Frauke Petry became the new party leader, redirecting the party from a mainly anti-Eurozone agenda to a mainly anti-immigration agenda. To some extent, this might be seen as a step of agenda appropriation. Although attempts at exclusion and rejection were made by mainstream and radical left parties, the salience of immigration has increased tremendously since PEGIDA emerged in 2014, especially with the intensification of the 'refugee crisis' in Germany a year later.

Competition

In this case, both political parties and social movements struggle to achieve a similar goal – for example, the former is seeking to attract members and voters and the latter to attract activists. Even though double militancy phenomena are common, in that time is limited, and in many cases both parties and movements might be attempting to attract members or activists from the same pool of citizens (Ramiro and Morales 2012), in most cases the struggle refers to the discursive/issue field, as with the AfD and PEGIDA interaction, in order to achieve a hegemonic position over a particular policy or access to popular support (resources).

Another form of competition between social movements and political parties is the evolution of a social movement into an electoral machine. More specifically, it is the situation when a social movement (usually a section of their leaders) decides to organise a political platform to compete with older political parties in elections. In this sense, the existence of competition approximates the transformative approach explained by Tina Hilgers (2005), where long-term presence in the public arena end up requiring social movements to either form a new political party to change the party system, as with the Sweden Democrats, or to attempt to influence an already existing party.

As summarised by Olga Gyarfášová for this Conclusion, in Slovakia the extreme right movement party is competing with the mainstream parties on who is the better representative of Slovak nationalist interests (a struggle over dominance in the discursive field). In the course of this competition, what was initially a movement transformed into a political party, most notably the Slovak National Party. The discursive field in this case is nationalism and nativism, i.e. defending the rights of the Slovaks, national sovereignty vis-à-vis the EU, and NATO membership.

Exclusion

Political parties might want to exclude certain movements and their demands from the official political space, even if there are no attempts on the part of a movement to interact with parties in the first place. This is the situation of radical/counter-cultural social movements (more on the left than right), which do not attempt to form ties with the political sphere, but rather try to create spaces at the margins of mainstream politics.

Given the focus of our book, the individual chapters do not primarily focus on possible sub/cultural elements of the radical right. Where they do, as in Hungary and Sweden, it is cooperation between politics and the radical right cultural milieu that is found to define the situation more than exclusion. Andrea Pirro has consequently summed up for this Conclusion that besides the significance the populist wave in Hungary has within the political field, it also has an important effect on cultural contents, which testifies to how closely integrated the institutional and the social extreme right are. In fact, in Hungary, one of the keys to the mainstreaming and success of radical right networks is the expansiveness of the national scene and the cultural industry built upon it.

Agenda setting

This is traditionally understood as an activity that social movements engage in to get new issues on the agenda, when parties are not opposed to accepting new issues and/or possible cooperation with social movements. Like other interaction types, there are numerous examples of this situation, which can, of course, later change, when political parties eventually take action, and either try to cooperate or appropriate the newly politicised issue. Depending on how movements react, we can also end up with a situation of competition over the issue and/or terms of interaction.

As summarised by Manès Weisskircher and Lars Erik Berntzen, PEGIDA influenced the German party system as an agenda-setter, making immigration an issue that other parties had to engage with. Extra-parliamentary mobilisation might have played a similar role in the Czech Republic during and after the migrant crisis, but some other important institutional players, such as the President, also worked hard to put immigration at the centre of the political agenda. A similar logic has been identified by Pietro Castelli Gattinara in the case of Italy.

Attack

We can expect that, in many cases, political parties will avoid reacting or responding to a mobilised demand or action put forward by a social movement against the parties. In some cases this is because the issue raised by the movement is irrelevant to the core constituency or to the values of the party, or because the cost of reacting to the demands might return no benefit to the party. For example, catchall parties in government at the national level probably do not have many incentives to react to local social movements demanding specific reforms that they have no control over. It seems that in the case of the Right to Housing movement in Spain national parties did not react to the local demands made by the 'Platform of People Evicted from their Houses' until the movement got media coverage at the national level.

In our book, this logic can be identified, for example, in the Slovak case and in Poland too. As summarised by Ben Stanley for this Conclusion, in the case of Kukiz'15 (the main example of a movement party), Law and Justice have largely focused on agenda appropriation (in the form of attempting to establish owner-ship of the issue of opposition to refugee relocation) and on competition with Kukiz'15 for the support of radical right voters. On the other hand, Kukiz'15 has recognised that it is at a structural disadvantage when it comes to competing with Law and Justice over key issues. Its chief interaction with Law and Justice, as with all the other political parties, is to attack them as elements of a 'partiocracy' that Kukiz'15 still considers itself to be outside.

No interaction

This is a theoretical possibility, but from the point of view of this book, it is not an interesting type of parallel existence of parties and movements. In our understand-ing, it is a rather rare phenomenon, since parties and movements interact on a number of issues and social problems. In fact, they interact even if they are not in some type of formal or visible cooperative or competitive relationship. At the very least, movement mobilisation helps form public opinion, which political parties follow and need to take notice of if they want to maintain their political existence.

Notes

1 The work of O. Císař on this chapter was done as part of the research project 'Activism in Hard Times' funded by the Czech Science Foundation (no. 16-10163S). We would like to acknowledge the contributions by the authors of the individual chapters to this Conclusion. Their contribution is always indicated by the author's name.
2 For this and the following points we are indebted to Maik Fielitz and Abby Peterson.

References

Alberoni, F. (1984) *Movement and Institution*, New York: Columbia University Press.

Arzheimer, K. (2015) 'The AfD: Finally a Successful Right-Wing Populist Eurosceptic Party for Germany?', *West European Politics*, 38(3): 535–56.

Azzellini, D. and Sitrin, M. (2014) *They Can't Represent Us! Reinventing Democracy from Greece to Occupy*, London: Verso Editions.

Bailey, D. (2017) *Protest Movements and Parties of the Left: Affirming Disruption*, London: Rowman and Littlefield International.

Bartolini, S. and Mair, P. (2001) 'The Challenge to Political Parties in Contemporary Democracies', in Diamond, L. and Gunther, R. (eds) *Political Parties and Democracy*, Baltimore, MD: John Hopkins University Press.

Bustikova, L. and Kitschelt, H. (2009) 'The Radical Right in Post-Communist Europe. Comparative Perspectives on Legacies and Party Competition', *Communist and Post-Communist Studies*, 42(4): 459–83.

Caiani, M. (2017a) 'Nationalism, Populism and the Re-Birth of Nationhood in Europe', in Grimmel, A. (ed) *The Crisis of the European Union: Challenges, Analyses, Solutions*, London: Routledge, 91–103.

Caiani, M. (2017b) 'Radical Right Wing Movements: Who, When, How and Why?', *Sociopedia, Sociopedia.isa*, Sage: London.

Castiglione, D. and Warren, M. (2006) 'Rethinking Democratic Representation: Eight Theoretical Issues', *Centre for the Study of Democratic Institutions* (University of British Columbia), 1–18.

Cavero, G. (2015) *Movements vs. Parties: an Attempt of Classification and Evidence from Four EU Countries*, Paper presented at the ECPR Conference, Montreal, 26–29 August 2015.

Císař, O. and Navrátil, J. (2017) 'Parties in the Streets: Conservative Movement Politics in Poland and Hungary', Paper presented at the ECPR Joint Session of Workshops 2017, University of Nottingham, 25–30 April 2017.

Císař, O. and Vráblíková, K. (2019) 'National Protest Agenda and the Dimensionality of Party Politics: Evidence from Four East-Central European Democracies.', *European Journal of Political Research*, forthcoming.

Cox, L. and Szolucha, A. (2013) 'Social Movement Research in Europe-the State of the Art', *Perspectives on Europe*, 59–63.

Crouch, C. (2004) *Post-Democracy*, London: Polity.

Dalton, R. (2007) *The Good Citizen: How a Younger Generation is Reshaping American Politics*. Washington, DC: Congress Quarterly Press.

Del Águila, R. (1994) 'Crisis of Parties as Legitimacy Crisis: A View from Political Theory', *Symposium on Political Parties: Changing Roles in Contemporary Democracies, Center for Advanced Study in the Social Sciences, Juan March Institute*, December 1994, 1–39.

Della Porta, D. (2012) 'Critical Trust: Social Movements and Democracy in Times of Crisis', *Cambio* II, 4(December): 33–43.

Enyedi, Z. (2014) 'The Discreet Charm of Political Parties', *Party Politics*, 1–11.

Giugni, M., Koopmans, R., Passy, F., and Statham, P. (2005) 'Institutional and Discursive Opportunities for Extreme-Right Mobilization in Five Countries', *Mobilization: An International Quarterly*, 10(1): 145–162.

Hilgers, T. (2005) 'Competition, Cooperation, or Transformation? Social Movements and Political Parties in Canada', *Critique: A Worldwide Journal of Politics*, Fall, 1–13.

Hutter, S. (2014) *Protesting Culture and Economics in Western Europe. New Cleavages in Left and Right Politics*, Minneapolis, MN: University of Minnesota Press.

Ignazi, P. (2004) '*Il puzzle dei partiti: più forti e più aperti ma meno attraenti e meno legittimi*', *Rivista Italiana di Scienza Politica*, 34: 325–346.

Inglehart, R. and Norris, P. (2017) 'Trump and the Populist Authoritarian Parties: The Silent Revolution in Reverse', *Perspectives on Politics*, 15(2): 443–454.

Inglehart, R. (1977) *The Silent Revolution: Changing Values and Political Styles Among Western Publics*, Princeton, NJ: Princeton University Press.

Jackman, R.W. and Volpert, K. (1996) 'Conditions Favouring Parties of the Extreme Right in Western Europe', *British Journal of Political Science*, 26(4) (Oct), edited by Cambridge University Press, 501–521.

Júlíusson, A.D. and Helgason, M.S. (2013) 'The Roots of the Saucepan Revolution in Iceland', in Cox, L. and Flesher Fominaya, C. (eds) *Understanding European Movements: New Social Movements, Global Justice Struggles, Anti-Austerity Protest*, London: Routledge, 189–202.

Kaldor, M. and Selchow, S. (2012) 'The 'Bubbling up' of Subterranean Politics in Europe', *Subterranean Politics*. Edited by London School of Economics and Political Science.

June 2012. Available at: http://www.gcsknowledgebase.org/europe/ (accessed 27 February 2014).

Katz, R. and Mair, P. (1995) 'Changing Models of Party Organization and Party Democracy. The Emergence of the Cartel Party', *Party Politics*, 1: 5–27.

Katz, R. and Mair, P. (2009) 'The Cartel Party Thesis: A Restatement', *Perspectives on Politics*, 7(4) (December): 753–766.

Kriesi, H. and Pappas, T.S. (eds) (2015) *European Populism in the Shadow of the Great Recession*, Colchester: ECPR Press.

Kriesi, H., Grande, E., Dolezal, M., Helbling, M., Hutter, S., Höglinger, D. and Wüest, B. (2012) *Political Conflict in Western Europe*, Cambridge: Cambridge University Press.

Lubbers, M., Gijsberts, M. and Scheepers, P. (2002) 'Extreme Right-Wing Voting in Western Europe', *European Journal of Political Research*, 41(3): 345–78. (http://doi.wiley.com/10.1111/1475-6765.00015).

Mair, P. (2002) 'Populist Democracy vs. Party Democracy', in Yves Mény and Yves Surel (eds) *Democracies and the Populist Challenge*, Basingstoke: Palgrave MacMillan, 81–98.

Mair, P. (2003) 'Political Parties and Democracy. What Sort of Future?', *Central European Political Science Review*, 4(13): 6–20.

Mair, P. (2009) 'Representative versus Responsible Government', *MPIfG Working Paper*, 8: 1–19.

Mazzoleni, O. and Voerman, G. (2017) 'Memberless Parties: Beyond the Business-firm Party Model?', *Party Politics*, 23(6): 783–792.

Mudde, C. (2007) *Populist Radical Right Parties in Europe*, Cambridge: Cambridge University Press.

Mudde, C. (2016) *On Extremism and Democracy in Europe*, London: Routledge.

Mudde, C. and Kaltwasser, C.R. (2013) 'Exclusionary vs. Inclusionary Populism: Comparing the Contemporary Europe and Latin America', *Government and Opposition*, 48(2): 147–178.

Ramiro, L. and Morales, L. (2012) 'Examining the 'demand' side of the market for political activism: Party and civil society grassroots activists in Spain', *Party Politics*, 1–24.

Rammstedt, O. (1978) *Sociale Bewegung*, Frankfurt: Suhrkamp.

Rucht, D. (2018) 'Observations on the Relationship between Political Parties and Social Movements', Paper presented at the SNS Lunch seminar series, Florence, 28 February 2018.

Streeck, W. (2014) *Buying Time. The Delayed Crisis of Democratic Capitalism*, London: Verso.

Taggart, P. and Kaltwasser, C.R. (2016) 'Dealing with Populists in Government', *Democratization*, 23.

Tejerina, B., Perugorría, I., Benski, T., and Langman, L. (2013) 'From Indignation to Occupation: A New Wave of Global Mobilization', *Current Sociology* 6(4) (April): 377–392.

Urbinati, N. and Warren, M.E. (2008) 'The Concept of Representation in Contemporary Democratic Theory', *Annual Review of Political Science*, 387–412.

Wainwright, H. (2013) *Essay: Political organisation in transition.* Available at: http://www.redpepper.org.uk/essay-political-organisation-in-transition/ (accessed April 2014).

Minkenberg, M. (2018) 'Between Party and Movement: Conceptual and Empirical Considerations of the Radical Right's Organizational Boundaries and Mobilization Processes.' *European Societies*, https://doi.org/10.1080/14616696.2018.1494296.

INDEX